Journey through the New Testament

Journey through the New Testament

Joyce Peel

Published by
The Reverend Eileen Wheeler

A CIP catalogue record for this book
is available from the British Library

Peel, Joyce
Journey through the New Testament

ISBN 0 9539449 1 3

Printed by
The Burlington Press
1 Station Road, Foxton,
Cambridge CB2 6SW

Published by
The Reverend Eileen Wheeler

To

John Byrom

Acknowledgements

I am deeply grateful for the continual interest, encouragement and prayer support of so many of my friends. Special thanks are due to Canon John Byrom, who read my script chapter by chapter offering most helpful theological comments, and sending me extracts of material I could not otherwise obtain. Thanks also to Dr Eric Franklin, sadly deceased, who read the completed manuscript and freely offered me a masterly criticism with very helpful suggestions.

I am also grateful to the Librarian of the Community of St Mary the Virgin, Wantage, who loaned me so many books, and to Canon Andrew Mayes who also lent books from his personal library. I am specially grateful to him for agreeing to write a Foreword at very short notice. I am also indebted to the Revd Murdoch MacKenzie, for his comments to be found on the back cover. Thanks too to Jean Blackford and Margaret Dawe for permission to use their photographs of the Holy Land.

Finally a big thank-you to the Revd Eileen Wheeler for agreeing to act as publisher.

Contents

Foreword		viii
Introduction		x
1	**St Mark's Gospel**	**1**
2	**St Matthew's Gospel**	**22**
3	**St Luke's Gospel**	**40**
4	**St John's Gospel**	**62**
5	**Acts of the Apostles**	**93**
6	**Mission to the Gentiles**	**111**
7	**Problems of a Gentile Church**	**134**
8	**The Road to Rome**	**152**
9	**Four Letters from Prison**	**174**
10	**After the Apostles**	**202**
11	**The Epistles of John and Hebrews**	**225**
12	**The End Unveiled**	**255**

Foreword

You hold in your hand a key that will unlock a door to untold spiritual treasures. You hold in your hand a tool which will enable you to apply God's truth to your life. And above all, you hold now a map for the most exciting journey you can ever make.

For this book is an invitation to a journey that can transform your life. With its help, you will travel confidently through the awesome territory of the New Testament, and allow it to make its impact on your life. Like a good map, this book highlights key landmarks on the journey, alerting you to crucial cross-roads and points of decision which the first Christians had to face, and which now await you too.

This book will be a great encouragement to you in your personal pilgrimage of faith. Each chapter offers you ten penetrating questions for your own private meditation - questions that will challenge you deeply and enable you to recognise the application of God's Word to your own situation. But you do not travel alone. Perhaps you have the opportunity to study with a group (if not, start one!). There are a further set of questions which will animate lively group discussion and reflection about issues which touch all our lives. This really is, at once, a super resource for groups and a powerful stimulus to individual growth.

This book springs from the eventful spiritual journey of its author. It arises from her rich experiences as a teacher and dramatist in India, her work as a counsellor in Britain, and her passionate concern for the spiritual development of individuals and churches which I have been privileged to witness these last ten years. My own work among the clergy and the Christians of Sussex reveals to me that this book meets an urgent need among post-Alpha and post-Confirmation groups looking for a challenging introduction to the New Testament, and among Christians of all ages wanting to grow in discipleship and understanding. Joyce Peel's book offers a rare combination of depth of insight and accessibility of thought, for it communicates knowledge and wisdom in language which is at once incisive and refreshing. It is both highly informative, imparting a wealth of background information, and powerfully invigorating, as you allow yourself to be led afresh to an encounter with the living Word of God.

Do not delay. With map in hand, step out on this journey right now. It may change your life!

Canon Andrew Mayes
Bishop of Chichester's Officer for Continuing Ministerial Education

Introduction

Christian bookshops are full of books on the New Testament written by eminent scholars. Why then write another when I am neither? In this introduction I hope to give my reasons.

First, this book is a sequel to an earlier book on the Old Testament. Behind it lay quite a story. After twenty-seven years as a C.M.S. missionary in South India, I settled in a parish in East Sussex, where I helped to start a bible study group. After some time I suggested that we might study an Old Testament book. One of the group protested. The O.T. was boring. Why should Christians study a Jewish book full of bloody battles and a sub-Christian idea of God? But I had fallen in love with the O.T. thanks to some brilliant studies on Amos I had heard as a student at Oxford. I told Kate, the protestor, that I'd be happy to share my enthusiasm with her. The result was a series of weekly sessions during which she became as enthusiastic about it as I was. The book aimed to share this more widely. It proved popular, especially with House Groups.

I had gone to India as a teacher, but I was at heart a dramatist. After eleven years, God, in a wonderful way, called me into full-time work developing drama in the church. The Bible has all the dramatic ingredients: people in conflict, with God, with others, and with themselves. Actors use their imagination to enter into the characters of those they portray. Over the centuries basic situations do not alter much, neither do people. My actors' knowledge of the bible was mostly drawn from memories of Sunday School. They now made the surprising discovery that these stories related to their own situation and adult problems. For a few, this experience was life-changing.

I had started by writing and producing two epic dramas, first on the whole O.T., followed by one on the Life of Christ. They were acted by different villages and institutions. The actors made another surprising discovery. The Bible was not a collection of stories, but one great story of God's plan of salvation for mankind. As I later discovered, it was a drama in three Acts.

Act 1: the Call of Israel, covered the O.T.
Act 2: the perfect fulfilment of the plan by Jesus, covered the gospels.
Act 3: the rest of the N.T., which showed the plan being worked out in the life and mission of the church.

Here was another reason for writing this book. The average church member's only encounter with the Bible is through snippets read at Sunday services. Unconnected, and deprived of their context, they are speedily forgotten. Even those keen enough to read daily bible notes, are still confronted with snippets. Some notes go through a whole book, but do not link them all together as a whole. The N.T. books, like those of the O.T. vary in date, style, and point of view. This dramatic theme could bring out both their development and underlying unity. Instead of acting experience, questions could help to draw out their relevance both for individuals and the present-day church and society.

But the New Testament is not just a dramatic story. The teaching is profound and the letters especially deal with deep matters of doctrine. My own struggles to re-think and re-express them helped me to communicate with others, as I discovered when, immediately after this, I was invited to join in a mission to London University. Pastors however may be wondering about my theological background and viewpoint. To return to the image of a Journey, they do not want their flock led astray.

Brought up by keen church-going parents, I am simply "C. of E.", with no party label. The question, "Is your church *High* or *Low*?", asked at an Anglican conference, shocked me. What matters, I thought, is whether it is alive or dead. One of my favourite texts is 1 Cor. 3:21-23: "All things are yours".

To the evangelical wing I owed my practice of daily Quiet Time. I'd been fed by C.M.S. Conferences, St Aldates, and the University Church Oxford. The catholic wing had introduced me to the great spiritual writers and mystics, and the value of Retreats. Working in South India, with Leslie Newbigin as my bishop, strengthened my ecumenism, and the charismatic renewal of the sixties was a life-changing experience. But I am still grateful to John Robinson. His book, "Honest to God", forced me to rethink my beliefs from scratch and learn to express them in non-theological language.

Another reason for this book was to present the Gospel of salvation, not watered down, but strong and open enough to welcome the questioning of enquiring minds. I could not ignore the findings of modern biblical scholarship without dishonesty, especially when it enriches our understanding with a more accurate knowledge of the text and its background. The discussion of critical problems however is not part of my chosen brief. Miracles happen today. I have experienced them. Explanations don't explain them away. But I can't accept the fundamentalism that regards the bible as infallible. Today this teaching is attractive to those, especially the young, hungry for religious certainty. Only God is infallible. The biblical writers, though truly inspired by the Holy Spirit, were still men. Neither do I believe in the infallibility of the church or of individual inspiration given by the Spirit. The N.T. books were accepted as authoritative by the church after experiencing their truth over many years. Being open to truth is not the same as being "swayed by every wind of doctrine". Jesus is the litmus test. Bible, Church and personal inspiration by the Holy Spirit, need to be held in balance, to correct, support and enrich each other, in their witness to Him.

A final practical word about the chapters. In seeking to emphasize the development of the church, the books are not studied according to their biblical order, and the early epistles are fitted into their narrative context in Acts. Some adjustments were necessary to make them more equal in length. Revelation was not the last book to be written, but it discloses the End, both of the Journey and the Drama. The End is not a terminus, but a final fulfilment. We are living in the "end times" now.

A brief summary of Act 1. The Call of Israel.

If you arrive at a theatre late and miss the first act, a lot of what goes on in the other acts isn't fully understood. So, for those who may find themselves somewhat in that position, here is a short summary giving some necessary clues.

God's Plan of Salvation makes its first appearance in the story of Abraham, who responded to God's call and promise with obedience and faith. (Gen. 12:1-4) This reversed the doubt and disobedience of Adam and Eve which made such a plan of salvation necessary. We can interpret their story as a story of ourselves.

The promise made to Abraham was ratified by the Covenant made at Sinai, after a mighty act of deliverance of the Israelites from Egypt. The Ten Commandments were given, and the people warned that loyalty to God and His Law would lead to life, disloyalty to death. (Deut. 30:15-19)

Once in the Promised Land, most of the Israelites opted to be like the inhabitants and worship their gods who would, they believed, give them what they wanted: prosperity, and pleasure. Very modern! They disregarded the warnings of the Prophets, and in 587 BC they were conquered and taken into exile in Babylon. About fifty years later, freed by the Persians to return home, they were given a second chance. Sadly, despite early enthusiasm, old disloyalties began to return. Apart from a short period of independence, they were conquered again, first by the Greeks, then by Rome. What was the answer to sin? How could God's promises be fulfilled? There were different and conflicting viewpoints based on past experiences.

First there was the Law given to Moses. Under the Greek persecution, many died as martyrs in upholding it. But love of it, voiced in the Psalms, degenerated into rigid legalism, and preoccupation with trivial detail that encouraged hypocrisy. The Priests trusted in the Temple sacrifices, offerings of thanksgiving, communion and atonement for sin. But sin continued and people's lives were unchanged.

The Prophets attacked both legalism and empty ritual. They called for true repentance, a change of heart, and moral and social reform. Their call went unheeded. Reform did not last. Only God could change hearts.

What about the everlasting Kingdom that God had promised to David? Here too were conflicting views. Was it to be politically independent and fought for? Was Ezra right in seeking to exclude foreigners with their corrupting influence? Or should they be welcomed, according to the visions of Isaiah? How can you witness to those with whom you won't mix? Another question relevant for today!

Some hoped for God to send His "Annointed One", the Messiah, to establish the Kingdom. Others, despairing of this, thought only a cataclysm, a new heaven and new earth, could bring it about.

When the O.T. era closes, all the strands of God's Plan of Salvation reach an impasse. This is typical of the ending of the first Act of a play. The different characters, with their conflicting purposes, get knotted up. Impasse is reached, and the curtain descends, leaving the audience wondering how on earth it can be resolved. What often happens is that a new character is introduced. The others reveal themselves by the way they react to him, and the plot takes a new turn. Thus the catalyst determines the final outcome of the play.

So in Act 2 - *the Gospels* - the curtain rises on the advent of Jesus, through whom God's Plan of Salvation is both revealed and brought about. As we travel through the Gospels, we will be noting how all these themes of the O.T. are confirmed, corrected, and given a new coherence. We will also see how all those who come in contact with Jesus find themselves exposed by their reaction.

Joyce Peel
Wantage
March 2002

Chapter 1

St Mark's Gospel

St Mark's Gospel is short. Both his style and method of presentation is dramatic. It is exciting to read it through at one sitting, as if it were entirely new to you.

The early ministry. Chapter 1.

The Gospel opens with a trumpet call, a joyful proclamation and summons to action.

The Good News is Jesus. His name means Saviour. He is the Christ, the Messiah, the anointed one, the long-expected King. He is the Son of God. Nothing tentative or hesitant here. Believe or reject him. Neutrality is impossible. His coming is the fulfilment of O.T. prophecy. (Mal. 3:1. Is. 40:3)

John is the Forerunner sent to prepare his way. His royal road must be cleared of every obstacle. People must prepare a pathway for him in their hearts or, in their pride and self-centredness, they will miss seeing him. There must be a right-about-turn in their orientation. Spiritual insight depends on being loosed from past presumptions, and being open to God, newly at work in our midst.

The word Baptize means being plunged into water, swamped by total immersion. It signifies a total dying to one's past way of life. For Jews of that time, baptism was only given to those who wanted to adopt the Jewish faith. But for John, and for the early prophets, being born a Jew wasn't enough. Neither is it enough for us to be born into a Christian family. John knew that even the baptism he gave wasn't enough. Water can wash away superficial dirt. It takes fire to refine the alloy within. By effort we can reform our actions. Only the Holy Spirit can change our hearts.

"And immediately", Mark's most characteristic expression, John's words are transformed into action. Jesus makes his entry. The Holy Spirit descends on him. He is baptized, and he hears the voice of God declaring, "You are my beloved Son".

Jesus, the catalyst, has come to bring healing and fulfilment to the conflicting strands of the O.T. He does it by turning them all upside down and inside out. He is the Upside-Down Man par excellence! Otherwise, why should the one and only sinless person go down into the waters of repentance? The waters of Jordan had been polluted by the sins of the crowd, but Jesus emerged unstained. It was an act of total identification with ordinary humanity.

After thirty years of preparation, about which Mark tells us nothing, Jesus' ministry now begins. He has, at most, only three years in which to complete his mission. Did he know his time would be so short? Certainly, not a day, not even a moment was wasted. Mark's repetition of the word "immediately", nine times in the first chapter, conveys a sense of urgency.

The first thing the Spirit does is to drive Jesus into the wilderness for a head-on conflict with the power of evil. Alone, fasting and praying, Jesus exposes himself to attack, as he ponders over how he is to accomplish his mission. Matthew and Luke describe in detail the methods he was tempted to adopt, and how he rejected them. Mark, instead, shows Jesus, at critical points of his ministry, actively demonstrating his rejection of these methods of achieving worldly power, and choosing the way of love. The inevitable outcome of this was the cross.

Again, "immediately", Jesus starts to call a selected group of men to be his disciples. In three years he can only pioneer the way of salvation. They must be trained to understand and live by it, and then teach it to the rest of the world. Fishermen are usually tough, independent-minded and loyal. They would need these qualities for the job. From St John's Gospel we learn that they had had about six weeks to ponder that experience before he called them, and, like Abraham, to follow him to God knows where, and to face God knows what.

In the rest of what we read in chapter 1 (note that Mark did not write in chapters), we are given a thumb-nail sketch of a typical day in the early ministry of Jesus. It starts with a visit to the synagogue where Jesus is invited to speak. The teaching of the Rabbis consisted of explaining the text of scripture by quoting famous Rabbis of the past, whose authority was unquestioned. Jesus spoke on his own authority. His teaching was fresh and surprising. But he was the local carpenter's son. He had had no theological training. Where did he get this authority from? That question stays with us to the end.

Then, immediately, there was fresh cause for astonishment. A man, possessed by an evil spirit, screamed at Jesus, and was instantly healed by a simple authoritative command.

Going to Peter's home for lunch, Jesus found Peter's mother-in-law down with a fever. He raises her up and she too is healed instantly. He spends the rest of the evening healing, by word and touch, the sick and demented folk who crowd at the door. He must have gone to bed exhausted, yet, long before dawn, he is up and praying alone on the hillside.

In his success lay the danger of being side-tracked. The healing of minds and bodies was part of his ministry. Like today, it is the aspect of healing that most people seek. But Jesus had come to bring the healing of salvation. The two words come from the same root. It is a healing of wholeness, which means the restoration of our relationship with God. Jesus stuck to his own priorities. For him this meant continual journeying.

Early opposition. 2 - 3:6.

With dramatic contrast Mark leads us from scenes of crowd enthusiasm to those of mounting hostility, as the Scribes and Pharisees challenge Jesus' authority with regard to the Law of Moses.

First comes the healing of the paralytic. With his gift of spiritual insight, Jesus saw the sin that lay behind the disease. With his word of forgiveness he released the man from his burden of guilt. To the Pharisees this was claiming the power that belonged to God alone. The healing of the man's paralysis was proof that the burden had gone. The Pharisees were silenced, but not pacified.

Then comes the dinner party thrown by Levi, ie Matthew. (Matt. 9:9) Newly called to discipleship, he was eager for Jesus to meet his friends. Eating together creates a bond of relationship, especially for Easterners. Jews would not eat with Gentiles or sinners. The sin of tax collectors was not just that of exploiting their power. As the job was farmed out to the highest bidder, this was an obvious temptation. But it meant working for the Romans. They were seen as traitors, helping in the exploitation of their own people. Jesus had identified himself with the whole of sinful humanity, however outcast and despised. He won them back to God, not by rebuke or moral re-education, but by loving them and accepting them as brothers.

Fasting was the next issue. Jesus fasted as an aid to prayer, not in order to follow tradition or gain merit and public approval. New situations call for new and more appropriate practices. Fixity must give way to flexibility.

The next confrontation was over something even more petty. To rub ears of corn is hardly work. But countless rules, that defined the application of the Law, counted it as such. Jesus silences his critics again by quoting scripture. His claim that the Son of Man is Lord of the Sabbath was rightly taken as a claim to have authority to reinterpret the Law. It had been given, he said, to benefit people, not to enslave them.

The last incident is the most serious. The leaders of the Pharisees were now actively seeking an opportunity to accuse and destroy Jesus. Again the Law of the Sabbath is the issue. To heal was also forbidden. Confronted by Jesus' challenge, his accusers remain silent, and Jesus responds with a look of anger and grief. Then he asks a searching question that exposes their murderous intent. The drama mounts to a turning point. Jesus' religious opponents join with the worldly Herodian Party, their natural enemies, to seek Jesus' death. Opposition to Him often makes strange bedfellows. But Jesus' time is not yet. He withdraws.

Conflicting Claims. 3:7 - 35.

Mark switches back to the enthusiasm of the crowds. But Jesus' priority is now his disciples. He selects twelve and retires to a mountain where he starts giving them special training. He plans to send them out on a Mission. The word apostle means one who is sent. Their first need is to stay close to him.

Returning, Jesus is again besieged by a clamouring multitude. Imagine the excited cries of the healed and the demented shrieks of the demons being expelled. Such frenzied scenes often occur. They did in the days of John Wesley and do so today. Those who accused Jesus of blasphemy for forgiving sins, now call his healing satanic. Such a deliberate confusion of good and evil is unforgivable because it makes repentance impossible. Those who fear they have committed the "unforgivable sin" cannot possible have committed it.

As the hours went by with no break for rest or food, even Jesus' mother and family must have thought him beside himself and in need of some protection and control. They claim family right of admittance. His reply must have been shattering. His human family has no special rights or privileges. All who do God's will are members of his family. Many Christians today can testify to this family of faith as having, for them, a deeper reality than that of their own human family.

Early training. a. Through Parables. 4:1-34.

As we have seen, the disciples were called first to be with Jesus, to listen to his teaching and watch him in action. Mark now selects four parables of the Kingdom to illustrate the fundamental lessons they had to learn.

In the parable of the Sower, the seed is faithfully sown. The harvest depends, not on the seed or the weather, but the ground on which it falls. What mattered then was faithful preaching. The O.T. prophets were warned that they would not be heeded, but they still had to speak out. Jesus himself knew that his words mostly fell on unprofitable soil. But, where the soil was well prepared, the harvest was rich and abundant. What mattered was faithful preaching and painstaking preparation of hearts.

Why did Jesus say that he used parables so that the crowd might not understand, and so not repent and be saved? This may be explained by the Jewish way of thinking that is apt to diminish the difference between what God purposes and what results. "God hardened Pharaoh's heart" is another example. Here perhaps an alternative suggestion may be of value. To hear and understand means being faced with a decision, to accept or reject. Knowingly to reject God and his salvation, is so terrible that it may be better that such understanding be withheld until the heart is ready to accept. Listening to a parable, we can enjoy the story, taking it at its face value, or we can begin to ponder and delve. We can see as much, and as deeply, as we need, or want to see at that time. Our search and understanding grow together. The greater our need, the more desperate our search.

This leads to the next parable. The light you receive is for sharing. The more you share, the more you receive. Stop sharing your faith, and you will be in danger of losing it. Experience bears this out.

The third parable teaches us that, while we may till and water the soil, we cannot make the seed grow. (cp. 1Cor. 3:6-7) Converting hearts is the work of the Holy Spirit, and not, apart from prayer, our responsibility.

Reaping the harvest is. The fourth parable provides encouragement. From small beginnings, great things grow. Through the faithful witness of this small band of men, a world-wide church will come into being.

Early training. b. Through Miracles. 4:35 - 6:6

The Gospel is not a system of doctrine or ethics. It is Jesus. Its power depends on our recognising him for who he is. The following incidents show how Jesus led his disciples to discover this.

First comes the storm at sea. Jesus, tired, sleeps in the boat, his head on a cushion, a nice touch of an eyewitness. A violent storm suddenly blows up. Even these fishermen, used to such storms, are terrified. They wake him up. It is interesting to compare this situation with that of Jonah chapter 1. Jesus commands the wind to cease. Then he rebukes them for lack of faith. Awed, they wonder at this new aspect of his authority. "Who is this?", they ask.

The mad man, or rather his demons, know the answer. They cry out, "Jesus,

Son of the Most High God." But Jesus silences them. The mystery of his person is only to be revealed by the Holy Spirit of God. Note the contrast of the pig-keepers, concerned only for their property, who see Jesus as a menace, and the healed man who wants to follow him. Jesus, however, sends him out as a witness. Unlike the disciples, who are not yet ready, he can witness through a transformed life, the most effective witness of all. As we shall see later, it was evidently effective.

How can we experience Jesus' saving power? While the crowds who jostled Jesus experienced nothing, a woman, with a faith as great as her need, pushed through them. She touched only the hem of his robe, but his healing power flowed into her. It wasn't just something psychological, Jesus felt the power's flow. He turned to face her. Her faith had, as it were, pressed the switch.

We can thank God for this interruption. Without it, Jesus might have reached Jairus' house before his daughter died. Was the child in a coma, or could Jesus, from a distance, halt the process of death? The raising of Lazarus, as told in St John's Gospel, points to the latter.

Mark now shows us how, in Jesus' home town, superficial familiarity had led to such an absence of faith that not even Jesus could do much. This is probably why, in post-Christian Europe, so few miracles take place in comparison with places where Jesus Christ has only recently been made known.

Early training. c. Learning by doing. 6:7-56

The disciples are now to start learning by doing. They are sent out in pairs to preach and heal. When they started, were they scared, until they discovered his authority was able to empower them? Joyfully they returned with a story of success. Notice their use of anointing with oil, known for its healing qualities. Did they learn its sacramental use from Jesus? (Luke 10:34. James. 5:14)

It is dangerous to preach repentance to the powerful. The Baptist's violent death was a warning to them of what they, as well as their master, would face. Mark uses the story of John's death to raise again the question of Jesus' identity. Herod had decided that, in Jesus, John's spirit had been reincarnated, and was still dangerously at work. No wonder that the Herodians, who cared little for the Law of Moses, joined with the Pharisees to plot against Jesus' life.

Jesus understood both his disciples' need of a rest, and the wisdom of withdrawal. But there was no escape from the crowds. His compassion allowed Jesus no rest for himself. For hours he held them, teaching with his stories. Then, when hunger set in, and dusk approached, his disciples called for a halt. His response was to challenge them to a new leap of faith. They were to feed the hungry multitude. First they had to measure their resources; five loaves and two fishes. These they gave to Jesus. He blessed, broke them, and gave them back to share with 5,000 others. How did they feel as they began the distribution of these pathetic crumbs? Some people believe that their generosity provoked the crowd to respond by producing their own rations, hidden for fear of having to share them. This too would have been a miracle with significance for us all. But science no longer claims that physical miracles are impossible. Not only had Elisha worked a similar miracle, but stories of such amazing multiplication of shared food have come out of the recent revival in Indonesia. With God all things are possible, even for ordinary people like us!

Some scholars believe that the feeding of the 4,000 is a repetition of the same incident. Neither Luke nor John record it, though Matthew follows Mark. But some lessons are so difficult to absorb that they have to be repeated. Again the disciples are caught in a storm at sea, but this time Jesus is not in the boat with them. In his Name they had healed the sick and cast out devils. Could they not then, in his Name, have commanded the wind to cease? It never occurs to them. They labour on in their own strength. Jesus comes to them, walking on the water. Panic stations! Is he a ghost? He enters the boat, and stills the storm. Again the disciples are astounded. "Who is this man?" Can a man walk on water? Many saints, such as Teresa of Avila, experienced the power of levitation, but gave it no significance. This Son of God is truly Son of Man. Clothed in the limitations of our humanity, he opens up to us new dimensions of life transformed and empowered by God.

A mixture of experiences. 7:1 - 8:26.

As events follow each other in breathtaking succession, we need to notice their pattern, woven together by a very skilful dramatist. Jesus is seen dealing alternately with three groups of people: the enthusiastic crowd, the hostile religious leaders, and the disciples, faint but pursuing. To the crowd he shows compassion. He teaches and heals them, using different methods with different individuals. He spits on the eyes of the blind man, spittle being regarded as a healing salve. With the man who is deaf and dumb, he uses visual actions. To check up on all the methods used in all four Gospels makes a fascinating study, especially for those engaged in the Church's healing ministry. With the exception of the Demoniac, in every case Jesus commands silence. He sought to avoid the pressure of the crowd's inexhaustible demands. He would not let his mission be deflected by them, nor did he trust their adulation.

With the Pharisees, Jesus acted, while they reacted, exposing their hostility, their priorities and motivations. The issues become growingly important. The complaint that Jesus' disciples ate without first washing their hands, is not a concern for hygiene, but for ritual and tradition. Jesus quotes the prophets. It is the heart that needs to be cleansed. The intention of the Law can be negated by rigidly narrow interpretation. They would, for example, allow a man to escape responsibility for providing for his parents, by nominally gifting his money and possessions to the temple, while retaining its use for himself. Jesus weighs in to attack their hypocrisy. Detailed reference to the excretory system leads to the comment, "He declared all foods clean". This broke down one of the chief barriers dividing Jew from Gentile. It was to become a major issue for the early church.

The next confrontation was over a demand for a sign. Here we see clearly how the temptations in the wilderness, which Mark omits, face Jesus in his ministry. The crowd demands bread, the meeting of their physical needs. But all Jesus' acts of compassion are signs of the Kingdom. Many today first come to know Jesus through an experience of healing. But healing, exalted into a Gospel, is a false side track. What the Pharisees want is not such an outflow of love, but some proof of Jesus' Messiahship, ie "Throw yourself down from the pinnacle of the temple." Jesus offered no such proof. Had he done so they would not have believed it. (cp. Lk. 16:31) His divine authority has to be recognised by spiritual insight, which is a gift of God. These men were no seekers. They were plotting to kill him. Jesus turns his back on them.

So we come to the third group, the disciples. They are reaching a critical moment in their journey. Jesus seeks an opportunity to be alone with them. They had still so much to learn. He withdraws to Sidonia. Then this woman, a Gentile foreigner, starts dogging their footsteps and invading their privacy. Jews often referred to foreigners as dogs. We call them Wogs, or Frogs!

Jesus knew that his earthly ministry was limited to Israel. (cp. Matt. 10:5-6. Jn. 12:20-23) He was faced by a dilemma. One act of compassion might open the floodgates. Denial might confirm pride and prejudice. With his reply, note that the word chosen for dog refers to a domestic pet. May we not see a humourously raised eyebrow questioning the disciples' attitude? They might have used a ruder word! The woman responds with persistence and trust. Jesus appreciates both. Principles make good guides but false gods! Jesus was free to be both flexible and spontaneous.

He now moves east to Decapolis, perhaps to avoid the Pharisees rather than the crowds. Strict Jews would not enter Gentile territory. Possibly we now see the effect of the healed Demoniac's witness, in the welcome the people there gave to Jesus. Thence he moves north to Caesarea Philippi.

The Turning Point. 8:27 - 9:13.

Here Jesus, at last, confronts his disciples with the crucial question, "Who do you say that I am?" Peter makes his momentous confession. "You are the Christ." What did the title mean to him?

Like "Messiah" it means "anointed". Kings of Israel were anointed, as are sovereigns of England today. It was a sign of God's authority, and the theory of the Divine Right of Kings was based on it. At the time of Jesus, the term referred to a human *Son of David* who would restore the Jewish Kingdom. A psalm, dated 50 BC, not in the bible, says that the Messiah would overcome his enemies, not by military force, but by the word of his mouth. But that was not the popular view. The word was political dynamite. Jesus calls Peter blessed, for it is the Father who has revealed the truth. But he tells his disciples not to reveal it to others. Jesus had rejected Satan's offer of the kingdoms of this world. Today we see Lucifer being worshipped in a bid for world power. This lies, generally concealed, behind the New Age movement.

Jesus now starts speaking clearly about his forthcoming suffering and death. Peter violently rejects this. He, and the other disciples, cling to their political hopes. They quarrel about power and precedence right up to Jesus' death. Even on the Mount of Ascension they are still hoping for a political kingdom. Jesus again turns worldly ideas on their head. To save one's life is to lose it. To lose one's life is to save it. The power of the cross, of self-sacrificing love is the greatest power on earth.

The coming of the Kingdom in glory points to Pentecost. But to strengthen their faith Jesus gives three of his closest disciples a glimpse of his glory. Moses and Elijah are with him. In Luke's account we learn that they were talking about his approaching death seen as something he would accomplish, implying an active victory. Here the emphasis is on the Voice. Jesus is the fulfilment of both the Law and the Prophets. He also has authority both to reinterpret and supercede them.

Jesus tells them to say nothing about what they have seen until after his death. The disciples are mystified. The deaths of both Elijah and Moses were shrouded in mystery. They were obviously still alive. Elijah was supposed to return before the coming of the Messiah. This was the OT's last word. (Mal. 4:5) Jesus points them to the Baptist as fulfilling Malachi's prophesy, just as the Baptist had pointed them to him.

Humiliation and Humility. 9:14-50.

Spiritual highs are usually followed by spiritual lows. The disciples descend the mountain to find the others at a loss. They had tried and failed to heal an epileptic boy. The power of Jesus, it seemed, had ceased to flow. Loss of faith is contagious. It spread through the crowd. Could even Jesus heal the boy? The blockage lies in the word *if* which Jesus repeats. The father could offer only a crumb of faith, but it was enough. The boy was healed. What had gone wrong? Had past success made the disciples over-confident, not that the power to heal was theirs, but that it would always flow through them. Only prayer and a humble constant openness to God, would keep the channels clear.

Jesus now returns very quietly to Galilee. Though he continues to warn them of his coming death, the disciples are still looking for a political kingdom. They quarrel as to which of them will get the top jobs. Jesus set a child before them. To serve God's Kingdom is to serve children, or, as Mother Theresa has shown, the poor, the outcast, and the dying. Upside-down values again! Jesus uses all who serve others. In the world, top jobs are given by the leader only to his inner circle. John tries to disqualify an outsider, who is healing in Jesus' Name. Jesus rebukes, not the man, but John. He welcomes all who serve others for his sake. There is no contradiction here with a similar saying recorded by Luke. (Lk. 11:23) While to do good in Jesus' Name is to be for him, to do nothing is to be against him. Then, as now, responsibility for monstrous crimes lies, not just with their perpetrators, but with the silent crowd.

In most traditional societies, the seriousness of a crime is reckoned by the status of the person wronged. A king or nobleman is given greater redress than a servant. For Jesus, to destroy the faith of a child was a crime worthy of death. Better for the criminal to die before, rather than after, the event. Physical handicap, popularly regarded as God's punishment for sin, can be transformed into spiritual blessing, yet another upside-down valuation.

Salt, a cleansing and preservative agent, was an essential ingredient of sacrifice. (Lev. 2:13) Jesus was telling his disciples to sacrifice their worldly ambitions, and so live at peace with each other. From now on, to follow him means treading the Way of the Cross.

Road to Jerusalem. 10:1-52.

The journey south, towards Jerusalem, now begins. According to John's Gospel, Jesus had visited the city several times, attending major festivals. Mark omits this. For him, there is only one journey, the journey to the Cross.

Though, at first, Jesus stays to the east of Jordan, he is immediately faced by the Pharisees, seeking to accuse him of subverting the Law of Moses. He confronts them openly on the issue of divorce. Moses, or rather the Laws attributed to him in the Book of Deuteronomy, allowed divorce. This was a watering down of God's Law (Gen. 2:24) to adjust to man's weakness. In holding up God's original intention, Jesus has put his own authority above that of Moses. Echoes of "This is My Son. Listen to him."

Those who think Jesus is more easy-going than his Father, and that the Law of Love breaks down the Mosaic Law, are wrong. It was a breaking upwards, raising it to a higher, more spiritual level. The family is the basic unit in which love can be experienced and taught, a foundation of personal security. Today, Satanists both fast and pray to the Devil for the break-up of family life, especially that of the clergy. We see the terrible results in the abandonment of, and cruelty to children, whose loveless background breeds the anger and violence, later vented on society.

The innocent trustfulness of children is the basic pattern of a right relationship to God. To the disciples, the children were just a nuisance. For a second time, Jesus holds them in his arms, as an example of faith. Mobility downwards, not upwards, was to be their pattern: standing the way of the world once again on its head.

The rich young man provokes a similar reversal. All his life he had tried to obey the Law and be a good man. Jesus loved him. But true goodness flows only from God. It flows to us through Jesus. Jesus calls the young man to follow him and share his life. What a privilege! What a risk! His wealth and possessions held him in a bondage of family cares and responsibilities. Mark does not give us the *Sermon on the Mount*. Its teaching is portrayed dramatically.

The disciples are stunned. They thought, as many do today, that sins are mainly caused by poverty. They had left their all, though it wasn't very much. Their promised reward is great. Like Jesus, having broken from the exclusiveness of their human family, they could share in the wider fellowship of his church, both in its richness and suffering.

The road now turns westward towards Jerusalem, the centre of hostility. The disciples are afraid, more perhaps of Jesus himself than of the dangers ahead, which still seem unreal. Again Jesus warns them of his approaching death and resurrection. They can't accept his scenario. The request for the best seats by James and John arouses a furore. Matthew lays the blame on their mother. This is understandable, but doesn't let them off them hook. Little did they realise what Jesus meant by sharing his baptism and his cup. (Lk. 12:50) Were the privileged places to be given eventually to the two thieves? Again the same reversal. Not lordship but slavery is the symbol of greatness. In Mark 10:45, we find perhaps the key to his gospel. Note that, in Mark's context, the implied alternative to "many", is not "all", but "few".

Before describing Jesus' entry into Jerusalem, Mark gives us one more incident that highlights, by contrast, his earlier scenes. In Jericho, Jesus is confronted by a blind beggar. His cry of faith contains the Messianic title that now will not be silenced. When Jesus calls him, Bartimaeus throws away his only possession. When asked what he wants, he asks, not for money, but for sight. Healed instantly, he chooses to follow Jesus on his way to the Cross. The fact that he is given a name indicates that he may later have become a Christian well-known to the early church.

The last days in Jerusalem. 11:1 - 12:44.

Mark's account of Jesus' three year ministry has taken up ten chapters. The last week of his life, including his death and resurrection, take up six. The pace slows down, but the pitch of intensity rises.

Jesus has carefully prepared both the timing and the manner of his entry into Jerusalem. He fulfils the prophecy of Zechariah, (Zec. 9:9) of a King, riding on a donkey, coming in peace not war. It is an excited triumphal procession. Hosanna means "Save now". They are expecting Jesus, as Messiah, to usher in the Kingdom immediately. He fulfills the prophecy of Malachi (Mal. 3:1) and enters the temple. He hears the noise, and sees the corruption. But it is too late in the day for effective action. He retires for the night to friends outside the city. It was a loving sanctuary in which he could pray and prepare for what was to come.

The fig tree pictured the temple. Outwardly, making a grand show, inwardly it was corrupt and fruitless. Long before the fruit season, signs of fruit formation are visible. The temple, and possibly the tree, were barren.

But for the temple this was the time for fruit. The Messiah had come to claim it. Malachi's prophesy (Mal. 3:2) was given forcible action. Jesus, soaked in the scriptures, expressed his anger, quoting Isaiah 56:7 and Jeremiah 7:11. For the first time we see Jesus attacking the priests on their own ground. Profits from the market and the money changing went toward the upkeep of the temple, no doubt feathering their own nests as well. But the priority given to money raising, and the methods used, negated the whole purpose of their existence, ie, to bring people to God. Their fury is understandable, but, with Jesus surrounded by the joyful and expectant crowd, they could do nothing.

The next day Jesus returned to the temple. One wonders if the merchants had returned too! The temple authorities demand to know the grounds of his authority, a question that had been raised from the beginning of his ministry. His counter question exposes their political pragmatism and insincerity. Jesus' authority, like all true spiritual authority, is inherent, recognised only by spiritual insight.

The parable of the Vineyard follows on from the incident of the fig tree. In this case there was a fully ripened harvest. Jesus had seen it. (Lk. 10:2) But those in charge of it wanted to keep it for themselves. The religious leaders clung to their authority to preserve their power. This was the basic sin of Eden, still worming its way inside Jesus' disciples.

Again it is the crowd that protects Jesus. Their hopes of him still run high. So all Jesus' enemies now combine to get him into trouble with Rome. For Jesus to speak against the tax would be sedition. To support it would lose him the popularity of the crowd. It was a clever question. Temple taxes had to be paid in temple coins, which accounts for the money-changers. Only Roman coins, with their blasphemous image of the Emperor's head, could be paid to Rome. But this was the normal currency. They all had it in their pockets, and could produce it when asked. His reply was unanswerable. Their hypocrisy was disclosed, and their authority challenged. There was no doubt that the harvest and the temple were God's.

The Sadducees now entered the fray. They were the priestly party which collaborated with Rome. They sat lightly to the Law and did not believe in any resurrection. Their weapon was ridicule. Again, Jesus goes on the offensive. They neither know the Scriptures nor the power of God.

One lone scribe remains to ask an honest question. What is the greatest commandment of the Law? Jesus quotes Deuteronomy 6:4 and Leviticus 19:18. Love of God and Man is the underlying principle of the Law and the basis for its interpretation. The scribe's thoughtful reply draws a significant commendation. "You are not far from the Kingdom of God." Love is also the key to the heart of God.

Jesus now talks about his authority to the crowd. They had hailed him as the

Son of David. But in Psalm 110:1, David calls the Messiah Lord. The Messiah is greater than David. His Kingdom too will be greater. Misunderstanding this, they are delighted. How can they be helped to understand the total reversal of values his Kingdom implies? Even his disciples could not take it in.

Jesus warns them against the love of worldly honour and respect indulged in by the scribes. Then he draws his disciples' attention to the ostentatious offerings of the rich, and, in contrast, to the widow's simple offering of two copper coins. God looks, not at the amount, but at the heart that lovingly gives its all.

Warnings of the Future. Chapter 13.

He and his disciples have hardly emerged from the temple when the disciples demonstrate their utter incomprehension. Newly up from the country, some of them may well have goggled at the temple's magnificence, just as today tourists goggle at York Minster. Jesus warns them of its coming destruction. He could read the political signs of the times. He may even have had clairvoyant foresight of the siege of AD 70 and the horrifying scenes of fire and sword that led to a total destruction of temple and city by Trajan. The Roman soldiers then set up their standards in the temple area, and sacrificed to them, It was a sacrilege similar to that of the Greek Antiochus Epiphanes, who, in BC 167, had erected an altar to Zeus where the altar had been. (Dan. 11:31. 1Macc. 1:54-57) Jesus' warning to flee was remembered by the Christian community, and many of them did flee, and so survived.

During this period soon after Jesus' death, his disciples would be persecuted by both Jews and Romans. Jesus and his gospel is divisive. Families would be split, and members would betray each other. But persecution was to give them opportunities to witness to people in high places. They were not to be anxious. The Holy Spirit would give them, at that time, words to say. Here lies the secret of Jesus' unerring response to all his critics. Today we live at a time of world-wide persecution. Unending are the stories of such courageous and effective witness.

Also ahead, as today, lay wars, earthquakes and famines. These are to be seen as birth-pangs of a new age. In such times of crisis, false Messiahs would arise, as they still do today.

The second series of disasters refers to the end of time and the return of Christ. Not even Jesus knew when this would happen. It is the false Messiahs who predict it with a certainty that events disprove, and so lead their followers to disillusionment, and even self-destruction. "Take heed", Jesus warns. His

"Watch" is thrice repeated. Heaven and earth will pass away, but his words, never. Jesus saves us from fear of the future. He is the Lord of Time.

Preparation for Death and Arrest. 14:1-52.

For Jesus himself, death is less than a week away. What a beautiful act of love prepares him for it. The valuable flask is broken. The precious ointment flows out and fills all the room with its perfume. It is an act of self-giving love that is a foretaste of his own. Some of the disciples thought it was a waste. Their suggestion was practical common sense. Here again we see a reversal of worldly standards. What God values is the spontaneous generous giving of a loving heart.

For Judas, this was the last straw. In John's Gospel Judas voices the objection, and it is the voice of a thief. Mark is not interested in Judas' motives, though he records that the priests gave him money. What matters is that he is the betrayer. It is the relationship with Jesus that counts. The awfulness of his betrayal is emphasised by Jesus' knowledge that his betrayer was one who was dipping his bread in the same dish. To the eastern mind, this in itself was unpardonable. But to betray Jesus! It would have been better for such a man never to have been born. When Mark wrote this, Christians were facing the persecution Jesus had predicted. Some might be tempted to betray, if not Jesus, then their brothers in Christ. To Jesus, it would be the same thing. (Matt. 25:40)

Time now gathers speed. Mark's account of the final events is so terse that, when the end comes, readers, not already dulled by familiarity, will share the disciples' shock.

Jesus had carefully prepared both the place and timing of his last meal with his disciples. Mark links it to the night on which the Passover Lamb was sacrificed. The Passover meal celebrated the passing over of the Angel of Death. Saved by the blood of the lamb smeared on their door posts, the Hebrews passed out of Egypt into freedom. (Exod. 12:1-17) It also celebrated the Covenant God made with them at Sinai. This too involved a blood sacrifice. The life of an animal was released to bond together God and His people. It was also celebrated by a meal. (Exod. 24:3-11)

Jesus gives the Passover Supper a new meaning. His blood is poured out to create a new covenant, an at-one-ment of Man and God. His broken body is the food that nourishes us on our journey into our freedom in Him. This is the climax, not just of Mark's Gospel, but of the whole Biblical Drama of Salvation. Salvation is both forgiveness, deliverance from sin, and restoration into a relationship of love and trust in God, that was lost at the Fall. (Gen. 3)

The Valley of Decision (Joel. 3:14) is now reached. Into it descend Jesus, his disciples, his enemies, the crowd, and even the Romans. It is the place where decisive action takes place. A lifetime of small decisions, implemented by words and actions, build up to a climax.

Jesus knows his disciples will all fail. This had been foretold in scripture. They will not fail because they are fated, but because they are fallible. They do not know themselves. But Jesus knows them. He warns them and also gives them hope. In this Valley their actions will teach them self-knowledge. Only their self-confidence will be destroyed. The confidence in Jesus they had enjoyed when he first called them will be raised to a new certainty.

In Gethsemane, Jesus grapples with human weakness. He was not immune. His understanding of Scripture and his knowledge of men had prepared him for the cross. He had accepted it and repeatedly foretold it. By word and deed he had moved deliberately towards it. Now his vivid imagination alerted his nervous system to violent protest. The Tempter would fill his mind with specious reasons urging withdrawal. It was still possible to escape. He did not pretend or cover up with a stiff upper lip. Tears, sweat and childlike entreaty expressed his feelings. Then came final acceptance, followed by a deep calm.

He had asked his disciples to watch and pray. Exhausted by sorrow and bewilderment they had fallen asleep. When their testing time came they were unprepared, and panicked. For Judas, the climax of his betrayal was the kiss, a pretence of love and loyalty. It was as if the guards behind him had nothing to do with him!

In Mark's Gospel, Jesus' response is silence, though, when the guards seize him, he questions their need for such a show of force. It was they who were afraid. Was it of the disciples? The followers of a political Messiah might have been expected to put up greater resistance than the pathetic effort that was made. Or did they fear that a crowd might gather?

As Jesus is led away, the disciples flee. But why this reference to a young man who, slow off the mark, had his garment seized, and ran away naked? It is generally thought that this is Mark himself, a disguised signature!

Trial and Crucifixion. 14:53 - 15:39.

It is now the turn of the Chief Priest and Council to face final exposure. According to the Law of Moses a sentence of death needed the agreement of two witnesses. (Deut 17:6) This was not forthcoming. Their accusation that Jesus had threatened the temple was a mixture of confusion and downright lying. (Mk. 13:2. cp. Jn. 2:19-21)

Jesus remains silent until the High Priest finally asks the one pertinent question, "Are you the Christ, the Son of the Blessed?" A man on trial should not be asked to incriminate himself. But this was the moment Jesus had been waiting for, his time to witness to the truth. Jesus quotes from Daniel 7:13. In this context, the title, Son of Man, was even more powerful than the title Son of God. To the Council it was blasphemy, rightly deserving the sentence of death. It was their final judgement on themselves.

So we move to the drama taking place in the courtyard of the High Priest's Palace. Though Mark does not say so, (cp. Jn. 18:26) it was Peter who had cut off the guard's ear. It was a futile gesture but showed at least a kind of rash courage. It took a more thoughtful courage to return and expose himself to the danger of recognition. He himself could have been arrested. Was it fear of this that led him to deny? The fact that Mark conceals that it was Peter who had wielded the sword, indicates that Mark did not think so. And Mark was probably Peter's scribe. Peter had boasted that he would die with Jesus. Had a fight developed in the garden, he might well have done so. Isolated, picked on by women, it was the mockery he was called upon to share with Jesus. That was too much for him. Boaster, blusterer, and coward, these were the hard truths about himself which Jesus had always known. Yet Jesus had loved and called him. It was the shame, not just of this self-knowledge, but the awfulness of betraying such love, that broke him down. His love for Jesus was literally Peter's redeeming feature.

Swiftly the scene changes to the Praetorium. The Roman Governor, called to sit in judgement on Jesus, finds himself in the dock of his own conscience. He knew the charges were false and were motivated by envy. His attempt to evade the issue by appealing to the crowd fails. The priests had manipulated them. It was easy. Jesus had not fulfilled their high hopes. Their shouts of Hosannah had proved hollow. Disappointed, their mood swings to hostility. They too, in the Valley of Decision are exposed. As for Pilate, when his sense of justice conflicts with his political need to please the crowd, he puts his political survival first. Pilate's truth is revealed by his action. He delivers Jesus to be crucified.

Jesus too is exposed, to humiliation piled on humiliation. The soldiers' mockery and the scourging, leaves him too weak to carry his cross like the other two criminals who are crucified beside him. He refuses the drink of myrrh, which would have helped to deaden his senses. Stripped of his clothes, for which the soldiers dice, he is held up, naked, for all to see. Priests and passers-by taunt him, their words echoing the Tempter. "Throw yourself down. Come down from the cross." Prove your claims by a miracle all can see.

Darkness descends. It is a double darkness. The sense of God's presence is blacked out. It was the one horror Jesus had not foreseen. Out of that darkness comes the terrible cry of dereliction, the only one of the Seven Words that Mark records. No cry of accomplishment, no quiet prayer of trustful commitment lightens the scene. All the more dramatic is the centurion's final verdict, "Truly, this man was a son of God."

"Who is this man?" All through the Gospel this question has haunted us, as it haunted all those whom Jesus met. Mark had opened with his own uncompromising declaration of faith. How significant that, at the end, almost the same witness is given by a Gentile. The centurion had seen none of Jesus' miracles, and heard none of his teaching. Jesus, silent, weak and helpless, unable to move hand or foot, achieves recognition in his death. At that moment the veil of the temple was torn. It screened off the Holy of Holies, where God's Presence was concealed in darkness. No one could enter except the High Priest, and that only once a year on the Day of Atonement. Because of Jesus' death on the cross, the way to God lay open to Jew and Gentile alike. The centurion's witness is the climax and the purpose of Mark's wonderful book. Like all great drama, its end lay in its beginning.

Resurrection and Aftermath. 15:40 - end.

Only now does Mark introduce us to that band of women who had followed Jesus and looked after his material needs during his ministry in Galilee. Three of them are named. They had followed him to Jerusalem, and were there at the cross, standing some distance away from the crowd. The disciples had fled, all except one, but the women stay on. Even after Jesus' death there is still a ministry they can perform. Their love is practical.

Joseph too makes his first and only appearance. It is from John's Gospel that we learn that he was a member of the Council, but had not consented to their verdict, and from Matthew that he was secretly a believer. In contrast to the disciples, Jesus' death gave him courage. He goes to Pilate and asks to be given Jesus' body for burial, thus saving it from a criminal's common grave. Pilate is surprised that death has come so soon. He grants the request, a small salve for his conscience perhaps. Mark, as usual, sticks to the bare facts.

Five actions follow, all difficult and time-consuming; acts of love and respect.

The women watch. The following evening, the Sabbath ended at 6 o'clock, they go to buy spices, which they then prepare. Next morning, before dawn, they go to the tomb. They worry about how they would be able to move the stone. To their astonishment, it is rolled away. A man in white, tells them Jesus is risen. They are to go and tell his disciples to go to Galilee, where they will see him. The women, terrified, flee, and say nothing to anyone.

Mark's Gospel ends here. The following verses were added by another hand. Mystery!

Did Mark die at this point? Were the final pages lost or stolen? Various endings, some heretical and shocking, have been found. The one we are given is a second-century completion made from stories taken from the other gospels. This brings us to the question: who was Mark, and why did he write his Gospel?

His full name was John Mark. As we have seen, he was probably the young man in the garden. His mother was Mary, to whose house Peter went after his miraculous release from prison. (Acts 12:12) It may well have been the house where the Last Supper was held. Mark was also a cousin of Barnabas. (Col. 4:10. King James' A.V's "sister's son" is revised in other versions.) He went with him and Paul on their first missionary journey. (Acts 13:5) The going was apparently too hard for him, and, at Pamphylia, he turned back. (v. 13) When a second journey was planned, Paul refused to take him. This led to a quarrel with Barnabas, who parted from Paul, and took Mark with him to Cyprus.

Despite Mark's early failure as a missionary pioneer, Paul later came to value him as a fellow worker. (Philem. v. 24) He asked for him to come and be with him, (2Tim. 4:11) and valued his loyal service. (Col. 4:10) Mark ends up, as far as the biblical record goes, in Rome, with Peter, who refers to him as "my son". (1Peter. 5:13) Mark therefore would have relied largely on Peter for his facts.

Mark's purpose in writing his Gospel was to teach the church the important facts about Jesus, before the last eyewitnesses died out. Christians were having to witness to those who had never known Jesus, or even heard of him. It was missionary work of the highest order. His facts he may have got from Peter, but his writing skills were his own. Writing in Greek, in a style almost crude in its simplicity, he makes use of Aramaic words spoken by Jesus, such as *Talitha cumi, Ephphatha*, and *Eli lama sabachthani*, thus heightening the dramatic effect. In fact, as we have already noted, Mark had all the skills of a playwright. Who now would dare to say that his work as an evangelist was less important than that of Paul?

The one thing the early church did know about Jesus was that he had risen from the dead. Unlike so many people in English churches today, they not only knew intellectually, but they had personal experience of his presence in the power of the Holy Spirit. Mark was in Rome, writing for Christians who were suffering persecution and even death for their belief. Maybe he deliberately ended his Gospel with the women's silence. His readers would know what happened next. Rhoads and Michie, in their fascinating book *Mark as Story* suggest that his abrupt ending might be a deliberate incitement to go out and witness boldly, whatever the cost.

Summary

In Mark's Gospel we have seen Jesus demonstrating his authority, both in action and in his teaching. The crowd and his disciples are awed. The religious leaders angrily question and reject. Jesus shows compassion for the crowd and mercy for sinners. His anger is directed against self-righteousness, legalism and hypocrisy. Where does his authority come from? Who is he?

The turning point is reached when Jesus questions his disciples, and Peter answers "You are the Christ". Then comes a big change. After a momentary glimpse of his glory, we are shown Jesus going resolutely towards Jerusalem and his death. He leaves the crowd behind. The disciples he seeks to prepare.

After his arrest in the garden, Jesus ceases to initiate. Passively, he demonstrates the patience of God, allowing evil, accepting suffering as its consequences, and sharing its pain with humanity. Jesus' authority stems from his Sonship. God himself is revealed on the cross. Is this a trite aphorism, blasphemy or a mind-blowing, world-shaking truth?

Such a revolutionary Gospel needed more than one writer to present its multifaceted truth. It was a Gospel for all people, but it needed to be related to the Jewish hope of a Messiah who would set up God's Kingdom on earth. Jesus' attitude to the Law also needed to be explored further. This is the special contribution of Matthew's Gospel which we will study next.

The relationship of Mark to 1 Peter is left to chapter 10.

Questions for private meditation

1. Do you have a sense of God's calling for your life? (1:16-19)

2. Is there anyone you know whom people look down on whom you could befriend? (2:17)

3. "Our first need is to stay with him". What helps us to do this? (3:13)

4. What has Jesus done for you, that you could tell others? (5:20)

5. What resources do you have that God might be calling you to share? (6:37)

6. In the context of your own life, what meaning has "losing your life to save it"? (8:35)

7. Is anything blocking the flow of God's peace into you? (9:28)

8. Are there still any bondages in your life, for which you need the freedom Jesus can give you? (10:22-25)

9. Have your actions taught you truths about yourself? (14:71-72)

10. Would you think it a sin to question God? (15:34)

Questions for group discussion

1. What worldly methods does Satan tempt the church to use today? (1:12-13)

2. Does your church have a sense of call to mission? Is it being side-tracked? (1:16-19)

3. Do you experience your church as a Family of faith? (3:31-35)

4. In your congregation are there people whose lives have been visibly changed by Jesus? Should public personal testimony be encouraged? (5:18-20)

5. Is there still a place for door-to-door evangelism? If so, what should be the approach and training for it? (6:7)

6. Is there a healing ministry in your church? What form should it take? (6:54-56)

7. Can the topsy-turvy values of Jesus be seen in your church by those outside it? (9:35)

8. Has the church watered down the Laws of God and teaching of Jesus on marriage to adjust to our weakness and pressure of modern society? (10:2-9)

9. How can your church be further helped to know the scriptures and the power of God? (12:24)

10. Jesus, nailed to a cross, achieved his greatest work. How can this affect our attitude towards physical weakness and disablement?

Chapter 2

St Matthew's Gospel

A letter written by a 2nd century bishop asserts that Matthew the Apostle made a collection of the Sayings of Jesus. This would have been before Mark's Gospel was written. St Matthew's Gospel, however, appeared 25 years later in Syria. Its author is unknown, but will be referred to as Matthew. Unlike Mark, he is not an eyewitness to the events he describes.

Matthew's Gospel, like that of Luke, includes almost the whole of Mark's Gospel which forms their common base. They also both include what are probably Matthew the Apostle's "Sayings of Jesus", about 200 of them. But Matthew's Gospel has special features of its own.

First, there are the continual references to Old Testament prophecies. Then there are a number of parables relating to the Kingdom of God, and some stories about Peter that are to be found nowhere else. Matthew is writing to Jewish Christians. He wants them to see how their Christian faith is rooted in the Old Testament, and how Jesus, both in word and deed, had fulfilled the Scriptures. He also wanted to justify the claim that the church was the New Israel which had supplanted the old. (1Peter 2:9. Ex. 19:5-6)

The Old Testament is full of *begats*, and this gospel starts with almost a whole chapter of them. What a boring contrast to Mark! But while Mark is proclaiming Jesus as Son of God, Matthew is proclaiming Jesus as King of the royal line of David. To Jewish Christians his ancestry is important. God had promised David an everlasting Kingdom. (2Sam. 7:12-13) Later, Matthew quotes Jesus as pointing to a still greater sonship. (Matt. 22:41-45) But the begats go back further, to Abraham, the Father of all the faithful, both Jew and Gentile, his descendants through whom the promised blessing was to come to the whole world. (Gen. 12:2-3)

Because of the importance of this royal descent to his readers, Matthew centres the story of Jesus' birth on Joseph. Inheritance can be passed on by legal adoption. Though Matthew quotes Isaiah 7:14, the word translated "Virgin" in the A.V. only means a young woman. (cp R.S.V. and other modern translations.) The miracle of the Virgin Birth relies on the story about Joseph. The importance of the quotation lies in the name Emmanuel. The name for Mary's son is to be Jesus, meaning Saviour. As King, he will save his people, not from political oppression, but from their sins.

Right from the start we see the danger of this title being misunderstood. Wise men come from the east to pay homage to the new-born King of the Jews. Herod, known as "the Great" had been made King by Rome. He had already slaughtered most of his family out of jealous fear they might supplant him. He plans to stamp out this new threat with typical guile and ferocity. Note that the Wise Men had already consulted the Old Testament both for interpreting the star and for choosing their gifts. (Num. 24:17. Is. 60:6)

Dreams play an important part in the story. There are four of them. Psychoanalysts, like Jung, have shown their importance in revealing what lies in our subconscious. The Pentecostal revival has also led to people today experiencing dreams as a way of receiving God's guidance. Christians, fleeing Nazi and Communist persecution, testify to having been given very precise instruction enabling them to escape.

When Matthew turns to the preaching of John the Baptist, he adds to Mark's account John's solemn warning to the Pharisees and Sadducees. He calls them a brood of vipers. Their repentance must bear the fruit of changed lives. Complacent reliance on their physical descent from Abraham is useless. God can raise up sons of Abraham from the stones on which they were standing. When Matthew wrote, children of Abraham were being raised up daily from Gentile soil. The tree of physical descent had been cut to its roots. New shoots, springing from Abraham's faith and obedience, were already producing a spiritual harvest.

Matthew also adds one significant detail to Mark's account of Jesus' baptism. John tries to defer to him, but Jesus, like King Cophetua, steps down. What Mark implies by an action, Matthew puts into words.

The wilderness temptations are described in detail. All were policies that Rulers, both Roman, and those of today, normally use: bread and circuses for the crowd; "miracles", engineered for the gullible by the priests, and, above all, the unscrupulous wielding of power, that we associate with the name Machiavelli. As in the Garden of Eden, the Tempter seeks to create doubt: "If you are the Son of God." Jesus refutes him by quoting scripture. Note well that the Devil can also quote texts but ignores their context. Jesus goes to the heart of the matter. Satan, rather than Rome, is the Usurper of God's Kingdom. In Dostoievsky's "The Brothers Karamazov", a story is told about the Grand Inquisitor. Jesus, reincarnated, protests against the burning of Christian heretics. He is put on trial by the Inquisition. He is told that, by rejecting the methods of worldly power, he has condemned his church to weakness and ineffectiveness. The church, having reversed the decision Jesus made in the desert, now flourishes. For the sake of its continuing success, he must again be put to death.

The Sermon On The Mount. Chapters 5 - 7.

The Beatitudes are not a new Law. They are a recipe for true happiness. Such happiness involves a total reversal of worldly values. It is the happiness of Man Right Side Up: emptiness not self-fulfilment, gentleness not pushiness. God not Self takes centre stage. It is from Him all happiness flows. Even persecution can bring joy, as the apostles quickly discovered. (Acts. 5:41) Disciples are to be Salt, to counteract the world's corruption. They are to be Light, shining out God's love and goodness, which most people have neither seen nor experienced.

It is only in the light of this reversal that Jesus' ambivalent attitude to the Law can be understood. This was a vital matter for Jewish Christians to take in. Jesus does not abolish the Law. He not only affirms it, but extends it to cover thoughts and motives. The standards of the Pharisees are not good enough. Jesus equates murder with hatred, adultery with lust. Who can now claim innocence? The root of sin lies in the heart. If love reigns there, not even an enemy can be excluded.

Similarly, piety is not to be paraded. Prayer is essentially the heart directed in love towards God, and so to others. Thoughts and desires count with God, rather than words and gestures. Resentment blocks the flow of love from God to us, as well as from us to others.

The Law forbade idolatry. To worship Baal was taboo. To worship Mammon was respectable. It is often the besetting sin of the pious. The Pharisees with whom Jesus came into conflict, were lovers of money. (Lk. 16:14) Such love draws hearts away from God, a seductive form of idolatry.

To centre our lives on God is to trust Him. So Jesus tells us not to worry. To worry about the future is not only futile, it also makes it difficult to discover God's guidance in any sensible planing.

Jesus also warns against a negative critical spirit. Our judgements are often biased projections of our own hidden faults. We misjudge people's motives. Only God sees into the heart and knows the pressures of their background and their inner struggles. To help another with a personal problem requires a very loving and humble spirit. Sensitivity is needed to know if and when such help is needed, and if we are the right person to give it. "Pearls before swine", portrays, with humorous irony, the conceit and contempt of would-be do-gooders.

Matthew's order at this point seems strange. It is not followed by Luke. (cp. Lk. 6:31) It might make more sense to put the teaching on asking God after the teaching on anxiety. "Do unto others" seems to fit better at the end of chapter 5.

All this teaching points to the path leading to the Kingdom. It seems impossibly difficult, but Jesus walked it. He was himself the Way. (Jn. 14:6). It led to a cross, a mysterious paradox of death leading to life, not in the future, but confronting us now. (Matt. 10:39)

Does the warning to judge false prophets contradict the earlier teaching to "judge not"? To judge means to make a decision about as well as to condemn. They are to be recognised by their fruit. We can judge the truth of their teaching, and leave other judgement to God. False Prophets often deceive themselves. They may be able to cast out demons in Jesus' Name, and yet themselves be cast out of the Kingdom. Today, the Press loves to publish stories of those who have apparently been "Working mightily in the Lord", and yet have been indulging some secret sin. Stone-throwing promotes sales! Nevertheless, what counts with God are not spectacular deeds, but a humble, loving and obedient heart. Does this contradict Jesus' words to John? (Mk. 9:39-40) The difference lies in the well-meaning ignorance of the one, and the self-confident arrogance of the other.

Matthew concludes this section of teaching with the parable of the Two Houses. Jews laid emphasis on obedience to the Law. Jesus laid his emphasis on the heart. Love was the Law of his Kingdom. It is Love that harmonises the O.T. conflict between the Law and the Prophets. However, the relationship between love and action is delicate and this problem has caused division in the church which has lasted to the present day. The Sermon on the Mount ends with the crucial importance of active obedience, working out what God works within. (Philip. 2:12-13. James 2:14-17) Practical obedience is the test of truth.

Jesus in Action. 8 - 12.

In the next five chapters, Matthew gives illustrations of Jesus' healing ministry, his choice of twelve disciples, and his early conflict with the Pharisees. He arranges his material in alternating blocks of incident and teaching material. He is not much concerned with chronology or the development of narrative.

Most of the incidents are copied from Mark's Gospel, but with some significant omissions and additions. The former are mainly the details given by an eye-witness; the pillow in the boat, the letting down of the paralytic with ropes through the roof, the Aramaic words used in the raising of Jairus' daughter, and the command that she should be given something to eat. Matthew introduces us to two blind men and two demoniacs, rather than one, but he does not tell us how Jesus sent the healed Demoniac back to his village to witness to his own people.

Matthew is more concerned with Jesus' mission to the Jews, and their rejection of the Gospel. He records how Jesus told his disciples to pray for God to send labourers into his harvest. As so often happens, they became the answer to their prayers. He also commanded them to visit only the homes of Israelites. Those who refuse to hear will be judged more harshly than the people of Sodom.

The Pharisees demanded that Jesus should first prove his credentials by giving them a sign. In Mark's Gospel, Jesus refuses. Matthew and Luke differ from him by qualifying his refusal with the offer of the sign of Jonah. The three days and three nights in the earth are a prophecy of the time bridging the interval between Jesus' death and resurrection. The Pharisees made nothing of this sign, either then, understandably, or later.

A further warning is given to those who experienced the healing and deliverance ministry of Jesus and his disciples, but would not open their hearts to him. The heart, like nature, abhors a vacuum. If God is not invited in, evil returns uninvited. The end is worse then before. "I've tried Christianity, and it didn't work. So I've given it up." Those who talk like this are the hardest of all to bring back.

Three additional incidents are included in these chapters. The first illustrates the shining faith of another Gentile, this time a Roman centurion. Jesus is amazed. He had met nothing like it among his own people. This is followed by a contrasting story of two men. One offers to become Jesus' disciple. The other, Jesus himself calls. Both are double-minded. They have neither the faith nor the readiness to pay the cost of burning their bridges.

The third incident concerns John the Baptist. Isolated, and in prison, he is afflicted by doubts. Is Jesus really the King who is to come? Will he indeed establish his Kingdom? John too sends to Jesus, asking for a sign of reassurance. John had burnt his bridges. Why else should he be languishing in Herod's dungeon? It is a cry of faith coming under attack, and Jesus responds. John's messengers are to tell John what they have seen. The signs, prophesied by Isaiah, are being fulfilled. The Kingdom is visible, here and now.

Jesus then gives his own testimony to John. Quoting from Isaiah and Malachi, he points to John as the Forerunner. But the least in the Kingdom of God is greater than he. Its privileges belong to those who trust and follow their King, even when they don't understand him, even when they are isolated, in prison, and in danger of death. How trivial are the excuses of those who don't want to believe, who sit on the side-lines, uncommitted. The ascetic life-style of John, the party atmosphere, generated by Jesus, are equally attacked. Either way, they won't play. They are lookers on.

Jesus praises God for His upside-down scheme of things. Clever philosophers, learned theologians, for all their studies, can be blind to spiritual truths, plain as a pike staff to a simple believer who receives it through Jesus with a child-like heart. It is they, who, coming to him, find rest from their burdens and release from their strain.

Parables of the Kingdom. Chapter 13.

Matthew returns to another block of teaching, now given in parables. To Mark's parables of the Sower and the Mustard Seed, he adds five more. The parable of the Tares relates to the problem of evil within the church, springing out of false teaching. One of the earliest problems the church had to meet was the insidious infiltration of Gnosticism. Gnostics believed that the body was merely a temporary home for the soul, and was morally neutral. Only the soul could be saved, and that, by knowledge and wisdom. So it was OK for the body to indulge itself in adultery and gluttony. The soul would remain unaffected. It was an attractive doctrine, especially to Greek converts, but the resulting behaviour scandalised Jewish Christians reared on the Ten Commandments. It cut clean across the teaching Jesus gave in the Sermon on the Mount. In this parable, the tares are sown by the Evil one. Were the servants at fault for sleeping, for not noticing and preventing such infiltration before such dangerous teaching took root? Maybe they could have given greater warning and more positive teaching. But censorship, and the closing of minds by community pressure, was, and is, totally contrary to the methods of Christ, though his church, as Dostoievsky pointed out, has frequently resorted to it.

So, what should the church do? Judge and expel their erring members? "No" says Jesus. "Wait for the harvest. Leave judgement to God." Wheat and weeds look very alike, especially in their early stages. It is not easy to distinguish them apart. There are those whose sins of the flesh are a sad burden. They love God, but have to struggle with bad habits, bad backgrounds, and weakness of faith. Julian of Norwich says that in such sinners there is a part of the will that never consents to sin. It is on this part that God looks with loving compassion, "free from blame". There are others who have never experienced the love of God. They join the church, but continue to act as they please. "Judge not" says Jesus, lest even one blade of wheat be rooted up.

Similar teaching is given in the parable of The Great Catch. The Gospel is preached to all. Crowds may respond for all sorts of reasons, emotional or practical. We have all heard of "rice Christians" who seek baptism for material advantage. Many are called, but few are chosen. We must leave the throwing-out to God. This problem of the inclusive and the exclusive church is a very real one, now as well as then. Later we will see how Paul wrestles with this problem in his letter to the Corinthians.

The growth of the Kingdom is not just a matter of size and spread, of numbers and geographical extension. It secretly transforms societies from within. Attitudes to slavery changed long before slavery was abolished. In India, Mother Theresa has transformed attitudes to the derelict poor dying in the streets. Attitudes towards the mentally ill have been similarly changed. A small group of prayerful believers can renew a local church, dying as a result of formality or faction. Note Jesus' warning that the Devil can also mix his leaven into the dough. (16:5-7)

Two more parables relate to those who value the Kingdom of God above all else. One man discovers it in a field by accident. He leaves it hidden while he goes and sells everything he has in order to buy the whole field. Many converts have heard of Jesus accidentally by being handed a tract, or hearing a broadcast. They have faced loss of friends and family in order to learn more about Jesus and accept him as Lord. The merchant is a seeker and connoisseur. He is rich, but, like Paul, after finding Christ, he considers his past treasures as dung. But note what Jesus has to say about the scribe, trained for the Kingdom. His former learning has value. Once it has been offered to Christ it can be used in his service. Like Thomas Merton, many have given up some talent to serve Christ, perhaps in some community, and have found themselves required to exercise it again fruitfully in a new context.

Events leading up to Peter's confession, and its aftermath. 14 - 17.

The death of John the Baptist, and the feeding of the 5,000, follow Mark's record. But the storm at sea has two significant additions. The first is the story of Peter's attempt to walk on the water. If Jesus, as Son of Man could do it, so could his followers. Already they had healed the sick and cast out demons. Peter, ever the leader, venturesome and rash, is prepared to have a go, but wisely, only if Jesus calls him. Jesus does call, and Peter gets out of the boat. It is when the wind and waves loom larger than Jesus, that he begins to sink. One cry for help, and Jesus is beside him, raising him up. They enter the boat together, and the storm ceases. It seems hard that Peter should be rebuked for lack of faith, but to a disciple, discouraged by failure, what could be more heartening than such a challenge?

Matthew notes that the disciples worshipped Jesus, and called him "Son of God". Was Peter's later confession not unique? For Greeks, "Son of God" was an ascription of divinity. But such semi-divine beings were two-a-penny. For the Jews, it referred to Judah's anointed King. (Ps. 2:6-7) It was not, in Jesus' day, regarded by them as a description of the Messiah. It is not clear whether anyone but Jesus heard God's voice at his baptism, though John saw the Spirit descend. (Jn. 1:32) Demons recognised him, but Jesus silenced them. The disciples, increasingly awed by his authority, were wondering who he was. Jesus had spoken of his Father in a way that was unique. Is this why the title, never used by himself, burst from his disciples' astonished lips?

Peter is again brought to our attention as the disciple who asks the question relating to food. Peter was later to be a key figure in the controversy that raged on this subject. (Acts 15. Gal. 2) The Pharisees are blind guides. "Leave them alone", counsels Jesus. Rooting them out is God's business, not theirs.

The following incidents are taken from Mark, but, when we come to Peter's confession, there is an important difference. The confession is unique, for Peter uses the title "Christ", ie "Messiah". This too means "Anointed One", but it was also clearly recognised as the title of the King, who would usher in the Kingdom of God. The story of Herod and three Wise Men makes this quite clear.

What is new are the words of Jesus about Peter and the church. "Peter" means "Rock". Was the church to be built on Peter, the man, who became the first Bishop of Rome? Or did Jesus mean that it would be built on Peter's faith? Roman Catholics and Protestants have been divided on this issue. But to separate the two makes a nonsense. The church is built on both. Peter is also given the Keys of the Kingdom. Centuries have been spent arguing about who holds these Keys. What is more important is to understand what the power to bind and loose entails. Jesus accused the Scribes and Pharisees of binding burdens on men with their laws and traditions. Jesus loosed and released them. How do the different churches today interpret this power to bind and loose?

For Matthew, what is important is the founding of a new community. The word "church" translates the Greek word *ecclesia,* meaning an assembly of people. In the O.T., qualified by "of Yahweh", it refers to Israel as the bearer of the divine Covenant. The early Christians used it to mean the Messianic Remnant, the reconstituted People of God.

This is a turning point, not only in the Gospel story but of the Bible as a whole. It is a turning point in world history. God is building his Kingdom on a new assembly of people, who accept Jesus as their King. At this point in the story it has not yet been brought into being. It is not even understood. Peter still sees the Kingdom in terms of the old. Jesus had to die and rise again before either were possible.

Because of Peter's importance, especially to Jewish Christians in the early church, Matthew adds another incident to bring him to our notice. Jesus did not approve of the temple tax, but preferred to pay it rather than give unnecessary offense on an unimportant issue. Whether his instructions led to a minor miracle, or to the sale of a catch, is not so important as Jesus' sense of priority. Matthew is reminding us that Peter is a fisherman whom Jesus called to catch men, and draw them into his Kingdom.

More teaching on the Kingdom. 18 - 20:16.

The new community is to have three distinguishing traits: childlike humility, a loving tender concern for the least of its members who might go astray, and a readiness to forgive.

A shortened version of the parable of The Lost Sheep is followed by detailed instructions about how to cope with an erring brother: no criticism behind the back, no gossip, tut-tutting, or even raised eyebrows with exchange of looks. Sensitive and humble concern for the brother's dignity is to be expressed in a private talk, followed if necessary by a further meeting with one or two witnesses. Only if this fails is the matter to be brought before the church. If the brother refuses to listen even to the church, then he is to be regarded as an outsider, still to be loved, prayed for, and won back to Christ.

The parable of The Unforgiving Servant has a stern ending. It is not the Lord who punishes. The servant, who has rejected mercy, is handed back to the Law. (cp Matt. 5:25-26) The Law is not abolished, but transcended by love. The parable illustrates both the teaching and the life of Jesus. (Matt. 6:14. Lk. 23:34)

On the matter of adultery, the teaching of Jesus, in Matthew's Gospel, has been said to be more lenient than Mark's. Adultery seems to be accepted as grounds for divorce. But there is no real difference. Adultery lies in the second marriage. Other versions of Matthew's text say that, if a man divorces his wife, he makes her commit adultery. This is because it would not be possible for a divorced woman to live alone.

A significant addition is made to the reward promised to his disciples. When Jesus sits on his throne, they too will sit on thrones judging the twelve tribes of Israel. When the Gospel was written, Jews were persecuting the Christians. The writer may have seen this saying as giving the New Israel the right to condemn the Old. (cp. Romans chap. 11, where a different view is expressed by Paul.)

The parable of The Labourers in the Vineyard is yet another illustration of the upside-down viewpoint of Christ's Kingdom. It is hardly in accordance with the principles of the T.U.C! But perhaps today, when the misery of unemployment with its sense of meaninglessness and rejection is understood, it may find easier acceptance. The repentant thief enters the Kingdom only just before he dies. He is the first to enter Paradise with Jesus. The reward for all is the same, the joy of being with the Lord. Who could ask for more?

Parables of the Kingdom told in Jerusalem. 20:17 - 25:46.

Jesus' entry into Jerusalem is as Mark tells it, with a few small additions. The disciples are told to bring both the ass and the colt. This is a more exact fulfilment of Zechariah's prophesy. It would be hard for Jesus to sit on both! Mark's eye-witness account is more likely to be accurate. Matthew alone tells us how children sang Jesus' praise in the temple. When the Pharisees protested, Jesus himself quotes Psalm 8. Jesus had a deep respect for children, and the story has the ring of truth.

The first parable of The Two Sons is more of a simile. Jesus calls on his hearers to make their own judgement. Which did his father's will? Obviously the first, despite his initial rude and negative reaction. He repented and did the job. The other only gave lip service. Harlots and thieves will enter the Kingdom before the Pharisees. What a reversal of judgement! Would church folk today be less shocked if confronted with such teaching in real life, not just in a biblical text?

The parable of the Wicked Tenants comes from Mark's gospel with one small change. When Jesus asks his hearers what the owner will do to these tenants, it is they who give the verdict. "He will put the wretches to death and let out the vineyard to others." No wonder the Pharisees feared the crowd. Under the outward public respect given to them lay contempt and hostility. Jesus underlines the crowd's verdict by being specific. In the O.T. Israel is portrayed as God's Vineyard. The spiritual fruit of its long history, and its nurture, will now be handed over to the church.

Jesus tells four more parables about those who will find themselves excluded from the Kingdom. In the parable of the Marriage Feast most of them exclude themselves. Instead of a joyful privilege, they find the invitation a bore. They had more pressing and interesting things to do. The savage punishment was typical of the times. Josephus, in his "Jewish Wars", gives horrific descriptions of contemporary events. If the Jews had accepted Jesus' Kingdom of peace, instead of rising in revolt, the Romans would not have destroyed their city.

But what of the man without a wedding garment? He could not plead poverty. A wedding garment would be provided, as Moslems today lend long robes to sleeveless women tourists who visit the Dome of the Rock in Jerusalem. In Zechariah we read how Joshua the High Priest is stripped of his filthy garments and clothed in rich robes, (Zech. 3:1-4) and in Isaiah we read of God clothing us in garments of praise and salvation. (Is. 61:3,10) This parable is a warning to those who think they can enter the Kingdom without first accepting forgiveness and the new life in Christ. Many would like to get into heaven bringing their favourite sins with them. Such infection would turn heaven into hell!

The parable of the Foolish Virgins is a warning to those who are not prepared for Christ's coming. Physical sleep was not the problem. All ten slept. But five had not prepared for the long wait. They ran out of oil. How long we wait for someone can be a measure of how much we care for them. Usually the first thing we start to give up on in our spiritual life is time spent in prayer. Oil is a symbol of the Spirit, with whose infilling we need to be continually renewed. Our spiritual battery quickly runs down. Then, when the moment of opportunity for action or decision suddenly arrives, we are too dull of spirit to recognise it and respond. This is another reason why Jesus weeps over the city. (Lk. 19:41-46) By AD 70 the doors were slammed. They were the doors of the city, slamming them in. There was no escape.

The parable of The Talents tells of an opportunity not only lost, but rejected. The third servant regarded his Lord as a tyrant who exploited his servants. In his absence he wasn't going to lift a finger. There are those who think of God like this, as a hard taskmaster. In Jesus, God's love shines forth unmistakably. Once again we see that, when love is rejected, we fall back into the arms of the Law. The Master acts accordingly. We also see that the more we use God's gifts in his service, the more opportunities to serve him we are given.

The last parable is that of the Sheep and the Goats. This is the only one that specifically deals with the Last Judgment. What comes across forcibly is everyone's surprise. God's love freely flows into us, but if it doesn't flow out, sin must be blocking it. Christ has identified himself with the poor, the needy, and the lost. To serve them is to serve him. This is what, in our day, Mother Theresa has so vividly demonstrated.

All these parables have a harsh end, a casting-out into darkness, wailing, and gnashing of teeth, misery and fury. This is first mentioned after the parable of the Tares. In Mark's Gospel, Jesus says some harsh things about the Pharisees. Matthew expands this into a whole chapter of Woes. John had called them "Vipers". Jesus does the same. (Matt. 12:34) Julian of Norwich tells us that, in her Revelations, she saw no anger in God, only love. How can we reconcile this with what we read here? It is a mystery. God's nature, and our final judgement, is beyond our understanding. But anger is not the same as hatred. It is the fiery reverse side of love's coin. Its opposite is indifference. We know that Jesus wept and died for all. He will not force us to accept and be transformed by his love. His Woes are not threats, but warnings of the inevitable consequences of our own chosen way of life.

Betrayal and Denial. 26:1 - 27:10.

The first difference we notice from Mark's account is the interest in Judas. At the Last Supper, after Jesus had spoken of a betrayer in their midst, Judas, last of all, asks, "Is it I?". Jesus, in his answer, indicates "Yes". From his reading of Psalm 41 verse 9, Jesus believed that he would eventually be betrayed by one of his friends. (Matt. 26:24) According to John, (Jn. 6:64) Jesus had known from the beginning that this would be Judas. Did Jesus choose him so that the Scriptures might be fulfilled? Perish the thought! There must have been great possibilities in Judas as well as weaknesses, as there were in all the disciples. Jesus may have recognized in Judas a tendency towards dishonesty and distrust, but, being led after much prayer to choose him, he had done all he could to heal him through acts of love and trust. He trusted him with the common purse. John called Judas a thief. (Jn. 12:4-6) Was Judas jealous of John. Did he fear to be exposed by him? At the Last Supper, Jesus gave Judas a final chance, warning him that he knew of his intention. John tells us that Jesus even honoured him by proffering him a special sop. (Jn. 13:26) Later, in the Garden, when Judas betrays him with a kiss, Jesus responds by calling him "Friend". With his question "Why are you here?", he probes into Judas' heart. There is no answer, but, after Jesus is condemned, Judas repents of what he has done.

"I have betrayed innocent blood." What had he thought Jesus was guilty of?

Some think that he had hoped Jesus would have brought in the Kingdom by some sort of show of miraculous force. Had he stolen for political reasons? Was his betrayal an attempt to force Jesus' hand into a showdown? Or was he an idealist who feared Jesus might do this and betray his own principles? In either case, he did not trust Jesus, and so tried to manipulate him. By this time, all the Gospel writers agree that the Devil had entered into him. Had he waited, he might, like Peter, have received forgiveness from the Risen Lord. But, though he repented of his action, he had not repented of his pride. Pride, sown by the Devil, makes it impossible for us to forgive ourselves, or live with exposure. Hence his suicide. Compare this with Peter. Peter was self-confident and boastful, frequently telling Jesus what he ought to do. But underneath lay humility, and a deep love of Jesus. Shame and self-knowledge led him, not to death, but to renewal of life.

As for the priests, they knew that Jesus was innocent of their charges. (Jn. 11:49) Their reaction to Judas was, "What is that to us?". Their motives were a combination of envy (Matt. 27:18) and anger at his public criticism, and challenge to their authority. As for the money, their attitude was legalistic. As for Judas, they had manipulated him to serve their purpose. They had no further interest in him. In all this we see the religious leaders betraying the Messiah, and, with him, their rich inheritance, which pointed to him, and found its fulfilment in him.

A significant addition is made to Mark's account of the Last Supper. The cup, which is the blood of the New Covenant, is poured out for the forgiveness of sins. This brings to mind the whole sacrificial system of the Law. Sacrifices for sin only covered sins unwittingly committed and ritual breaches of the Law. They did not cover deliberate wrong-doing. The New Law of the Kingdom was concerned with the sins of the heart. For such sin there was no sacrifice, no forgiveness. Jeremiah had understood the deceitful wickedness of the heart. (Jer. 17:9) He foretold the coming of the King, The Lord our Righteousness. (Jer. 23:6) He spoke of a New Covenant that would be written on men's hearts.

The Prophets had mostly denounced the sacrificial system for the very reason that it failed to change hearts or behaviour. But their ethical teaching met with similar failure. Jesus was now the Sin Offering. As Son of Man, he poured out his life of sinless obedience, that all our sins might through him, receive pardon, and that we, through him, might truly become Sons of God.

In the account of Jesus' arrest, Matthew adds two important sayings to Mark's record. The first is, "All who take the sword shall perish by the sword." Jesus did not reject all use of the sword for self-defence. He even told his disciples to buy one. (Lk. 22:36) Two swords were enough for defence, so long as they did nothing to provoke attack. But neither Jesus, nor his Kingdom can be defended or established by force. Contrast Mahomet who, when his life and work were threatened, resorted to war. But Islam is a religion based on Law. Love goes willingly to the Cross.

The other saying, which follows immediately afterwards, refers to legions of angels. They were at the ready, but Jesus refuses their help. Angels are with us today, and, as many can testify, they do occasionally intervene to defend us from danger. There is a time to escape and live. There is a time to suffer and die. (Eccles. 3:1-8) What matters is that we allow God to work his will through us.

Trial and Crucifixion. 27:11-54.

Two incidents are added about Pilate. First is the warning given him through his wife's dream. It made him even more reluctant to sentence Jesus. Mark tells us that he surrendered to the crowd because he wanted to please them. His past actions had made him very unpopular. Matthew's reason is that Pilate feared a riot. This is a second reminder of the real possibility of a violent uprising to set up Jesus as a political king. The Devil probably could have made good his promise, had Jesus cooperated. Pilate tries to disassociate himself from the evil consequences of his action by publicly washing his hands. It is an unconvincing act, but Matthew is not concerned with blaming Rome. He records however the horrific words of the crowd, in which they take the responsibility for Jesus' death upon themselves and upon their children. Did they actually say this? Matthew was not an eyewitness. Was he perhaps recording their continuing rejection of Jesus, and their persecution of the early Christians by stoning, or, when Emperor worship was enforced on all but Jews, by reporting them for non-compliance to the Roman officials who might otherwise have left the Christians alone?

Throughout the centuries, these words have been used by the church to justify its own persecution of the Jews. It is only in this century that the Pope has publicly disclaimed this view and asked forgiveness of the Jewish people for all the church's crimes against them. It was the sins of all of us that brought Christ to his cross. It is our continuing rejection of both him, and his Law of Love, that still crucifies him today. "In as much as ye do it to the least of these my brothers, ye do it unto me."

The crucifixion story is told in the words of Mark, with one significant addition. Mark tells us that Jesus refused the wine mingled with myrrh. Matthew says he tasted it, and only then refused it. He might have drunk it had it not been laced with a drug to lessen the pain. Jesus chose to drink the cup of pain and sorrow to its dregs. In the "Showings" given to Julian of Norwich, Jesus told her, "If there was anything more I could have suffered for you, I would have done so."

The story of the tombs being opened, and the appearance of the dead to many in the city, is peculiar to Matthew. Was it a fabrication of overwrought minds, growing in conviction as the stories circulated? This is typical of many such stories which evolve out of disturbing events. Or did the descent of Jesus into the world of the dead lead, in fact, to such disturbances? Even today, many can testify to seeing loved ones who have died appearing to them in some crisis, to warn or encourage. While the Bible forbids us to summon them, and the church sets its face against Spiritist practices, such visitations may be given us by God, as a form of angelic ministry.

Resurrection and Ascension. 27:55 - end.

So we come to the resurrection story. It differs from that given in Mark's gospel in many ways. There is the sealing of the tomb, and the witness and the bribing of the guards. It must have been a hefty bribe, for sleeping on duty could be a capital offence. If they were temple guards, rather than Roman soldiers, and the narrative seems to leave room for this possibility, then the problem would not be so great. Their story however was proof that the body was not there. If it had been, the authorities could have exposed it, and disproved the disciples' claims.

The other big difference is that the women heard the angel's message with joy. They ran off to tell the disciples, and, on the way, met Jesus. How can we reconcile these accounts? Many efforts have been made to do so, but they are not very convincing. Luke however agrees that the women did tell the disciples, but were not believed. Some of the disciples ran off to see the tomb for themselves. They found it empty. This, more or less, accords with John's Gospel, where the story is expanded.

Matthew also tells us that the disciples got the angel's message and went to Galilee where they saw Jesus, not by the lakeside as John records, but on a mountain. Strangely, while some worshipped, some doubted. In both Luke's and John's account of Jesus' resurrection appearances, there were initial difficulties in recognizing him. (Lk. 24:16. Jn. 20:15) Would this perhaps explain why, in Mark's gospel, the women, who met Jesus after leaving the tomb, said nothing to anyone? Did they not believe their own eyes, and ears!? When we encounter something totally outside our experience, we often doubt our senses, rather than take on the task of rethinking all we have known in the past.

It is here, exalted on a mountain, that the King proclaims his universal authority in heaven and on earth. He issues a royal commission to his followers. They are to call all people to enter his Kingdom. It is no longer to be a Jewish Kingdom but a Universal Kingdom of all nations. The baptismal formula was that of the writer's day. The earliest Christians were baptized into the Name of Jesus only. (Acts. 2:38. 19:5) With the Command goes a Royal Promise. Jesus will be with us to the End of Time. That is why, perhaps, the Ascension is not recorded. There is no real departure.

Summary

In this Gospel Matthew shows Jesus the catalyst resolving some of the problems of the O.T. Jesus continually quotes from the scriptures, starting with his rebuff to the Devil in the wilderness, and ending with his last cry on the cross. He uses scripture in prayer, in teaching, and, with telling effect, in his reply to the questions and criticisms of his opponents. He fulfils it by his actions, sometimes deliberately with careful preparations, as in the case of his entry into Jerusalem. Matthew quotes many other texts as prophesies fulfilled. Not all of them are relevant but the number of them is remarkable.

Jesus' attitude to the Law is expounded in the Sermon on the Mount. He came not to abolish but to fulfil. His standards of morality are higher than those of legalism for they are applied to the heart. When the heart is cleansed there is freedom for flexibility. For those whose hearts reject God's love, the letter of the Law remains.

Jesus knew himself to be the Messiah but he kept this a secret. The word had dangerous political overtones. His view of the Kingdom was totally different. Matthew illustrates this in the parables he selects.

God reigns in the hearts of His people. People were confronted by the Kingdom in the person of Jesus. By their response to him they were preparing to enter or reject it now. The Kingdom had no walls of exclusion. People built walls around their hearts to exclude the claims of God. They excluded themselves. Note that while Mark and Luke speak of the Kingdom of God, Matthew speaks of the Kingdom of Heaven. Heaven is both eternal and in the here and now. Thus another problem raised in the O.T. is resolved.

All this depends on the Holy Spirit at work in people's hearts. St Luke's

Gospel stresses the centrality of the Spirit in Jesus' life and ministry. So now it is to his Gospel that we turn.

The relation of St Matthew's Gospel and the problems of the Church in Antioch is dealt with in chapter 10.

Questions for private meditation

1. What influence has your own ancestry had upon you? (1:1-17)

2. Make a list of your favourite texts. What does this tell you about yourself?

3. What happiness have you found in the qualities listed in the Beatitudes? (5:1-11)

4. Prayer is the heart directed in love towards God. Do words help or hinder you? (9:38)

5. How can a Christian be "salty"? (5:13)

6. Are there any instances in which you might be the answer to your own prayer? (6:7)

7. In your church, are you a player, or do you watch from the side-lines? (11:16)

8. Have you a favourite fault you would like to hold on to?

9. What is the present state of your oil supply? (25:1-9)

10. Is there anything you can't forgive yourself for? Would it help to share this problem with a priest or a friend? (27:3-5)

Questions for group discussion

1. What aspects of Jesus' teaching would you stress to meet the special needs of your own society?

2. When is the quoting of texts helpful, convincing, tiresome, and misleading? (4:1-10)

3. How would you refute Dostoievsky's Grand Inquisitor? Does the church to-day try to settle for a compromise?

4. How can we stop worrying? Do we see it as a sin? (6:25-34)

5. Select some problem in your church. How could you relate love and action in seeking to solve it? (7:21)

6. How can your church act as leaven in society? (13:33)

7. How would you explain the parable of the Labourers in the Vineyard to those who complain of its unfairness? (20:1-16 may help)

8. The opposite of love is not anger, but indifference. Discuss.

9. The goats are condemned for inaction. What opportunities is your church failing to recognise? (25:45)

10. What do you do with your doubts? What value have they? (28:17)

Chapter 3

St Luke's Gospel

St Luke is the Beloved Physician (Col. 4:14) who accompanied St Paul on some of his missionary journeys. They met at Troas, and their teaming-up is indicated with subtlety by the changing of the pronoun from "them" to "we". (Acts 16:6-10) He was with Paul on his journey to Rome, and stayed with him to the end. (2Tim. 4:11) A Greek, and a Doctor of medicine, Luke was a highly educated man. He is the only one of the Gospel writers to write in beautiful prose style. He is a careful historian, as his Preface shows. Whether Theophilus, (lover of God) is the name of an individual, or, more probably, a generic title to cover all God lovers, is not clear. But Luke is writing primarily for Greeks. The Acts of the Apostles is a sequel to his Gospel.

Tradition has it that Luke was also an artist, and that he painted the Virgin Mary. It is quite possible that he knew her personally, and so could have learnt from her the events recorded in his first two chapters. His introduction also authenticates the eyewitness testimony of other Gospels.

Like Matthew, he used Mark's Gospel as a base, and included many of the sayings compiled by Matthew the Apostle. Instead of stringing them together in blocks of teaching, Luke very carefully fitted them round incidents, thus giving them both a fresh interpretation. He also added material of his own. Besides the birth stories, the best loved parables are found in his Gospel: The Lost Sheep, The Prodigal Son, and The Good Samaritan. He emphasises stories favouring the Gentiles, and gives teaching on prayer and the Holy Spirit. The humanity and tender compassion of Jesus is stressed. By tradition, the Gospel Writers are linked to the four Creatures that surround the throne of God. (Rev. 4:6-7) Mark is often linked to the ox for he shows the Son of God as a Servant. Matthew is usually the Lion King, John the high-flying, far-seeing eagle, and Luke is the one with a human face.

The Birth stories.

As we have noted, these could have come from Mary herself. They give her point of view. Joseph remains in the background. There is no mention of the shame Mary had to endure. Foremost in all the events is the Holy Spirit. He will fill John the Baptist from his mother's womb. His overshadowing will cause Mary to conceive. He inspires Zechariah to prophesy. He reveals to Simeon that he will live to see the Christ, and inspires him to come into the Temple and recognise the Child, when his parents came to present their offering.

While angels appear to Joseph only in dreams, they appear to Mary and the shepherds as waking experiences. Gabriel is even named. He is God's Messenger, first met with in Daniel. (Dan. 8:15-16, 9:21) When the Book of Daniel was written, between 167-4 BC, belief in a hierarchy of angels was well established. In the same book we also meet Michael. (Dan. 10:21, 12:1)

Luke also stresses prayer. Zechariah and Elizabeth must have prayed for a child for decades. After the age of child-bearing was past, they would have given up, maybe thinking their prayers had not been heard. But the answer had only been delayed. Why? For God's right time, for another miracle. Way out west, a Roman Emperor was to decree that a census be made for tax purposes. This forced Mary and Joseph to travel to Bethlehem in time for the birth of her son. Thus the prophecy of Micah was fulfilled. God's long arm reaches over time and space.

Faith goes hand in hand with humility and obedience. Zechariah had to learn these qualities by being dumb. Elizabeth showed it in abundance when she greeted Mary. Mary's response to the angel's message typified her whole life. It is reflected in the prayer of her Son in the Garden of Gethsemane. "Be it unto me according to Thy will." "Not my will but Thine be done."

The Good News is for the poor and simple. The birthplace is amid cattle. The first visitors are shepherds. The birth is heralded by song. Mary's song echoes that of Hannah. (1Sam. 2:1-10) It celebrates God's reversal of values. Zechariah's song celebrates His faithfulness in fulfilling the Covenant, not by political liberation but by deliverance from sin. The angel's song proclaims the joyful news that, despite the Fall, God still takes pleasure in His people. Simeon's song celebrates Jesus as the fulfilment and glory of their treasured inheritance. But he is also to be Light to the Gentiles.

Simeon had waited long years for Christ's coming. Like Anna, he spent much of his time in the temple. He would know only too well the rigid legalism and political expediency of the various religious parties. He must have known that this Child would expose their religious hypocrisy. He may even have been one of the very few who saw in Isaiah's Suffering Servant, a prophecy relating to the Messiah.

The sword that would cut Mary's heart was very close at hand. According to the Law, the presentation of offerings for the first-born had to be made sixty-six days after the birth. Joseph and Mary may well have planned to stay on in Bethlehem for the event and return home immediately after it. If Matthew's account of the Wise Men is to be fitted in to Luke's story, then they must have been just arriving. The flight into Egypt and massacre of the Innocents would have followed almost immediately.

The Divine Call. 2:41 - 5:11.

Only Luke gives us one short but significant glimpse of Jesus' childhood. A Jewish child becomes a responsible member of his community at the age of twelve. Jesus had been well trained for his Bar Mitsva. He knows the scriptures and has meditated on them deeply. He is eager to learn more, and asks searching questions. Already his answers are original enough to astonish those learned men. So does his reply to his anxious parents. Could he not have warned them? But, maybe, the divine call to stay in Jerusalem was sudden. It seems his parents had gone on ahead. Jesus had to make his first responsible decision to put obedience to his Heavenly Father before all else. This was the right time to do so. Jesus expected his parents to understand and accept this. In all other matters he remained their obedient child.

All four of Luke's special characteristics are to be seen in this account of Jesus' baptism. Note his concern for historical details. Modern research has found difficulty in equating some of these facts with records from secular sources, but there is much we do not know. Note also Luke's longer quotation from Isaiah. "All flesh shall see the salvation of God", not just the Jews. The Baptist gives practical advice as to what repentance involves. It isn't just being sorry, but involves showing practical concern for the poor and weak. This too was the message of Isaiah. (Is. 1:16-17) Lastly it is while Jesus is praying that the Holy Spirit descends.

And now, what a shock! We run into a whole chapter of begats. Matthew put his at the beginning. Why does Luke interrupt his story by putting them here? And why don't the two genealogies agree?

Matthew's list starts with Abraham, Father of the Jews. Luke's goes back to Adam, Father of all mankind. The two lists, from Abraham to David, agree. But, while Matthew traces Jesus' line back to Solomon and the Kings of Judah, Luke traces it back to Nathan, Solomon's elder brother. Solomon's style of worldly glory was not to be the model for that of Jesus. The true facts of Jesus' genealogy we probably won't ever know. Both lists differ from the one given in 1 Chronicles 3:17-19. What matters here is the point Luke is making.

After the Exile, both lists lead us to Zerubbabel. He was of the royal line. Encouraged by the Prophet Haggai, he led the Jews to rebuild the temple. Many of the people of his day hoped that he might be the Messiah. But the prophecy about him (Zech. 4:7-10) is significant. The Kingdom was to be built, not by power, but by Spirit. The" headstone" links up with Psalm 118:22, which Jesus quoted in reference to himself. The temple of his Body and the church was to be established by Grace. His, ie the Messiah's hands, would complete it. Who indeed shall despise the day of small things? How the mustard seed has grown! There is more in these begats than is obvious at first sight.

Luke again emphasises that it was the Spirit who led Jesus into the wilderness where he was tempted to take those worldly short cuts that would lead nowhere. It was in the power of the Spirit that he returned to Galilee, and began to teach and preach. Only Luke tells us how he returned to Nazareth and outlined the programme he intended to follow, based on the prophecy of Isaiah, 61:1-2. Matthew only refers to it in the context of Jesus' reply to the Baptist's question from prison. Luke presents it as a clear policy statement. It is a message of hope to the downtrodden, practical as well as spiritual. It was inclusive and offered to the Gentiles as well as to the Jews. The time of opportunity was now. Note the omission of Isaiah's warning of God's vengeance. Isaiah's warning had been the central message of the Baptist who proclaimed the traditional teaching of the O.T. prophets that the Day of the Lord would be the Day of His anger. Jesus, in contrast proclaimed it as the Day of God's favour. This led to a tragic rift between them which may lie behind John's message from prison and Jesus' reply. (Lk. 7:20-23). It also explains Jesus' later comments on the limitations of John's greatness. (Lk. 7:28)

It was Jesus' hearers who tried to take vengeance on him for such inclusiveness. God's goodies were for them alone. They tried to throw him over a cliff, but the awesome power of his spirit was too much for them. He passed through the furious crowd unscathed. John Wesley had a similar experience. So did my own great grandfather, vicar of a docklands church.

The call of the four fishermen differs from the other two Gospels. Jesus first makes use of one of their boats. It was Simon's. After he had finished teaching, he told Simon to "launch out into the deep", and let down the net. Luke obviously expects his readers to interpret this at two levels. Typically, Simon makes a protest, but obeys. The result is a miraculous catch. Simon is totally out of his depth. Faced by the awesomeness of Jesus he falls on his knees. Is it really so strange that he should ask Jesus to leave him? Moses, Elijah, and many others were scared when confronted by God's close and awesome Presence. Yet, without such an experience of launching into the deep, Simon would never have become Peter the Great Fisherman!

A mixture of Teaching and Healing. 5:12 - 9:62.

While reading the rest of chapter 5, and the stories already made familiar by Mark and Matthew, do not overlook Luke's small addition of verse 39. What gentle understanding Jesus shows of those who find it hard to accept his revolutionary teaching.

In chapter 6 we get Luke's version of the Beatitudes. The poor are not spiritualised. The land was being trampled on by war and bled white by taxes. There were rich and poor, and not much in between. It was the poor who responded to Jesus. The rich were unaware of any need. It is hard to proclaim the Gospel to an affluent society.

Luke adds a contrasting list of Woes. He shows Jesus warning the comfortable and complacent of their pain and sorrow when they finally realise what they have missed. But he omits Matthew's references to the casting out and weeping and gnashing of teeth. (cp Lk. 7:9. Matt. 8:10-12)

Part of the Sermon on the Mount is here represented as the Sermon on the Plain. Those who have visited the site will see no contradiction. Half-way up the hill, on which the Church of the Beatitudes is built, the land flattens out, convenient for a crowd to sit.

It is interesting to note how Luke gives some of Jesus' sayings a different context to that given by Matthew. The saying about the measure you give, being the same as the measure you receive, is linked, not to sharing the gospel, but with forgiveness. The blind leading the blind relates to those who try and remove motes from their brother's eye, rather than to legalists imposing food regulations. Today, as we read and pray over Jesus' teaching, the Holy Spirit applies it to our own situation, as Jesus promised He would. (Jn. 14:26) But we need to test that it is the Holy Spirit, and not our desire to prove our point of view! No saying can be taken out of the context of the Gospel as a whole.

In the account of Jesus' meeting with the centurion, (7:1-10) an added detail illustrates Luke's interest in all that brings Jew and Gentile together. It is the Jews that bring him to Jesus. He had built their synagogue, and was a God-fearing man who favoured them and their religion. They considered him worthy of "crumbs falling from the children's table". (Matt. 15:26-27) But they hardly expected the praise by which Jesus raised him to the high table!

Besides appreciation of Gentiles, Luke also shows Jesus' compassion for widows. The raising of the widow's son at Nain, is a story special to Luke. It was a chance meeting. Jesus' help was neither expected nor sought. His intervention was an act of pure compassion, given to the poor as well as the rich. (cp. Lk. 8:40-56)

It was also for sinners. Jesus was ready to dine with anyone, rich or poor, respectable or despised. The rich did not often invite him, nor did the Pharisees often play host. Had he invited Jesus just to test him out? He did not offer him any of the basic courtesies normally offered to guests. To him, the woman was nothing but a prostitute, whose very touch was pollution. To Jesus, her action was a sign and measure of the love and forgiveness that had reached her. The measure of sin forgiven was now the measure of her joy and gratitude.

Luke appreciates the service of women, and mentions them early in his story. The other two do not mention them until after the crucifixion. Among them were women of status and wealth, who used their assets to serve Jesus and support his work.

In the rest of chapter 8, and most of chapter 9 we meet material recorded by Mark and Matthew. But note the few changes that Luke makes, no doubt deliberately. As a doctor he omits Mark's derogatory comment that the woman who touched Jesus had spent all she had on doctors, and had only become worse. They'd bled her dry!

Luke continually refers to Jesus praying. He notes that only after Jesus had been praying alone did he ask his disciples that momentous question about his identity. Similarly, it is as he is praying that he is transfigured. (9:18 & 28) Luke tells us that Moses and Elijah were talking with him about his "departure that he was to accomplish at Jerusalem." What a significant way in which to describe his death! It finds echoes in Luke 9:51 and John 10:18 as well as the loud cry of triumph in John 19:30.

Jesus now chooses to travel towards Jerusalem by way of Samaria. It was a shorter route and would be free from the hostility and plots of the Jewish leaders. Pious Jews avoided all contact with Samaritans, a people of mixed race and religion. Hostility was mutual. It was because Jesus was bound for Jerusalem that the Samaritans shut their doors against him. The reaction to this by James and John explains the nickname, Boanerges, which Jesus gave them. (Mk. 3:17) Why not call down fire from heaven? Elijah had done it. (2Kings 1:9-12) The harshness of Jesus' rebuke is omitted, as is his similar rebuke to Peter. (cp Lk. 9:55-6. A.V. reduced in R.S.V. to a footnote & Matt. 16:23). The incident foreshadows the acceptance and passive strength of Jesus in facing insult and rejection in Jerusalem.

Chapters 10:1 - 12:12.

Only Luke records the Mission of the 70. The instructions given to them are almost identical with those given to the 12. Luke also records the Mission of the 12, so it is not a variation of one event. When the 12 returned they were tired. (Mk. 6:30) When the 70 returned they were exhilarated by success. Jesus' reply gives a glimpse of his timeless pre-existence. (Rev. 12:9) He has given them authority to tread down serpents and scorpions, typical representatives of evil. This is found in the additional verses of St Mark's Gospel, (Mk. 16:18) where it is linked to the Ascension and Jesus' final commission to preach the Gospel to the world. Luke chooses to end his gospel on a different note. Here, Jesus warns his disciples to rejoice in their salvation, rather than in the spiritual gifts that flow from it. The latter can sometimes turn men's heads with tragic consequences.

The belief in a Book of Life, in which the names of the saved are inscribed, is first mentioned in Exodus. (Ex. 32:32) It is referred to in Psalm 69:28, and in the book of Daniel, (Dan. 12:1) so it has a long history: the Devil loves to sow doubt in people's hearts. Jesus wanted his followers to rejoice in assurance of their salvation, despite their faults and failings, and not to agonize as to whether their names were written there or not.

So we come to one of the most loved of Jesus' parables. It has a sting in its tail, and can be easily misunderstood. While working in India, I asked the wives of Ordinands to divide into groups and each to act out the story in a modern setting. They all complacently identified the Good Samaritan with a Christian. But in the story, told to a Jew, the Good Neighbour was a man the Jew most despised. Whom would we cast in that role? Note the time, the trouble and continuing care given in the name of common humanity and human compassion.

India has also helped me to understand the Martha and Mary story. When I visited homes, the women would all disappear into the kitchen to make coffee, a long process. By the time they brought it, and watched me drink it, it was almost time to go. Traditional social obligation took precedence over a more appropriate personal response. It is easier to serve Jesus actively than to sit and listen to him silently.

The story of the sisters leads appropriately to a section on prayer. The Lord's Prayer is given in a shortened version. Luke's concern is for perseverance in praying. The verbs, ask, seek, knock, are given in a continuous tense, ie "go on asking". The two parables illustrate the point. At what point do we, perhaps like Elizabeth and Zecharias, give up? What a sad haunting question Jesus asks in the last verse! Note the significant difference between Luke 11:13 and Matt 7:11.

Two small additions to Matthew's story (Matt. 12:43-45) are given in Chapter 11. There is the emotional outburst of a woman, and Jesus' response, which is similar to that which he gave when his mother and brothers tried to see him. (Lk. 8:21) Blessed are the actively obedient.

It is interesting that Luke, who gives such prominence to Mary in the birth stories, should repeat this seeming put-down. Apart from those early stories, Mary is hardly mentioned in the Gospels except by St John, where she stands at the foot of the cross. Luke implies that she was present at Pentecost, (Acts 1:14, 2:1) but she received no special resurrection appearance. The exaltation of Mary only developed many years after her death, and was linked to the growth of a theology that made her an almost symbolic Woman to contrast with Eve.

Another surprising detail is that Jesus' attack on the hypocrisy of the Pharisees in their concern for outward rather than inward cleansing, is set in the context of a dinner party given by a Pharisee at which he is a guest. Jesus is more concerned with speaking truth than being tactful. Beloved in the home of Bethany, and honoured in the homes of Levi and Zacchaeus, with the smugly pious, Jesus could be an uncomfortable and too perceptive a guest!

Both Mark and Matthew link Jesus' warning against the leaven of the Pharisees, with their demand for a sign. In Luke's account Jesus clearly states that he is referring to their hypocrisy. This is no contradiction. Their demand for a sign was itself hypocritical. Hypocrisy means a covering up. The disciples are told they are not to cover up the Gospel but to proclaim it from the housetops, whatever the cost. It is in this context of evangelism and persecution that the Holy Spirit is promised. He will inspire their witness. Those who recognise His voice and, for their own purposes, knowingly denounce it, have cut themselves off from their only hope of forgiveness.

Chapters 12:13 - 13:35.

In the rest of chapter 12 we see how beautifully Luke weaves together sayings, culled from the Sermon on the Mount, with sayings and parables special to himself. Meaning is added by juxtaposition and contrast. The man who wants Jesus to intervene in a land dispute is rebuked for covetousness. Jesus doesn't take sides. There is no solution to territorial disputes when national pride and greed for land and its resources take precedence over humanity. Pile up a fortune. Conquer a province. Death makes personal ambitions meaningless. In contrast, Jesus' followers are told to trust God for their minimum necessities. Then, like St Francis they will discover they are rich.

Next, Luke takes up the theme of watchfulness. In place of the story of the Foolish Virgins, he gives a beautiful picture of a returning Master who girds himself, and graciously serves his own servants. Here is a foretaste of Jesus washing the feet of his disciples. It is Peter who asks whether the parable is for Jesus' disciples or for all. Jesus goes on to be more specific about those who are to act as stewards over his household, the church. No mention is made of expulsion or gnashing of teeth. (cp. Matt. 24:50-51) Punishment will vary according to their understanding of what was required of them. It is good to contrast verse 48 with a similar saying in Luke 8:18. The earlier related more to the parable of the Talents and the loss of what goes unused. The more God gives us, the more He will expect from us. I find Luke 12:48 the most frightening saying in the Gospels.

Jesus had his own inner battles to fight. Verses 49-50 give a glimpse into his sense of frustration. He longed for the time when he would be free to heal and save, and draw into his Kingdom people of every race and nation throughout the world. Through his church, baptized by the Spirit, he would kindle a fire that would blaze throughout the centuries and would never be put out. But none of this could happen until after his death. (Jn. 12:24, 32) This was the cup and the baptism he both dreaded and longed for.

When trials come we ask why? In the last verses of chapter 12 we read of Jesus asking people why? It is the most searching of questions. It probes into our deepest motives. It challenges us to self-knowledge, confession and repentance. Other questions can be evaded by facts. "Why" is inescapably confrontative.

The first "Why" reveals hypocrisy. They cannot read the signs of the times because they do not want to. The foundations of their world were being shaken. In the words of Amos, by putting off the evil day they were bringing it nearer. The second " Why" reveals greed that lies hidden behind many claims for civil justice. Pounds mean more than People. Bankruptcy of both may result. This is a favourite theme for novels and plays. For another pertinent "Why", look back to Luke 6:46. Later the priests and scribes foresaw a still more dangerous "Why", and tried to avoid it by silence. (Lk. 20:5-7)

Chapter 13 starts with another question Jesus asked. It was rhetorical. Everyone knew the answer. Calamities were generally explained as God's punishment of those concerned. It is an attitude prevalent today. People's first reaction to tragedy is so often "What have I done to deserve this?" (cp. Jn. 9:1-2) Human sin may cause an accident or disease, but the sin of sufferers is not to be measured by their suffering. However, all persistent turning away from God's love eventually leads to spiritual death.

The following illustration may raise a question. God is usually portrayed as the owner of the vineyard. Is God impatient? Is Jesus the vine-dresser who seeks to appease Him? Parables are not meant to be pushed this way. They are not allegories, though some may have allegorical features, such as the Sower. Most parables have one overriding point. Here the point is to warn the hearers that in Jesus, they are being offered their last chance. Soon he would be dead, and they would have to live with the awful truth that the longed-for Christ had come and they had crucified him. This could harden their hearts still further. (nb. Acts 2:37) Far from saving themselves and their city they were dooming both to destruction. (Jn. 11:47-50) To return to the question, we should never contrast a harsh God with a more merciful Jesus. In Jesus the nature of God, as far as we can understand it, is fully revealed. Again we are shown the loving heart of Jesus as he cries out in pain. Half-way down the road from the Mount of Olives, at the turn where the city first comes into sight, is the Church of Dominus Flevit ('Jesus wept'). Instead of an altar frontal, there is a beautiful mosaic depicting a hen with outstretched wings protecting her chickens. The anger Jesus showed to the religious leaders sprang from a loving and anguished heart.

The healing of a woman with a bent back is special to Luke. Spinal deformity can have many causes. Jesus diagnoses this case as a bondage of Satan. This does not rule out psychological pressure. We talk of being crushed by our burdens, of being ground down by the exploitation of society. Even families can crush and exploit their members. Jesus is all compassion for this daughter of faith, and initiates her healing. There are countries where cows are more valued and cared for than wives. Cows are more expensive to replace.

The narrow door is like the narrow gate. (Matt. 7:13) Its shutting finds echoes in the parable of the Foolish Virgins. "Where do you come from?" is an interesting question. We use such a figure of speech to explore our basic assumptions. It seems as if the Jews regarded themselves as automatically eligible for the Kingdom. (cp. Lk. 3:8) Christians are apt to do the same. At funeral services we are usually given the benefit of the doubt! In this case Luke does refer to the gnashing of teeth. It is the anger of envy and frustrated presumption.

Are we shocked at Jesus calling Herod a fox? Jesus was no enemy of foxes. (Lk. 9:58) For us they have a reputation of being sly. Herod wanted to meet Jesus, but more out of curiosity than a desire for his death. (Lk. 23:8) Mark tells us however that, early on, it was the Pharisees who took the initiative to plot with some of Herod's followers to destroy Jesus. (Mk. 3:6) "Fox" could refer to a jackal, an animal that feeds on what others kill. Here, it is the Pharisees who are being sly. Jesus knew that it was in the city of Jerusalem that the Messiah must die. He would be there when the time was right. Until then he walked in safety.

Chapters 14-17.

Chapter 14 starts with another dinner party, given to Jesus by a Pharisee. This is the third that Luke records. At the first, Jesus warned his host that his inhospitable reception pointed to his state of unforgivenness. (Lk. 7:36-47) At the second, his host is confronted with hypocrisy. (Lk. 11:37-41) This third Pharisee is shown up on three counts. Had the man with dropsy been invited? The guests were all watching Jesus. Were they setting him up? If so, he met them on their chosen ground, and reduced them to silence. Jesus also noticed their scramble for the best seats, and spoke of the wisdom of humility in this regard.

The call to invite the poor rather than one's friends can create a problem for us in present day society. The "poor" might resent it as condescension. There is a need to build up a mutual relationship of respect that involves a mutual sharing. Today, what Jesus might rebuke are the business dinners that are planned, not just to provide opportunities for business discussion, but to extract social and financial advantage.

Luke links this incident and teaching with the parable of the Great Banquet. It is sparked off by the hollow ring of another pious bromide. Most people don't want the feast God has prepared for us. Luke omits all the hard additions making other points. (Matt. 22:11-14)

The warning against any expectancy that following Jesus will be a comfortable joy ride, is now given to all, not just to the disciples. All must count the cost. The hopes held out by today's triumphalist preachers are false.

Nothing needs to be written about the three wonderful stories in chapter 15. They speak for themselves. It is not surprising that they have been recorded by the one whom St Paul called the Beloved Physician.

The next chapter is mostly concerned with money. The story of the dishonest steward raises several questions. Was he wasting his master's goods by inefficient accounting, extravagance, or by lining his own pocket? Under threat of dismissal, his actions are decisive, and effective. Was Jesus the master who commended him? Probably yes. The commendation is not for dishonesty but for shrewdness. The steward had made a wise investment. Note that it is not holy to be careless of money, nor is it unholy to be shrewd. The steward's motives were selfish, but Jesus is commending the generous use of money to make friends with people and help those in need. When, at Heaven's gate, we are asked what good deeds we have done as evidence of our faith, it will be nice to have friends to speak up on our behalf! (cp. James 2:17) As a counterbalance to avoid any misunderstanding of the parable, teaching is given about stewardship of money and the impossibility of devoting oneself to money and to God. Those who scoffed at this would justify their pursuit of riches by looking upon their success as a sign of God's blessing. Jesus warned them that God was not deceived!

The story of Dives and Lazarus is another warning about complacency about money. It is a fearsome story, especially now that our cities are full of homeless young people sleeping in doorways, and the TV brings millions of starving refugees into our sitting rooms. Dives not only did nothing, he didn't care. No doubt familiarity caused him not even to notice Lazarus. It was the way things were. Even after death, Dives still presumes that he can treat Lazarus as a servant. Jesus' final tag about the resurrection proved true. Miracles prove nothing to those unwilling to believe.

What can we make of Jesus' saying about the violent taking the Kingdom by force? The Law and the Prophets had created a mind-set that the scribes and Pharisees had mixed with concrete. The Gospel, with its offer of the unconditional love of God, was overwhelmingly attractive, but a violent effort of thought and action was needed to break through to the new freedom. But Jesus goes on to teach that freedom is not license. The Law and Prophets remain. As Bishop Fison once said, when we make a break, it must break up not down.

Do we think God owes us something when we have served Him, some earthly reward perhaps, or, at least special protection in times of trouble? Do we think that, after a lifetime's service, we can put our feet up and retire on a pension? If so chapter 17 verses 7-10 will give us a rude shock. If this sounds hard, read again Luke 12:37. The sayings are not contradictory. The attitude of the Master relates to that of the servant. There is also a rich reward for those who give God unconditional service, as Jesus makes clear. (Lk. 18:28-30)

We have already noticed that Luke chooses stories that favour Gentiles and Samaritans. Jesus healed ten lepers, but only one, a Samaritan, returned to thank him. He shamed his fellow outcasts. Once they were healed they would no longer be his fellows, for the Jewish ex-lepers would now outcast him. But Jesus honoured him.

Luke adds new insight into the Pharisees demand for a sign. In Mark, Jesus refuses them. In Matthew, he gives them only the sign of Jonah. Luke tells us that there was no need for a sign, for the Kingdom was, in Jesus, visibly among them. Some manuscripts give, "The Kingdom of God is within you". This is probably a later interpretation, given in the context of the Holy Spirit. (Jn;14:17)

Parables and examples of Vindication. Chapter 18.

In chapter 18 we meet the parable of the Unjust Judge. At first sight it looks like that of the Importunate Friend. (Lk 11:5-13) But the earlier parable is set in the context of prayer for our needs to be met, so that they can supply the needs of others. Luke sees this as primarily a prayer for the Holy Spirit. This later parable is a prayer for vindication against an adversary. It could be dangerous when put into our own personal context. In Luke's context it is an encouragement to those who suffer persecution for Jesus' sake, to go on praying, even when God seems to be deaf, or doing nothing to help. God hears and cares, though He may not physically rescue. Jesus wasn't rescued. But God will vindicate. We can trust His timing. (cp. Jn. 16:8-11) Jesus has been speaking of his own sufferings and death, only a few days away, and the Last Judgement, that in terms of our times could be delayed for centuries. But Jesus was vindicated only three days later, by his resurrection, though only in the eyes of his disciples. The agony and martyrdom of his church still goes on today. Individual persecutors like Saul are still being converted, and the church is being strengthened, but in the eyes of the world there is no vindication. Hence the cry of the martyrs. (Rev. 6:9-11) So we have to hold on, come hell and high water, praying and believing that, in the end, Christ, through his Body, will be vindicated. How sad is Jesus' question. Even he did not know all the answers. (Lk. 18:8)

The parable of the Pharisee and the Publican is notorious for its dangers in interpretation. How easy it is to thank God that we are not like that Pharisee. Note the Pharisee's strident "I" and the Publican's humble "me". Humility can't be learnt by thinking or trying. According to St Thérèse of Liseaux, it is best learnt by practise, ie by being constantly humiliated. In the parable it depends on the focus of attention, not on self, either one's virtues or one's sins, but on the holiness and infinite mercy of God. The parable is another example of Jesus' reversal of human judgements.

Luke goes on to illustrate this parable. Zachaeus was hated as a traitor, working for the Romans, extorting as much in taxes as he could to serve the Imperial Power, lining his pockets in the process. Society creates its own anti-social elements. Why do men take such jobs that earn them public loathing? He was short, perhaps even somewhat deformed. Children can be cruel. At school, had he been despised and called "dwarf"? Isolated, inwardly hurt and angry, Zachaeus could find in his job an opportunity for revenge. This might ease but could not heal his hurt. His desire to see Jesus was so great that he was ready to face further public mockery. Jesus noticed this strange little man up a tree and saw through to his deep need for acceptance. By calling him down, and inviting himself to a meal at his house, Jesus publicly accepted him, and so shared with him in the crowd's criticism. Love not blame called forth Zachaeus' repentance. Both the love and the repentance were expressed, not just in words, but in deeds. This is the salvation Jesus came to bring, the transformation of hurt and damaged lives. So, if we feel hurt and damaged, we can say, as Julian of Norwich puts it, "It is just for people like me that Jesus came to save."

There are a few changes in Luke's version of the parable of The Talents. All are given the same amount of capital, and when the buried money is given to the man who has made the most, there is some protest. As we have seen, God's justice is not that of the world. The harsh reference to the citizens who sent an embassy of protest against their new ruler would ring bells of memory. The Jews had protested against the Emperor's appointment of Herod's son, Archelaus, as Ethnarch of half the kingdom. According to Josephus, on his return, he punished them brutally. Jesus told the parable to his followers as they were nearing Jerusalem. It was to reassure them that there would be a final reckoning with those who reject the loving purpose of God revealed in the Lordship of Christ. The vindication would, to the faithful, be speedy. (Lk. 18:8) The reckoning might be longer delayed.

The Last Days in Jerusalem. 19:28 - 22:62.

As Jesus rides down the Mount of Olives, the shouts of the crowd recall both the words of Psalm 118:26 and the song of the angels at Jesus' birth. Jesus said that if they were silenced, the very stones would cry out. At the same time, with clairvoyant certainty, he could see the horrors of the siege, the toppling of the walls, and the massacre that was to follow. How can one bear to live with such foreknowledge? It is good so few of us have this gift.

Nothing new is added to the story of Jesus' last days in Jerusalem. One significant detail is omitted, that of the woman who poured ointment over his head. Luke had earlier recorded the story of the repentant prostitute, who had poured such ointment over his feet. Luke may not have wanted any link to be made between her and the woman in Bethany, whom John identifies as Martha's sister Mary. In our journey through the three Gospels we have seen what a wealth of new meaning can be garnered by comparing them. This is especially true when we come to the Last Supper. Mark records simply Jesus' main words and actions. Matthew adds that the cup is poured out for the forgiveness of sins. Luke tells us that we are to do this in remembrance. This agrees with what Paul had written earlier. (1Cor. 11:23-25) It is a meal celebrating the night of Israel's deliverance from Egypt. It was food for their journey into freedom. From now on, it would be, for his disciples, a celebration of a new deliverance, not from Egypt, but from the power of sin. Tonight Jesus will celebrate with them. Tomorrow he will suffer the cost. Luke also sees the Lord's Supper, not just as a foretaste of the Kingdom, but as its foundation. As sharers in his trials, and now, sacramentally, in his death and resurrection, he assigns to them a Kingdom as his Father had assigned it to him. It is a feast that Jesus has long desired to eat with his disciples. Only Luke gives this insight into Jesus' inner feelings. Only Luke mentions two cups. The first Jesus would have shared. It is a cup of celebration and joy drunk early in the meal. The second cup, given after the bread, he would not have shared, for it symbolised his life blood, to be poured out in sacrifice.

The disciples are still arguing about which of them will be the greatest. Jesus tells them that leadership is not lording it over others, but being their servant. The Messiah is the Suffering Servant. Their true greatness is that, for all their faults and foolishness, they have faithfully followed him, and shared in his sufferings. The Mother Superior of an Order of Nuns was asked what commendation she would most like to receive from her Lord, and she quoted the words of verse 28.

There follows another example of Jesus' foreknowledge. Satan has demanded the right to test Peter. As with Job, permission has been given. When wheat is sifted, only the chaff is lost. Jesus tells Peter he has prayed for him. So confident is he that his prayer will be answered, that he gives Peter a foretaste of his final re-commissioning, another example of Jesus living out his teaching. We shouldn't presume that he found this easy. In the event, Peter, in his failure, lost nothing but his brash confidence in himself.

So we come to Gethsemane. Here Luke again gives us further insight into Jesus' deepest emotions and experiences. As a boy, Jesus must have seen many crucifixions. His sensitive mind must have been deeply affected. In the garden, he does not pretend. He prays out of his humanity. Escape was still possible. But was there any other path for the Messiah to tread? He knows there isn't. Prayer for Jesus meant aligning his will with his Father's and mastering his doubts and fears. Like us, he too had to battle with himself. Luke tells us that an angel appeared to strengthen him. This did not remove the problem. The agony continued. He was strengthened to go on praying, until his spirit conquered, and the battle was won. Then a great peace and calm resolution took control. How did Luke know about this intimate experience? The disciples were sleeping. Did Jesus, after his resurrection, share this experience to strengthen them for the martyrdom most of them would suffer? Here. as elsewhere in his Gospel, Luke shows us, not only his great compassion, but his special concerns as a doctor, and his interest in angels.

The other writers tell us that Jesus reproached Judas, not for betrayal, but for doing it with a token of friendship. From Luke we learn this was a kiss. Only he tells us that the disciples asked if they should use the swords Jesus had advised them to bring. Peter doesn't wait for an answer. Luke, kindly, withholds his name. Jesus halts Peter and heals the man's ear. Their swords were only for their own self-defence. They were not to provoke attack. Helpless, frightened and shocked, they all run away.

But Peter returned. In Luke's pregnant phrase, he "followed at a distance." Better than not following at all. If he hadn't followed, he wouldn't have met, or failed, the test Satan had prepared, or learnt from it. It was past midnight. Shivering with cold, he moves close to the fire, a fatal move, for it lights up his face, and he is recognised. He moves away to the darkness of the porch, but he doesn't escape. Luke notes that he had a whole hour to decide whether or not to withdraw to safety. He has enough loyalty to stay, but not enough to swallow his former denials. At a third challenge he makes a lonely confession of total ignorance. There was, after all, the little matter of his slicing off the guard's ear! Poor Peter. He'd done better than most of the others.

Trial and Crucifixion. 22:63 - 23:56.

So we come to Luke's account of Jesus' trial and death. He was not an eyewitness, but he knew those who were, and he was a careful historian. He tells us much that the other two do not record.

First, "Jesus turned and looked on Peter." What a pregnant phrase! Was that face conjured up in Peter's conscience, or was it real? Careful reading shows that Jesus was first taken to the High Priest's palace, but nothing could be done immediately. The Council members had to be summoned. Night trials were against the Law. So, until dawn broke, Jesus was taken down to the guard's quarters and prison. Yes, the High Priest had a prison. Some time before dawn, when cocks crow, he would be taken back to the Palace. By one of God's coincidences, he might well have seen Peter just as he made his third denial. There are however two problems. One is, that the mockery and return of Jesus to meet the Council, is put after this. The other is, that the other two Gospels state that the Council members had already been summoned, and Jesus was illegally tried at night. Can this be resolved by the account given by the Gospel of John? There we learn that there were two trials, first before Annas, and later before Caiaphas. (Jn. 18:12-28) Jesus may have looked at Peter as he was being led off to Pilate.

There are also significant differences between the ways in which Jesus responds to the demand to reveal his identity. Mark tells us that Jesus' answer is a straightforward "I am". His reference to the Son of Man, taken from Daniel, raises this title, which he had always used for himself, though not in this exalted context, to the same high level as Son of the Blessed, ie God. In Matthew's account Jesus only speaks when put on oath. When asked if he is the Christ, the Son of God, his answer could mean "Those words are yours." This is made clearer in his answer to Pilate when questioned about his kingship. But, again, it is the prophesy in Daniel that expresses his view of himself best. It was enough to bring about his conviction for blasphemy. The title of Son of God can be misunderstood. To a Moslem it is deeply offensive. To the Greeks of Jesus' day, and to Hindus today, it is too common. Multiple gods have sons by the score. The Person of Jesus Christ cannot be defined in words, any more than God or the Holy Trinity can be so defined. We are confronted by mystery. As the anonymous author of "The Cloud of Unknowing" puts it, "By love He can be gotten and holden. By thought, never", let alone by words! Hence the importance of the challenge Jesus gave to his accusers, which Luke alone records.

As Paul's travelling companion, Luke had often experienced the protection of the Roman authorities. He describes the brutal assaults by the Jewish guards, but not by the Roman soldiers. The mocking is done by Herod. The trial before Herod is unique to Luke. While presenting a frivolous picture of the King, it gives Jesus a double bill of "Not Guilty as charged". In this, Herod and Pilate were united. Only Luke gives us the details of the false charges made against Jesus by the lying witnesses. Not only are they the opposite of the truth, but they come close to the charges that would have been made against Barabbas, whom Luke records as being an insurrectionist and murderer. Ancient authorities note that his name also was Jesus. It was quite a common name at the time, a variant of Joshua, both meaning Saviour. So the crowd had to choose between being saved by violence or through suffering. Like most crowds, they were easily stirred up to choose the former. The same choice has confronted the church ever since.

Luke shows us how Jesus went on showing this suffering love right to the end. He describes Jesus' meeting with the women of Jerusalem. "Weep not for me, but for yourselves", he tells them. It is Luke who records Jesus' prayer of forgiveness, even as he was being crucified. It was not just for the soldiers he was praying. (cp Peter's speech Acts 3:17) He responds to the prayer of the penitent thief with a promise of being with him that day in Paradise. Finally, after the cry of dereliction, which Luke does not mention, Jesus dies, committing himself into his Father's hands in perfect trust. It was a prayer that his mother would have taught him to say every night before going to sleep. It is from Psalm 31 and is still repeated in the service of Compline, the night prayers of the church.

The centurion's final verdict that "This man was surely innocent", would, for him, be more valid than to call him a Son of God. The sons of Greek and Roman gods were morally far from innocent. In Matthew, the comments of the Centurion and others are the result of the darkness and the earthquake. In Luke the centurion is moved by the sheer goodness that flowed out of Jesus throughout his ordeal. There is a tradition that this centurion later became a Christian. If so, the germ of his comment, recorded by the other evangelists, would have been present in this verdict. Note how it links up with the verdict of Herod and Pilate. The verdict of the Jewish Council is reversed mainly by Gentiles. Luke, writing for Gentiles, makes this very clear.

Resurrection and Ascension. 24:1 - end.

In his account of the resurrection, Luke starts by following Mark, except in a few minor details. But he tells us that the women did go and tell the disciples, who didn't believe them. Luke's great contribution is the story of the walk to Emmaus. It is presented in great detail, with superb dramatic skill.

The strange thing about the resurrection stories is not that the disciples couldn't believe what the women told them, still less that the details differ. Ask any group of bystanders to describe in detail a deeply emotional experience some time after the event, and such discrepancies will always appear. No, the really strange thing is that Jesus is not at first recognised. Did his resurrection body look different, or was there a veil over the eyes of the beholder? His body certainly bore the marks of his wounds. Luke tells us that Jesus even ate fish to prove to them he wasn't a ghost. John also implies that he ate with them. Yet he appeared and disappeared, regardless of doors and walls. The new knowledge opened up by post-Newtonian physics has introduced us to a mysterious world where such strange mutations can no longer be dismissed as impossible.

In Matthew's Gospel, Jesus is shown continually quoting from scripture. At the end of Luke's Gospel, Jesus gives a summary of all its teaching and prophecy about him. He gives it twice, first to Cleopas and his companion on their journey, then again to the disciples gathered in the Upper Room. Greek Christians might have thought that they did not need to read the Old Testament. Many Christians today think they can ignore it. They dismiss it as Jewish History, full of outdated and sub-Christian beliefs. But the whole of Jewish history, as interpreted in their scripture, was God's preparation for Christ's coming. It was through studying it that Jesus learnt what his calling and destiny as Messiah would mean. It was his thought-world. He affirmed, corrected and reinterpreted it. But if we are truly, as Paul puts it, grafted into him, then his roots will become ours. (Rom. 11:17-18). If we are to stand strong in adverse times, and in a hostile society, our roots need to be grounded deep.

It is in this context of the scriptures, that the disciples are to preach, in Christ's name, the gospel of repentance and forgiveness of sins. His death and resurrection make both possible, melting hardened hearts, and giving assurance to fearful consciences. The disciples are witnesses who will speak from personal experience. Compare this very personal charge with the command to preach, teach and baptize, given in the other gospels. Many Christians today are against preaching to people of other faiths. They say that all religions are equal, and teach more or less the same things. That is not true. They do not all teach the need of everyone to repent, nor do they all provide the assurance of full forgiveness, and the offer of new life. Mostly they encourage their adherents to earn salvation, by leading a moral life and doing good works. Despite the clear teaching of the Gospels, popular Christianity seems to do the same. Without love, this can be a recipe for self-righteousness. For those in bondage to failure, and evil habits, from which they cannot escape, this is not a Gospel of good news. Only from the Cross does the loving forgiveness and acceptance of God shine forth for those who are broken, rejected by society, and by themselves. Only such a visible revelation of God's love has the power to restore them, and us, to hope and new life. Only those who have themselves experienced this, can proclaim it with authentic conviction.

While Matthew puts the final scene in Galilee, Luke sets it firmly in Bethany, on the Mount of Olives. (Acts. 1:12. cp Mk. 11:1) Matthew concludes with Jesus' promise to be with his disciples to the end of the age. The final verse in Mark witnesses to the fulfilment of that promise in the experience of the church. In Luke, Jesus' promise points clearly to Pentecost. His final command is not to preach, but to wait. Thus Luke ends his gospel by foreshadowing the event with which his sequel opens. The Holy Spirit is another Catalyst. It is He who empowered Jesus. From now on, He will empower his church.

Summary

While Matthew links his stories to O.T. prophecies that point to Jesus as Messiah, Luke is more concerned with the breath-taking wonder of the Incarnation: the Spirit enabling Mary to conceive and give birth to the Son of God. Without her response of humble obedience, this could not have happened. In Luke's sequel, the Acts, he shows how the Spirit enabled the church both to be born and to give birth by offering Christ to the world. Though in Acts, Mary is hardly mentioned, her response to her calling provided a model for the church.

Whether or not Luke ever painted Mary in colour, he certainly painted her with restrained artistry in words. "She pondered all these things". Luke's emphasis on prayer prompts us to do the same. The questions are appended as an aid. Luke similarly paints several other miniature portraits, of Zechariah and Elizabeth, Simeon and Anna and, later, Martha and Mary. Imagination, used to explore their feelings and relationships, is another form of pondering. They become our friends as we share in their experiences.

Jesus however is central. As we read Luke's Gospel, we are led to ponder on the human face of God. As he speaks to individuals, look for the expression on his face and listen to hear the tone of his voice. Above all notice how in his life he demonstrates the Beatitudes.

In studying this Gospel we have continually compared the different contexts and interpretations given to the stories and actions of Jesus by Matthew. Both have been accepted by the church as equally inspired. The caution given in my comment on Luke 16:9 needs to be heeded if fresh interpretations, given to fit contemporary situations, are to contribute new facets to the wholeness of its truth.

In John's Gospel we see a radically new interpretation. Like Luke, John is concerned with the mystery of the Incarnation, and with Mark's question: "Who is this man who speaks and acts with such authority?" But, while showing Jesus in all the vulnerability of his humanity, it is the mystery of Jesus as the Logos, the Word of God, that John explores, together with his relationship with his Father.

Questions for private meditation

1. What has repentance involved for you? (3:10-14)

2. Do you allow the Holy Spirit to direct and empower you in every aspect of your life? Are there any no-go areas? (4:1)

3. What does "launching out into the deep" mean for you? (5:4-9)

4. In your Christian life, what gives you the greatest joy? Spend some time thanking God for this.

5. Have you assurance of salvation? What is the difference between assurance and presumption? (10:20)

6. The more God gives, the more He expects. Ponder this. (12:48)

7. Are you accountable to God for the use of your purse? (16:1-9)

8. What is the difference between "God is on my side" and "I am on God's side". Is either assertion safe? (18:3 cp 12:13-14)

9. Should we pray "deliver us from temptation" or "deliver us in temptation"? (22:31-32. 43-46)

10. Has your heart burnt within you as you read the scriptures? What was the consequence? (24:32)

Questions for group discussion

1. What experience, if any, have members of your Group had of obedience to God clashing with family claims? (2:48-50)

2. How do we take the Gospel to an affluent society? (4:18)

3. Has emphasis on God as a Loving Father eclipsed our sense of His awesome-

ness? What do we lose thereby? (5:8)

4. In applying scripture to our own situation, how do we distinguish between the Spirit's guidance and our own point of view?

5. How can death be an accomplishment? Illustrate from the lives of those you have known. (9:31)

6. Why is our first reaction to trouble so often to ask, "What have I done to deserve this"? Does God owe us anything? (17:7-10)

7. How would Jesus view our tolerant society? (12:51-53)

8. Is God concerned as to how we invest our capital? (16:1-9)

9. What have we learnt from our humiliating experiences? (18:14)

10. Protestants have sometimes been accused of seeing the Lord's Supper as only a Remembrance Service. What active power has remembrance? (22:19)

Chapter 4

St John's Gospel

When we start reading the 4th Gospel we find we are entering a new world. The first three Gospels present a similar viewpoint (*Syn-optic*). They describe Jesus' ministry, touring the towns and villages of Galilee. From a collection of stories and events they select examples of healing miracles, parables and pithy sayings. They trace the growth of opposition to his claims of authority. Finally he enters Jerusalem, only a few days before his death. In contrast, John, not only records several visits to Jerusalem, one very early on in his ministry, but he confronts us with long discourses and theological controversies, full of contrasted abstractions such as Light and Darkness. Are these really the words of Jesus? How could the writer remember it all? Stories and pithy sayings are easy to remember, though not always in their original context. But these complicated disputes, were they made up by the writer?

Until fairly recently the opinion of some biblical scholars was that the author lived in the 3rd or 4th century, long after the events, and his work is the result of his meditation on the meaning of events recorded by others and the experience of the church. However, a papyrus fragment from John's gospel, since discovered in Egypt and dated c. AD 132, has proved that it could not have been written later than 100 AD. Archaeological studies have also confirmed the author's historical accuracy. Where his record differs from Mark, in terms of time and place, John's is the more reliable. It is as if he were making a deliberate correction.

The Gospel claims to be based on the witness of the beloved disciple, who, after the fall of Jerusalem, went to Ephesus, and lived to a great age. Another hand claims to have penned the Gospel, (21:24) as Mark penned the memories of Peter. He may have been John the Elder, who also lived in Ephesus.

It has generally been assumed that John the Galilean fisherman was the beloved disciple. This assumption has been questioned. To go into this is not part of my brief so, where the gospel refers to the beloved disciple, I shall do the same and reserve the name John for the Gospel that bears his name.

So we return to these long discourses. It is likely that the disciples would have asked questions and talked over these matters both before and after such confrontations, which may, in various forms, have taken place many times. The beloved disciple, so called, not because Jesus had favourites, but because he had the most sensitive understanding of Jesus, would for many years have pondered over these controversies, and refined them to extract their essence.

Another thing to note in the Gospel, is the importance of the number seven. It has symbolic meaning. Four, represents earth, and three, the Trinity, indicates Heaven. Seven joins them together. John selects 7 Signs which reveal the glory of Jesus, and 7 "I AMs", which reveal his identity. John's symbolic language does not always rule out an additional literal interpretation, as in his pregnant comment "and it was night". A more common mistake of the casual reader is to take such comments at their surface value.

The Prologue. 1:1-18.

Matthew takes us back to Abraham, Luke, to Adam. John takes us back behind the big bang of creation, to the pre-existence of Christ.

The Word of God is a recurring theme of the O.T. God speaks, calls, commands and promises. He can shout to the whole world, and whisper secretly to the inner ear. His Word is effective, It can hammer, pierce, refresh and allure. It is creative. "God spake", and it was so.

The Hebrew word is here translated by the Greek word Logos. Logos also expresses the meaning behind the word, the rationality behind creation. Physicists today are increasingly awed by the sheer mathematics of the universe, the perfect balance of equations, down to strings of point noughts. The same is true in biology and chemistry.

The Jews, influenced by Greek culture also had a word for this concept, Wisdom, which they pictured as female. John has chosen a word of profound meaning to Jew and Greek. Meaningful life depends upon this Word of God, as Jesus made clear when he quoted Deuteronomy 8:3 to the Tempter. This life-giving Word is the light given to all. How else could men's spiritual awareness grow? How could the unbeliever ever respond to the gospel if the Light was not already within him? It is tragic that so many failed to recognise it. The artificial light of a city blots out the stars. Worldliness and prejudice have a similar effect. But those who, with joyful recognition, say "Yes", are born to a new kind of life. They have power to become children of God, though this becoming may take more then a lifetime!

Now comes the shock. "The Word became flesh". So far philosophers of all religions could concur. Truth is safely abstract. John uses the most earthy of words, flesh, something you can roast and eat. Jews are equally shocked. So are Moslems. To proclaim Jesus, Carpenter of Nazareth, as the Cosmic Christ, the pre-existing agent of Creation, a part of God Himself, was blasphemy.

How could John write this? He himself was a Jew, a strict monotheist. Yet he wrote it about a man he knew, and had lived with for three years. What had convinced him? Strangely, he does not mention the resurrection. He speaks of Grace, Truth, and Glory: Grace, God's free unmerited love, drawing men back to Himself; Truth, lived as well as understood; Glory, the shining radiance and glowing beauty of true goodness and holiness. John has seen and experienced all this in Jesus. Wave over wave of grace had rolled over him. No law-keeping or moral behaviour had led to such newness of life. Through knowing Jesus, he had come into a new relationship with God.

The Witnesses. 1:19-51.

The first witness to Christ was John the Baptist. No description of his person or of his teaching is given, only his witness to Jesus. When the authorities question him about himself, his replies get shorter and shorter. He is a Voice, as foretold by Isaiah, pointing to One who will come after him.

"Among you stands One." It is clear that the baptism has already taken place. Before that John had not known the true identity of his deeply respected cousin. The baptism is described as it was experienced by John. The sign of recognition is that the Holy Spirit should descend and remain. Many prophets had been filled with the Spirit at peak moments. In this permanency Jesus was unique. He could never be caught out in an off moment. John's witness is that Jesus is the Son of God. He is the image of his Father, a perfect reflection of His identity.

Events follow fast. "The next day". No time to fit in the 40 days in the wilderness. The Baptist points to Jesus as the Lamb of God, who takes away the sin of the world. How huge a meaning is implied in so small a phrase: the fulfilment of the sacrifices and the Law; sins, not only forgiven but taken away at great cost. Most shocking to John's hearers would be the gift of this salvation to the whole world. His audience must have been stunned.

The next day Jesus returns. Again John points to him with the same words. Two of his disciples follow his pointing. Jesus turns and asks, "What do you seek?" They can't answer his question. They were motivated by instinct rather than thought. Their reply is practical. "Where are you staying?" "Come and see," replies Jesus. This interchange is typical of the author's deep layers of meaning. So they go with Jesus. But first Andrew is off to find his brother Simon. What an astonishing witness. "We have found the Christ." It is a personal witness, made after so short a contact. He brings him to Jesus who instantly recognises both Simon's weakness and his potential strength. "You are. . . . you will be." The old adage "you can't change human nature" is true. We can't. But Jesus can. Living with Jesus can have a transforming effect.

The next day, (cp Mark's "immediately") Jesus goes to Galilee. The call of the four fishermen is not mentioned. Their meeting with Jesus by the Jordan, explains their instant response in the accounts given by the other gospels. Jesus calls Philip who goes off and witnesses to Nathaniel. Nathaniel's first reaction is sceptical. Philip repeats Jesus' invitation, "Come and see." Again there is instant recognition. Jesus sees Nathaniel's transparent honesty. Nathaniel responds by making his own confession of faith. Jesus does not deny the title Son of God. He clarifies it by referring to Jacob's Ladder. Through Jesus, God descends to man, and man ascends to God. In all this we see a repeated pattern of salvation: witness, the call to come and see, recognition, acceptance, and resulting witness.

The suddenness of this contrasts with the gradual recognition of Jesus portrayed by the other gospels. In Matthew it reaches a climax in Peter's confession. John's climax is rather different. (Jn. 6:66-69) John's concentration of events clarifies a basic Christian experience which is actually quite common. Our faith does not grow in a well-ordered fashion. It can begin with a flash of insight. This can fade, and we are back in the mundane. Doubts and questions have to be wrestled with. It may take years of struggle before we repossess that first joyous illumination. The process is different for us all.

The first sign. Water into Wine. 2:1-12.

Jesus' miracles were never performed to stun men into belief, ie stones into bread. John calls them signs. They revealed his glory to those who already had faith. But his reaction to his mother's request was not just a refusal to solve a social problem. He speaks of "his hour" being "not yet". His hour always refers to his death. Only then would he provide the wine that was to be his life-blood, poured out for the world. Mary's total trust transforms the situation. (cp Mk. 7:24-30) His action would be, not just a solution, but a sign. Water used for washing feet, another link with the Last Supper, as well as with Baptism, becomes Wine, symbol of joyous celebration of new life in the Kingdom of God. The puzzled steward notes that the best wine has been kept to the last. Ordinary wine, like bread, was part of the staple diet. There were many holy men and women in O.T. times. Jesus commenting on John the Baptist, said he was the greatest of them all. But the least in the Kingdom of God is greater than he. (Lk. 7:28) Through Jesus a new rich quality of life was now possible.

Cleansing the Temple. 2:13-25.

Unlike the other writers, John records three visits to the temple, not one. (2:23. 6:4. 13:1) This makes it clear that Jesus' ministry must have lasted three years. He also records visits to a feast of Tabernacles, (7:2) a festival of the Dedication of the temple, (10:22) and an unnamed feast. (5:1) Most of the important events take place in Jerusalem, e.g. at the Pools of Bethsaida and Siloam. So do most of the discourses. It is in the city that the great battle between Light and Darkness, Faith and Unbelief, is fought out.

The other Gospels make the cleansing of the temple the climax of Jesus' entry into the city. It leads directly to his arrest and death. Why did John choose to place it earlier? It may be a deliberate correction. The building was begun in BC 26. The Jews said it had taken 46 years to build. This would take us to the date AD 20 at the earliest. If Luke is correct in his dating (Lk. 3:1), the crucifixion was three years away. An additional symbolic motive was possible. It was another sign, to complement the sign given at Cana. There, water for purification, representing the Law, was transformed into the Wine of the Gospel. Here, the system of animal sacrifices is supplanted by Jesus, who is himself both sacrifice and temple. Only John records that Jesus drove out the animals, only he tells us what Jesus really said about the temple's destruction within three days. His body was the temple. They, his opponents, would be the destroyers.

John notes that those who saw his signs *believed*, but that Jesus who saw into men's hearts, did not trust them.

A visit by night. The New Birth. Chapter 3.

Old and New now meet in a personal encounter. A member of the ruling class pays a visit to Jesus the carpenter prophet. He opens with a polite compliment. Who is the *we*? In those early days there may have been one or two councillors like Joseph of Aramathea perhaps, who were open to enquiry. Or was the *we* really an *I*? Certainly the majority of the council were hostile, why else the visit by night? Was it merely for coolness and freedom from crowds?

Jesus cuts through the flummery. "Unless a man is born of Water and Spirit, he cannot even see the kingdom of God", let alone enter it. Jesus is astonished that a religious leader should be so lacking in spiritual understanding. If Nicodemus had hoped for a theological debate, he was not only disappointed, he was reduced to the position of a non-starter. His knowledge was only intellectual. It is difficult to share spiritual experience with someone who has none. Words bounce back, unless the Spirit gives them wings. Like the wind, the Spirit is beyond man's control. The organised church is wary of him. It has tried to domesticate Him by confining His activity to sacraments within its own control. It is typical of John that he releases the sacraments from such confinement.

Verse 13 onwards is probably John's commentary on all this. From the contrast of earthly and spiritual birth, he goes on to the contrast of life and death. The Serpent, a symbol of Satan, was, in Egypt, worshipped also as a god. Its venom brings death, but can become a healing salve. Pinned to a pole, it is the symbol of the medical profession. The Israelites, plagued for their sins, looked up at the bronze serpent and were healed. (Num. 21:5-9) So Jesus, bearing our sins on the cross, heals and saves. Evil is transformed into good, death into life. Verse 16 is probably the best loved verse in the Bible.

So we are led to another of the Prologue's contrasts, light and darkness. Darkness is not God's punishment for sin. We choose it when we turn away from God to do our own thing. Adam and Eve hid from exposure. Darkness is our camouflage. Even religion can act as camouflage to conceal our lack of spiritual life.

The baptism controversy illustrates the danger, both of control and camouflage. It could have led to theological argument and party faction. But the Baptist continues to point to Jesus. He rejoices in his own eclipse. Jesus' response was to withdraw.

The Water of Life. 4:1-42.

Water is not only used for washing, but to quench thirst. In the O.T. God is called a Fountain of Life. (Jer. 2:13. Ps. 36:8-9) Isaiah prophesies of the joy in drawing water from the wells of salvation. (Is. 11:1-10. 12:1-6) It is good to stop and study these verses. Jesus did. Sitting by Jacob's well we see how he fulfills them.

What a contrast to the previous encounter. From the cool evening air in a city, we move to a well just outside a village, blazing in the heat of midday. In place of the learned Pharisee, we encounter someone whom he would have despised for her race, her morals, and even for her sex. Jesus cuts through all these barriers, to meet both the woman and her need. He takes the initiative, starting by asking her for water. He is hot and thirsty. She can help him. His revolutionary humble approach astonishes her. He drinks water that Nicodemus would have regarded as polluted by her bucket. A caste Hindu still feels the same about those once called "untouchables". Jesus has provoked her to question him. Note the delicate skill by which he arouses further curiosity, and a desire for what he could give her. While causing her to expose her sin, he also commends her for truthfulness. Note also how she tries to evade, first by raising a hoary controversy. Jesus takes it to depths that strip away the camouflage. She falls back to an equally hoary form of indefinite postponement. Jesus then shatters the darkness with a revelation of light. "I am he." The day of salvation is now. She believes, and, like Andrew and Philip, dashes off to tell others. What a glorious witness she has to give. Jesus knows her sin and accepts her without condemnation. Because of her faith, the spiritual life which Nicodemus lacked has already started to well up within her, as Jesus had promised. It is, as Isaiah had prophesied, a promise for all nations, for Jews and Samaritans also.

The Second Sign. The healing of the Official's son. 43 - end.

From Samaria Jesus returns to Galilee, not to Nazareth, but to Cana. News travels fast. A royal official had heard of Jesus' miracle there, and comes from Capernaum to ask him to go there and heal his son. Jesus' words are directed to the whole crowd. The N.E.B. turns them into a question. Jesus puts the official to the test, giving him a command and a promise. Like Abraham, he believes and obeys. At that moment his son is healed.

This story is one of the milestones in my own spiritual journey. We receive God's promises and accept His gifts by faith. This is especially true in receiving forgiveness, healing and the gift of the Holy Spirit, hence the importance of thanksgiving. After prayer and ministry people often say, "I don't feel any different", so they refuse to believe any gift has been given. Of course some gifts, like forgiveness depend on prior conditions being met, but then, "standing on the promises of God" as the old hymn puts it, they need to launch out in faith and obedience, ready to take risks.

The Third Sign. The Word of Life. Chapter 5.

Jesus has returned to Jerusalem, and we meet him at the Pool of Bethesda. The man had been sitting there for 38 years. He believed that the waters could heal, but, without a friend to help him, he was always elbowed out by the rush. Yet there he stayed. He had evidently committed some grave sin. A bad conscience can cause some kinds of paralysis. (cp. Mark 2:5) Such an illness can also be a form of camouflage. It is a bid for sympathy and help, and can be manipulative. It can also become a way of life. We talk possessively of "my arthritis" or "my back pain". Jesus asked the man if he wanted to be made well. To be healed means change, taking back responsibility. The man gives a seemingly convincing excuse. As usual, Jesus cuts through it with an immediate challenge. His words have life-giving authority. (Is. 55:11) The man gets up and walks. His appearance in the temple shows that he recognises that his healing has come from God. His witness to Jesus stirs up trouble. Jesus is accused of working on the Sabbath,

Here we meet the first Discourse. One reason for the strict Law of the Sabbath, was the belief that God rested on the seventh day of Creation. Even today, some believe that God set off the Big Bang, and then left the cosmos to develop on its own. The theory of fixed laws to control it has been blown apart by the discovery of Random Mutation. Random, or Purposeful? God continues to reveal Himself through our growing understanding of the laws of creation. The Name He revealed to Moses, "I am that I am" also means "I will be what I will be". Jesus makes it clear that God never ceases to work, so neither does he. This further claim, whether stated or implied, stirs up more trouble.

Here we are given a glimpse into the prayer life of Jesus. It was more than times of special quiet. It was a continuous unbroken communion. In every situation Jesus was aware of God at work. As he heard and saw, so he acted: God's Word enfleshed! Jesus is the Word of Life. The life he gives is abundant and eternal. (Jn. 10:10,28) It is a new kind of life, that starts now, (11:25) as it did for the woman at the well.

Jesus is also our judge. Does this conflict with "I judge no one"? (Jn. 8:15) The answer lies back in John 3:19-20. To come into his presence is to experience judgement. A masterpiece of art or music has the same effect. In our reaction to it, we are ourselves exposed and judged. It is those who are the most dogmatic who are usually the most ignorant and blind.

Jesus now speaks of the witness that has been given to his claims. First there is the Baptist. Even among the rulers, some, like Nicodemus, had believed John was a prophet. Then there are Jesus' works, signs of his glory. Thirdly there was the voice of his Father. John would be referring to the Voice heard at Jesus' baptism and transfiguration. The only Voice he mentions was heard by nobody but Jesus. (Jn. 12:28-30) Finally, there were the scriptures, which his hearers had studied and venerated. Yet they had totally failed to see that, in almost every book, these pointed to Jesus. Why were they so blind? Jesus tells them. Their eyes are on each other and on their own reputations. Famous scientists have been similarly blinded to truth discovered by rival colleagues.

The Fourth Sign. Bread from Heaven. Chapter 6.

Bread and water are the two basic needs of life. In the desert, God, through Moses, provided his people with both. We have already seen Jesus promising the Water of Life to the Woman of Samaria. Here we see him promising Bread.

The story of the feeding of the five thousand is one of the very few stories told in all four gospels. John's version has significant differences. It is Jesus who raises the problem of the crowd's need. He tests Philip by asking him how it is to be solved. Only here do we read of the boy who was willing to give the little he had. Most important of all, we read that Jesus himself gave the loaves to the crowd, though obviously the other gospels are correct when they say that the disciples actually handed them round. In verse 4, John clearly links this meal to the Passover, and in his version of the Last Supper, he omits the giving of bread and wine. This is an example of his deliberate freeing of sacraments from a constrictive interpretation. The last difference is that the crowd reacts by trying to make Jesus king. This explains why Jesus sent his disciples away, though John omits stating this, while he stayed to try and quieten the crowd, after which he withdrew to pray. (cp. Matt. 14:22) The Temptations are another deliberate omission. Two of them here confront him in a concrete situation. His motivation for providing food was not to stun the crowd into belief. He turned his back on power.

Walking on the water is not one of the seven signs. As with Mark and Matthew, it is a continuation of the previous event. When Jesus enters the boat, John records that "immediately" they found themselves at the place where they were going. Jesus, in the Ark of Salvation, brings us safely to our destination immediately, for our destination is himself.

The second Discourse takes place the next morning. Jesus ignores the crowd's curiosity, and challenges them to labour for the food of eternal life. They interpret this in terms of religious observances. What more should they do? But the basic "work" is to believe and trust in Jesus. This is an active commitment which gives value to all other actions. These include the Opus Dei, the daily

Offices of the church,

So we come to the first of the great I AMs. Jesus himself is the Bread of Life. To eat is to absorb into the heart. (Ezek. 3:1)

How can the crowd, with no experience of Pentecost, swallow such teaching? Only the Father, through the Spirit, can draw us to Himself. (cp Matt. 16:17) Here we reach the turning point of John's gospel. First, for the crowd. Jesus has refused to be the king who would restore the nation's independence. From now on they withdraw their support. Then for the religious leaders. They would hear of the event and fear a repetition. Jesus might change his mind. Their determination to destroy him hardens. Thirdly for the disciples, now swollen to quite a crowd. How could they go on following him, when they couldn't understand him? Only the twelve remain. To them Jesus addresses a sad question. "Will you also go away?" In this gospel, Peter's great Confession is to Jesus as the Word of Life. Peter didn't understand Jesus with his mind. But he knew, by experience of living with Jesus, that Jesus and his words were food for his soul. There was no one else. He spoke for them all. Except Judas!

Controversy at the Feast of Tabernacles. Chapter 7.

Knowing that the Jewish authorities are out to kill him, Jesus stays in Galilee. When his family go up to Jerusalem for the Feast of Tabernacles, he tells them he will not go with them. It was not the right time for publicity. Tabernacles was a jolly and chaotic family festival, with everyone building booths in which to camp. Arriving alone, unrecognised, Jesus would be able to find out for himself what the crowd was thinking about him. Opinions differed, but were muted for fear of the authorities.

Suddenly Jesus emerges into the limelight, and starts teaching in the temple. The third Discourse begins. Familiar themes are developed. What is the source of his authority? Verse 17 is basic. Spiritual discernment depends upon a heart set on doing God's will. Concern for their own reputation, hypocrisy and disobedience, has blinded them. Violently they deny that anyone wants to kill him, but such plotting was common knowledge.

Where does Christ come from? The scriptures point to Bethlehem, certainly not to Nazareth! (Jn. 1:46, 7:52) Jesus' miracles may have gained him a few supporters, but they do not recognise God in all he says and does. Their faith is like seed on stones.

With all this commotion, the authorities send officers to arrest Jesus. His veiled reference to his departure mystifies them all. Is he referring to his death, or to his ascension, or both? (Jn. 16:16) His final word is the promise of the water of life, not just a well-spring, (cp. 4:14) but rivers of it. The gift is now specifically linked to the gift of the Holy Spirit.

The officers return without making an arrest. They have been deeply impressed by Jesus. The authorities obviously do not know of Nicodemus' secret belief. He has at least the courage to make some form of legal protest.

The Light of the World. Chapter 8.

As noted in chapter 4, the lovely story of the woman taken in adultery, is not by John. It needs no comment. From verse 12 the fourth Discourse begins.

The design of these discourses, in fact of the whole gospel seems to be spiral. As we have noted, we meet the same basic questions and answers. Without repentance and faith, we are blind to God's truth. But at each circling of the spiral, new revelation is given. So let us concentrate on what is special here.

First comes another great I AM. Jesus is the Light of the World. Whatever truth is found in other religions, its source is the Light of Christ. (Jn. 1:9) But only in Jesus is the fullness of Light to be found. Only by following him can we walk in the light. How active is this expression!

Jesus warns his hearers that, if they don't believe, they will die in their sins. At a Christian Writer's School in India, I met a Brahmin convert from Nepal. Disillusioned by all the empty rituals he had to observe, he left home and wandered into India seeking a teacher who could satisfy his spiritual hunger. Outside a church in Darjeeling he saw a huge placard proclaiming the Forgiveness of Sins. This spoke to his deepest need. The Pastor led him to Christ. "In no other religion," the Brahmin told me, "can you find such forgiveness offered." All over India one finds people desperately trying to earn forgiveness, with no assurance of receiving it.

The forgiveness Jesus offers is free, but it is not cheap. It cost him his death on the cross. From the cross his Light and Truth shine out in saving power. To believe and accept his forgiveness means following him, and being ready to share his cross. But Jesus promises that those who continue to follow will know the truth which will set them free. Jesus' audience is offended. Despite Roman rule and despite their fear of their own authorities, they claim to be in bondage to none. But sin is a bondage. Forgiveness isn't enough. Jesus gives us power to overcome, if we really want it!

A modern expression, "where are you coming from?", probes the origins of our thoughts and actions. Jesus speaks to Jews who have partly believed, and are turning away. (cp, 2:23-25) What was the true source of their identity? Not Abraham. Not God. Their deeds reveal it. It is the Father of Lies, Satan. Similarly, the deeds of the sinless Jesus, reveal his true identity. It is that of God.

In verse 51 we have another emphatic promise. If we continue following Jesus, we shall not see death. Eternal life starts when we are born again. (Jn. 3:16) As usual, his words are taken literally, and misunderstood.

The discourse ends with Jesus' astonishing claim to pre-existence. This would indeed be blasphemy, or madness, were it not true! (Jn. 1:1-14)

The 5th Sign. The Healing of the Blind Man. Chapter 9.

In this chapter we are given a dramatic illustration of the conflicts already discussed; darkness versus light, blindness versus sight.

The disciples see the man as a subject for discussion. The 2nd commandment speaks of the sins of the parents being visited on the children. In terms of punishment, both Jeremiah and Ezekiel had refuted this. (Jer. 31:29-30, Ezek. 18:19-20) Today, we recognise that there can sometimes be a causal connection. Sexual sin, addictions, and even anger and resentment, can affect the unborn child. Here Jesus refutes any implication of sin. He sees the man in need of compassionate action, that the glory of God may be seen in him. Jesus knew that he had only a few months left in which he would be free to act. When light is present, it is day. When light is absent, night falls. (cp Jn. 13:30. Lk. 22:53) Action would end, Passion begin.

Jesus anoints the man's eyes, and sends him to wash at the Pool of Siloam, which appropriately means "sent". The man obeys, and returns healed. In the following dialogue how clearly the characters are depicted: the argumentative and incredulous crowd, the man, sticking to the facts, the parents dodging away from involvement, and the Pharisees, fighting their way out of a corner.

First they try denial. Then, after scaring the parents, they try to scare the man. "Give God the Glory" was a way of putting him on oath. He is to swear support for their judgement that Jesus is a sinner. He answers back aggressively. Ironically, their pressure causes his belief in Jesus to grow from Healer to Prophet and finally to Man of God. Equal to Moses! This, from an ignorant beggar, was too much. They curse him as a bastard, and throw him out of the community.

Jesus, hearing this, seeks him out, and leads him into a full declaration of faith. The blind man ends by receiving both physical and spiritual sight. The Pharisees, who claim they already have both, are declared blind beyond possibility of healing.

The Good Shepherd and the Door. Chapter 10.

We now come to the 3rd and 4th of the great I AMs. The Shepherd is one of the most tender of the OT's description of God's relationship with his people. The Patriarchs were shepherds. Moses learnt the skills and patience needed to lead his unruly people, by serving as a shepherd in Midian. David was the beloved Shepherd King, and Psalm 23, attributed to him, is the best loved of all the psalms. Later, Israel's autocratic rulers, and their syncophant priests and prophets, were denounced by the true prophets as false shepherds. Ezekiel's bitter accusations, in chapter 34, ends however in a promise that God Himself will come to be Israel's Shepherd, a promise fulfilled in Jesus. (Ezek 34:15)

Jesus calls each of his sheep by name. He does not drive them. He leads, feeds and protects them. They know and obey his voice. Note Jesus' significant statement. No one can take his life from him. Freely he lays it down for his flock. He has power to lay it down, and take it up again. (cp. Jn. 19:30) He also has other sheep, Samaritans and Gentiles. These he will gather and all will be one flock under one shepherd. He will give them eternal life. None will be able to pluck them out of his hand, for it is God's hand.

What of the Door? At night, shepherds often barred the entrance to the fold by lying there. An enemy can break in only "over my dead body". Those appointed to care for God's flock must come through Jesus. Any other approach will disclose their wolfish motives. Many power-seeking self-proclaimed Messiahs had come and led their followers into armed rebellion. The result was roads lined with crosses. Personal ambition can still motivate those seeking high office in Christ's church.

The chapter ends with another short Discourse. It is the Feast of the Dedication. John notes that it is winter. Like "night" this is an evocative word with deeper meaning. Jesus has again claimed oneness with his Father. His enemies who have already called him a Devil, and tried to arrest him, now turn to violence. Jesus quotes Psalm 82. Verses 6 and 7 make it clear that they are called gods because they are all sons of God. However, because of their sins, they will die like men. Eternal life is given through belief in Jesus.

Jesus escapes both stoning and arrest, and returns to the Jordan. Some follow him. There, by the waters of baptism, they come to believe.

The 6th Sign. The Raising of Lazarus and its effect. Chap 11 - 12:20.

Lazarus is very ill. His sisters send a message asking Jesus to come, and save his friend. They are confident that he will do so. Jesus loved them, *so* when he heard, he stayed where he was two days. That *so* is astonishing. He didn't delay for fear of arrest. That is made quite clear. He deliberately waited until Lazarus died. As with the blind man, a seeming tragedy would be transformed into a revelation of God's glory. It would also be a sign, prefiguring his own death and resurrection.

By the time Jesus reached the outskirts of Bethany, Lazarus had been dead four days. Jesus must have somehow held on to him with an invisible thread, preserving his body as well as his soul in that mysterious paradisal sleep. (cp Mk. 5:39. 1Thes. 4:13)

News of his arrival is brought to the sisters. Typically, it is Martha who goes to meet him. Her agonised cry, later echoed by Mary, must have been continually repeated throughout those agonising days. Yet still they trust. Martha believes in a future resurrection, but that is small comfort to her now. Then comes Jesus' 5th great "I AM". Resurrection Life is present with us NOW in Jesus. It isn't surprising that Martha can't understand. But if Jesus says so, then it must be true. Her trust in him is absolute.

Joined by Mary and the mourners, they come to the tomb. There, "Jesus wept." It is the shortest verse in the Bible. Why did he weep? He wasn't weeping for Lazarus, as the mourners thought. Was he weeping for the sisters? I think perhaps he was rather weeping with them, sharing in their pain. His tears may have been intensified by his knowledge that he could have spared them this. So often it is through our times of suffering that we are given a new revelation of the glory of God. When, in pain, we are tempted to feel bitter, let us remember those tears. This sign also prepared them for Jesus' own death and resurrection. Maybe his tears were also for the sorrow they would suffer again, for him.

The time for weeping ends. Now is the time for them to exercise their faith in action. "Roll away the stone." Martha, ever practical, still voices apprehension. Jesus reminds her of his promise. Trustingly, she allows them to roll the stone away. Jesus then gives thanks to God. Another sign of faith is to anticipate God's answer with thanksgiving. Such a prayer Jesus prays aloud, for the sake of the crowd.

Then his loud command rings out, and "the dead man came out." It was left to his friends, and perhaps to Martha, to free him from the constricting bandages they had so lovingly wrapped around him. Jesus frees us from the bondage of death and sin. But there are some bonds, laid on us by others, that only they can remove. Sometimes they are bonds of love!

As always, Jesus' action is divisive. Some believe, while some go off to report his action to his enemies.

It is one thing to restore to life a widow's son in the obscure village of Nain, or even raise the daughter of a minor official in Galilee after only a few hours of death. But to raise a man who has been dead four days, and whose tomb is only two miles from the city, is quite another. Jerusalem was astir. The greatest Jewish Festival was approaching, A Messianic uprising was a nightmare possibility. So was a Roman backlash, bringing the end of the limited social and religious self-regulation still permitted. The Council meets to plan Jesus' arrest and death. There were, evidently, not just two, but apparently several members who were secret believers. (Jn. 12:42) They would have noted Caiaphas' words, and later remembered them in a prophetic light. "One man should die for the people". It was no longer safe for Jesus to stay in the city. He withdraws to a town on the edge of the desert. Note the 6th discourse which ends the chapter.

The Upper Room. Chapter 13.

And so we come to the Upper Room, and Jesus' last meal with his disciples. As already noted, no mention is made of bread and wine. Not only had the other Gospel writers described the Lord's Supper, but it was already being re-enacted weekly by the church. In Jesus' first discourse, the essence of Holy Communion had been expressed in terms of moment by moment absorption of Jesus into our hearts, minds and souls. (cp Ezek. 2:2-3. Ps. 36:18) What is more strange is that none of the other writers mention the foot-washing. All speak of the disciple's continued argument over precedence, and of Jesus' rebuke, but not of his action.

John sets this action in the wide context of Jesus' total awareness of his situation. Note the emphatic repetition. "He knew" his hour had come. He knew that Judas had decided on betrayal. He knew his own origin and destiny. He had come from God and was returning to God.

The whole of John's gospel proclaims Jesus as the Logos, the eternal creative Word, one with the Father in authority, life-giving power and judgement. Yet he shares our human "flesh". He is tired, hungry and thirsty, and he weeps. So it is the Eternal God Himself who stoops to wash His disciple's feet! Because of their faith and continuing obedience, Judas excepted, they are essentially clean. Only the daily coating of dust from the streets needs to be washed from their feet.

Contrast the false humility of Peter. He thinks he knows but he doesn't understand. He keeps telling Jesus what to do. He can't "let go and let God."

John has already emphasized Judas' betrayal as Satanic. (Jn 6:70-71) Jesus had long known of it. Though he knew his gesture would fail, he still offers Judas a last chance, a hand still stretched out in love. The sop, given to a guest by the host's own hand, was a mark of special favour. This is the only food John mentions. It could only break or harden Judas' heart. Judas takes the sop, and Satan enters into him. (cp. I Cor 11:29) Jesus, ever courteous, gives him an opportunity to withdraw without public exposure. Judas goes, and for him, it is "night".

The atmosphere lightens. Glory can now begin to break through. Jesus, at last, has time to talk freely with his disciples. In the following three chapters, his last Discourse, he prepares them, not just for his departure, but for his return, and continued presence with them, through the coming of the Holy Spirit.

The Way, the Truth, and the Life. 14:1-26.

The Passover Meal was a yearly remembrance of Israel's deliverance from slavery. The exodus from Egypt was followed by the giving of the Law at Sinai. It transformed this despised people into a free nation, a People of God. Jesus had given his disciples a new Meal for the remembrance of a second deliverance from sin. This too was followed by the giving of a New Law, not of Ten Commandments, but One, which contained their essence. The Law of Love would bind them into a new community, the Body of Christ, the church. Love, not Law, was to be the mark by which they were to be recognized.

To love one's neigbour as oneself, was not a new commandment. Coming from Leviticus 19:18, Jesus had quoted it to the young lawyer. But his disciples are now told they must love each other with the same kind of love with which Jesus had loved them. This gave love a totally new dimension. It would seem impossible.

It is in this context that Jesus speaks of his departure and return. Chapter 14 verse 2 is usually read at funerals, and taken as referring to life after death. True, but we must not limit it to this. In Jesus, eternal life is now. So, what is impossible for us, is made possible in Jesus. This leads on to the next two I AMs, and teaching on the coming and work of the Holy Spirit.

First, Jesus is the Way. Jesus is never stationary. He goes ahead, preparing a way for us to follow. Psalm 16 speaks of a Path of Life, leading to joy. Isaiah (35:8-10) when speaking about the coming of God to save his people, tells of a Highway, the Holy Way, on which the redeemed could safely walk. It may lead us, in practical terms, in different directions. This can sometimes seem puzzling, as when, in the 2nd World War, some Christians felt called to fight, and some to be pacifists. They could still love one another, for they recognized that those who differed from them were walking on the same Highway. Sometimes it can mean that we are called suddenly to change direction. This too can cause problems, as it did for the Corinthians. Paul had to explain that, in Jesus, it was always *Yes*. (2Cor. 1:15-20) We can trust that God always knows what He is doing! Jesus does not just show us the way, or walk on it ahead of us, He is the Way. If we keep close to him, we are safely on it too.

Jesus is also the Truth. Whoever does God's will can know the truth. (Jn. 7:17) Truth is not a set of facts or propositions to be assented to intellectually, though this may be a by-product. Truth is a Person. Jesus was Truth. The Truth of God was expressed in his every word and deed.

God's Word is life-giving. Jesus is also the Life. God's life flowed continuously through him, perfectly expressed in terms of our humanity. This perfect union, claimed in all his discourses, is now given simply in answer to Philip's question. "To have seen me, is to see the Father."

Even more mind-boggling is the implication of this for his disciples. The works that Jesus has done, they can also do, and even greater works. This is not ground for easy confidence that we can work "miracles". Jesus had said faith could move mountains, but he never moved one! "Mountains" are of course figurative, but boundaries are also set. The works of Jesus were those that God was working through him, and, as such, were the outcome of perfect obedience to God's will. Also, power for us to "do likewise" is dependent on Jesus, having returned to the Father, empowering his disciples in response to their prayer.

This leads on naturally to teaching about the coming of the Holy Spirit. The Spirit was already with them, through being in Jesus. After Pentecost, He will also be in them. As Advocate, He will be their Counsellor and Protector. In and through Him, Jesus, and his Father, will be with them for ever.

Verses 27-31 should really follow on after the end of chapter 17, but John has his reasons for ending as he does. Peace, Shalom, is a word of farewell. It is an expression of total well-being.

The True Vine. 15:1-17.

Israel saw itself as a fruitful Vine, which God had planted in the land He had given them. Psalm 80. 8-11, expresses their complaint that God had allowed it to be uprooted. (verses 12-13) But, in The Song of the Beloved and his Vineyard, Isaiah complains of this Vine's unfruitfulness. He warns it of such a possible fate. (Is. 5:1-10) Later, Jeremiah speaks of a Vine that has run wild because of idolatry. (Jer. 2:20-22) Jesus now declares that he himself is the true Vine. The faithful Remnant had dwindled to One, but, from this One, new and fruitful branches will grow.

It is only the life of Jesus within them that renders them fruitful. Deprived of sap, branches wither and die. They are then cut off and burnt. But fruitful branches are also cut off, pruned to produce more fruit. All through life, we experience such pruning. The good is cut away to make room for the better. Our activity becomes more concentrated, and we learn to "centre down".

Our most important activity is to abide in Christ. Only then can his love flow through us, and out to others. Only then can we truly pray "in Jesus Name", and have confidence that our prayers will be answered. Only then will our service have enduring results. Here also is the source of joy. To abide is to love. To love, is to obey.

The work of the Holy Spirit. 15:18 - 16:12.

Jesus chose his disciples, not just to be his friends, but to be his witnesses. It is in this setting, of his teaching in the Upper Room, that he warns them of their own imminent persecution by the Jewish authorities. (cp. Lk. 21:5-20) He is not leaving them alone. The Holy Spirit will be with them, not only as Advocate, ie Protector, but as Co-Witness. He will guide them, teach them and give them words of authority. It is He who will convict men's hearts of sin, and reverse human judgements. Above all, He will glorify Jesus.

There is much more Jesus wants to say, but they are too sorrowful and perplexed to take in what he has already told them. The Holy Spirit will teach and remind them. He will also warn them of things to come. So Jesus is free to speak more clearly about his departure. In less than twenty-four hours, he will be gone. Within three days, he will be back. So soon will their anguish be turned into joy. We are back full circle to where Jesus started. (cp. 14:1-3) It all sounds reassuring. They tell him they now understand and fully believe. Alas, neither is true. When it comes to the crunch Jesus will be left utterly alone; alone with God. That is enough for him. When their own time of testing comes, they will share both his confidence and his victory. He leaves them with the gift of his Peace.

The High Priestly Prayer. Chapter 17.

The scene in the Upper Room ends with Jesus' long prayer. In it the whole purpose of his Mission is summed up. First he prays that in his suffering and death, God may glorify him, so that he may glorify God. His disciples had seen Jesus' glory in his active life, in his signs and in his Transfiguration. It was essential that they should now also see his glory on the cross. Humiliated, helpless, mocked, and hanging on a tree, as one cursed by the Law, (Deut. 21:23. Gal. 3:13) what glory could they see? It was a hidden glory, but they would see it later. The whole of the world's sin, its lies, jealousy, cowardice, cruelty and hatred, were focused on Jesus as he hung there. In agony of mind and spirit, he bore its full weight, absorbed it, and transformed it into a channel for the greatest outpouring of love and forgiveness the world has ever known. Satan's final assault was utterly defeated. The victory of Jesus over sin and death was complete.

A priest saw a man enter his church and stand gazing at a window depicting God enthroned in glory. As the priest approached him, bitter and angry words burst from him. "What does He care, up there on his throne, away from it all?" "You need to look at another window," the priest replied, and pointed him to a window showing the crucifixion. A long time later, the man returned and told him that this had saved his faith.

Jesus then prays for his disciples. They had stuck to him faithfully, and, without always understanding him, they believed that God had sent him, and that all he had done and said, was from God. He was leaving them, but, with his Spirit within them, they would be lamps, through which his glory would continue to shine. (cp. Matt. 5:14-16)

So Jesus prays that God will keep them. Three times the word *keep* is used. "Keep them in Thy Name, which Thou hast given to me." In other words, may all the qualities of God, that they had recognised in Jesus, now be seen in them. He prays that they may be kept "abiding", one with him, as he is one with his Father.

Jesus does not pray that they may be kept from coming persecution. It will be, for them, a sharing in his cross, and a source of joy. (Acts 5:40-41) Instead, he prays that they may be kept from the Evil One. (cp. Matt. 10:26-28) By abiding, and by invoking the Name of Jesus, they, and we, are given power to expose the Devil in his many disguises, and overcome his attacks. His power has been broken.

Now Jesus prays that they may be sanctified and consecrated. To be sanctified, is to be made holy, to be so close to God that one is always available for His immediate use. To be consecrated means to be devoted, to have given oneself lovingly and exclusively to another person. For our sakes, Jesus gave himself totally to God. He held back nothing. There lies the rub. We like to sing, "All to Jesus I surrender", and other such hymns. We think, or mean to mean them. But later, our actions too often disprove this. It is good to know that Jesus prayed for us, and is still praying. (Heb. 7:24-25)

For he ends by praying for all who, through their preaching and witness, will come to believe in him. It will include people of all races, languages and cultures, and so includes us. He prays that we may all be as truly one, as he and his Father are one!

Verse 23 has been a motivating force behind the movement for church unity. This was especially true in South India. Dr Ambedkar, leader of India's vast underclass, advised his people to leave Hinduism, which regarded them as outcasts, and suggested they might become Buddhist. A great many did so. When asked why he had not pointed them to Christianity, he replied that, as Harijans, (outcasts) his community was united. As Christians they would be divided. This seared the conscience of many church leaders, and gave great impetus towards the eventual setting-up of the Church of South India.

But the unity Jesus prayed for was something far deeper and more personal. The unity his disciples were to have with each other was to share the quality of his own unity with his Father. It was into this unity that they were all to be caught up. Then the Father, united with Jesus, will, through the Spirit, be also in them. They are thus to be enfolded into the Holy Trinity. This is beautifully portrayed by Rublev's Icon, in which the Three Persons are sitting at a table, and we, and the whole of redeemed humanity are invited to occupy the empty place.

This prayer, known as the High Priestly Prayer, contains all the elements of our celebration of the Eucharist: the Thanksgiving, Gloria, and Intercession, Offertory, Consecration and Holy Communion. It is, in fact, a Eucharistic Prayer.

The Arrest, Trial, and Crucifixion. Chapters 18 & 19.

The scene changes to the Garden. No mention is made of Jesus' Prayer of Agony. Omission is not denial. John has earlier referred to Jesus' human dread. (12:27-28) He wants us to read coming events in the light of Jesus' Priestly Prayer, which now immediately precedes them. This is probably the reason why the last verses of chapter 14 are placed where they are.

Note the renewed stress on Jesus' knowing. (cp. 13:1-3) Such knowledge implies both acceptance and power to respond wisely and creatively. Judas knew the place, and his plan of betrayal. Jesus knew God's plan lying behind the events, and his own purpose in fulfilling them.

When the armed band arrived - Jewish guards backed by a Roman cohort - Jesus goes forward to meet them. "Whom do you seek?" he asks. When they answer, "Jesus of Nazareth", he replies "I AM he." Was it this implied Name of God, or Jesus' majestic presence, that gave his use of it momentary credence, that awed and felled those Jewish guards to their knees?

Jesus' concern was for the safety of his disciples. Peter's brave but rash attack could have brought disaster. Only John names him, significantly giving both his names. John had reason for naming him. (cp 18:26-27) Jesus halts him. The cup of suffering and death he has willingly accepted from his Father's hands.

The other gospels tell us that all the disciples fled; but later, Peter returned, in Luke's pregnant phrase, "following at a distance". John however, mentions another disciple, who was with him. This disciple was known to the High Priest, and so could gain entry into his palace. Leaving Peter at the door, he went in to secure for himself a place, from which he could witness the trial. He then returned and gained admission for Peter. Leaving him safely, so he thought, provided with warmth and shelter, he then returned to his privileged view point.

Poor Peter! One of those by the fire had not only been in the garden, but was a relative of the man whose ear Peter had cut off. Only John mentions the man's name. Did Marcus, whose ear had been healed by Jesus, later become a Christian? Peter is cornered. Again he denies. The cock crows. Once was enough.

Who was this other disciple? Traditionally he has been identified with John the apostle. Today many scholars believe it more likely to have been an unnamed disciple of some status. The word translated as "was known to" indicates more than a casual acquaintance. This would explain his easy access to the Palace.

John's account of what follows makes it clear that it is Jesus who is putting the Jewish rulers on trial, not vice-versa. Jesus questions the High Priest's action in questioning him, rather than witnesses. A prisoner's testimony can't be used as incriminating evidence. Slapped by the guard for what he considered effrontery, Jesus also questions him as to the right fulfilment of his duties. Slapping a prisoner was not included in his official regulations! Nothing else about the trial is given any mention.

Jesus is next taken to the Roman Governor for sentencing. The Jewish leaders would consider themselves defiled were they to enter a pagan building. They had no such concern for moral defilement. Pilate has to come out to them. They expect him to sentence a man to death purely on their say-so, without even knowing the charges made against him! Pilate puts the matter back, literally, into their own court. It was not true that they had no power to put anyone to death. Public stoning, though possible, (cp. 8:1-7, 59) would involve cooperation by the crowd. This would be both dicey and dangerous.

Pilate withdraws into the Praetorium, calling Jesus to follow him. For Jesus, there was no defilement in places. Pilate must have known that the Jews were accusing him of claiming to be the Messiah. He asks Jesus if he is in fact a king. Jesus replies, as he so often does, with a counter question. Is Pilate personally seeking an answer, or is he merely repeating an accusation made by the Jewish authorities? Jesus will not defend himself, but he will meet Pilate's need.

Pilate wants no personal involvement. Theoretical claims hold no interest. What has Jesus done to arouse such hostility among his own people? That's what he wants to know. Mark tells us that Pilate knew the real motive was envy. (Mk. 15:10) Again Jesus will not answer to defend himself. Instead, he reassures Pilate that there is no need to fear an armed uprising. Jesus' kingly rule lies in the hearts of men. His Kingdom is a Kingdom of Truth.

"What is Truth?" Pilate brushes the question off as irrelevant philosophy. But Truth, in the Person of Jesus, was standing before him. Pilate is being challenged on his own ground, as were the High Priest and Guard before him. He is being required to do truth, by freeing a prisoner he knows to be innocent.

Not easy! By now a crowd has gathered. Pilate hopes to persuade them to use their Passover privilege to call for the release of Jesus. Their leaders had anticipated this. Their agents had been busily at work, instructing the crowd to call instead for Barabbas. Frustrated, Pilate tries to pacify them by having Jesus flogged, and exposed to ridicule. "Behold the Man", he cries, pointing to a mock king, bleeding, and crowned with thorns. For John, his words have another meaning. Behold Man as God created him to be, clothed in divine dignity that nothing and no one can strip from him.

This strategy only increases the fury of Jesus' accusers. The real charge they had intended to conceal bursts out. "He has made himself Son of God." They hadn't expected this piece of Jewish theology to cut any ice with Pilate, but it did. Like many educated Romans of his day, he was superstitious. The Romans had gods galore, who sometimes appeared in the guise of men, rewarding or causing havoc. Even a cynic may fear to take risks. Pilate retreats back inside the Praetorium, for further private interrogation.

"Where are you from?", Earth or Olympus? In such a context no reply was possible. Jesus remains silent. Angry at such apparent disregard, Pilate flaunts his power. What irony! Pilate must already have been aware that the situation was rapidly moving beyond his control. Jesus tells him that he would have no power over himself were it not given him by God. If the Jews pressurise him into giving an unjust verdict, their sin will be greater than his.

Their roles are reversed. Pilate is in the dock. Jesus pronounces judgement. But it is a merciful judgement.

Pilate makes one last attempt to save Jesus, and his own integrity, but the Jews play their trump card. Pilate had already got himself into trouble with his Roman masters. Such an accusation, if made against him to Caesar, would not only end his career, but probably also his life. Rome wanted the Jews kept peaceful. How could Pilate rebut such a charge to Caesar, hundreds of miles away? All he could do was to exact some revenge. Knowing their hatred of Roman rule, he goads them into acclaiming Caesar as their King. Then he hands over Jesus to be crucified.

Jesus is led outside the city, like the Scapegoat driven from the camp, (Lev. 16:21-22) bearing our sins on his back. He is crucified between two thieves. Are they given the privilege desired by James and John? (Mk. 10:35-40)

Seven words were spoken from the cross. The other gospels had recorded four. John gives us three more. The first shows his loving concern for his mother. He gives her into the keeping of the disciple who had always been closest to him. Jesus' brothers, her natural protectors, did not then believe in him.

The second Word, "I thirst", is a quotation from Psalm 22:15 and Psalm 69:3. The scene at the cross fulfills so much of what is pictured in these psalms. Jesus certainly did not quote them in order to fulfil them! But, all his life he had loved and continually prayed the psalms. These two may well have been in his mind during those long dark hours. Psalm 22:1 provided natural expression for his cry of dereliction, and Psalm 31:5 for his final committal. The church has seen, in this Word, his thirst for the world's salvation. Certainly he did have such a thirst. But there may have also been physical need. One of the torments of death by crucifixion was thirst. Jesus' parched throat needed refreshment in order to make the loud cry, that all the other evangelists record. Only John gives words to that cry. "It is finished", not in the sense of "It is over at last", but "It is accomplished". Jesus' work on earth was complete. It was a cry of victory, and he shouted it out as loud as he could. Note that Psalms 22 and 69 both end on a note of triumph.

All the gospels make it clear that Jesus' death was a willed action, as he had said it would be. (Jn. 10:18) Hanging on a cross strained the heart and made breathing increasingly difficult. Life could only be sustained by continually pressing up with the feet, and by keeping the head raised. When Jesus bowed his head, breathing would have become impossible. The two thieves clung on to life. When their legs were broken, they would have died of heart failure.

John sees in these events fulfilment of scripture, but far more than that. The bone that must not be broken was that of the Passover Lamb. (Ex. 12:43-46) The Baptist had pointed to Jesus crying "Behold the Lamb of God". Then John shows Jesus, at the beginning of his ministry, cleansing the temple, and claiming that his body was the true temple that God Himself would raise up. Not only that, Jesus drives out the animals used for the sacrifices. As the Lamb of God, his sacrifice of himself, once for all, will take their place. Finally, at the end of his Gospel, John makes clear that the day and the time of Jesus' death coincided with the time when the Passover lamb was slaughtered. The Passover meal would have taken place on the Friday night, which is a reason for John not mentioning it. His emphasis was elsewhere.

John also saw the piercing of Jesus' side as a fulfilment of a prophesy by Zechariah. (Chap. 12. v. 10) This is set in the context of a siege of Jerusalem, a disaster Jesus had predicted. It speaks of the people's repentance, and an overflow of God's compassion. Later, it goes on to prophesy about a Fountain opening up, to cleanse them from sin. (Zech. 13:1) The church connected this Fountain with the blood and water that flowed from the side of Christ, and these were seen as symbolising the two great sacraments of salvation, Baptism, which included the gift of the holy Spirit, and Holy Communion. These are the three Witnesses referred to in 1 John 5:8.

After Jesus' death, his friends in high places emerge from their hiding, and see to his burial. Joseph goes to Pilate to ask for permission to take possession of the body. The chief priests had already been to complain, unsuccessfully, about his inscription. Pilate acceded to Joseph's request. Mark tells us that he was surprised that Jesus was dead so soon. He had summoned the centurion for confirmation. This could explain the spear thrust. (Mk. 15:44-45) From Matthew we learn that the Chief Priests disturbed Pilate again, asking for the tomb to be guarded. He was given no peace!

John emphasises the lavish quantity of the spices, and the grandeur of the new tomb, set in a garden. It probably belonged to Joseph. Here is another prophetic fulfilment. The Suffering Servant would make his grave with the rich. (Is. 53:9) The N.E.B. alters this to a more natural reading, but other translators have stuck to the surprising prophecy.

The 7th Sign. The Resurrection. Chapter 20.

When Jesus "cleansed" the temple at the beginning of his ministry he was challenged to give a sign of his authority. (Jn. 2:18-19) Here, at the end of the Gospel, we are given the sign he promised. As we have already noted, the details of the resurrection as told by the four evangelists, cannot be reconciled from the viewpoint of historical and chronological accuracy. It is wiser to approach them theologically, and dramatically, to find out what impact the Risen Jesus made on those to whom he appeared. They all had to learn something new about themselves, as well as about him.

First to see him was Mary of Magdala. She visited the tomb twice. On her first visit she was stunned with grief to find the stone rolled back, and the body of Jesus gone. She runs to the disciples crying, "They have taken away the Lord, and we don't know where they have laid him." Three times she reiterates this horrific fact.

The "we" implies that the other women had been with her. This accords with Mark 16:8 which also says they were too terrified to say anything. But who are "they"? There is irony here. The Jewish authorities spread the rumour that the body had been stolen by the disciples. The author of the Gospel, writing many years later, would know this.

Peter and the beloved disciple race to the tomb to see for themselves. Later, Mary returns alone. This time she goes inside the tomb, and sees two men in white, seated in the inner chamber by the burial clothes. They ask her why she is weeping. She answers, but shows no surprise or interest in their presence and turns away. Then, Jesus appears at the entrance. I have stood inside such a tomb and understood how the rising sun would blind her tear-filled eyes while casting his face in deep shadow. The same question. The same reply. Still her only concern is the whereabouts of the body. She wants to take it into her possession. She, who clung to Jesus so closely in life, still clings to his body after death. How many who suffer bereavement do the same!

"Mary!" He calls her by name, in his own unmistakable way. *Rabbuni!* This is a Hebrew but also a typically Galilean word, meaning my Master. It has a touch of possessiveness. It is also a title used in prayer exclusively for God. Another hint of double meaning?

Mary has to learn not to cling bodily, either to the Jesus she had known and loved in the past, or to him in his intermediary state. After his Ascension, she can cling as much as she wants! Now, she has to show her love by leaving him, and taking his message to his disciples, whom now, for the first time he calls his brothers. He is on his way to His Father and theirs. Mary obeys. Her first words are those of joyful witness, "I have seen the Lord!"

We return to the two disciples. They have contrasting experiences. Peter arrives second but enters first. They have no need for angels or young men in white. Peter, overwhelmed by shame and grief, is beyond seeing anything. His companion has faith to believe without them. The two came together. They return separately, Peter, in puzzled sorrow, the beloved disciple in joyful eagerness, to share his wonderful news with his new Mother.

Later that same day, Jesus appears to his disciples in the Upper Room. They were fearful, and, at first, incredulous. Only when they saw the marks of his wounds did they believe. Those scars of love will be Jesus' distinguishing marks for all eternity. Joy then drives out fear. Jesus gives them his Peace, his Shalom, twice. Then he gives them their new commission.

He is sending them out, as his Father sent him. He empowers them, by breathing into them the Holy Spirit. *Pneuma* means both breath and wind. John knew all about the Spirit's coming at Pentecost. His Gospel sets the gift of the Spirit in this earlier context to emphasise that it is the gift of the Spirit of Jesus. Through his indwelling Spirit, Jesus himself will be present within them always, as he had promised only three days earlier. Gently the disciples are fuelled. At Pentecost, fire will set them alight.

The only power specified here is that of forgiving and retaining sins. The power to retain has been sometimes interpreted as the church's power to withhold absolution and to excommunicate. (cp. Matt. 16:19) We can see this rather as an awesome responsibility laid upon all Christians, both to proclaim and demonstrate the forgiving and merciful love of God. If we fail to do this, then we, like the Pharisees, will be binding burdens of sin upon people's backs. Alternatively, those who refuse to accept the offer of God's forgiveness, bind their burden of sin upon themselves.

A week passes. Then we encounter Thomas, who had been absent at that meeting. One wonders why he was called the Twin, and who his twin was. Had he also a need to cling? John tells us that Thomas, thinking Jesus' delay in going to Bethany was due to danger from the Jews, had suggested they go and die with him. (11:16) But he too fled from the garden. He was honest to question what he didn't understand, (14:5) and he was certainly very outspoken about his disbelief of the disciples' report. But, when Jesus appears, and graciously invites him to touch his scars, Thomas is the first to worship Jesus as "My Lord and my God". The rebuke that follows is gentle. It sets off, by contrast, the blessedness of Christians, who, like John, would believe by faith alone.

An important detail in this story usually passes unnoticed, because it is implied, not stated. Unseen by them, Jesus must have been with them at that earlier meeting. How else would he know what Thomas had said? His constant unseen presence, with them, was something his disciples had to know and depend on, before his Ascension.

The last story is about Peter. Jesus had already appeared to him privately. (Lk. 24:34. 1Cor. 15:5) Peter needed the reassurance of forgiveness before he could face the others, or understand anything. They had gone to Galilee, as directed, to meet with Jesus there. Waiting was hard for Peter. Long before dawn, he was up. He'd go back to his old job, fishing, something familiar that he was good at. The others join him. Peter is in charge again.

The experience that preceded the disciples' original call is repeated. Only Luke had recorded it. Has the writer transposed it to this later occasion to remind us of it, now that they are being called to a new Mission? Or did the miraculous event happen again? What is clear is that the disciples had to learn that success in their new mission would depend entirely upon their obedience to the guidance of their risen Lord.

Typically it is the beloved disciple who first recognizes that the Stranger on the shore is Jesus. Typically, it is Peter who jumps impetuously into the water, wades ashore and then returns to help haul in the nets. Also typical is the action of Jesus, who serves them with food, turning a shared offering of bread and fish into a sacrament of renewed communion. There are echoes of the feeding of the five thousand. So few were the members of Jesus' chosen band, so slender their earthly resources, so gigantic both their task and their need. But by Jesus they would be amply supplied.

Jesus then draws Peter aside. Calling him by his old name, Jesus uses the word given in Greek as *agape*, meaning the pure self-giving love that Jesus had both demonstrated and commanded. Faced by the second question, Peter no longer claims to love Jesus more than the others. The only word he dare use is that of friendship, *phileo*. The third time Jesus asks the question he uses the same word. It is as if he were asking, "Can I count on even your friendship?" No wonder Peter is grieved. He will claim nothing. Jesus can see into his heart and knows the love that is there.

Peter had been called to be a Fisher of Men. Now he is called to be a Shepherd. For this he would need new and different qualities. Christ's flock, consisting of both old and new sheep, Jews and Gentiles, would need patient, loving and individual care. Jesus, the Good Shepherd had laid down his life for his sheep. He warns Peter that he must be prepared to do the same. Tradition has it that when Peter was sentenced to be crucified, he asked to be crucified head downwards, as he was not worthy to die the same death as his Master. Here it is noted that he was to glorify God by his death just as Jesus had done.

The early church expected the Return of Jesus would take place soon. The Scribe surfaces to correct a popular belief that the beloved disciple would live to see it. According to tradition, he did however live to a great old age.

In verse 24 the Gospel is given authenticity by the double witness required by the Law. (cp. Jn. 8:17-18.) The witness of the Scribe is supported by that of an eyewitness, that of the beloved disciple. Verse 25 makes it clear that what is recorded has been selective. This is a repetition of what is stated in chapter 20 verse 30.

Chapter 21 seems to have been added later. There are many reasons for thinking this. Here it is enough to point out that the last two verses of the previous chapter seem to bring the gospel to a natural conclusion. The writer's purpose is clearly stated. It is to bring his readers to the same saving knowledge of Jesus Christ as that confessed by Thomas.

Summary

John's Gospel has been popularly regarded as the most spiritual of the Gospels, but it is a spirituality that is earthy. By the time it was written, the church was having to counter Gnostic teaching that kept spirit and flesh apart. John's Gospel seeks to oppose this by binding them together. "The Word made Flesh".

John also makes a distinction between the world that God loves and for which Jesus died, and worldliness. Jesus was in the world but not of it. The two uses of the word in chapter 17 makes the distinction between them quite clear.

If Luke reveals the human face of God, John shows the divine face of humanity. The upside-down man, who set the world's system of values on it's head, is now presented as Man right-side up, walking tall with God as his Father. In other Gospels, Jesus' opponents ascribe his powers of healing to Beelzebub. Here we see Jesus forcing them to expose themselves as children of the Devil. Reversal of roles is also seen at Jesus' trial, where his judges find themselves judged.

In the other three gospels the main opposition comes from the scribes and

Pharisees. They were the recognized teachers of the Law, their authority centring on the synagogues. Jesus challenged both their legalistic interpretation of the Law and their moral authority, accusing them of hypocrisy, the besetting sin of moralists, especially those in high positions. In John's Gospel, criticism of the Pharisees is, in certain places, toned down. The Baptist's virulent attack on them is omitted. In Nicodemus we meet a more liberal-minded member of their Order, represented also in Acts by the renowned Gamaliel. In Mark we meet the scribe of whom Jesus said, "You are not far from the Kingdom of God." (Mk. 12:34)

In John's Gospel the main opponents of Jesus are "the Jews". This refers to those who lived in Judea and the environs of Jerusalem. They are contrasted with the Galileans, "a people accursed who do not know the Law." (Jn. 7:48-52) Jesus is shown to have visited Jerusalem three times, and most of the important events and discourses took place there. The Sadducees, the priestly party, become increasingly important as leaders of the opposition. It is Caiaphas the High Priest who engineers Jesus' death for political rather than religious reasons.

Unique to John's Gospel is the resolution of the O.T. problem connected with the temple. Only John records what Jesus really said about its destruction, which was misquoted at his trial. He himself is the Temple that, finally, can never be desecrated or destroyed, and in whom God's glory is eternally present. It is also John who emphasises the High Priesthood of Jesus, who is also the Lamb, whose sacrifice consisted of a life of perfect obedience, and a death freely offered, thus fulfilling all the sacrifices of the past.

In the High Priestly prayer, Jesus witnesses to his unity with the Father in the Holy Spirit. This unity has shone through the 7 signs, and been asserted in all his discourses. Finally, Jesus breathes the Holy Spirit into his disciples, empowering them, as he was empowered, and sending them, as he was sent by his Father, to proclaim the gospel of forgiveness of sins.

How this empowerment was experienced, and how the disciples began to carry out their commission is recorded in the Book of Acts, and is the subject of the following chapter.

The story is told that, when Jesus returned to heaven, the angels asked him what plans he had made for his work to be carried on to its completion. "I have left that to my disciples", he answered. "But what will you do if they should fail? " they asked. "I have no other plan", he replied.

The prognosis was not too good. The disciples were still easily frightened.

According to Matthew, even at the Ascension, some of them were still doubting. Luke tells us that they were still asking Jesus when the Kingdom of Israel would be established. (Acts 1:6)

Another Catalyst was needed to transform the situation. This role was taken by the Holy Spirit, to be given at Pentecost. His advent had been foreshadowed in two of the Gospels. Mark and Matthew say nothing, but Luke had planned a sequel. His Gospel foreshadows by showing how the Holy Spirit was the guiding force in Jesus' own life, and how, at his Ascension, Jesus promised his disciples that he would send his Spirit upon them. He told them to wait, and not embark upon their mission until the Spirit had come. The Book of Acts begins where his Gospel ends. It is Act 3 of our drama, and shows how all Jesus' predictions about the Holy Spirit were fulfilled.

Questions for private meditation

1. If Jesus asked you, "What are you seeking?", what would you answer? (1:38)

2. Have words from scripture ever come into your mind to give light to any particular situation? (2:22)

3. Make a list of those from whose labours you have benefited. Thank God for them. (4:38)

4. How much do you depend on the good opinion of others? Would you hesitate to take a Christian stand for fear of offending them? (5:44)

5. Is there anything God may want to say to you that you don't want to hear? (9:33-34)

6. Do you think of the Father as being different from Jesus, and vice-versa? What did Jesus mean by saying "I and my Father are one"? (10:30)

7. How much of our prayer is spent telling God what to do? (13:6-10)

8. How have you experienced God's pruning? How does He do it? (15:2)

9. How would you explain to a seeker the victory that Jesus won on the cross, and how has it affected your life? (19:30).

10. What is the Gospel according to you?

Questions for group discussion

1. Can the enthusiasm of converts to witness to their secular friends get smothered by churchy activities? (1:45-46)

2. "We heard - we believe - we know". Is faith static? How does it keep on growing? (4:42)

3. Is the inward and spiritual grace of sacraments confined to their outward and visible sign? How does the Group view the Christian position of Quakers and members of the Salvation Army?

4. "Right judgement depends upon a will set to obey God". Discuss. (7:17-24)

5. "Forgiveness is free, but not cheap." How does this tally with your experience of forgiving others?

6. What light do you see in other religions? How do you relate this to Jesus as Light of the World? (8:12)

7. What remaining bonds does the church need to remove from those set free by Christ? (11:44)

8. What were the special qualities of the love Jesus had for his disciples? (15:12)

9. Is guidance ever infallible? Does God bring good out of differences? (16:13)

10. Jesus' resurrection appearances cannot be explained, nor explained away. Share doubts and convictions on this subject.

Chapter 5

Acts of the Apostles

Like the Gospel, Luke opens his second book with a personal note. It is addressed to the same Theophilus, and is clearly a sequel. His Gospel ended at the Ascension with Jesus' last commands to his disciples. They were to preach repentance and forgiveness of sins in His Name, to all the nations. But first, they were to stay in Jerusalem until the Spirit had empowered them.

The Book of Acts starts with a repetition of that final scene, but new and interesting points are made. Luke tells us that he had previously recorded all that Jesus had begun to teach and do before he was taken up. This implies that, through the Holy Spirit, Jesus would be continuing his ministry through his disciples. We also learn that he had been appearing to them for forty days, speaking of the Kingdom of God. He could have taught them a lot in such a lengthy period. All the more surprising is it that, at the end, they were still asking him about the restoration of the Kingdom of Israel. Note that Jesus did not say this would never happen, but only that the timing of future events was known to God alone. Have we seen it happen in our day?

Their business was to wait for the Spirit's coming. In the Gospel, He is to "clothe them with power". Here He is to baptize them. (cp. Lk. 3:16) Two additions are made to the Ascension. Here, it is a cloud that hides Jesus from their sight. All through the O.T. the Cloud both symbolised and concealed the glory of God. The scene recalls the Transfiguration. Jesus is now received into the glory and the concealment of his Father.

The other addition is that of the two Messengers, and their promise of Jesus' return. The phrase, "In the same manner", has led to much idle speculation. Only two things are certain. Jesus will return, and both the manner and the timing will surprise us. (Matt. 24:42-44)

So the disciples return to Jerusalem, to wait in prayer for an event they can't either imagine or control. Peter however can't just wait and do nothing. He organises an election. Was the election of Matthias really God's will? Churches that have chosen him as their Patron Saint obviously think so. Or did Jesus himself select the apostle who was to take Judas' place? Paul's call and commissioning was unique. Luke narrates it in chapter 9. Later he records two of Paul's own descriptions of this momentous experience. (Acts 22:2-21. 26:12-18) Paul almost certainly believed this, (1Cor. 9:2) though it appears he knew that some disputed it.

In church elections today, praying for guidance is one thing. Waiting to receive it is another.

Wind and Fire. Chapters 1 & 2.

The story of the Spirit's coming is thrilling to read. Like the Cloud, Wind and Fire had always been symbols of God's glory and power. Experiences today, such as those during the Revival in Indonesia, show that such striking manifestations are not unique.

The gift of tongues, long dismissed by liberal theologians as emotional gabble, is now a gift possessed by many ordinary people, and bishops! It can become, or be heard as recognisable languages. In South India, I met a Pentecostal, Tamil-speaking lady evangelist. She told me of an experience she had at a Tent Meeting while preaching about the Cross. She saw a man enter at the back of the tent, and felt led to change from Tamil into tongues. She continued to think of the Cross, but the words that flowed from her lips she no longer controlled or recognised. At the end of the meeting the man came forward and spoke to her. He told her of his amazement at hearing her speaking in perfect Bengali, his own mother tongue. It is unwise to explain away the more mysterious gifts of the Spirit, just because they may be outside our own personal experience. The Jews who mocked on this occasion, may well have heard nothing but a meaningless babble. Mockery is more spiritually destructive than hostility or honest disbelief.

For the disciples, who probably included Mary, Jesus' Mother, other women, and possibly over a hundred others, (1:14-15) the initial experience was an explosion of joy, too great to be contained by mundane speech. They literally had no words to express it. Not even a string of Halleluias would do! The Spirit liberated them to allow a flood of joyful sound to pour through them. They were blown out of the room, perhaps on to an upstairs veranda, with an intense flame of desire to share this dynamic new life with others. The Greek word for power, *dunamis*, gives us our words dynamite and dynamo. The Spirit's power is explosive. It can destroy rigid structures of mind and of society. As a controllable force, it generates both light and energy.

God's timing is perfect. At Pentecost, Jews poured in to Jerusalem from all over Asia. What an opportunity! The Spirit also inspires rational speech, raising it to new levels. Peter was no orator, but Jesus had promised that, when the time for witness came, the right words would be given them. Peter spoke fluently. He handled Old Testament quotations with the confidence of his Master. Verses from Psalms and Joel sprang to his mind spontaneously. We need to learn from Mother Hubbard's sad experience, to keep our cupboard well stocked, through daily bible reading! Verses that may say nothing to us at the time, can meet a later need, as the Spirit brings them to our remembrance.

The Spirit also gave Peter boldness. The man who, out of fear, had denied his Lord, was transfigured. He gave it to them strong! "You crucified him." How many of his hearers had been part of the crowd that shouted for Barabbas? "You crucified him, but God raised him up. Of that we are all witnesses." That was the key message: resurrection, a fact based on personal testimony. God had overturned men's judgement. The man they had mocked and crucified was vindicated and declared Lord. Another work of the Spirit was to convince men of sin. (Jn. 16:8) However convincing the preaching, or apt the quotations, only the Spirit has access to the secret workings of men's hearts and minds. We can't convert. It is dangerously easy "to win the argument and lose the man". The Spirit winged Peter's words like darts, bang on target.

"What shall we do?" We like to think of the Spirit as bringer of peace, but He is also the disturber. He shatters our complacency and cuts to the heart.

Peter's answer was simple. "Repent and be baptized." Don't wail over your past. Change direction. Accept the love and healing poured out for you on the cross, by making a public profession of faith. Then, oh what a wonderful promise, they too would receive this gift of his Spirit, to empower them to share Christ's risen life, and witness to others.

Three thousand people responded. What an impact they would make, returning home from that Festival, changed men, telling of a Harvest Ingathering, not of wheat, but of souls.

Why do these things not happen today? The answer is that they do, but the secular press doesn't report them. Sometimes its silence is deafening! Jesus, alive in his world today, is as threatening to our established way of life as he was in Jerusalem two thousand years ago. Where his disciples today fulfil the same conditions, they meet the same response. At the beginning of the 20th century, a small group, waiting in persistent and expectant prayer, united in heart, mind and obedience, gave birth to a new Pentecostal outpouring of the Spirit. But the timing is always God's, and the manner of the Spirit's coming varies. He can come with storm force or as a warm breath, like dew, or like a fresh spring of living water. So often we lack faith to receive Him. We want spectacular evidence, or a special feeling before we believe He has come. We put the cart before the horse. Faith must precede feeling.

The fire kindled at that first Pentecost began to spread throughout the city. It was not just the signs and healing miracles that drew people. The attraction lay also in the quality of life shown by the Christian community: their prayerfulness, their desire to learn more about Jesus, their togetherness, men, women and slaves, equally accepted. Most impressive was their generosity, and glad sharing of resources. This was important, for many were greatly in need. Many of those first converts would find themselves in the same position as the blind man Jesus had healed, (Jn. 9) cast out by the community, losing friends, property and work, as are converts from Islam and Hinduism today.

Then the situation exploded.

Healing the lame man. 3:1 - 4:31. 5:12-42.

He must have sat there begging for years. Jesus must often have passed by, but he had not cried out for healing. Peter and John too must have passed him daily, hardly noticing his beggar's whine.

But on this occasion, the Holy Spirit stopped them in their tracks. Again, it was the right time and the right place. The lame man only expected money. His eyes were on their hands and purses. The first step towards healing was personal encounter. "Look at us." The compassion of Jesus shone through their eyes. His authority rang out through Peter's voice. His power flowed through his outstretched hand. The beggar was not just healed, but transformed. Dancing around them, he entered the temple praising God. The astonished crowd gathered round the two disciples, crediting them with miraculous power. Peter was driven to deny such power was his.

For the second time, the Spirit had provided him with a platform, and a large audience. His preaching was an answer to their question. Their question was provoked by his action in obedience to the prompting of the Spirit. Such prompting and such provocation leads to attentive ears, and often to an active response. Five thousand people were converted, more than on the day of Pentecost.

The temple officials were incensed. Jesus, who had threatened their profits, Jesus the blasphemer, whom they thought they had done away with for ever, this Jesus was being proclaimed as alive and active, infinitely more dangerous than before.

Peter and John were arrested, together with the man who had been healed, and a meeting of the Sanhedrin was summoned for the following day.

Once again Peter is provided with a ready-made audience, this time of Top People. Their question gives him a perfect opening. He and John would have spent the night in prayer, trusting in Jesus' promise that the right words would again be given. They were: direct, incisive, scriptural, and bold. "Jesus alone is Saviour. There is no one else."

The healed man was standing there before them. What could their accusers say? What impressed them most was the boldness of the disciples. Such ordinary common men of little education; fishermen! The members of the Sanhedrin were accustomed to awed and unquestioning respect. Never had anyone dared to confront them like this, except Jesus. They recognised his spirit in these men. It made them both angry and cautious. After private consultation, they decided to take no action. After all, no crime had been committed. They would only threaten and forbid any further such teaching.

"Is it right for us to obey God or you?" Peter challenged them to judge that for themselves. The answer he and John must give is plain. The Council could only respond with further threats.

It is interesting to wonder why Luke names Alexander and John. Did they later become Christians? Did the Spirit use Peter's question to disturb them?

Jesus had warned his disciples that witnessing to him would lead to persecution. Now the Holy Spirit, like a gust of wind, blew them outwards. They called together their fellow apostles to report on the situation, and to pray. Note how constant is the strength they draw from scripture. There is no sign of fear or indecision, no prayer even for protection, only for boldness in proclaiming Jesus, and for God to continue to heal and work signs and wonders through the power of his Name.

The result of this prayer was another Pentecostal outpouring. Not only were they refilled with the Spirit, but the room itself was shaken. I experienced this phenomena at a healing meeting in a private house. The air shimmered as if with electricity, and passed amongst us by touch. I have learnt that this is not an uncommon experience in a Pentecostal meeting.

God gave them the boldness they asked for. Skip to chapter 5 verse 12 and you'll see He gave them the signs and wonders as well. Now, all the apostles met together in Solomon's Porch. No one dared to join them, but all admired them. Multitudes more came to believe. The news had spilled out beyond the city, and crowds were coming in from the surrounding towns, bringing their sick to be healed. It was just like the days of Jesus' ministry. All were healed, and demons were cast out.

We don't know how long this went on. We know the Jewish leaders feared the crowds. But they were jealous of their power and authority, which was slipping away. They were eventually driven to arrest the apostles, apparently all twelve of them, and lock them up for the night.

What are we to make of their release by an angel? Angels are messengers of God and can be human. A believer amongst the prison guards could perhaps have effected such a rescue. But today, Christians have told similar stories of angels rescuing them from Communist and other such prison camps and prisons. The Czech husband of a friend of mine experienced a miraculous deliverance through a quite extraordinary series of events, inexplicable to non-believers. He learnt later that a group in England had been praying for his deliverance.

In the case of the apostles, it wasn't so much a rescue as a sign. They returned to the temple and continued to preach. Officers of the guard were sent to re-arrest them. It was no enviable task. The crowd could have turned violent. They need not have feared. The apostles went with them willingly.

Again they were questioned by the Council. What were they trying to do? Rouse the people against them? Extract vengeance for their leader's death? What irony! The apostles did indeed want the blood of Jesus to cover them, but with forgiveness not condemnation. Again they insist that they are constrained by obedience to God. They have to declare that the risen Jesus is Saviour and Lord. Their witness is the witness of the Holy Spirit, given to all who believe and obey him. The implication of this further assertion is clear. Shutting up the apostles will not shut up the gospel. Countless others will be similarly empowered to proclaim it.

But the Council had no mind to abdicate. They felt no need of forgiveness, and were out for blood. The situation was saved only by the wisdom of Gamaliel, a learned and highly respected Pharisee. He ordered the apostles to be taken outside. Then he counselled patience, and trust that truth would eventually prevail. If the new movement was based on a lie, it would fizzle out. Gamaliel could at least conceive the possibility that the story might be true. In which case violent repression would be futile and spiritually dangerous.

The Council submitted to Gamaliel's advice. They ordered the apostles to be beaten, and then released, with a repeated command that, from then on, they were to keep silent on the matter. Wasted effort! The apostles positively exulted in their beating, and continued to preach in the temple every day.

Problems of the early church. 4:32 - 5:11. 6:1-7.

We have seen that one of the outstanding features of the early Christians was their generosity. Most of the apostles were probably married men with families to support. They had left their work to follow Jesus, and were now committed to full time preaching. During Jesus' ministry, a group of wealthy women had helped to support them. Now, thousands of converts were flooding in to form a new congregation, (Gk. *ecclesia*) or church, from the Latin. Many as a result may have faced eviction from their homes and destitution. They had to rely on the support of their new Christian brothers in a more fortunate position.

Spontaneously a new society came into being, based on the communist principle "from each according to his ability, to each according to his need." It differed from Communism in that it was voluntary, and was actively practiced. Barnabas is named, and his action is an illustration of this.

But converts are not free from temptation, and, when the Spirit is most active, the Devil can be relied upon to counter-attack. Typically the first sin to be recorded is that of pride.

Ananias and his wife wanted the kudos of appearing to be more generous than they were. So they lied about the profits of their sale. The Devil is, after all, the Father of lies. However, one of the gifts of the Spirit is that of knowledge. (1Cor. 12:8) This is a flash of insight, an interior awareness of a hidden truth about a person or his situation. Sometimes it is given in a picture that comes into the mind. Jesus showed this gift when speaking to the woman of Samaria.

Peter thus knew that Ananias had lied. His question uncovers Ananias' motive, and his rebuke, the seriousness of the sin. The shock of exposure may have brought on a heart attack. Ananias' death was not the punishment of an angry God, or of a judgmental church leader. As with Judas, it was the consequence of guilt, the Devil's substitute for repentance. The speedy burial illustrates the fear and horror of the bystanders. Even the corpse was a contamination. It was disposed of in three hours, before Sapphira returned.

Peter gave her a chance to tell the truth, but she too lied. Again the gift of knowledge revealed that this was not just ignorance. She and her husband had together agreed on the deception. Did they think they could get away with it? If the sale was to an outsider, how could anyone know? It was tempting, a challenge to the Spirit. Peter's prediction of her death should not be seen as a curse so much as another form of the same gift of knowledge. Sapphira's death was caused by the same shock and guilt that had led to the death of her husband, sudden knowledge of which was the crowning blow.

If the first sin led to dishonesty, the second led to division. Hebrews and Hellenists were both Jews, but in language and culture the latter were Greek. They felt discriminated against, for their widows were being overlooked in the giving out of food.

The problem was not settled by Peter, but, on his instructions, by the whole church. Everyone trusted the Twelve. To entrust the food distribution to them would have been an easy solution. But the Apostles had a right sense of priorities. Like Moses, (Ex. 18:25-26) they delegated. There were others, filled with the Spirit, who had the necessary integrity. The whole church could be trusted to select seven of them to do this service. It is remarkable that all those chosen had Greek names.

They were set aside for this work by democratic choice and by guided recognition of their worth. The choice was confirmed by the laying on the Apostle's hands, and prayer for a special gift of the Spirit to enable them to perform their work. Service is also a gift of the Spirit. (Rom. 12:7) As a result, unity was restored, and the number of disciples multiplied.

Disunity hinders evangelism, hence Jesus' prayer. (Jn. 17:20-21) Racial differences, coupled with injustice, cuts us more closely than denominational difference. But the Holy Spirit can sweep barriers down. In this dispute the Spirit was allowed to take charge every step of the way. The church emerged stronger than before.

The witness of Stephen. 6:8 - 7:60.

Stephen was one of the Seven chosen to distribute food aid. Integrity and faithfulness are fruits of the Spirit. (Gal. 5:22) They grow naturally out of a life surrendered to God. Wisdom equips us for service. (1Cor. 12:7 cp 1Kings 3:7-13) Stephen was also given gifts of preaching and working miracles. These stirred up both faith and hostility, especially within the Hellenist community. Unable to counter his arguments, his enemies resorted to plots. It was a replay of the trial of Jesus, the same accusations and the same use of false witnesses.

Stephen's defense is given at length. Is Luke's record based on Saul's memory? Was Saul one of the Cilicians who accused Stephen? His home town, Tarsus, was in Cilicia. It might also have come from Alexander and John. Already impressed by Peter and John, did they now recognise in Stephen the face of an angel? Were they converted by his witness and his death?

Stephen addressed the Council initially with respect. His recapitulation of Jewish history appears irreproachable. In fact, it was dynamite. God's covenant with Abraham, that he would father a nation, and inherit the land of Canaan, was given long before the covenant of circumcision. It was a covenant based on faith not Law. Secondly, the men God raised up to set his people free: Joseph, Moses, and later the prophets, all suffered rejection by their own people. Thirdly God's laws were continually flouted. Right up to the Exile in Babylon, the people continued to worship the Calf and other idols. (Amos 5:25-27) As for the temple, even Solomon who built it, knew that God could not be contained within it (1Kgs. 8:27) as Isaiah, whom Stephen quotes, confirms. (Is. 66:1-2)

Finally, Stephen turns on his hearers. The Law they are upholding has always been denied by their lives. As they rage in fury against him, Stephen is given a vision of Jesus in glory. They will hear no more. They block their ears, drag him out of the city, and stone him to death. Like his Master, he commends his spirit into God's hands, and dies, praying for his enemies to be forgiven.

There were two immediate consequences of Stephen's martyrdom. One was the disturbance of Saul. The violence of his fury points to a violence of inner conflict. The manner of Stephen's death witnessed to Jesus with a power that not all the arguments of Saul's brilliant mind could withstand. It illustrates the comment in a preacher's notes, "When your argument is weak, shout loudly" - or act violently!

The second consequence, linked to the first, was the persecution of Christians in Jerusalem. As a result, the Believers, apart from the Apostles, scattered to all the surrounding districts, taking the Gospel with them.

The same thing has been happening today. While newspapers report only of African refugees flooding into adjacent countries, Christian leaders, sharing their plight, speak of revival, the expansion of the gospel, great numbers of new converts and the establishment of new churches. About all this the secular press is silent.

The witness of Philip. Chapter 8.

Philip was one of those scattered like a seed, to produce a spiritual harvest in Samaria. Like Stephen, he was one of the Seven, chosen to "serve tables". He too had gifts of healing and exorcism. It was these gifts that first attracted people to the gospel. In India, and in many other parts of the world today, people have been initially won to Christ after seeing such signs of deliverance performed in his Name.

But Simon, a local magician, saw these signs as a superior magic. He tried to discover Philip's secret, and to get in on his act. For him, baptism was not a dying to self and a rising to new life in Christ. It was a ritual, giving him contact with a new source of power. He stuck to Philip like a burr, with envious desire to emulate his miracles.

He soon learnt that Philip was not the Master Magician. He could heal, but not impart his power of healing to others. Strangely, the Spirit did not descend on those whom Philip baptized.

News of mass conversions in Samaria however, soon reached Jerusalem, and drew Peter and John to visit the new converts. They had learnt from Jesus not to despise Samaritans as semi-pagans, but to treat them with respect. John would never forget his sharp rebuke. (Lk. 9:52-55) At the Ascension, Jesus had told them they were to be his witnesses, starting in Jerusalem and spreading to all Judea and Samaria, and to the ends of the earth. The wind of the Spirit had now started to blow in Samaria. What a presage for the future!

When they got there, they discovered this blockage. What was wrong? Had something of Simon's spirit infected the crowds he had beguiled? Was it only the healing they wanted, rather than forgiveness and new life? Or was it that the coming of the Gospel to Samaria was such a radical and important event that the Spirit chose to withhold some of His gifts, until their conversion was confirmed by these senior apostles? As in the later case of the Roman centurion, conservative Jews might hesitate to accept the Samarian converts without this lead from those whose authority was unquestioned. In any case, the Spirit is sovereign. He cannot be pinned down by rules or rituals, or their absence. Luke makes this very clear.

In Simon's eyes, Peter and John were the Grand Masters of the secret arts. He tried to buy his way into their brotherhood. It is from his attempt to purchase spiritual power and gifts, that we get our word *simony*. Peter's response was stern. "To hell with you and your money!" But he did hold out the possibility of forgiveness should Simon repent. Simon however only wanted protection from what he saw as a curse. He did not repent. Later he won fame in Rome as a great magician. A statue was erected in his honour, but it did not survive very long. Peter's glorious monument, built close to the site where he was martyred, is with us today.

The Spirit's timing is perfect. After the apostles had returned to Jerusalem, Philip was given a compelling nudge. "Take the desert road to Gaza."

What? Leave his new converts, badly in need of teaching, and set off for the wilds with no reason given? Philip didn't hesitate. The Spirit could shepherd the flock without him. Later missionaries have found this difficult. Too often they have stayed on too long, thereby stunting the growth of their converts. It was just as well that Philip obeyed, blindly and immediately. Had he delayed, he might have missed that chariot, and the gospel would not have reached Ethiopia until many years later.

The Spirit had everything prepared; the eunuch with his embryonic faith, and interest in the scriptures, the text he was puzzling over when Philip reached him, that second nudge to make Philip contact him, and ask what he was reading, and finally, the pool of water, scarce in the desert, reached just at the perfect time! What a good thing that Philip was not plagued by theological problems about baptizing uncircumcised Gentiles! He followed his leading and went ahead. How could he refuse? Then they parted. The eunuch went on his way rejoicing. Philip walked on in a daze. They never met again. What an experience of faithful obedience, and divinely planned coincidences!

Saul's conversion. 9:1-31.

Meanwhile the Spirit was dealing with Saul. Furiously fighting his fears and inner disturbance, he is stopped in his tracks by a vision of Jesus himself. Blinded by the light, and brought to his knees, Saul has to confess that Jesus is Lord. He enters Damascus a helpless prisoner. Ironic in view of his intended activity there! Like Jonah, like Jesus, he experienced for three days a form of death.

Now it is Ananias who gets a nudge. "Go and lay hands on Saul and restore his sight." Understandably Ananias is reluctant. He argued, but he went. God can cope with our objections. It gives Him a chance to clarify His intention. What matters is our obedience. Note how gently Ananias approaches Saul, calling him brother.

Healing was no easy let off. Saul had been picked for a purpose. He was to preach Jesus to the Gentiles. In doing so, he would have to face the persecution he had inflicted on others.

It is clear from his account in Galatians that Saul's first significant action was to make for the Arabian desert. Like Jesus in the wilderness, Saul needed space and silence to pray and rethink his whole understanding of Scripture, and of his way of life. Led by the Spirit, he needed no other teacher. (Gal. 1:15-24) Later, he returned to Damascus, astounding the Christians and confounding the Jews. All his gifts were now used to expound Scripture in order to prove that Jesus was indeed Christ, the Messiah.

The reaction of the Jews was predictable. To escape assassination, Saul had to leave the city by night, let down over the wall in a basket. It was a blow to his pride, worse than countless beatings. (2Cor. 11:24-32)

Only after three years did Saul go up to Jerusalem. The church refused to accept him. They did not believe his story. They suspected him of being a spy, seeking to infiltrate and betray them. Only Barnabas, "Son of Consolation" believed him. This lovely generous-hearted man took Saul to the apostles, vouched for him, and won his acceptance.

In Jerusalem too, Saul's bold preaching led to threats on his life. His new friends had to provide him with a safe escort out of the city and as far as Caesarea. From there he was packed off home to Tarsus. Another humiliation. Zeal is not enough. Saul had a lot to learn.

Luke omits from his account Saul's years in Arabia. He also omits another important fact, or rather he postpones it. He allows Saul to tell it in his own words when, years later, as Paul, back in the city, he was defending himself against another furious mob. It was while he was praying in the temple, on that first visit, that Saul fell into a trance, and experienced a second vision of Jesus. He was told to leave the city, for the people there would not listen to him. He was given a different, but equally costly mission, to take the gospel to the Gentiles. Luke's postponement of this fact is no accident. He is not only a master of prose, but, like Mark, he has the skill of a dramatist. This revelation was the climax of Paul's testimony.

Back now to Saul. He had believed that, having been such a strict Jew, and a previous persecutor of the Christians, his people would listen to him. The opposite was true. Back in Tarsus he had to face another inner wilderness before he was ready to embark on his new mission.

Peter and Cornelius. 9:32 - 11:18.

Step by step, the Holy Spirit was driving the church to burst the bonds of Judaism. Philip was the first to baptize a man who, though classed as a "god-fearer", was still regarded as a pagan. Peter, as Christ's leading apostle, would have to be convinced before this big change would be generally accepted by the church.

So the Spirit starts nudging him in the right direction. He visits Lydda, where he heals Aeneas, and the people there turn to the Lord. Hearing of this, a group of disciples in Joppa ask him to visit them and lay hands on Tabitha. Lydda and Joppa are coastal towns lying between Azotus and Caesarea. Philip must have passed through them. (8:40) Did Peter hear any rumour of what Philip had done? If so it must have aroused questions in his mind. Peter's decision to stay with Simon the Tanner was already breaking a taboo. Tanners were regarded as unclean. It was preparation for a still greater change.

Meanwhile, God was at work on Cornelius. Like many other Roman centurions stationed in Palestine and mentioned in the Gospels, he was an intelligent and devout pagan, attracted to the Jewish religion with its monotheism and high ethical teaching. Cornelius could visit the synagogue, but would be excluded from fellowship. No Jew would enter his house, let alone share a meal with him.

In the middle of the afternoon, taking no doubt his usual siesta, he had a waking vision. An angel appeared who told him to send for one called Simon Peter, staying in Joppa at the house of Simon a tanner. The detailed instructions gave the vision strong authenticity. Such an experience is not unknown even today. Cornelius acted immediately. He sent a soldier, and two servants to find and fetch this man, of whom he had probably never heard before.

Once again, God's timing was perfect. The next day, Peter, hungry and waiting for his dinner, dozes off. His dream, thrice repeated, drives the message home. "What God has cleansed, do not you call common." At that moment Cornelius' men arrive and invite Peter to visit a pagan home!

Forewarned by the Spirit, Peter knows what he must reply. First he invites them into Simon's home to stay as guests. Did they have to overcome some distaste themselves? The next day, Peter sets off with them, taking other disciples with him. If he has to learn and do something new, they must share the experience.

He arrives to find Cornelius waiting for him with a small band of family and friends. Knowing the rules, Cornelius, with sensitive courtesy, had come out of his house to meet his guest. Humbly, this Roman officer kneels to Peter as to a god. Peter raises him up and, before declaring the gospel to him, demonstrates it by entering Cornelius' house.

"We are all here in the sight of God, to hear what He has given you to say." What an invitation! Again the Spirit has provided the right place, and the right occasion.

Peter, equally humble, starts by sharing what God has been teaching him. Then he refers to the facts about Jesus which Cornelius might possibly know. He might have heard favourable reports from a fellow centurion stationed at Capurnaum, as well as twisted reports given him by Jews.

Peter then gives his personal testimony to Jesus' death, resurrection, and the forgiveness of sins. While he was still speaking, the Holy Spirit fell upon them, tongues and all! Peter hadn't got as far as telling them about the Spirit's coming at Pentecost, let alone about His gifts. Until then, Peter had only experienced the Spirit being given after baptism. He hadn't had time to mention that either. The Spirit demonstrated His freedom by reversing the usual procedure. Responding to the Word by faith was enough.

Who could now refuse them baptism? None of his friends could object. How wise of Peter to have brought them. So Peter, the Rock on which Jesus said he would build his church, stepped boldly out of line. What Philip had done spontaneously, Peter did with conscious deliberation. The Holy Spirit had masterminded both occasions.

Returning to Jerusalem, Peter, unsurprisingly, found himself in hot water. Pagans were accepted into Judaism only after being circumcised. Many Hebrew Christians assumed that the same rite should be imposed upon Gentile converts. Peter told them how his own reluctance had been overcome, and described the events in Cornelius' house. "Who was I to withstand God?" It was much the same reply as he had given to the Sanhedrin. For a time at least, the conservatives were silenced. Perhaps it was a one-off! But, as Jesus had promised, his Spirit was guiding them into all truth; thoughts and practices that were new. The new wine was bursting the old wine skins!

New dangers and new opportunities. 11:19 - 12:24.

As the church grew, so did the persecution. The Jews now put pressure on Herod Agrippa to intervene. He was a grandson of Herod the Great, who was made Tetrarch of Palestine and later given the title of King. He is not to be confused with Herod Antipas, the son of Herod the Great, to whom Jesus was sent for trial. He had since been banished. Herod Agrippa the First, was deeply unpopular with the Jews, and this was his chance to curry favour. So he executed James, who became the first apostle to be martyred. Finding this a popular move, Herod arrested Peter with the same intent.

Like the Sanhedrin, Herod had not reckoned with the power of prayer. For the second time Peter was miraculously delivered. When he knocked on their door, his praying friends could not believe their prayers had been answered so soon. The maid, who answered the door, thought he was ghost.

This time Peter does not court further publicity. Herod had shown he could and would take life. Peter's mission was now too important. Leaving a message for James, the Lord's brother, who was now one of the main leaders of the church in Jerusalem, Peter moves away to another place. As for Herod, his sudden death was seen by the church as an act of God. He was struck down, not for his persecution, but for his pride. He had accepted the attribution of divinity from the syncophant citizens of Tyre and Sidon.

Meanwhile, persecution had been driving the gospel still further into the Greek cities of Asia Minor. At first, the Believers, known as "Followers of the Way", spoke only to Jews. Then, some who had come from the islands of Cyprus and Cyrene, began preaching to Greeks too. They met with a great response, especially in the city of Antioch.

Hearing of this, the church in Jerusalem sent Barnabas to investigate and deal with the situation. He was himself a Cypriot. When he saw the great things the Spirit was doing in Antioch, he rejoiced. He was a man with an open mind, and full of the Spirit. Had Peter's report on the events in Caesarea taken place before this? Barnabas saw the situation as an open door and a great opportunity. Courage was needed to go forward, to encourage and guide, though not to control. That was the Spirit's prerogative. Then he remembered the man he had befriended, a man God had specially called to mission to the Gentiles. Saul, with his youth, enthusiasm, and outstanding gifts, was just the man for the job. Barnabas set off to Tarsus to find him, and ask for his help.

How wonderfully the Spirit draws threads together. Both bad and good get drawn into a pattern that could never have been conceived in advance. From being a problem, Antioch became the first church in which Jews and Gentiles discovered unity in Christ. It was here that they were first called Christians. Those who saw them wondered, and said, "See how these Christians love one another!"

This love was not parochial. Neither was it impractical. When a prophet named Agabus visited them from Jerusalem, and foretold a world famine, the Christians in Antioch didn't even wait for it to happen before sending aid to the impoverished brethren there. They commissioned Barnabas and Paul to go to Jerusalem and deliver their offerings personally. It was a grateful gift of material help, in return for the spiritual riches they had received through the sharing of the gospel.

Finally, the church in Antioch, became the launch pad for a Mission to the world. That is the story to be told in the next chapter.

Summary

In the Gospels we see Jesus as Man recreated in God's image. But was such recreation possible for ordinary sinful people like ourselves, not virgin born? To this Jesus gave a resounding "Yes". We must be reborn in the Spirit.

So, in these early chapters of Acts, we see people being reborn as the Spirit came upon them. It was a gift. The initiative was always God's. The Spirit came in different ways, but experience showed that there were some necessary conditions for receiving Him, such as faith, obedience and expectancy. All this is seen in the disciples at Pentecost as they waited together on God in prayer.

What difference did the coming of the Holy Spirit make? Five things clearly emerge. First was the change in the lives of the disciples. They had a new boldness to witness and a new authority to heal in Jesus' Name. They exercised gifts of the Spirit: wisdom, knowledge and discernment, as well as tongues. They rejoiced in suffering. In all these things they were recognizably like their Master. (Acts 4:13)

Secondly, change was seen in the way they acted. They were alert and obedient to the nudges of the Spirit. The Spirit initiated actions that opened up new doors of opportunity. He was in charge of operations.

A new society, the church was born. Those who believed were baptized both with water and in the Spirit. They met regularly on the Lord's Day, to break bread in remembrance of the Lord's death, and in celebration of his risen presence. Special ministries came to be recognized, deacons were commissioned for service.

A pattern emerged in the way their mission was received. Jesus had warned them of persecution. Many suffered. Twice Peter was miraculously delivered from prison. His time was not yet. The infant church needed his leadership. James however and Stephen were put to death.

The wind of the Spirit used persecution to strengthen the church and scatter the seed of the Gospel. The reversal of roles, found in the Gospels, is repeated as Saul the persecutor becomes Paul the Apostle to the Gentiles, the death of Stephen playing a part in preparing for his conversion.

Lastly, despite these wonderful happenings, the problem of sin remained. Though Jesus was tempted, he never succumbed to evil. He taught the need to be continually filled with the Holy Spirit, together with constant prayer and watchfulness. The main temptation came from love of money and power. Above all, the Devil sought to divide them. Only the Holy Spirit and His gift of love could preserve their unity.

In the following chapter we see how the same principles and problems continue, as Saul, now known as Paul, launches out on his missionary journeys. From now on he, not Peter, is the central character of Luke's story. In Paul's letters we see him wrestling with new problems arising within a growingly Gentile church.

Questions for private meditation

1. Do you wait on God, giving Him freedom to speak or to remain silent? (Chap. 1)

2. As the gifts of the Spirit are promised to all who believe and are baptized, what prevents you from possessing all your possessions? (Chap. 2)

3. What opportunities for witness has (does) the Spirit open up for you? (Chaps. 3 & 4)

4. How do you feel when others are praised, or your services go unrecognised? How do you cope with such feelings? (Chap. 5)

5. Are you concerned for the fair and equal treatment of any minority group in your church? (Chap. 6)

6. Has God ever spoken to you from the Old Testament? (Chap. 7)

7. What "nudges" of the Spirit have you experienced? How do you know they come from the Spirit? (Acts 8)

8. Was your conversion experienced as a decisive event or a series of events, and/or as a process still going on? (Chap. 9)

9. Has God ever challenged your religious prejudices and practices? How flexible are you? (Chap. 10)

10. How central is the Spirit to every aspect of your life?

Questions for group discussion

1. How can prayer for guidance at church meetings be made more meaningful? (Chap. 1)

2. Note the different ways of expressing the Pentecost experience in 1:5, 2:2-4, 4:31, 8:14-17, 10:44-46. Which do you find most helpful and why? Why is the church so afraid of it? (Chap. 2). Since Christmas and Easter are powerless without Pentecost, why has this Festival been so neglected?

3. In the early days of the church, actions provoked questions which opened opportunities for a valid witness. Should this be a pattern for the church's evangelism today. (Chaps. 3 & 4)

4. "Guilt is the Devil's alternative to repentance". Discuss. (Chap. 5)

5. How prayerfully are church members voted on to the church council and supported afterwards? (Chap. 6)

6. How relevant is the Old Testament to the church today? (Chap. 7)
7. What experiences have members of the Group of the Spirit's "nudges" and perfect timing? (Chap. 8)
8. Is conversion ever really sudden or complete? (Chap. 9)
9. When is it right to break church rules? Give examples. (Chaps. 10 & 11)
10. Would "Acts of the Spirit" be a better title for this Book?

Chapter 6

Mission to the Gentiles

Acts Chapters 13-20. Galatians. 1 & 2 Thessalonians.

Let us look more closely at the leaders of the church that was Paul's launch pad. The twelve apostles were men of widely different backgrounds. The same is true of the leaders at Antioch.

There was Barnabas, a Levite trained in the Law, but open-minded. Simon, called Niger, was he from Africa and perhaps black? Was he the same as Simon of Cyrene who carried Jesus' cross, as so many Blacks have to carry it today? Lucius, certainly from Cyrene, was Roman, or at least Greek in culture. Manaean was an aristocrat brought up in the court of Herod. Saul was a man of two worlds. Brought up in Tarsus, a sea port and university town with a Greek culture, he was educated in Jerusalem, the centre of Jewish orthodoxy. There he had been trained as a Rabbi under the great Gamaliel. They included prophets, likely to disturb the status quo, and teachers, more likely to maintain it. We find them together, worshipping, fasting, and waiting in silence for a word from the Spirit.

The word, when it came was costly. They were told to release their two best and most experienced leaders for missionary service abroad. Neither were starry-eyed volunteers, but, had they been experiencing a restlessness, a growing awareness of a secret nudge? Had they even been waiting and praying for the church to recognize and give support for such a calling? Or did it come as a bolt from the blue?

Support they certainly received. The laying on of hands was a form of blessing. It was also a commissioning for service, and a channel through which the Spirit could flow, to empower them for it? (cp. 6:6 and 8:17) Their sending was a joint action of the Spirit and the church.

From now on Saul is known as Paul, (v. 9) the Greek version of his name. He and Barnabas took with them a young man, not so clearly called or sent. What we know of John Mark has been given at the end of the Gospel that bears his name. They had brought him with them from Jerusalem when they returned from their mission. Did Mark ask his cousin to take him, or did Barnabas suggest it, thinking it would provide him with a good training in preaching the Gospel? If so it didn't work out, and Mark soon turned back. (13:13) But perhaps, if he had never started out on that mission, and faced failure, he might never have discovered his real vocation. No experience is wasted.

The first missionary journey. 13:4 - 14:28.

Their first port of call was Cyprus. This was Barnabas' home territory. They seem to have confined themselves to preaching in the synagogues. Ironically it was the hostility of a false prophet-cum-magician that aroused the curiosity of the Roman Pro-Consul. He invited them to visit him and explain their teaching. Again, notice how wonderfully the Spirit reverses the situation. The more Elymas contradicts, the stronger Paul speaks out. Was it cruel of Paul to strike the man with blindness if only for a time? Paul himself had been so struck. For him it had been a blessing, a time when he learnt to see more clearly. The Pro- Consul, seeing this sign, believed. The first Gentile convert was not a Greek, but a Roman.

The next important stop was Antioch in Pisidia. By that time John Mark had left them and gone home. Here a pattern was set that was to be repeated time after time. First they visited the synagogue where, as visitors, they were invited to give a message. Paul is the speaker. Like Stephen, he gives a scriptural summary of Jewish history, though without any slant of criticism. He presents Jesus as the descendent of David and the promised Messiah, pointed to by John the Baptist, but unrecognised by the Jewish leaders. He proclaims the resurrection and the good news of forgiveness of sins. The sacrifices of the Law only covered inadvertent failures of ritual observance, but it is for forgiveness and acceptance that our guilty souls cry out. No wonder the natural response of most of Paul's hearers was a desire to hear more.

So the second stage is reached. Crowds come, not just Jews and proselytes, ie devout converts to Judaism who had accepted circumcision, but almost the whole city. The Jewish leaders are filled with jealous anger. They contradict and vilify Paul. Henceforth the synagogue is barred both to him and Barnabas.

Just as well, for it could not have contained all the eager followers. Paul warns his revilers that Jews had been given their chance. Now they would concentrate on preaching the gospel to the Gentiles. So the third stage is reached. The Gospel spreads rapidly, not only in the town, but throughout the region round about.

We don't know how long this happy period was allowed to continue, or when the fourth stage was reached. Persecution followed. The Jews stirred up leading men and devout women of high social standing, and drove the apostles out of the district. Following Jesus' instructions, they shook off the dust from their feet against them, a strong symbolic gesture, and went on to the next town.

At Iconium the third stage continued for a long time, but slowly the Jews were able to turn some of the Greeks against Paul, and the town was divided. He and Barnabas then went on to Lystra.

At Lystra they met a pagan crowd, untouched by Jewish teaching. The healing of a cripple led the apostles to be hailed as gods, Zeus and Hermes, walking the earth disguised as men. Greek myths were full of such manifestations. But when their offer of worship was repulsed with horror, and Paul called them to abandon such a vain religion, and to worship one God the Creator, the mood of the crowd changed to hostility. Then it was easy for Jews, who had pursued the apostles from Iconium, to stone Paul, and drag him out of the city, leaving him for dead. It was "Hosanna" and "Crucify" all over again. Gentiles, quite as much as Jews, expect their God, or gods, to fulfil their desires and expectations.

The attempt to stone Paul at Iconium had not succeeded. This time it seemed that it had. The new disciples gathered round. Were they praying that he should be raised from the dead? If so, this is the first example of Group Prayer for healing. Those praying were not leaders, but very ordinary converts. The story of Cornelius had shown that the Spirit showers His gifts on the newest of believers. The power of healing is God's. It is channelled, through the prayer of faith.

Paul got up. Had he been only concussed, it would still have been a miracle. He walked back into the town where he rested for the night, and the next day, together with Barnabas, walked on to Derbe. There many believed and became disciples.

What courage it took to return to all those towns where his life had been threatened! But in each there were many disciples who needed teaching and encouragement. No doubt, they too would suffer persecution. They needed to be bonded together into a strong fellowship of believers, a church, an *ecclesia*, called out and chosen. They would need wise leaders whom they could trust. So, when the apostles returned, in each place, with prayer and fasting, they appointed elders, *presbuteroi.* Then, after committing them to the Lord, they moved on.

At last they returned safely to their sending church. At Antioch they reported on all that God had done with them - not what they had done for God! The doors into the Gentile world were wide open. Faithful believers were flowing in. Like oil lamps, glowing in the dark, these small churches were witnessing in place after place. Great opportunities lay ahead.

The Council of Jerusalem. 15:1 - 35.

Wonderful, but-. Yes, there is always a but. We have seen how Philip had happily baptized the Ethiopian, with no regard for theological niceties. We have also seen how Peter had to face hostile criticism after he had baptized Cornelius. The Christian leaders had accepted this, perhaps as a special dispensation. But now Gentiles were flocking into the church. There was even a possibility that they might one day come to outnumber Jewish believers. They lacked the strong moral teaching based on religious sanctions that was given in Jewish homes. Circumcision, with its commitment to the Law, could be seen as a practical, as well as a theological matter. In the city, a number of Pharisees had joined the church. They were adamant that the practice of circumcising Gentile proselytes must be maintained.

What was worse, some men had visited Antioch saying that, without circumcision, nobody could be saved! Paul and Barnabas argued with them in vain. Finally, they decided to go up to Jerusalem and consult with Peter and the other leaders. The church in Jerusalem welcomed them, and they were able to report on their mission and its success. It was then that the Pharisaic believers put forward their point of view. All the new converts must be circumcised, and told they must keep the Law. Paul and Barnabas were horrified. The imposition of the Law, with its rules covering every aspect of life, would completely cut off the converts from their own society. It could even halt the flow of new believers into the church.

Wisely, they left it to Peter to defend their cause. They had met him since his experience in Caesarea, so they knew they could rely on him. Peter made the two really relevant points. The Law with its hundreds of commands and prohibitions was a burden that even Jews had found too heavy to bear. As Christians, they believed that they would be saved by the grace of Christ just as the Gentiles would be. There was a great silence. Then they all listened to Paul and Barnabas as they shared their experience of what God had been doing through them.

It was James, whose opinion settled the matter. Not only was he honoured as the Lord's brother, he was also deeply respected by Pharisees, in and outside the church, for his strict observance of the Law. Now that Peter was travelling so much, James was recognised as the leader of the church in Jerusalem.

Gentile believers, he said, should not have the Law of Moses imposed on them. He may have referred them to The Talmud, which speaks of the Law of Noah, as God's Law for the Gentiles. It consists of the last five of the Ten Commandments. James proposed that only three restrictions should be laid down. There should be no involvement with idols, or prostitution, and the meat they ate should be bloodless. Blood was life, and was sacred. (Gen. 9:4) Only then would it be possible for Jewish and Christian believers to eat happily together. It could be seen as a concession of courtesy, rather than of Law.

This decision was accepted unanimously. A letter containing it was given to Paul and Barnabas, to take back with them to Antioch. It also declared that those who had come with upsetting teaching had not been sent by them. The letter began, "It seemed good to the Holy Spirit and to us". Would that all church decisions could be thus recorded! We have much to learn from the Society of Friends in this respect.

Paul's Letter to the Galatians.

Sadly the matter did not end there. Jews, like those who had disturbed Antioch with their teaching, did not accept the Council's ruling. They continued to stir up trouble.

This was not helped by Peter's own ambivalence, when he himself visited Antioch. It is not certain whether the occasion Paul describes in his letter happened before or after the Council. (Gal. 2:11-14) In any case, the decision only freed Gentile believers from the demands of the Law. It was presumed that Jews, already circumcised, were still bound by it. Hence the ruling on kosher food.

The logic of this would lead to there being two classes of believers. If interpreted strictly, it would mean that Jewish Christians could not eat with their Gentile brethren, even if the food were kosher. The Lord's Supper was celebrated within the context of a Love Feast. Unity was expressed in every aspect of life. What would happen to that?

Paul and Barnabas had eaten with Gentiles without question. When Peter visited them, he happily fell in with the practice. But, when stricter brothers came from James on a visit, Peter decided that, for the short time they would be there, it would be wiser to eat at separate tables. Otherwise they would return and report such laxity, and there would be further trouble and division. As a pillar of the church, Peter could not risk this.

Most agreed with his arguments, "even Barnabas!" (2:11-14) Obviously a sore point. Paul was outraged. Not only was it hypocrisy, it was a betrayal of the

Gospel, a denial, (dangerous word for Peter!) of the basic belief that we are saved by faith. The grace of Jesus Christ revealed on the cross is all sufficient. As a modern theologian has pointed out, our salvation does not depend on Christ, *and* adult baptism, episcopacy, or *and* anything. We are saved by Christ, full stop.

Paul had to face Peter openly. This wasn't easy. Paul was a younger man. He had had theological training and his mind was razor sharp. A rebuke from him could have aroused in Peter a sense of inferiority, leading him to use his status as the Rock, to put his foot down. Paul wasn't even one of the twelve. Having organised Matthias' election, Peter would have to uphold Matthias' position. Peter was also stubborn. In this the men were alike.

But Peter was humble. He loved his Lord. Paul's personal pride and ambition had been "crucified with Christ." (2:20) There was no power struggle between them. Paul trusted in the Spirit to use his words to speak to Peter's heart. Peter must have felt hurt, but there was no rift between them.

When Paul heard that his beloved converts in Galatia had been led astray, he wrote them the passionate letter in which this incident is described. Those who were disturbing them had sought to undermine Paul's authority, so his letter opens with his claim to be a true apostle, called, like the others, by Jesus Christ himself. The Galatians had been told that he had only been appointed by a Gentile-dominated church in Antioch. In order to achieve popular success, he had changed the gospel as it was preached in Jerusalem, by telling them they were free from the Law. As a result, the gospel they had received was defective. Their salvation was therefore in doubt.

Paul is furious. "May they be cursed", he cries. Jesus too could be angry with those who shook the faith of children, and these were Paul's children in the faith. He loved them passionately. They had loved him too. How could they so easily be turned against him? (4:12-20)

Faced by their foolishness, Paul tells of his own conversion by direct revelation from Christ himself. Only years later had he visited Jerusalem and met Cephas. Note his use of the Hebrew form of Peter's name. He had also met the ultra-orthodox James. Both had accepted him and the gospel he preached. He also tells of a later visit with Titus. Does this refer to the visit taking the relief offerings, or the visit to the Council? No demand was made for Titus to be circumcised. The three "pillars", which included John, had accepted both himself and Barnabas in equal fellowship, called to an equal but different sphere of mission. (1:11 - 2:10)

Paul then describes his confrontation with Peter at Antioch. This leads to teaching on the essence of Christian belief. We are not saved by the works of the Law, but by faith in Jesus Christ. When we justify ourselves, we try to prove that we are OK. Try convincing God of that! Draw up a list of your good deeds, remembering that God looks at the heart, and reads our secret motives. Is our hope, "I'm not as bad as some"? Or do we hope God will lower his standards a bit? After all, he is a loving Father. Yes, but God is also Holy. He is a God of Truth. Children need to own up to their naughtiness, knowing that this makes no difference to the love their parents have for them.

If we can bank on free forgiveness, won't this encourage us to go on sinning? We can sin as we like and, like the thief on the cross, by making a deathbed repentance, that is if we are given the chance, we can get away with it - an idea expressed by Heinrich Heine's famous aphorism, "God will pardon me. It is His trade." Can we look at the cross, see God's love, and the cost of such love, and say that to Jesus? Embraced by such love, we die to our "oughts and shoulds", our comparison of ourselves with others and our self-justification. Thankfully, and freely, we can let his love flow into us, and begin to transform us. This is no dry doctrine. Passionately, Paul shared his own experience. "I am crucified with Christ, and now Christ lives in me."

Having shared his own experience, Paul now appeals to theirs. (3:1-5) The wonderful things that the Spirit had been doing amongst them were the result of faith, not of keeping the Law. He illustrates his point with Abraham. He received his call, and the promises by faith, long before he was circumcised. (cp Gen. 12:1-4, 15:2-6 & 18, 17:1-2, 9-11) The Law hadn't even been given. A later covenant could not cancel the first. In any case, to keep the whole Law was impractical. All Jews were selective in their observance. That wasn't obedience.

So why was the Law given? Paul likens it to a school-master. Children need rules, or they run wild. That doesn't lead to freedom. The rabble of slaves, that were suddenly liberated from Egypt, needed to learn discipline, and to know right from wrong. Adults are supposed to have learnt to discipline themselves. But we discover that our unruly passions and desires possess us and we are in fact, not free. (cp. Jn. 8:34-36) If someone says "I ought to do this", one can be pretty sure they won't. Love is the great motivator, and we receive this love by faith. Education, culture, race and sex make no difference to this. In Christ we are all one, children of one Father, "Abba", the equivalent of a child's "Daddy". (3:19-4:7)

Paul now returns to his personal relationship with these churches. (4:8-20)

Despite being a Jew, he had eaten their food. They had loved him despite some distressing ailment. We don't know what it was, but it was humiliating, epilepsy perhaps. (2Cor. 10:10, 12:7) Why then are they now shutting him out? It is these new teachers who are flattering them, to win their support. Like scalp-hunters, they want to boast of their converts. In fact the Galatians are cutting themselves off from the freedom given them in Christ.

After this display of emotion, Paul returns to argument. (4:21-5:1) Rabbis were accustomed to interpret scripture allegorically. Today many find this unconvincing, though some preachers still use it. Paul quickly turns from this to direct teaching, based on his own personal authority, "I Paul say to you." (5:2-12) If they accept circumcision, then they no longer believe that Christ has already saved them. Their faith and freedom are lost. They are back in bondage. Is it this false teaching, or Paul's costly witness, that will act as leaven and permeate the church? Paul's hope lies, not in his letter, but in his Lord.

A strong argument made by the upholders of the Law, then and now, is that to teach people that God loves and freely forgives them, however bad they are, only encourages them to continue in their bad ways. Paul deals with this problem at length in his letter to the Romans. Here he deals with it practically. (5:13-25)

If we love God, and want to live in His presence, then we can't go on deliberately doing all that shuts us out from Him. The nasty sins Paul lists are not a recipe for happiness. To this the TV Soaps all bear witness. Self-indulgence only enslaves.

Only when we "lose our life" can we "save it". Christ's life, like sap from the vine, seeps through the branches to produce fruit. Love and Peace aren't qualities we can acquire by text book study or effort (cp books on "how to be popular"). The fruits of the Spirit grow naturally. But they need to be desired, accepted and put to use.

Even Christians can be judgmental. Our faults and failings do not miraculously disappear. Old habits die hard. Growing to maturity in Christ takes time. (6:1-10) So Paul ends by asking his brothers to be gentle with those who fall. Humbly and gently they should raise them up. Harsh criticism pushes them further down. Our faults are our burdens. We all have to bear them, but we can help each other by sharing the load. This is another aspect of sharing the gospel. We reap what we sow. Sow seed of the Spirit and we will reap a harvest of eternal life. Sow seeds of the flesh and we reap inevitable corruption.

Paul evidently dictated his letters. It seems that he also suffered from bad eyesight. His final words, written in his own hand, sum up his message. Those who preach circumcision, glory in the flesh, which includes pride in the success of their preaching. He, Paul, has died to all such glory. He glories only in Christ crucified. The marks he bears on his body are the scars of the beating and stoning he has suffered for the gospel. *"No wound? No scar? Yet, as the Master shall the servant be. And pierced are the feet that follow Me; But thine are whole: Can he have followed far Who has no wound or scar?"* (A. Carmichael)

Call to Macedonia. Chapter 16.

The Council having concluded, Paul was itching to be off again, to encourage these young churches with his personal presence. We have seen how his disagreement over taking Mark with them had led to his separation from Barnabas. His new companion, Silas, had been sent with Judas, to accompany Paul on his return to Antioch. Some texts include an extra verse, telling us that, when Judas returned to Jerusalem, Silas decided to stay on.

So Paul's second, and much longer journey began. Little did he know how far it would take him.

At Lystra they found young Timothy. His father was Greek, but his mother Eunice, and his grandmother Lois were devout converts. (2Tim. 1:5) Paul decided to invite Timothy to come with them, thus replacing Mark. Then, surprise, surprise, (!) he has the young man circumcised!

Paul had used the freedom of Titus in his argument with the Galatians. Why the difference? In the case of Titus it was the church that had to learn to accept him. Timothy would be sharing in Paul's mission to the Gentiles. Jews would be more likely not only to shut their own ears, but to try to shut the ears of Gentiles, if the gospel was taken to them by an uncircumcised Greek. To win men for Christ, Paul was ready to be all things to all men. Ambassadors for Christ must learn to adjust, in all matters not contrary to the gospel. (1Cor. 9:19-23)

As they travelled they began to learn that the Holy Spirit could close doors as well as open them. They were "forbidden" to speak in Asia. Was this an inner constraint, or a series of coincidences upsetting their plans? They found themselves driven on to the great seaport of Troas. There, in a dream, it became clear. Leaving Asian Christians to take the gospel to Asia, they were to venture into new territory, and cross over into Macedonia.

Note the important change of pronoun in verse 10. Luke, the author, has joined them. How did Paul meet him? Did illness impel him to call in a local doctor? Paul left Luke in Philippi for a long time. The pronoun changes back in verse 40, and only returns to "we" in chapter 20:6. This suggests that Philippi may have been Luke's home town. We don't know what brought him to Troas. Was he the man seen in Paul's dream?

What adventures they met with in Philippi! There was no synagogue there, so the Jews met for prayer by the river bank. The first convert was Lydia. She was a wealthy merchant. Purple dye was very expensive. It was the colour of the Imperial robes. Lydia offered them hospitality in her home.

They found themselves followed round the town by a slave girl. Possessed by an evil spirit that gave her clairvoyancy, she was paraded by her masters, to answer questions and tell fortunes. They made a lot of money out of her.

In the gospels, we see how evil spirits recognised Jesus, who commanded them to be silent before driving them out. Paul had the same experience, and freed the girl from her possession.

The men cared nothing for the girl who was now useless. Their profits were gone. What lies they told to stir up the crowd against the apostles and force the magistrates to give them their revenge! Philippi was a Roman city, with the privilege of self-government. Such privileges could be lost if law and order broke down. Paul and Silas were summarily beaten and thrown into prison.

Why, we may ask, did Paul not claim his rights as a Roman citizen? (cp 22:25-29) Was he shouted down? Or did he not want to escape, leaving Silas to take the beating alone? After the earthquake, it is clear from the pronoun (16:37) that, by then, he knew that Silas also had citizenship, but he might not have known before. If so, did Silas, not knowing about Paul's, keep silent for the same reason? An intriguing thought.

What a witness those two brave men gave to their fellow prisoners. Instead of the usual cursing and groans, there were songs of praise. Today, many Christians, imprisoned for their faith, are winning their fellow inmates for Christ. One Chinese pastor was released because his witness was converting so many, that his jailors could not cope with it.

When the earthquake struck, they neither panicked, nor tried to escape. They even kept the other prisoners with them, thus saving them from savage punishment after re-arrest, and saving the jailor from suicide. Punishment for losing a prisoner was death.

The situation is now reversed. The Jailor and his family are baptized, and minister to their one-time prisoners. The terrified magistrates order their release, but find Paul won't go quietly. Jesus had rebuked his judges, and the guard who slapped him, for failing in the proper conduct of their office. Paul demands, and gets, a personal apology. Then he and Silas leave the city, while Luke and Timothy remain to nurture the new converts.

A rich Jewess, a Greek slave, and a Roman jailor, had nothing in common but Christ. Paul's letter to the Philippians shows how greatly he loved them, and cared that the love and unity they had discovered should be preserved. (Phil. 1:27. 2:1-2. 4:2-3)

Three Greek Cities. Chapters 17 & 18.

Paul and Silas went on to Thessalonica. The familiar pattern was repeated: preaching in the synagogue, Gentile acceptance, Jewish jealousy and rejection, persecution, rabble rousing and involvement of the city authorities.

The accusations are now more specific. It is not just a matter of upsetting customs, but of proclaiming a new king. Pilate had rejected with contempt such a charge against Jesus. He didn't believe Jesus posed any threat to Rome, though he couldn't afford to let a lying report to be sent off to Caesar.

Looking back on history, we can see that perhaps Pilate was wrong. The Kingship of Jesus does challenge the state, wherever it exceeds its powers and acts unjustly. Why else do dictators persecute the church? Even British Prime Ministers get angry when Bishops poke their noses into politics. "Render unto Caesar", they quote. But, can any aspect of life be shut off from God? Church buildings can be destroyed, and pastors and people jailed and put to death. But persecution fans the flames of faith. Time after time it is the dictator who falls, and the church which survives, though there have been exceptions.

"They have turned the world upside down." What a compliment to those preaching the gospel of The Upside-Down Man! If the world ignores us, or finds the church boring, is our witness being given faithfully?

The city authorities acted with caution. The three missionaries were left free to travel on to Beroea. There, many Jews as well as Greeks believed. Note how important the women are, both in believing and resisting the gospel. But again Paul is pursued by Jewish opponents. His spectacular conversion, his vast knowledge of scripture and rabbinical training, and his powerful leadership qualities make him their prime target. Paul was hurried away, with an escort of believers, who took him by sea to Athens. Silas and Timothy stayed on in Beroea until the escort returned with Paul's message that they should follow and rejoin him.

Athens was the home of Greek philosophy. Shades of Socrates and Plato still haunted the streets. Strange how abstract thought can coexist in the same mind with superstition. In India, a top Astronomer was asked by a missionary how he could combine his scientific knowledge with his practice of astrology. He said he thought it best to play for safety!

There were idols and altars galore. The Athenians were also playing safe. An Unknown God might take offense at being overlooked. That altar, so strangely inscribed, gave Paul his opening. The agora, a huge open market square in the centre of the city, was the place where the philosophers would meet daily for discussion and exchange of news. As slaves did all the work, there was little else for them to do.

Some of the philosophers, curiosity mastering their disdain, invited Paul to speak in the Areopagus, a court of Councillors, who were the guardians of religion and education. For the first time, Paul is confronted by the intellectual elite of his day.

Paul was well read in Greek literature. He may have attended the University of Tarsus. He starts from where his hearers are. Greeks as well as Jews believed in a Creator God. Paul quotes Greek poets, such as Epimenides, as well as Isaiah. He denounces idols, but then so did Socrates. Paul then speaks of Jesus as the Chosen One, raised from the dead. At this point, most of them laugh him out of court. Significantly, there is no mention of the cross, or of the forgiveness of sins. Some of his hearers offered to hear him again, or was this a polite form of dismissal. Very few believed.

Was this failure? Had Paul relied too much on intellectual argument, on meeting them on their own ground? Surely this was a good way to begin. But forgiveness is meaningless where there is no sense of sin. This is why Lutherans believe that teaching the Law must precede the Gospel. Greek gods were amoral rather than immoral. The one sin that provoked their anger was hubris, a proud presumption by which man dared to flout their authority. Hubris was basically the sin of Adam. Perhaps here was a link Paul might have used. Greeks exalted the reasoning mind over religion, but Socrates was put to death for teaching this. When the writings of Plato and Aristotle were brought to Europe, theologians like St Augustine and Thomas Aquinas tried to square them with Christian beliefs. But Greek and Jewish ways of thinking are poles apart. The leap of faith has to be made. What Bishop Newbigin has called a paradigm shift cannot be by-passed.

Paul, it seems, had his own doubts about that sermon. Going on to Corinth, he determined that, from then on, his approach would be very different. (1Cor. 2:1-2) He must have felt very down and discouraged. He was anxious about the fate of his new converts in Beroea. While he escaped, they had to stay and face persecution. When Silas and Timothy at last arrived, bringing good news, he must have been heartened. We can learn of his work amongst the Thessalonians, and how they had fared by reading the first of his two letters that he wrote to them from Athens.

1. Thessalonians.

In Thessalonica, Paul and his companions had proclaimed the Gospel, not just by word, but by the way they had lived. The Spirit had been powerfully at work, convicting hearts. Like Paul, and the first apostles, the converts there had learnt to suffer and rejoice. Their witness was not only the talk of the town, but of the whole district. To see lives transformed was News. Merchants and others, travelling by land and sea, "gossiped the gospel", by relating what they had seen there.

The accusations flung against Paul in Galatia had been used to smear his reputation there too. They were told that, hungry for power, he had won them by flattery. These were lies. As for the charge of greed, Paul was, as always, careful to earn his own living, and not depend upon hospitality, though he upheld the right of others to claim it. (cp. 1Cor. 9:3-18)

Those who think of Paul as a harsh moralist and abstract theologian, should read his letters more closely, the bits not usually read in church! Gentle as a nurse, loving as a mother, his converts are his glory and his joy. He was continually praying for them, and yearned to be with them again. It was Satan, not the Spirit that had hindered him. Silas and Timothy had come on to Paul at Athens, bringing news from Beroea. Then Paul had sent Timothy alone, back to Thessalonica, to see how they had been faring. When he returned with good news, Paul was over the moon with joy. But he still longed to come and see them himself. What a wonderful prayer he prays for them! (1Thess. 3:12-13)

In the following chapters, Paul deals with two problems. The first is dealt with briefly. Chastity was not a virtue practiced by the Greeks. Not Law, but their upward calling in God required it, and the Holy Spirit would empower them for it. The second, which he dealt with at length, concerned the Second Coming. Many believed, as indeed Paul did for a time, that the event would take place soon. The Thessalonians were worried about the fate of those who had died before it had happened. Jesus had promised that those who believed would never die, but have eternal life. To live in him was to have eternal life now. Paul assures them that, when the Last Trumpet blows, the dead in Christ will rise first. Those still living will be caught up together with them. According to 1 Cor.

15:52, it will all happen in a twinkling of an eye. The dead may even have the advantage of half a twink!

We need not be disturbed by Paul's pre-scientific cosmology. He may have believed in a heaven "up there". More likely he was speaking symbolically. How else can we speak of things totally beyond our experience! As we have seen, clouds have always signified God's mysterious presence.

In our own day, especially as the Millennium drew near. various cults predicted the day of Christ's Return, despite his teaching. (Mk. 13:32) It will come unexpectedly. We should always be ready to meet it, armed with faith, and unafraid.

2. Thessalonians.

It seems that Paul's letter did not solve all the problems in the Thessalonian church. Some seemed to get worse. Very soon he had to write again.

Their sufferings under persecution had increased. Paul is not saying that persecution is sent to make them worthy of God's Kingdom. The Greek construction implies that it is rather a proof of the genuineness of their faith. In God's eyes they are deemed worthy. It is true that such trials often do strengthen faith, as the persecuted church today can testify.

When Christ returns, they will enjoy rest in the glory of His presence. Those who afflict them will have to pay the penalty. We like to believe in salvation. We don't like to think about the other side of the coin, condemnation. If it were left to us, sin would be tolerated, in which case it would be goodbye to heaven! Jesus constantly taught that there would be both. (Matt. 25:44-46) Ultimately we are responsible for our self-chosen destiny. (Deut. 30:19. cp. Jn. 3:19) Paul then harks back to the problem of when Christ will return. It will not take place until the "Rebellion", and "The Man of Destiny" has appeared. He assumes they all know about this strange figure as he had given them plenty of teaching about it when he was with them.

Jesus had prophesied that there would be a period of great wickedness and sacrilege, as mentioned in the book of Daniel. (Matt. 24:10-16. Dan. 11:31) This sacrilege was the desecration of the Temple by Antiochus Epiphanes in 167 BC. He tried to stamp out the Jewish religion, setting up a statue of Zeus in the Temple, and ordering Jews to worship it. Jesus prophesied about the destruction of the Temple and city by Titus, which took place in AD 70. Before this, in AD 40, the Emperor Caligula tried to set up a statue of himself in the Temple and force Jews to worship him. He was restrained by the fanatical courage of the Jews, and merciful delaying tactics of the Roman Commander. Caligula died before he could compel Petronius to act. His successor Claudius, a sensible and moderate man, did not pursue such a mad policy. It was during the lull in persecution, brought about by his short reign, that Paul wrote this letter. The Book of Revelation, refers to the "Man of Lawlessness" as the Beast and as Anti-Christ. We will study the matter in more detail when we meet with it there.

What does Paul mean by God deluding men? The same problem is met with in the Old Testament, where we read "God hardened Pharoah's heart". This manner of putting things expresses the Jewish belief that, ultimately, God is responsible for everything. (cp. Amos 3:6) We have free will whether or not to harden our hearts, and we will be held responsible for our choice. But God is responsible for giving us this freedom.

The final problem to be sorted out was practical, and again related to belief in Christ's imminent return. Some people had decided to wait for it expectantly, by downing tools. They stopped working, and, presumably, existed by sponging on their neighbours, and being a general nuisance. Today there are sects that indulge in similar behaviour, and worse. They anticipate the "Rapture" by suicide. Paul's injunction is clear. No work, no food. This of course does not relate to those who want to work, but can't.

This letter contains three more lovely prayers. (2:16-17. 3:5. 3:16) We can offer these prayers for each other.

There is an extra emphasis on Paul's final signature. Is this related to the possibility of a forged letter they may have received? (2Thes. 2:2)

Corinth. Acts 18:1-18.

At Corinth, Paul met up with Aquila and his wife Priscilla. Together with other Jews, they had been expelled from Rome by Claudius in AD 49. According to the Roman historian Suetonius, there had been riots in the city between Jews connected with one named Chrestos. This is one of the first references to Christ outside Scripture. Even the moderate Claudius could not tolerate such imported riots in Rome.

Aquila was a tent maker. This was Paul's own trade. Every Jewish father had to see his sons were trained in some form of manual work by which they could earn a living. It wasn't enough to be an intellectual! Paul joined Aquila, and thus found his first converts in the city. Had they already some knowledge of Christ? They now became fellow workers, but not just in tent making. Their work place and home became a place for making known the Gospel.

Here, in this worldly and wealthy port, notorious for immorality of every kind, Paul and his friends found fertile soil. As elsewhere there was a large Jewish presence. They rejected and opposed the gospel, though Crispus, the ruler of the synagogue, was converted.

The Gentiles were very responsive, and were baptized in large numbers. Here, Paul had another vision. It was his fifth. (Acts 9:2-4, 9:12, 22:17, 16:9, 18:9-10) God told him he was to stay in Corinth and reap a great harvest. He was to speak out boldly, and no one would have power to harm him.

Rejecting an intellectual approach, and relying totally on the Spirit, Paul preached the foolishness of the Cross, with its reversal of human values. It left him feeling weak and afraid, but it resulted in a mighty release of power. (1Cor. 2:1-5) Spiritual truth can only be spiritually understood. (1Cor. 2:10-16) The Spirit has been called "The Go-between God". (John V. Taylor) Only He can take the speaker's words and feed them into the hearer's heart to kindle the spark of life.

Corinth was a Provincial Capital. Galleo, the new Pro-Consul of Achaea, arrived in AD 51. Only about twenty years had passed since the first outpouring of the Spirit at Pentecost, yet how the church had grown and spread!

Galleo's arrival prompted the Jews to mount an attack on Paul. Some rulers, like Pilate, and the magistrates at Philippi, felt insecure. All they wanted was peace and quiet, so they were open to arm-twisting. Not so Galleo. His brother was Seneca, the famous philosopher. Galleo threw Paul's accusers out of his Court. They vented their fury on Sosthenes, the new ruler of the synagogue. Had he encouraged or tried to stop them? Either way, he was a convenient scape-goat.

Paul stayed on for a time, and then took ship for Ephesus. Aquila and Priscilla went with him. After a short stay, Paul left them there, while he went on to Jerusalem. In accordance with a vow, he had shaved his head, and was hurrying on to get there for the feast of the Passover. He was still very much a Jew at heart.

Ephesus. 18:24- 19:41.

While Paul was away on his pilgrimage, Aquila and Priscilla amply justified his confidence in them.

Their witness was much strengthened by the arrival of Apollos from Alexandria. This city was the principle centre of Hellenistic culture. There was a large Jewish community there, and an interflow of ideas, thanks to its famous university.

As a preacher, Apollos had a lot going for him. He had a thorough knowledge of Scripture. He was eloquent, and full of enthusiastic conviction that Jesus was the Messiah. He knew of John's baptism of water and forgiveness but, and it was a big but, he knew nothing of the Spirit's baptism of power at Pentecost.

Easy to go home after a service, and pull both the preacher and his sermon to pieces over the Sunday roast. Aquila and his wife acted more constructively. They invited Apollos to a meal. There, gently, without inflicting the humiliation of criticism, they would have been able to tell him the facts he needed to know. He must have then been baptized into the Name of Jesus, and have received the Holy Spirit, with all His gifts.

Now, Apollos' natural gifts could be fully used. The church helped to send him on to Corinth. There his preaching proved so effective that he soon became ranked as an apostle equal in authority to Peter as well as Paul. Later, as we shall see, this led to quite a problem.

Meanwhile Paul, after visiting Jerusalem, had returned to Antioch to see his friends and report on the results of his second missionary journey. Then he set forth on his third and last.

First he visited Galatia and Phrygia. These were the churches he had planned to visit earlier, but the Spirit had prevented him, propelling him on to pastures new. Now Paul was free to revisit them, to teach them and strengthen their faith. He then returned to Ephesus. What a joyful reunion he must have experienced with Aquila and Priscilla!

They would have told him about Apollos. Paul met twelve men who must have been converted by Apollos before he had been fully instructed. Paul asked them "When you were baptized, did you receive the Holy Spirit?" Something must have been obviously lacking in their lives to provoke such a question. It is a pertinent question for a lot of church members today.

Notice the power of the Name of Jesus. Talk about "God" is easy. It is abstract, vast, imprecise. But "Jesus" is specific, challenging and powerful as a laser beam. His Name, which enshrines his character and his Spirit, reaches the hidden depths of the heart, provoking an active response. Into this Name, these men were baptized. Then, as Paul laid his hands on them, they were filled by the Spirit. Like the converts in Samaria, they were left in no doubt about this. Immediately they spoke with tongues and prophesied. These are the two gifts that can be manifested instantly. Maybe this is why they are given to those who may need such instant reassurance.

The Jews at Ephesus had, at Paul's first visit, showed considerable openness. Surprisingly, they had even invited him to stay on longer. But now, after three months of argument and teaching, some were so stubbornly opposed that Paul left the synagogue, and started teaching in a hall lent by Tyrannus. This gave him a larger audience, and he continued teaching there for two years.

Ephesus was a cosmopolitan city, famous for its Temple to Diana. This was not the chaste Huntress of Greek mythology, but a multi-breasted fertility goddess. The Guardians of the Temple were called Archons, and came from many cities. Like Mecca today, Ephesus drew pilgrims from all over Asia. Many were made rich thereby. Magicians, fortune-tellers, and practitioners of the black arts, all made a fortune out of ripping off the pilgrims.

Like Simon Magnus, they presumed that Paul was just another magician with knowledge of a superior magic. But, when the sons of Sceva tried to copy him, using the Name of Jesus, they came in for a shock. The evil spirits were not fooled. Exorcism can be a dangerous business without the protection of the Holy Spirit, and He will not allow the holy Name to be taken in vain.

The fear that resulted led to the burning of books of magic. Believers, who owned such books, had been still hanging on to them. In how many Christian homes today could books on magic, spiritualism, and astrology be found? In our libraries they crowd the shelves labelled Religion. Those who invite the Holy Spirit into their lives find He will not tolerate any rival.

There were others in Ephesus who also found Paul's preaching was affecting their pockets. Silversmiths, making miniature silver shrines for the goddess, were angered to see their profits were falling. One of them, Demetrius, roused the rabble. Seizing two of Paul's companions, he and his fellows dragged them into the open-air Theatre. They shouted and chanted the name of Diana, like football fans at a cup final, except that most of the shouters hadn't a clue as to what it was all about!

Paul was restrained from going into the arena. In the mind of the crowd, Jews and Christians were lumped as one. So the Jews, fearing that they too might be blamed for disrespect to the goddess, put up Aristarchus to defend them. He was shouted down, and the crowd went on with their clamour for another two hours!

The town clerk was forced to intervene. Paul was no iconoclast. He had smashed nothing, and insulted neither Diana nor her followers. It was unlikely that any charge made by the silversmiths would stick, even if they did bring the matter to court. They could hardly sue the Holy Spirit!

Letters to the Corinthians.

Paul evidently had a bad time in Ephesus. (2Cor. 1:8-11) He talks of having to fight with beasts. (1Cor 15:32) This is figurative speech. As a Roman citizen he would never have had to fight in an arena. But he may well have had a spell in prison. If so, it would have given him the respite he needed to write letters.

Problems of the church in Corinth were causing him both a headache and a heart-ache. His first letter, dealing with various problems there created by the surrounding idolatry, has been lost. There is reference to this letter in 1 Cor. 5:9. Some believe that a fragment of it is to be found in 2 Cor. 6:14-7:1 He sent it to them by the hand of Timothy. Alas, Timothy returned bringing news that things were worse. (1Cor. 4:17)

What, in our Bible, is called Paul's First Letter to the Corinthians, is therefore, in fact, his second. In it he dealt with many of their problems at length. Again, he sent it via Timothy. (1Cor. 16:10) It did not go down well. The Corinthian church resented Paul's interference, and denigrated his authority.

Paul then paid them a flying visit. It is not mentioned in Acts, but is referred to, both before and after it took place, in 1 Cor. 4:18-21 and 2 Cor. 2:1. It did no good. They mocked him as weighty and strong in his letters but pathetically weak in bodily presence. (2Cor. 10:9-10) Unlike Barnabas, whose imposing stature led the people of Lystra to think he was Zeus, Paul must have been smaller. We have already noted that he may have suffered from poor eyesight and epilepsy. Here some kind of speech defect is hinted at. Did he also stammer?

Returning to Ephesus, hurt and angry, Paul wrote a third letter. (2Cor. 10:1 - 13:14) This time he sent Titus, probably an older and more experienced man. It is a very personal and moving document. Provoked into asserting himself, by what he knows is futile boasting, he shames them by boasting, not of his exploits and successes, but of his sufferings. Among these he lists as a climax his burden of anxiety for all the churches. (2Cor. 11:23-28)

Paul's Farewells. The third Missionary Journey. Acts 19:21-20:38.

After the Silversmith's riot, Paul set off again for Macedonia by way of Troas. There he hoped to meet up with Titus. But Titus wasn't there. Anxiously he pressed forward, meeting him in Macedonia. What a relief! The letter he had penned with so much pain and prayer had born fruit. The Corinthians had repented. They had excommunicated Paul's detractors, and were anxious to see him again. Overjoyed, Paul sends them a fourth letter. (2Cor. 1:1 - 9:15) Again, he sends it via Titus. How warmly he speaks of this disciple who had mediated peace in that troublesome church. (2Cor 8:16, 17, 23) Now he can happily visit them again. This he did, and stayed with them for three months. (Acts 20:3)

A plot prevented him from sailing back to Asia by the most direct route. His friends go on ahead, leaving him to pay a farewell visit to Philippi. There at last he meets up again with his "beloved physician". What a lot they had to share. Together they embark for Troas. Note the change of pronoun back to "we". It was at Troas they had first met.

Waiting for them at Troas were many friends. They had come from Beroea, Thessalonica, Derbe and other parts of Asia. It was a time for goodbyes, for Paul knew that he wouldn't be coming back. A final Agape meal and Holy Communion service was held in an Upper Room. It was Paul's last chance to teach them. He went on talking until after midnight.

It was not surprising therefore that poor young Eutychus dozed off. He was sitting by an open window three floors up. The tragedy of his fall and apparent death, was transformed into resurrection joy, by what seems to have been a miracle. Paul's embrace reminds us of the method of healing used by both Elijah and Elisha. (1Kings 17:17-23. 2Kings 4:32-37) But this was a case, not of fever but probably of a cracked skull, and the healing seems to have been instantaneous. To Paul, such miracles were no surprise. He remounted the stairs to celebrate the broken Body of Christ in broken bread. Body and soul thus refreshed, Paul went on talking until dawn!

Luke and other friends now took ship for Assos. The "we" now excludes Paul, who had decided to foot it alone on land. Did he plan to meet other disciples en route, or did he need time to be alone? There had been no let up. Ships are crowded and noisy. Walking in solitude is conducive to meditation, thought and prayer.

Paul had much to pray about. He was planning to visit Spain, calling on Rome on his way. But the Spirit was warning him of troubles to come. One thing was immediately clear. There could be no final visit to Ephesus. That would only stir up more trouble. So he sends word to the Elders there, calling them to meet him at Miletus. He joined the ship at Assos, so, sailing to Miletus with his friends, they were all able to meet at Miletus together. Luke was present to record Paul's farewell address.

Paul speaks to the Elders of his three years with them. His conscience is clear. There is nothing with which they can reproach him. With tears, and amid many trials, he had boldly proclaimed the gospel to all. He tells them that he knows that imprisonment and danger awaits him in Jerusalem. This is his final goodbye. He prophesies danger for them too; the danger of false teaching. It would not be brought by outsiders. It would emerge from amongst themselves.

So, as shepherds, they must be watchful. Especially should they be on guard against the love of money. Poverty and generosity of spirit will help to keep both them, and the gospel pure.

Finally he hands them over to God. How difficult it is to let go, to love and to trust. Like Jesus his Lord, Paul lived what he preached. Together they prayed, wept and embraced. Then they parted. Paul's missionary journeys, as a free man, were ended.

Summary

In this chapter we see the Gospel spreading westwards into Greece and Macedonia. A similar pattern emerges of initial success, followed by persecution, which drives the missionaries further afield. Opposition first comes from leaders of the synagogues. Later riots are caused by those whose profits are threatened by Paul's preaching. Mostly Paul is protected by the tolerance and indifference of Roman authorities and by his Roman citizenship.

Paul entrusts his new churches into the care of local elders whom he commissions. Only when serious problems arise does he interfere by writing letters, or by a visit from himself or a colleague.

In Paul the Church had gained a great theologian, not a dry-as-dust academic but someone vulnerable, with a loving concern for his children in the faith. Three main problems arise:-

1. The relationship of Gentile Christians to the Law. A decision of wise compromise, made by the Council at Jerusalem, was agreed to, but could not be enforced. An active circumcision party dogged his footsteps upsetting his converts. Paul's arguments defending their freedom undermined the compromise. What was the importance of the Law even to Jewish Christians? Paul wrestles with this in his letter to the Romans. Factions began to grow up round different leaders which develop later. Meanwhile the circumcision of Timothy shows that Paul's theology is pragmatic as well as Spirit led.

2. Problems relating to the Return of Christ. At this point of time, Paul, like most people, probably thought it would be soon, but in his letter to the Thessalonians he is pragmatic. Only God knows when it will be, so let them use the remaining time working normally and growing in love, faith, and practical

holiness. Thus panic and idle speculation are both rebuked.

3. The problem of presenting the Gospel to Greek intellectuals. The crucifixion of the Messiah was not a relevant basis for talking to them about sin. When gods are amoral and immortality depends on secret knowledge, *gnosis*, how can God as Creator, and Jesus as the Logos be understood in terms of the cross and resurrection? Paul the Philosopher fails to convince the Athenians. It is Paul who is weak, who is crucified with Christ, whose preaching is so richly blessed at Corinth. The chapter ends with Paul, like his Master, setting his face to go to Jerusalem. Warned of danger and imprisonment, he is also conscious of an unfinished task and an urgent desire to visit Rome and the regions beyond. In chapter 8 we will see how both these futures are reconciled by the Spirit. But first we will take a closer look at the church in Corinth, and the special problems relating to this flourishing and predominantly Greek church.

Questions for private meditation

1. What have you learnt from your failures? Are mistakes ever wasted? (13:8-11. cp 9:8. 13:13. 15:36-40)

2 Do you have expectations of God as to how He ought to act in your life? What happens when He doesn't fulfil them? (Chap. 14:11-19)

3 How do you respond to rebuke: (a) deserved, (b) undeserved? (Gal. 2:11-14)

4. What does "Crucified with Christ" mean to you? What "scars of love" do you bear? (Gal. 2:20. 6:17)

5. How can you become more fruitful? (Gal. 5:22-26)

6. Do you tend to stick with your own set in church or do you seek to mingle with others?

7. Has your witness a cutting edge or is it bland?

8. How do you view your own death and those of others? (1Thess. 4:13 - 5:11)

9. Choose one of Paul's lovely prayers in 1 Thessalonians. Meditate upon it and pray it for your friends and church.

10. How can you tell if someone is actively alive in the Spirit? How do you react if they fall into sin? (19:1-6)

Questions for group discussion

1. Have the leaders of your church ever waited on the Lord with fasting and prayer? What do you think might happen if they did? (Chap 13:2)

2. How is your local church involved in the calling and sending out of missionaries. (Chap. 13)

3. What factors led to a successful outcome of the Council of Jerusalem? Do they apply today? (Chap. 15)

4. "Saved by Christ alone". (Gal 2:20. Acts 15:11) Should this be enough for Table Fellowship, ie inter-communion? Would you want to add anything to Paul's reply to the Jailor in Acts 16:30-31?

5. What loyalties and distinctions divide the members of your church? How can the divisiveness be overcome?

6. Underneath conflicts of principle lie conflicts of power. Discuss this in relation to church and other local conflicts.

7. Why did Paul's preaching produce riots? (Acts 16:19. 17:16. 18:12-18. 19:24-27) Why does our own meet with such indifference?

8. How can the church today speak of forgiveness to an amoral society? Is hubris our sin?

9. In what way is the whole of our life a preparation for our death? What teaching, if any, does your church give on this subject? (1Thess. 5)

10. Why is it so much easier to talk to people about God than to mention the name of Jesus? (Acts 17:22-34. see also 1Cor. 1:20-31)

Chapter 7

Problems of a Gentile Church

1 & 2 Corinthians

Values reversed. 1 Cor. 1 - 4.

Converts who transfer their allegiance to Christ, especially by sudden or mass conversion, usually find it takes longer to change their attitudes and system of values.

Most of the converts in Corinth were poor people or slaves. The Gospel offered them a new sense of self-worth and an inner freedom. Always it is the poor and outcast who are the first to respond to its message. The rich have too much to lose. As a rich Hindu once told a bishop, "I can't afford to become a Christian. I'd have to change my business methods." He at least knew the score. Many don't. Scratch a Christian, and under the skin often the continuing Hindu or pagan, ie the old man, will appear.

The Christians at Corinth, both slave and free, retained their Greek values. They admired physical beauty, the tall, well-proportioned, and athletic. Their education specialised in philosophy, logic and oratory, the cut and thrust of abstract debate.

After his experience in Athens, Paul had come to Corinth preaching Christ crucified. The cross turned all these values upside down. Wisdom and foolishness, strength and weakness, all had their connotations reversed.

Paul's greeting starts with a reminder of his special call, and claim to apostleship. He writes to them as already sanctified, ie set apart for God's use. They are called to grow into becoming what, in Christ, they essentially are. This is a better approach than pointing to people's sins and denying their Christianity. The Christians in Corinth are to grow, not only in holiness but in togetherness, not just with each other, but with all Christians everywhere. Male and female, black and white, slave and free, Jew and Gentile, all need God's grace for that.

Thanksgiving follows. Paul gives thanks for them, and for the many gifts with which God has endowed them. Paul always starts his letters with encouragement. Galatians is the one notable exception. Notice that his emphasis is on God's giving.

Party spirit. 1 Cor. 1:10 - 4:21.

This leads into the first problem, which was party faction. We have seen how Apollos had been sent to Corinth, and how his eloquence and success had led the Christians there to rank him as an apostle equal to Peter and Paul. He had certainly won a following, but was not necessarily to blame for the factious spirit of his admirers any more than Paul was. Do people enjoy basking in the reflected glory of their leaders, Paul's party, Peter's party, Wesleyans, Lutherans, Calvinists, Romans and so on? In one street in Birmingham, where there were a number of different churches, one advertised itself as "The True Church of Christ". As a priest acidly commented, "I don't know what they think the rest of us are!"

Paul first tackles the root of the matter. Their arguments as well as their rivalry are shown to be folly in the light of the cross. God's power lies in weakness. His wisdom is worldly foolishness. But only the Spirit can teach them this by transforming their minds. Party talk is baby talk. The Corinthians must grow up.

How are they to view their different leaders? Paul uses two illustrations. First, they are God's servants, given different duties. They sow or reap, but only God gives the harvest. (Mk. 4:26-27) Secondly they are builders. Paul laid the foundation stone which is Jesus Christ. Others build on it. Their work may or may not be solid and enduring. The Day of Judgement will reveal its worth. "Build for eternity", was the wise advice given by an old priest to a party of missionaries in training.

Were the soaring arches, sculptured pillars, and glorious glass windows of Chartres cathedral, created to evoke admiration for their creators, or to lift people's hearts to God? Faction is as destructive as Cromwell's men loosed on a medieval church.

God's people are God's Temple. As the varied treasures of Chartres combine to lift the spirit Godwards, so the various gifts of churches and leaders are riches to be combined and shared by all. Some denominations major on scripture, some on the Spirit's gifts, some on the church's rich traditions. In this more ecumenical age, Protestants, Pentecostalists and Catholics are learning to appreciate and learn from each other. Without each other's strengths, all suffer from the weakness of imbalance.

Case requiring Excommunication. 1 Cor. 5.

Today people are obsessed with sex. It screams at us from advertisements on hoardings and TV. Sexual practice is regarded as a private matter and anything goes. Toleration is the only moral must. Paedophilia is perhaps the one exception.

The immorality of Corinth was notorious. Prostitution flourished in its port and, as at Ephesus, in its temples. The gods, created in the likeness of men, were indifferent to morality. Ethics was a widespread branch of philosophy, but lacked effective sanction. The fact that so many of the Christians were slaves compounded the problem. What chance had they to be chaste or form a stable marriage?

Paul first deals with an urgent case of incest. The man concerned must be excommunicated, or the whole church will be contaminated. When they meet to take action, Paul will be with them in spirit, and so will the Lord. They will be acting in obedience to the highest authority.

Unlike the Galatians, the Corinthians were boasting of their freedom from the Law. They were feeding on the Body of Christ, sacrificed to save them from sin. How could they justify their immorality, greed, and constant quarrelling? They should have nothing to do with a brother who indulges in such evil.

There are Christian sects that pursue a policy of social segregation. They quote St Paul's words, "Come ye out from among them and be ye separate." In fact Paul was quoting Isaiah, who was calling the Jews to return home and not stay on in Babylon, where they had settled down comfortably and intermarried with pagans. (Is. 52:11. 2Cor. 6:17) Paul was using these words in the specific context of Christians marrying pagans, and not of social schism. We should be in the world but not of it, mixing with people freely, as Jesus did, yet never compromising with sin. However, for the church to ignore scandalous behaviour, openly persisted in, is to connive in it. Others will be tempted to emulate and the whole church will be smeared with sleaze.

Litigation. 1 Cor. 6:1-8.

Litigation was another cause for public shame. Lawyers abounded. The courts enabled them to display their oratorical skills as well as make money. The litigants were motivated by greed and a determination to stand on their rights and not be downed by anyone. Litigation is very much a problem in many of the young churches in Asia today. In India, converts have come from the lowest strata of society, and the Gospel, bringing education, has made many of them upwardly mobile, at least economically and politically. Frequently church disputes are taken to the secular courts. A Hindu Judge, well-read in the New Testament, once rebuked them saying, "Why do you bring these disputes before me, contrary to the teaching of Jesus?" (Matt 5:25-26. 18:15-17)

Paul's teaching here is clear and dogmatic. Those who indulge in immoral and greedy practices will not inherit the Kingdom of Heaven. In 2 Peter 2:22, such Christians are compared to a washed sow, returning to wallow in the mud.

Teaching on Sex and Marriage. 1 Cor. 6:12 - 7:40.

Paul's teaching on salvation by faith alone was open to misunderstanding. As noted already, he deals with this problem in detail in his letter to the Romans, which will be discussed in the next chapter. Here, he simplifies it by saying, "All things are lawful. Not everything is helpful." We are free to destroy our bodies by alcohol and drugs. But our bodies, renewed by Christ, are now part of His Body. Are we to take members of His Body, and unite them to a prostitute? Paul had a very high view of the physical body. He disciplined his own, to keep it in prime condition. It had important work to do. As St Teresa of Avila wrote, "Christ has no hands or feet but ours." In Paul's view, it is not only the church that is God's Temple. Individually, our bodies are God's Temple too. (cp. Jn. 2:20-21)

We now come to teaching that is more controversial. Notice the clear distinction Paul makes between what Christ has commanded, and what he, Paul, advises. Paul's letter brings us closer to Christ's command than does Mark's Gospel, written some time later. But Paul knew Mark well, and Peter, who had heard what Christ had said. Adultery is admixture. "Whose baby is it?" provided a theme for a popular Soap. Genes, emotions, loyalties, the sense of one's identity are all confused, making for unhappiness. Though we will always sin, ie fall short of the glory of God, yet the best is worth effort and sacrifice in every department of life. God is like a mother teaching her child to walk. It is not the fall that matters, but the getting up and starting again. In the words of Julian of Norwich, "If we fall, he catches us lovingly in his gracious embrace, and swiftly raises us."

Why was Paul so keen on celibacy? He has been called a misogynist, but his loving and high regard for so many women, who were his fellow workers, belies this. (Phil. 4:2-3. Rom. 16:3, 6, 12) Paul was totally committed to missionary outreach. Others, like Peter, could combine mission and marriage. They would have to travel at a gentler pace. Even young Mark couldn't keep up with Paul. His special calling was both physically demanding and dangerous. Marriage, for him, would have been a restriction, as it would have been for Jesus. It would have been unfair to the wife and children. Celibacy is a vocation to which some are called. It needn't result in loving less. If it does, something has gone wrong; enforcement perhaps. Celibacy can mean a widening scope for love's embrace. (Mk. 3:31-35. 10:29-30)

Paul now takes up various questions concerning marriage. In Aquilla and Priscilla, he had met up with a perfect missionary partnership. The end greetings of his letters point to the value he set upon such a Christian home. How important it is then, to choose one's partner, "in the Lord".

Gnosticism was a popular philosophy, stemming from the belief that body and spirit were separate and could not affect each other. It took two forms. One was to teach that immorality could not harm the soul. That heresy Paul had dealt with. The second was to advocate sexual abstinence, even for the married. The mediaeval Cathars, and some sects today, advocate this. "No", says Paul, "do not deny each other". It would only lead to temptation and distraction. "Better to marry than burn" recognises that not all have equal powers of sublimation. Some can, some can't, and some kid themselves. Hypocrisy in this matter is corrosively destructive. It is a burning issue in the Roman Catholic church today.

Today, all the emphasis is on "my body is mine to do what I like with; sex when I want it, and only when I want it." Paul turns this about. Sexual love is the gift of oneself, and love is always responsive to the need of others. This is equally true for both sexes. Revolutionary stuff!

Another problem was divorce. In the case of one of the partners becoming a Christian, and the other not, Paul allows a choice. The two are no longer truly one. Freedom can be given, though Paul advises against this. A Christian, usually the woman, can often win her partner through her prayers, and the witness of a more loving life, not, let it be noted, by argument or nagging. A recent report on the causes of conversion in Britain today, showed that the witness of marriage partners came top of the list. Mainly it consisted of wives, winning their husbands.

The influence on the children is equally important. Timothy's father was a pagan, but Timothy was brought up as a Christian by a saintly mother and grandmother. After long years of prayer, St Monica's patience and love led to the conversion, both of her husband, and of her famous son, St Augustine.

For those not married, Paul's advice is to stay put. His belief that the time before Christ's return would be short, affected both his attitude to marriage and to slavery. Obviously, in the long term, advice against marriage would be fatal to the Christian community. But, if the time was to be short, while normal work must continue, Christians should seek to be free of any unnecessary distraction. Cluttered lives leave no time for growing in the love of God.

Paul did not condone slavery. If freedom was offered, it should be accepted. But the preaching of the cross undermined the whole system. Relationships between slave and free, servant and master within the church, were slowly being transformed. This is illustrated by Paul's letter to Philemon. The upside-down effect of the cross was that the slaves were, in Christ, made inwardly free, while Paul, a freeborn Roman citizen, was a slave of Christ. (1Cor. 9:19) Political revolution does not equalise society, a fact well illustrated by Orwell's Animal Farm.

Food and Idols. Chapters 8 - 10.

The food problem was caused by the fact that meat on sale in the market would have been offered up at the temple. Also, most social functions took place at the temples, and included a meal. Thus, dining with pagan friends would cause a problem. What were Christians to do if pagan friends invited them to dinner? Should they go, and cause public embarrassment by rejecting what was set before them, or should they eat, and compromise their faith? The alternative was to refuse all invitations, and find themselves cut off from family and friends.

Jewish Christians would be likely to take a rigid stance. Their families and friends would be strictly kosher. The more educated of the Greek Christians would be likely to argue that, as other god's don't exist, idols are nothing. Nothing the body eats can harm the soul. They had the Lord's authority for that. (Mk. 7:18-20) Paul agrees that what we eat is not important, but love is, and so is our witness.

There may be no harm in a glass of wine or the odd cigarette, but to drink or smoke in front of an alcoholic or cigarette addict who is trying to break from addiction, is not an act of brotherly love. Paul is concerned for the "weaker brother", who, lacking such superior knowledge, would be burdened with guilt, if, egged on by others, he acted against his conscience. On the other hand, those who stuck to their principles might accuse those who ate of not being "proper Christians". Such accusations are still made by strict evangelical groups, who regard drinking and smoking as sins. But these are not "weaker brothers". They can enforce their views on others. The constraints of love are needed on both sides, if the fellowship of love is to be maintained in the church.

Later on in his letter, Paul takes up another attitude to idols. The idols themselves may be nothing, but sacrifices offered to them are, in fact, offered to demons. Power does flow through consecrated bread and wine, water and oil. Even today Satanists use these things, after investing them with demonic power. Paul tells the Corinthians that they need have no fear. Their faith in Christ protects them, so they can freely buy meat in the market, and, when they visit the homes of friends, they can eat what is set before them without question. But, if someone makes a point of telling them that the food has been offered to idols, then they should refuse it, and use the opportunity to give their Christian witness. The information may well have been provided to test them out! (1Cor. 10:18-32)

In chapter 9 we get two golden verses that give the key to everything that Paul has been writing. The first is, "Woe is me, if I preach not the Gospel." The Gospel must be truthfully proclaimed and witnessed to by everything we do. This is why he even resorted to boasting to assert his apostleship given him by Christ. This one dominating desire is the reason for his waiving all claim for material support, and for his flexibility in non-essential issues. It is his guiding motivation.

The other verse is, "So run that you may obtain the incorruptible prize". (9:24) That is the reason for self-discipline, and why over-indulgence in food, sleep, and sex is out. Early morning runs on a frosty morning are no fun. The athlete gets out of bed, not from fear of his trainer, but because he wants to win the race. Paul's goal is "the upward call of God in Jesus Christ". (Phil. 3:14) The basis of Christian morality is desire to please God in response to his love.

Paul warns that not all get prizes. Some don't even make it to the tape. Those early converts were over-confident of their salvation. They had been baptized in water and the Spirit. The gifts they had received were proof of that. So they were "all right Jack!" Such triumphalism is dangerous. Not even Paul had such confidence. (Phil. 3:12:14) Paul uses the experience of the Israelites in the wilderness as a warning. They were set free from slavery in Egypt, but, because of bondage to their own undisciplined passions, they wandered in that wilderness for years, and very few of them ever reached the Promised Land. (10:1-13) A man is saved from drowning as soon as he grasps the life-line thrown to him. But he has to keep holding on while it pulls him toward the shore. Only when he stands on the beach is he finally saved.

Regulation of Public Worship. Chapters 11 - 14.

As there were no church buildings, the early Christians met for worship in private homes. Some Christians were wealthy, and would have large houses, providing room for quite a large congregation, eg Philemon. (Philem. 2)

Jewish converts had behind them a tradition of synagogue worship. The Greeks had no such training. Lacking any regulation, worship had become chaotic. “We are free to be led by the Spirit”, might sound good. In practice it was more like a free-for-all. The Spirit disturbs, but He is also the Spirit who brings order out of chaos. (Gen. 1:1-5)

The first issue was the appropriate headwear for women. To us, this may, at first sight, seem ridiculous, but Paul’s instructions relate both to synagogue tradition and contemporary belief and practice. To walk unveiled in the street was the mark of a prostitute. Flouting public opinion was not the way to recommend the gospel. The principle applying to food, applied here. Our actions must help to promote both our unity and our witness.

In both Jewish and Greek society, women were subject to their husbands, both in custom and in law. Though Paul quotes scripture to defend this, he was well aware that such subjection was the result of the Fall. (Gen, 3:16) As in the case of slavery, new life in Christ created an equality of the sexes in terms of relationship. (cp. Gal. 3:28) Gradually this was to transform long entrenched attitudes, and change laws. But today, the frontal assault of strident feminism both alienates and divides. It not only breaks up marriages, but the institution of marriage itself.

Paul’s arguments reveal his conflicting ideas. Freedom and equality in Christ must, in practice, be limited by some respect for existing custom and social order, so long as these are not contrary to the will of God. Paul’s ruling only causes trouble when we apply it literally to our own very different society. But do we never dress to draw attention to ourselves in a way that can distract and sometimes shock our fellow-worshippers? Paul’s principles still hold good. Love holds together freedom and self discipline.

Paul next deals with the Lord’s Supper. (11:17-33) These verses give us the earliest account of it that we have. It is, first, a Remembrance of three things: Christ’s sacrifice on the cross for our sins, and the Institution of a New Covenant. It is also a Proclamation of his death, that turns all worldly attitudes and judgements upside down. Lastly it is a Communion, in which, as members of Christ’s body, we are united with him and with each other.

As we have seen, both Jews and Gentiles linked worship to a shared meal.

Jesus instituted his sacrament in the setting of the Passover Meal, and the early church celebrated it in the context of a Love Feast or Agape. People brought their food from home and shared it, as they often do at church lunches today. But at Corinth there was no sharing, no waiting for each other, or for a grace to be said. The wealthy over-indulged. Those with meagre rations were shamed. Those too poor to bring anything went hungry. After this, the celebration of the sacrament of unity was a mockery. The Body they failed to discern was that of Christ in each other. To Paul, this was so terrible, that he saw it as a cause of illness amongst them. Or was it a sickness of the spirit? Both perhaps. The two are not unconnected.

In many churches, the sharing of the Peace has helped to break down the very English attitude of "me, making my communion", which leads to people sitting as far apart from each other as possible.

As for desecration, it is not unknown for people to turn up for a midnight mass at Christmas, half drunk from a party. This is probably more rare today when church-going, even at major festivals, is less traditional.

Something was seriously wrong. The gifts of the Spirit were manifestly present amongst them, but they were being used to divide rather than unite. From problems relating to practice, Paul now turns to principles.

First, he warns them that they must learn to distinguish between false spirits and true. This is especially important when the gift of prophesy is being exercised. (cp 1Jn. 4:1-3) A test Paul gives is still used today with powerful effect. A Christian friend of mine, booking into a small guest house, had an uncomfortable feeling about it. Her host and hostess appeared normal and friendly, but something prompted her to say very quietly, "Jesus is Lord". For a split second, their faces were suffused by evil, and then returned to normal, She collected her unpacked cases and left. Later she discovered that they were Satanists.

While the gifts of the Spirit had been poured out richly, the fruits were not so apparent. (Gal. 5:22-23) The more spectacular gifts, especially the gift of tongues, had puffed up those who possessed it. Those who lacked it felt diminished, even excluded. Today, many charismatic churches have experienced the same divisiveness. This is why many clergy fear and discourage charismatic revival.

Paul speaks to us too. All belong. All are needed. Don't envy or despise the gifts of others. Front-runners need backroom boys. How many ground staff are needed to keep one plane in the air! (cp. Rom. 12:8-10) After a highly successful Mission, the church secretary complained to the Missioner that he had no spiritual gift. The Missioner asked him, "Who organised this mission? Who booked the Hall, planned the publicity, sent out invitations, and arranged my hospitality? " "I did", the secretary replied. Then the Missioner pointed him to the list of gifts given in 1 Cor. 12:27-30, where helpers and administrators are included. "God has given you the gift of administration", said the Missioner. "Where would we all have been without you?" The secretary was astonished. The list given in Romans 12:8-10, also includes benefactors. Where would we be without them and their gift of generosity? These passages are less often read in church. None of these lists are exhaustive.

An infected toe can confine an otherwise healthy person to bed. One aching tooth can devastate us. Church members are thus bound together in suffering and in joy. "We've won" cry the ecstatic football fans, when their team wins. How great the sorrow and humiliation of all the parishioners if their priest is found guilty of sexual misconduct. When this is highlighted in the press, the whole church suffers.

This squabbling over spiritual gifts was childish. Like the party rivalries, dealt with earlier, it sprang from pride and vanity. New Christians, emerging from despised social classes, who suffer from inner insecurity, are specially prone to such temptation. Humility is not a virtue that can be pursued by any direct method. The only remedy is love. Love is the one gift that all should desire most earnestly.

Chapter 13 is perhaps the most loved chapter in the whole bible. Comment is superfluous. A revealing exercise however, is to read it, substituting for "Love", the name of "Jesus". It fits in perfectly. Then read the passage again, substituting one's own name. Notice where the shoe pinches!

Love is the bonding of the church and its witness. "See how the Christians love one another"! What difference would love make to the chaos of their unstructured worship?

Paul himself had the gift of tongues, *more than you all*. But he never used it in public worship. He wanted all he said to teach and build up the congregation. He put it at the bottom of his list of gifts, a rebuke to those who put it at the top and were puffed up by it. If disproportionate space is given to it here, it is because, while being increasingly experienced in so many churches today, it is generally misunderstood.

On the day of Pentecost, tongues was both an ecstatic expression of joyful praise, and a mysterious means of communication between those whose mother tongues were different. There are many varieties of tongues. (1Cor. 12:10) Singing in tongues is a wonderful way in which a whole congregation is bound together in worship.

Another use of tongues is in prayer for healing, or other situations in which the will of God is not clearly known. Freed from the restriction of adding "if it be Thy will", one can pray "full out" as it were, confident that the Spirit, who does know, is doing the interceding. (Rom. 8:26) Praying in tongues is powerful. It can cause evil spirits to expose their presence. We need the protection of the Name of Jesus.

In Corinth, tongues were closely linked to prophecy. It required the presence of someone with the allied gift of interpretation. It can be a pathway for man's spirit, influenced by the Holy Spirit, or by other spirits, not holy. This is why there is need for spiritual maturity and wise discernment. In this, as in all things, Jesus, crucified and risen, is our litmus test. In Corinth, lack of interpreters was not the only problem. Prophets were loosing off in tongues more than one at a time. The gift was in danger of being degraded as a means of self-display. The use of tongues, when and where their use is appropriate, must be controlled by reason. It is not, as some think, emotional hysteria, though it can be taken over by this. Paul is concerned about what an outside visitor might think. Such seeming meaningless gabble would put him right off. The Holy Spirit, as said before, is a Spirit of order. Each prophecy should be followed by silence for its truth to be attested and absorbed. How good, and rare it is when such a silent space is accorded to the reading of scripture and to a sermon. Our churches seem to be afraid of silence, and our congregations unaccustomed and untrained to use it profitably.

Paul is quite sure that what he has written about this is "of the Lord". If we question his dictum about women keeping silent in church, there are two points we need to bear in mind. One is that a particular ruling, made for a particular society, at a particular time, may indeed be of the Lord, but it will lose its authority when enforced as an infallible dictum for a later age, and a different society. The Word of God is not letter or law, but a spring of fresh water, alive with the Spirit. (cp. Jn. 7:37-39, 6:63. 2Cor. 3:6)

Another practical point, valid even today, is that harm can be done when the wife of a Christian leader, and for that matter, a prominent politician, contradicts her husband in public. Public rebuke may occasionally be necessary, but private correction is less humiliating, and more effective. It has been said that behind every great man, there is a loyal and supportive woman.

Note verses 33, 36 and 38 of chapter 14. It was typical of this self-confident young church that they were ignoring the opinions and practices of other churches, and going ahead to do their own thing. There was an inevitable tension here, especially as the church grew larger. We have experienced this in the matter of ordaining women. Churches in different countries have come to have different opinions about this. One of the main arguments against it is that it is divisive. We have to recognise that people seem to be guided differently. How far is this due to our prejudices making us deaf to the Spirit? How far do we need to be led by different paths to the same goal? We need to have the humility to be open to respect each other's guidance. Can we combine this with the wisdom of knowing when to resist it?

Resurrection. Chapter 15.

Is there a life after death? This is the question that haunts us all. Paul had written "Love never ends". Does it survive death?

In the time of Jesus, most Jews had come to believe in resurrection. The Sadducees were a notable exception. For most of the Old Testament period, Jews believed that, when people die, they descended into a shadowy underworld, Hades, where a ghost- like life continued, cut off from God. It was rather like the Greek concept of Pluto's kingdom. In some of the Psalms, and in Job, there are flashes of something more hopeful, but it was the persecution of Antiochus Epiphanes in BC 167 that pressed the Jews into a more positive belief. The attempt to stamp out the Jewish faith with appalling cruelty is described in the books of the Maccabees, found in the Apocrypha, and is reflected in the Book of Daniel, with its story of the burning fiery furnace. So many faithful Jews died a martyr's death. God, who is faithful, surely would reward them, if not in this life, then in the next. How else could the Jews justify their belief in His character?

Christ's resurrection was the fundamental fact on which the Gospel was based. The Jewish authorities would not have been disturbed by a general belief that Jesus would share in the general resurrection. It was the assertion that he was alive now, and powerfully active, that they could not tolerate. (cp. Acts 23:6-9)

Paul is writing in response to a real problem of belief for some of the Christians in Corinth. From the opening verses of chapter 15 it is clear that they did not doubt the resurrection of Christ. In verses 3-4 we have the beginnings of an early baptismal creed, that Paul was probably quoting. The Corinthians had taken their stand upon their belief, and had experienced salvation through it. Paul's list of resurrection appearances contains some not recorded in the gospels, which were written later. He must have been told of them by Peter or other eyewitnesses. So what was the problem?

In our study of 1 Thessalonians, we have seen one aspect of it. Christ's coming was delayed. Believers were dying. What did sharing in his resurrection mean for them? Some scholars think that some of the Corinthians were only believing in the immortality of the soul. This was a common belief amongst the Greeks, and is increasingly popular today, especially with those influenced by Eastern religion. Others think the problem was due to gnostic teaching, that eternal life is something Christians can experience as a spiritual resurrection here and now. Paul would not deny this, but he certainly denied that there was no further resurrection yet to come.

Paul first deals with the consequences of such unbelief. He links our resurrection with that of Christ. If we don't rise, then Christ, who was truly Man, didn't rise either. The cross was then a defeat, not a victory, and we are still in bondage to our sins. Those who have given their lives for their faith have no hope of reward. If this life is all we have, why risk losing it? So "eat drink and be merry."

This was one of the options offered by Greek thought. Epicurus taught that, since there was no future life, we must make the best of this one. But he did not limit this to physical self-indulgence as some of his followers did. The Stoics taught that one should live bravely and nobly. One's honour will survive.

What we believe does affect our actions. People are prepared to die to preserve their reputations. Far more will die for love of another. Paul's certainty of resurrection inspired enormous courage and endurance. But he did not take it for granted or slacken his efforts. Rather it spurred him on. (1Cor 9:26-27. cp Phil. 3:14)

Paul then turns to the consequences of Christ's rising for us. He finds a link in his concept of Adam, old and new. The old Adam is our fallen humanity, sinful, rebellious, cut off from the Tree of Life. (Gen. 3:22-24) Christ, in the total obedience of a sinless life, is the new Adam. As we share in his death to self, we share in his new and risen life, now and for all eternity.

The problem of course is that the two Adams continue to struggle inside us. The old Adam "is dead, but he won't lie down." It all depends on who we believe we are. Paul writes to the Romans, "Reckon yourselves to be dead to sin". (Rom. 6:11) We'll come back to this later when we study this letter.

When we rise, what sort of body will we have? Will it be the wrinkled arthritic old body we are only too glad to have done with? What happens if it is cremated? Foolish questions, asked by foolish people, with materialistic minds.

Yet even today, such instinctive subconscious primitive fears may lie behind a preference for burial, and why the desecration of graves is regarded with such horror.

Jesus' risen body can afford some clues. He was recognisable, though, at first, "their eyes were kept from recognising him". His body also still bore the marks of the nails. In 2 Cor. 5:1-5, Paul speaks of a spiritual body in terms of a house, or rather a tent, as well as new clothes. He longs to put on the new clothes, and fears the exposure of nakedness. Our spiritual body must start growing within us now, just as a snake must grow a new skin before sloughing off the old one.

How can we be sure our spiritual body is growing? A physical body needs food. Spiritual food must be part of our daily diet. We need to feed on the Bread of Life in word and sacrament. Bodies are also made strong by exercise. The spiritual gifts God gives us need to be used. On Judgement Day, the reckoning will be of deeds not words. But, while efforts to earn and accumulate "Brownie points" have zero value, a single action, like giving someone a cup of tea, if it springs from genuine love, will not go unrewarded.

Giving. 1 Corinthians 16. 2 Corinthians 8 & 9.

Paul was deeply concerned that his converts should be noted for loving generosity to their needy brothers, especially those in Jerusalem. He had already, with Barnabas, taken them help from Antioch in anticipation of the famine predicted by Agabus. (Acts 11:27-30) The elders of the church there specially asked him to remember the poor, and this Paul was keen to do. (Gal 2:10)

Wherever Paul went, he urged his churches to make giving a regular part of their worship. Such giving was not to meet their own needs, as so much of our own church giving is today. It was for others. While visiting them for the last time, Paul collected up their offerings to take with him to Jerusalem, where he planned to be for Pentecost. Wisely, he had written to warn them of this in advance. Some churches were more generous than others, and Paul thought a spirit of emulation would be no bad thing. So he tells the Corinthians how generous the Christians in Macedonia had been.

Paul taught that giving should be regular, not sporadic, or based on impulse. The amount given should be the result of prayerful decision. He did not want them to be burdened, but, spare sowing leads to spare reaping. He rejoiced in the attitude of the Macedonians, who had begged to be allowed to give more than they could really afford. This was because, already, they had truly given themselves to the Lord. It is a known fact that, when revival comes to a church, one of the first of problems to be solved is that concerned with finance. Open hearts lead to open hands. Despite his tactics of emulation, Paul knew that it was gratitude for the overwhelming generosity of God in Christ, that would best motivate genuine desire to give. *Love so amazing, so divine, Demands my soul, my life, my all.*

How careful Paul is to ensure that those who handle these gifts are men recognised by the churches as being of the highest integrity. Sleaze can endanger the church as well as the state.

Paul ends his letter by calling on the Corinthians to welcome and honour those who work amongst them, and visit them in the name of Christ. They should be obedient, rather than contentious to such men. Do we jib at this? We like to do things our way. Leaders who are confident of the love and prayerful support of their congregation, are more likely to be open to their suggestions. In all the problems dealt with in this letter, Paul brings the same principles to bear; love and unity. These are the themes of Jesus' final discourse in the Upper Room, and of his High Priestly prayer. Only by sharing in his cross and resurrection can such gifts be received. Problems can be so complex. So many letters and books can be written about them. The solution offered by Christ, and by Paul, is simple, but both costly, and profound.

Jewels for all.

By now, most of Paul's second letter to the Corinthians, actually his fourth and last, has been discussed: his reason for delaying his coming, (Chap 1:15 - 2:4) his anxiety and relief when he met up with Titus, and heard of their repentance, (2:12-13. 7:5-16) and their obedience in excommunicating the man guilty of incest. (2:5-11) Paul now forgives all who have hurt him, and asks them in turn to forgive this repentant brother, and restore him to fellowship. As we have seen, chapters 8 and 9 deal with giving.

But in chapters 1-6 there are jewels to be found. We must not pass them by. They are not just for the Corinthians, but for all of us. Here are some of them.

When we share Christ's sufferings we share too in God's comfort. Both the suffering and the comfort are gifts we can share with others. (1:3-7)

We are an aroma of Christ to those who are being saved. (2:15-16) Notice how many TV ads show people turning in appreciation to mark those wearing some special perfume. Even so, our lives are to give out to others the fragrance of God.

We are letters of Christ, not written on paper with pen and ink, but inscribed by the Spirit on our hearts, for all to read. (3:1-3)

A glorious passage on the splendour of God, is too long to quote. (3:7-18) Unlike the splendour of the Old Covenant, the splendour of the New never fades. When Jesus died, the Veil of the Temple, which hid the Holy of Holies, was rent apart. Now, the Spirit enables us to gaze on his glory, and, as we gaze, we are changed into his likeness.

This is why contemplative prayer is so important. It is as if a man with T.B. were to spend hours every day lying on a sunny beach. Without being aware of it, the sun's rays penetrate his body and heal him. Alas, today, thanks to the holes in the ozone layer, the rays are now malignant! For centuries, this kind of contemplative prayer was confined to the enclosed monastic orders. Now it is being revived amongst ordinary Christians.

"We preach not ourselves, but Christ, and ourselves your servants for his sake." (4:5-7) Ours is a servant's status. We have this treasure in the earthern vessels of our human weakness.

The sufferings we undergo for Christ's sake are light and only for a moment. They are not to be compared with the weight of eternal glory that awaits us. (4:16-18) Incidentally, the Hebrew word *Kabod,* which, in the Old Testament is translated as glory, literally means weight.

We are not only servants. We are ambassadors for Christ, sent to call people to be reconciled to God through him. We have the high privilege of his delegated authority. (5:20)

"Our mouth and our heart is wide open to you," cries Paul. "Open wide your hearts also." (6:11-13)

Summary

Right from its birth the Church had to struggle with the problem of continuing sin. A distinction has to be made between sin as rebellion against God, and faults due to fallen human nature.

In writing to the Galatians, Paul refers to faults overcoming a brother who needs help to cope with his burden. The Thessalonians were renowned for their faith and generosity. Apart from the busybody idleness of those whose false expectations led them to down tools, the only sin rebuked is sexual immorality. To the Greeks this was normal behaviour, and the gods would certainly not frown upon it.

Conversion to faith in Christ does not automatically change accustomed behaviour or give freedom from faults of character, upbringing, and the natural tendency towards self-indulgence. Converts are "babes in Christ". Both they and baby churches have to grow up, a slow process that can take a lifetime. It means learning from one's own mistakes. Learning from those of others is difficult and rare.

Paul is dealing with new problems that would not have arisen in churches where the converts were all Jews, programmed by the Law. We see him laying down principles, both theological and practical, in order to solve a number of problems. The basic principle is love. In matters of principle Paul is dogmatic. In practical application he is pragmatic. In the next chapter, in his letter to the Romans, we see Paul the theologian working through the problems relating to Law and Grace.

In Paul's letter to the Corinthians we have our first glimpse of early church worship, and also the importance of individual churches keeping in line with the practice of other churches. The link could only be maintained by personal contact through letters and visits. Though Paul had founded the church in Corinth, his authority came to be challenged. Amid tears and prayer it had been restored, but this problem of maintaining unity and the exercise of authority in the church will grow.

The only doctrinal issue dealt with was that of the Resurrection. The concept of Christ as the Second Adam became important in relating the new life in Christ to the problem of continuing sin. Paul returns to this also in his letter to the Romans which will be studied in the following chapter.

Questions for private meditation

1. How far does Jesus influence your views on secular matters?

2. Do you think of yourself primarily in denominational terms ie Anglican, High, Low, Catholic, Evangelical, or simply as a Christian? (1Cor. 1:10-16)

3. How does your life-style witness to your faith?

4. What disciplines do you impose on yourself? With what motives? With what success?

5. Do you like to stand on your rights? (Acts 16:22-23. cp 22:25-29)

6. Do you think of your body as holy? How might that affect what you do with it? (1Cor. 6. 12-20)

7. Whom would you regard as "weaker brethren"? (1Cor. 8)

8. What is your dominating desire, and the basis of your morality? Do they reflect each other? (1Cor. 9:19-27)

9. What gifts has the Spirit given to you? How are you using them for God's glory? (1Cor. 12, Rom. 12:4-8)

10. In the light of 2Cor. 8:1-5, how do you view your own giving?

Questions for group discussion

1. Is there any Party spirit or any cliques in your church? How can this be remedied? (1Cor. 3 & 4)

2. How do the special emphases of Catholic, Evangelical and Pentecostal balance each other? What can they learn from each other? (1Cor. 14)

3. How far do the Soaps reflect and how far do they help to establish our amoral society?

4. Under what circumstances and conditions should the church excommunicate one of its members? (1Cor. 5)

5. Should litigation be initiated by Christians? (1Cor. 6:1-8)

6 How can the conflict between biblical teaching on sex and marriage and contemporary practice be resolved? (1Cor. 6:12-40)

7. What social evils has the church yet to recognise and seek to transform?

8. What pressures, inner and outer, limit our Christian freedom?

9. Are the gifts of the Spirit recognised and encouraged by your church? How are they administered and controlled? (1Cor. 12. Rom. 12)

10. Discuss your church's methods of raising money. Do they dictate policy or does policy flow out from it? (1Cor. 16:1-4. 2Cor. 9)

Chapter 8

The Road to Rome

Acts 21:1 - 25:12. Romans. Acts 25:13 - 28:31

Journey to Jerusalem and its outcome. Acts 21:1 - 23:35.

As the author of Ecclesiastes says, "there is a time for everything under the sun". (Eccles. 3:1) There is a time to escape from danger and a time to walk into it open-eyed. Like his Master, Paul knew how to do both.

For some time the Spirit had been warning him that danger and imprisonment awaited him in Jerusalem. Both in Tyre, and at Caesarea, where Philip's daughters prophesied, he received further warnings. The arrival of Agabus, and his dramatic gesture, was further confirmation to Paul's fearful disciples. They interpreted it as the Spirit's warning to Paul not to go ahead. Wishful thinking! Paul knew that it was not so. Instead of encouraging him, they were breaking his heart with their fears and opposition. At last he persuaded them to join him in his prayer, "Thy will be done".

On arrival at Jerusalem, Paul was given a great welcome by the church. He reported on his third journey to James and the elders. They told him that thousands of Jews were becoming Christians. Wonderful news! Like James, however, they were all enthusiasts for the Law. Unfortunately, they had heard that Paul was teaching that Christian Jews should no longer observe circumcision. This was not strictly true, though his teaching was undermining its importance.

"Demonstrate your loyalty, and calm the fears of these brothers", the elders advised him. On a previous visit to Jerusalem Paul had fulfilled a vow he had made, by shaving his head. He was therefore happy to join four men, who had taken a vow, and go with them to the temple to purify himself with them, paying their expenses.

He might have got away with this scheme, had not some Jews from Asia recognised him. They had heard his negative teaching about the Law. Having seen him in the city with Trophimus, a Gentile Christian from Ephesus, they supposed, wrongly, that Paul had taken him also into the temple. Seeing him in the temple again, they made an outcry and raised a riot. Dragging Paul out of the temple, they would have killed him, had not the Tribune, with a cohort of soldiers, intervened.

Adjoining, and dominating the temple, was the Antonia. Built by Herod the Great, it was used as a barracks, and housed a Roman garrison. The Tribune arrested Paul, and, finding it impossible to learn from the shouting mob what the row was about, had him chained, and taken into the barracks.

At first, the Tribune took Paul to be an Egyptian. Luke has linked together three groups of people. First, the Assassins were fanatical freedom fighters, more violent than the IRA. They mingled with the throng at festivals, and murdered their enemies with small daggers hidden in their clothes. Then they melted into the crowd undetected. Another group, like the Zealots, wanted to start a revolution. Claiming the inspiration of a second Moses, they drew a crowd into the desert. There, they claimed that God would show them signs to prove that the day of liberation was near. Then thirdly, an Egyptian rounded up four thousand of these gullible people, planning to lead them into an attack on the Roman garrison in Jerusalem. Josephus, the Jewish historian who was a friend of Rome, exaggerated their number to thirty thousand. To him these people were bandits. As with the IRA, it all depends upon one's point of view.

It is good to read Josephus' history of the Jewish Wars, and understand the violent political background of the events that we read of in the Gospels and in Acts. The growing number of revolts escalated into a very bloody war. Paul's trial probably took place early in AD 59. The destruction of Jerusalem was only eleven years away.

Paul was no political agitator. He boasts of his home city of Tarsus and of his Jewish ancestry in cultured Greek. The Tribune is impressed, and allows him to speak to the crowd, safely, from the steps of the Antonia.

Speaking now in Hebrew, the language of the Rabbis, and as a student of the revered Gamaliel, Paul tells his story.

They listen until he speaks of his vision and call to preach to the Gentiles. Then bedlam is let loose. The soldiers hurry Paul back into the safety of the Antonia.

To get to the truth of the matter, the Tribune orders Paul to be beaten and interrogated. This time, Paul claims his rights as a Roman citizen. Note his flash of very human one-upmanship. Unlike the Tribune, Paul was born free. Even binding him was illegal.

The Tribune is both afraid and mystified. He summons the Jewish Council, and arranges to bring Paul out to meet them on their own ground. He would be present, and a guard would be on call. Presumably the language used would be one he could understand.

The trial has echoes of that of Jesus. The High Priest orders Paul to be slapped. Paul, like Jesus, rebukes this illegality by quoting the Law. His own breach of it, name calling, was due to ignorance. Jesus himself had called the Pharisees whited sepulchres. Then, astutely, Paul alters the ground for their charge. Taking his stand on the resurrection, he divides the Council. Angrily Sadducees and Pharisees argue with each other, the latter siding with Paul, who is nearly torn in two between them. The guards again have to rescue him and take him back to their barracks.

The following night Paul has another dream. God is sending him to Rome to give his witness there. How strange and wonderful are the ways of God! As with Paul's vision in the temple, this vision clarifies and confirms something that had been growing in his mind for some time. He had been planning to visit Rome when he was in Corinth. (Acts. 19:21) Now, God Himself was strangely preparing his way.

The next nudge of events slips into place. Paul's nephew hears of an ambush being planned to murder his uncle. This is a rare glimpse we have of Paul's family. At the end of his letter to the Romans, he speaks of two kinsmen. The Tribune agreed to see this young man, no doubt expecting to be offered a bribe to secure Paul's release. What he heard made him fear for his own position. The situation was getting out of hand. Under the cover of night, protected by a huge armed escort, Paul is taken out of the city, and finally packed off to Caesarea, the Provincial capital. Let Governor Felix cope with the problem!

Paul's Trials in Caesarea. Acts 24:1 - 26:32.

Felix summoned Paul's accusers. Ananias wisely brings a Roman lawyer to argue his case. Tertullus knows how to flatter, but, lacking witnesses, he has no convincing case. He seems to have thought that Felix could force Paul to accuse himself!

Paul states the truth. Ananias at least had not stooped to coach lying witnesses to deny it. Again Paul takes his stand on the resurrection. What did Ananias, a Sadducee, make of that?

Unlike Lysias the Tribune, Felix knew quite a lot about the Jewish religion. His wife Drusilla was a Jewess. Her father, Herod Agrippa, had executed the apostle James. Had Felix also learnt something about Christ from Cornelius? Was Cornelius still stationed in Caesarea?

Felix postponed the case until Lycias should come. Did he ever come? There is no record of this, or of any trial. There was only an invitation given to Paul to speak about Christ to Felix and his wife. They were however both unsavoury characters. When Paul weighed in on justice and judgement, Felix was alarmed and sent him away. He too was hoping, not for salvation, but for a bribe.

Two years passed. Paul was given freedom to see his friends. We can be sure he did not waste his time. Luke, who was with him, would be able to write up all Paul could tell him about his missionary journeys. He would also be free to journey around to collect eye-witness accounts of the life and teaching of Jesus, and the early experience of the church, which he would use for his two books.

Felix goes. Festus comes. Compared to other Procurators, all appallingly savage and corrupt, he was better than most. His first act was to visit Jerusalem, where the Jewish authorities begged him to send Paul back to them for trial. Had those who had vowed to murder Paul by then starved to death? Festus was not fooled. He told them he would judge Paul at Caesarea.

So, for the third time, Paul stands trial. The same accusations are made, and remain unproven. Only in Jerusalem could witnesses be found. So Festus asks Paul, "Are you willing to go to Jerusalem to be tried there?"

To say *yes* would be to invite murder. To say *no* would sound both cowardly and unreasonable. But, as Festus put the question, the voice of Paul's vision must have shouted loud and clear. His Roman citizenship was part of God's provision for the fulfilment of His purpose at this most critical moment. Loud and clear, Paul claimed the privilege of every Roman citizen. "I appeal to Caesar."

There was nothing that Ananias could do. He left, and returned to Jerusalem, defeated.

The arrival of Herod Agrippa 11, gave Paul another opportunity to witness to the highest in the land. (Lk. 21:12) A grandson of Herod the Great, he was a friend of Rome, and was doing all he could to persuade his Jewish subjects to accept Roman rule, and not provoke a useless and bloody war. Berenice, a gentle and compassionate lady, was his sister. His other sister was Drusilla.

Why did Luke add yet another account of Paul's conversion? It is his third. For the church, it was the most important event since Pentecost. It was crucial to the expansion of the Gospel to the Gentiles. It was also a rare, though not unique experience, of Jesus appearing to people after his ascension.

Paul's account of his vision differs slightly from the narrated version, though, of course, both are recorded by Luke. Paul speaks of his companions seeing the light, but not hearing the voice. (Acts 9:7. cp 22:9) In this third account we learn that the men fell to the ground, and also that the voice spoke in Hebrew, not Aramaic, the language used by Jesus during his ministry. Paul combines his two versions, perhaps, to shorten and simplify.

On this occasion Paul takes his stand on the Messianic hope. He probably gave a long and detailed exposition of scripture to prove that Jesus had fulfilled all the ancient prophesies, including those that foretold a mission to the Gentiles. Such a passionate display of learning must have seemed totally out of place to Festus. Paul must be mad. But Paul knew that Agrippa, like himself, was a man of two worlds, an intellectual who had made a study of the Jewish religion.

Agrippa was "almost persuaded". (Acts 26:28. AV) To be fully persuaded, is to become involved and committed. With this light but dismissive comment, Agrippa is able to make a dignified exit. He will not risk being drawn in further.

His final word to Festus is however weighty. How dramatically Luke concludes this part of his story. But for Paul's appeal, he could have been freed. It was all part of God's plan. Paul's plea, and Festus' response, were irrevocable.

"You have appealed to Caesar. To Caesar you shall go."

The Letter to the Romans.

Paul's letter to the Christians in Rome preceded and paved the way for his visit. The first Jews who came to Rome were probably merchants. They were followed by immigrants and captives. Pompey brought over many as slaves. They multiplied, and, being politically astute, won for themselves various privileges, which included that of religious toleration. There was a close relationship between the Imperial Family and that of Herod the Great. He and his descendants received their kingdom from the hands of Rome.

We do not know who brought the gospel to Rome. Visitors from Rome had been in the crowd that Peter addressed on the day of Pentecost. There was a continual flow of people, especially from the main cities of Ephesus, Corinth and Antioch, where Paul had preached. We have seen how the riots over Chrestos led to the expulsion of all Jews from Rome in AD 49. Aquilla and Priscilla were probably Christians before they arrived in Corinth.

Paul had been planning to visit Rome for a long time. It would be a step on his way to Spain, the western limit of the known world, ie "the end of the earth". (Acts 1:8) His reasons for delay are given in Romans 15:18-22. Paul was a pioneer not a poacher. It is clear from the following verses, that he was writing towards the end of his third missionary journey, as he was collecting contributions from the churches to take to Jerusalem. He asks for prayer that he might be delivered from the dangers he knew awaited him there. He also seems to fear that the anti-Hellenists might refuse these gifts. The date is therefore 57/58 AD.

The mention of Phoebe (16:1) makes it likely that he was writing either from Corinth, or Cenchreae which is nearby. Three of the companions who send greetings were with him at that time. Gaius, (Acts 20:4) was one of the very few whom Paul had baptized in Corinth. Erastus too is linked to that city. (2Tim. 4:20. cp. Acts 19:22) It is clear from the rest of Romans 16, that Paul had a lot of friends in Rome. Even Aquilla and Priscilla are back there. The Emperor Claudius died in AD 54. His order for the expulsion of Jews was then probably rescinded.

This is Paul's longest letter. It reads more like a theological treatise. He is expounding the gospel as he preached it, to a church he had not founded. The conflict between the Jewish and Gentile Christians over Law and circumcision, was already in evidence.

The Jews in Rome were in close touch with Jews in Jerusalem. They had heard criticism of the Nazarene sect. The Greek word is *heiresis* from which we get our word heresy. They had not as yet heard anything about Paul. (Acts 28:21-22) No doubt they soon would! It was important that Paul should anticipate this, by getting both Jewish and Gentile Christians to understand and accept his teaching.

The themes he had argued so passionately with the Galatians, he now takes up with reasoned calm. His arguments are sometimes complex and rabbinical. Even Peter had problems with understanding him. (2Pet. 3:14-16) The English words used in translation can also be misunderstood. Modern translation can help to clarify.

Introduction and greeting.

What a lot Paul packs in! Every word counts. Verses 3-6 may be part of a baptismal catechism. Note how he checks himself. He must not seem to dominate. Encouragement is to be mutual. Paul found it easier to give than to receive. Churches in England are finding it hard to accept that they need the help being offered them by the younger churches of Africa and the East, though in length of Christian experience the two cases are not quite parallel.

If Jews looked down on Gentiles as pagans, Greeks and Romans looked down on Jews as barbarians. Both equally needed the gospel. What a glorious witness Paul gives in verses 16-17. Link this with 2 Timothy 1:12. Paul is not ashamed of the gospel of Christ. He has experienced its power and its trustworthiness. It is for all. In Christ, God offers us the gift of new life, lived in a loving relationship with Him. By faith this gift is recognised. By faith it is received. Here is the heart of his message. The rest of the first eight chapters are taken up with his attempt to argue and explain it.

The Judgement of God. 1:18 - 3:23.

The one thing we all have in common is our sinfulness. A Chinese Christian was asked how he could forgive the Japanese who had bombed and destroyed his home. He said that when he cried out to God for judgement upon them, he found himself in the dock beside them. Their common sinfulness bound them together as equally in need of God's mercy.

Pagans will be judged. Paul argues that they cannot plead ignorance of God's laws. We live in an ordered world. There are moral as well as physical laws, which, if broken, lead to disharmony and disaster. Society may condition us to different codes, but there is a moral streak within us. "The Light that lighteth every man" can lead individuals to rebel against the code of their society in favour of a higher code. Paul teaches that pagans will be judged by the highest code their innermost heart acknowledges. But idols that degrade God into an animal form are an excuse for bestial behaviour. A woman, watching a film of Nazis torturing Jews, cried out "Beasts, they are beasts!" Someone sitting next to her remarked, "Madam, do not insult the animals". When we surrender ourselves totally to our animal instincts, we destroy what makes us human. Then we fall lower than the animals. The most awful thing God can do to us is to give us up to pursue our chosen path of self-destruction. Maybe, it is only by suffering the consequences, that people will be led to unblock their ears. (cp. 1Cor. 5:4-5 cp. Is. 54:6-8)

As for Jews and Christians, we will be judged, not by our boasted Law and moral code, but by our obedience to it. (Matt. 7:21) Giving his quotation from Isaiah 52:5 a bit of a twist, Paul accuses those whose actions belie their beliefs of causing unbelievers to speak evil of God.

This teaching led Paul to say something very revolutionary. True circumcision is not that of the body, but of the heart. Jeremiah had foretold that God's Law would be inscribed on men's hearts. (Jer. 31:33) Through the Gospel, Christ's new law of Love was inscribed equally on the hearts of Jews and Gentiles, who responded by faith. This is relevant today with regard to baptism. I have heard a

Roman Catholic priest deny that Quakers and members of the Salvation Army are Christians if they have not been baptized. They might claim that they have been baptized in the Spirit, by repentance and faith. I think Paul would have accepted this, though he might have counselled water baptism for the sake of unity.

At this point, Paul foresees his readers asking, "Then what advantage has the Jew?" Paul has kept saying, "First the Jew, then the Gentile", but it seems more a matter of timing than of privilege. The Jews had inherited a high calling and great promises, but, without the obedience of a living faith, these blessings could inoculate them against receiving the challenging and life changing reality. A parallel situation can perhaps be found in the danger of conventional Christianity inoculating people against the discovery of real faith. Jesus said, "The first will be last". Paul's arguments to justify his reply, "Much in every way", are abstract and unconvincing. His real answer, found in verse 9, is "None at all". So what value has the Law? However much we try, we can never succeed in keeping it. Even when we are selective, we still have to face Jesus' teaching that the Law applies to thoughts and motives as well as actions. At this point even the most self-righteous amongst us must throw in the sponge.

The real value of the Law is to reveal to us our inescapable sinfulness and need of salvation. Despairing of self-effort, we recognize our utter dependence on the grace of God. This is not the same point as Paul's illustration of the Law as a kind of Schoolmaster. The emphasis in Galatians is on the habit of discipline which prepares us for the freedom of love. Paul concludes this section of his teaching with a brief summary. "All have sinned and fallen short of the glory of God". The Greek word for sin, *hamartia*, means missing the target. Sin isn't just thinking and doing bad things, it is failing to fulfill the purpose for which we were created, ie, to be like Christ.

The Gift of Grace. 3:24 - 4:25.

In the next three verses, Paul uses four dauntingly theological words. If we are to make sense of what follows, we must understand their meaning. First, *Expiation*. This is one of the two meanings of Atonement, ie, at-one-ment, the bridging of the gap between sinful man and God. The word used literally means "to cover" or "wipe away". This doesn't mean that God sweeps our sin under the carpet. He first exposes it so that we can confess it and receive His forgiveness. Then, in God's eyes, our slate is wiped clean. By faith, baptism gives us, as it were, an all-over wash. Total immersion, while not necessary as a practice, is a vivid symbol of this. But we still need Jesus to wash our feet daily. (Ps. 51:1-2. cp. Ps. 103:12)

How can the blood of Jesus wash away our sin? Beyond our full comprehension and efforts to define it, it remains a mysterious fact. For two thousand years, people of simple faith have believed it, and experienced forgiveness and salvation. Something of this we can understand when we look at the cross, and realize what our sin has done, and is still doing to Christ. Then his loving words of forgiveness strike home to our hearts. This is the work of the Holy Spirit. Our hearts crack open and Christ's healing life flows in. Then we know that we are at peace with God and at peace within ourselves. You can witness to this experience, but you can't explain it. (cp. 1Cor. 2:14)

The second is *Justification.* This word can be used in two ways. We say, "I was perfectly justified in getting a bit of my own back." We reckon ourselves right in our own eyes. But not in God's! Justification, as Paul uses it, means that, when we turn to Christ in faith, and receive his gift of forgiveness, then God reckons us as righteous, ie, "all right" in His eyes. In chapter 4, this word "reckon" is used ten times. Here lies the mystery, hidden in the loving heart of God. It is like a child, who loses his temper, stamps, kicks, howls, and hits out at his mother, while she continues to encircle him in her loving embrace. "You are all right darling", she'll say, "Mother loves you". The bout of temper will soon be over, leaving the child secure, and his relationship with his mother unscarred.

Righteousness is another. Paul uses this word in three ways. First, God's righteousness can mean his justice, as in Romans 2:5. It can also mean His saving power, as in 3:22-25. The righteousness of a person does not depend on law-abiding morality. That leads to self-righteousness. It depends on a right relationship with God. This undeserved, loving acceptance is a free gift, which is ours to accept by faith. Such faith is not an intellectual acceptance of a doctrine, but a personal trust in Jesus, and in what God has done for us through him. Lastly, righteousness can mean Christian ethical behaviour, and good deeds that spring from a love of God, and a desire to please Him, as in 6:13-19.

Finally, linked to Righteousness is *Redemption.* In Paul's day, this word was commonly used for the cost of freeing a slave. Christ has redeemed us from the slavery of sin and the power of Satan. His victory on the cross has set us free to become what God created us to be. Bishop Joe Fison, in a TV program, summed up the meaning of the cross in three simple aphorisms. It was a showing up of sin, a showing forth of love, and a show-down with Satan. This made more sense to me than any theological explanations that I'd previously heard.

Illustrations must not be pushed beyond the limit of their meaning. We must not ask, as many have done, to whom is the price paid, God or the Devil? Both lead to appalling theological conclusions. If a father jumps off the pier, and saves his child from drowning at the cost of his own life, we do not ask such a question.

Once Paul's language is understood, his teaching is clear. It is summed up in 3:23-24. Jew and Gentile are equally sinners deserving God's condemnation. Neither can earn forgiveness by obedience to the Law or to their own moral code. Like bankrupt debtors, no one has the where-with-all to pay. Forgiveness is a free gift of grace which has to be received by faith.

Paul now backs up his argument by reference to Abraham. He has already used this argument in Galatians. Here he adds a further argument from Psalm 32 verses 1-2. These, ascribed to David, were enhanced by his authority. "Happy the man whom God has freely forgiven".

Returning to Abraham, Paul points out that both circumcision and the Law were given later, the former being an outward seal of a Promise already given, not a condition for receiving it. So Abraham is father to all who share his faith and obedience.

As I travelled through Palestine, made so familiar to me through the Bible, I felt "this is my land, the land of my ancestors in the faith". All their experiences of God's providence, and all those glorious promises, are mine too. How wonderful!

How much is concentrated in chapter 4 verses 24-25! Our Christian belief is basically belief in God. He sent Jesus our Lord to die for our sins. He raised him from the dead. "For our trespasses" could mean "because of" or "on behalf of". The betrayal of Judas and the freeing of Barabbas aptly illustrates the distinction.

New Life in Christ. Chapter 5.

Therefore - the glorious news of forgiveness, and our own acceptance in Christ, warts and all, is only half the gospel. The other half is resurrection: the joyful hope of sharing in Christ's new life, and finally entering with him into the glory of God. It sounds incredible, but read Ephesians, 1:3-9, where Paul spells it out, giving it a cosmic setting!

So great a destiny involves unending spiritual growth. Thanks to the Holy Spirit at work within us, every experience is grist to our mill. Hurts and hardships can stretch and strengthen our faith. As usual, Paul writes from experience. (2Cor. 11:24-29)

In Galatians, Paul referred to Adam. He is the Archetypal Old Man. Seen in this light, we can recognise him in ourselves. His disbelief and disobedience are ingrained within us: the cause of our sin and spiritual death. Paul sees Christ as the New Adam, the New Archetypal Man, as God created him to be. (Gen. 1:27) Four times in Chapter 5 Paul uses the phrase "much more". We are "justified" by the cross, but much more are we saved from final condemnation, ie, safely pulled to the shore. (verse 9) We are reconciled by his death, but much more are we saved by his divine life, which fills us with joy. (verses 10-11) Much more are we given abundant grace. (v. 15). Much more, through this abundance, will we reign in life through him. (v. 17)

Saints may get tripped up by sin, but they can thank God even for that. It keeps them humble. It is also a sign that Satan thinks them worth attacking. Grace is always stronger. The greater the attack, the more abundant the grace. Though a battle may be lost, the war can still be won. The struggle for our completion, ie our perfection, goes on to the end.

This Part Two of the Gospel is not usually preached with the same confidence as the first. Is this linked to the difficulty found in teaching about the Holy Spirit? To confess that one is a forgiven sinner is not difficult. To admit to a desire for perfection is to stick one's head over the parapet. Why does Paul refer to "all" in verse 18 and only "many" in verse 19? Is it because this new life in Christ, though offered to all, is received by only a few? "We are excluded, not by what we are, but by our unwillingness to go further." (Iain Matthew: "The Impact of God").

Where does Law come into this? Why does Paul say, "sin reigned from Adam to Moses". The Law of Moses didn't stop it. If it had done so there would have been no need of Christ's death on the cross. "Where there is no Law, there is no condemnation." (verse 13) This is a hopeful message for today. Children abandoned, abused, and left to the harsh upbringing of the streets, are, in one sense, lawless. Many seem to have no sense of right and wrong. We easily condemn them, but who and what is really to blame? Home? Society?

Law makes sin worse. (v. 20) It certainly makes it more defiant. A Catholic Priest, who founded Boys Town for children who were handed over to him by the Courts, would tell them that they were good. "No, no", they'd reply, "we are bad". "You are good", he'd insist. "You want to be the best. Your only trouble is that you've got the wrong model. With Jesus as your Gang Leader, all your energies will be appreciated and used to the fullest extent. Then you'll know, what Jesus already knows, just how very good you are." No wonder so many boys were transformed while under his care.

There is a solidarity both in sin and salvation, in the Old Man Adam and the New Man Christ. The former leads to our sharing in his disobedience, condemnation, and death. The later leads to our being united in Christ's obedience, and, through his cross and resurrection, receiving the free gift of acceptance and eternal life.

The struggle against continuing sin. Chapter 6.

"When sin increased, Grace abounded." OK. So lets go on sinning. Then your amazing grace will be still more amazing. That's the attitude some of Paul's hearers took. At least that is what his detractors accused him of saying, a specious and dangerous argument. In baptism we have died to sin. How can we return to it, like a dog to its vomit? (2Pet. 2:22)

Our baptism involves a twofold commitment. We are to consider ourselves dead to sin, and alive to God. In the Musical, Oliver is invited to "Consider yourself one of the family." How we live and behave depends primarily on how we consider ourselves. Are we orphans, outsiders, bad? How unwise is the parent who tells his son "You are a bad boy". Better to say, "That thing you have done is bad." Keep calling a child bad, and he will strive to fulfil your expectations!

Secondly, we are to go on struggling. No matter how many times we fail, we must never give up. But this is a negative stance. Better far is a positive yielding to God: letting go of self, so that He can have His way with us. "Yield yourselves," ie present yourselves before God, implies a once-for-all decision kept up by an ongoing struggle. But it is a struggle of a different sort.

Sin comes in an attractive guise, but the final pay-off is spiritual death. No free hand-outs from the Devil! The wages of sin, however, consists of reaping the harvest we have sown. In Dorothy Sayers' "Devil to Pay", Mephistopheles finds himself cheated. He had bargained for a nice white Christian soul. What he gets is a bag of black rubbish. Spiritual diminishment may be so slow that it is hardly apparent. Gradually however, sin affects, not just the spirit, but the mind and body, family and other relationships, and finally the whole of our society. In contrast, our new life in Christ earns us nothing, but it opens us up to receive the gift of his wide embrace. This includes all we could ever want or hope for. It is beyond our imagining.

Paul's personal struggle. Chapter 7.

In this chapter Paul shares his own experience of this struggle. (Verses 1-13) He starts with two clear statements:

1. We are no longer bound by the Law. His analogy of the woman is rather confusing. It is the woman, ie the church, who dies to the Law by sharing in the death of Christ. Union with him can never be broken for he will never die again. Sharing his resurrection life, we can bear fruit for God through the Spirit.

In the old life, sin is made worse by the Law. *Dos* and *Donts* bring out our natural contrariness, the "Keep off the grass" syndrome. But rules can also kill the natural spontaneity of "the free child", to use a term taken from psychology. There is a danger that, in some Christian circles, a new convert can be confronted by so many *dos* and *don'ts* that their initial joy in discovering the grace of God can be diminished. The fruit of the Spirit is life-giving and springs from love. (2Cor. 3:6)

2. The Law is good. (vs. 7-12) From what has been said above, one might presume the opposite. "No" says Paul, "Law is good". It not only teaches what is wrong, but, in a backhanded sort of way, it leads us to discover this for ourselves, both by failure and success.

As a Pharisee, and vigorous upholder of the Law, Paul could boast of his success. But "Thou shalt not covet" is the one commandment that addresses the inner desires. Failure could be concealed by moral blindness or hypocrisy. Paul must have suffered a secret agony of helplessness. His boasted success was trash. (Philip. 3:6-8) Sometimes we learn from failure, sometimes from success. Attainment can disclose the emptiness of our ambition. Paul knew both experiences. He was ripe for conversion.

The problem of inner conflict. Verses 14-24.

Verses 15 and 19 strike a sympathetic echo in our hearts. We don't understand ourselves either. Paul wrestles with the problem on our behalf. But about what stage in his life is he writing?

There are two opinions about this. The first is that he is writing of his experience before conversion. The other believes it to refer to a continuing struggle with sin even after he was filled with the Spirit. I have neither space nor concern to discuss the arguments on either side. My interest is to draw from Scripture all that can help us on our pilgrimage. I think something emerges from both views that chime in with our own experience.

Many have gone through a transitional stage in their Christian life. Even after conversion and the joy of knowing God's grace, we can still find ourselves depending on our own efforts to be good. Then there comes a stage, akin to the second blessing, and renewal in the Spirit, when we learn what it is to "let go and let God". A boundary has been crossed. Deeply aware of being enfolded in God's love, our over-riding desire is only for Him.

Despite this, the struggle with sin goes on, and, after an initial period of peace, it may increase. From peak experiences we descend with a bump. The problem of continuing sin continues. Paul knew this when he addressed the unruly Corinthians as "sanctified in Christ", calling them to be what they really are. The greatest saints are those who are most conscious of their sin.

Paul delights in God with his mind. He is not referring to his intellect but his deepest innermost desire. Sin stems from his members, ie the natural desires of his humanity, not evil in themselves but open to invasion by evil. Hence he calls us to yield our members to God and not to sin. (6:13) This is not a conflict between spirit and body but between our overmastering desire for God and a multiplication of lesser temporary desires. This is a problem developed in later writings.

Out of the struggle comes Paul's moving cry, "Who will deliver me?" Bold comes his joyful answer. "Thanks be to God, through Jesus Christ our Lord." It takes a lot of falls to make a good rider. A small child, learning to walk, isn't scolded when he falls. God goes on forgiving, trusting and encouraging us. What matters is our relationship with Him. Our loving desire to please Him will save us from all presumption and abusing of His love. In Him we come to the end, not of struggle, but of all fear of condemnation.

The Role of the Spirit. Chapter 8.

This is the high point in Paul's letter. It gathers up all that has been said and brings it to a triumphant conclusion. Free from Law and condemnation, in Christ, God accepts us as we are. (5:1-2) The Devil wants us to doubt this. Guilty feelings are his substitute for repentance. We nurse our bad feelings and do nothing.

We are also freed from the power of sin. (6:14) We still fall, but can get up to continue the fight. Jesus, wearing the garment of our sin-prone humanity led a sinless and victorious life. In the power of his Spirit we can claim victory too.

The battle is fought in the mind, (7:22-23) hence the repeated emphasis on setting the mind, ie our deepest desires, on spiritual, not worldly matters. That doesn't mean thinking about God all day! Rather it means allowing God to think in us so that His Spirit influences our attitudes, opinions, and desires.

It isn't enough to believe in Christ and try to follow him. Only if his Spirit dwells in us do we belong to him. Note that when the Spirit comes, the other members of the Holy Trinity come in too. (cp. Jn. 14:23)

Through the Spirit, God's life flows into us. He can control our "unruly wills and affections" that can enslave and finally destroy us. He leads us on our journey into life back home with God. Through Him we rejoice in our Sonship crying Abba, the Jewish child's name for Father. Finally he strengthens us to face suffering. Paul had suffered more than most. His testimony, and the experience of the other apostles, (Acts 5:40-41) is supported by the witness of countless persecuted Christians today. Having shared Christ's sufferings, we also share his glory. This is what Jesus prayed for before his death. (Jn. 17:22-26).

Added to this is the hope for the whole of Creation being restored to the perfection of God's original Plan. Creation shared in the consequences of the Fall. (Gen. 3:17) Animals suffer appalling cruelty. Forests are destroyed by acid rain. The whole of Nature is composed of living matter. Plants as well as animals respond to loving care. Even rocks are alive. Nature groans for its liberation which depends on ours.

We have to go on hoping. Hope is our life-line. We hold on by faith and prayer. Even when we are too busy or too sick or miserable to pray, from deep within, inexpressible longings well up, sometimes unrecognized by ourselves, yet known to God. This is the Spirit praying within us. So often we pray for the wrong things. The Spirit knows our deepest needs. He prays within us, sometimes silently, sometimes through tongues.

Paul finally sums up our grounds for hope. First he recapitulates all God has done for us, giving it a cosmic setting. The only new word is "Predestination". According to Paul, God knew that Man would mess things up by misusing his God-given freedom, so God had His Plan of Salvation all worked out beforehand. Does fore-knowledge and fore-planning leave room for freedom? We must believe that it does. Libraries could be filled with the books written on this subject. It is a mystery lying at the very heart of God's Being.

Julian of Norwich wrote, "All shall be well, and all manner of things shall be well." God's touch is a Midas touch turning all into gold. Every experience can help to mould us according to His purpose for our lives, that is, if we will let it. Our lives may seem broken and fragmented, but God lets nothing go to waste.

If God is on our side, then what have we to fear? Who can accuse us, condemn us, or separate us from His love? Even in suffering and persecution we are more than conquerors. Out of the depths of his experience of this, triumphantly Paul cries out, "Nothing can separate us from the love of God in Christ Jesus our Lord."

After all this, the rest of the letter may seem rather an anti-climax. In one sense it is, but, from the heights we descend to the plain to face the practical problems of life. It was for this the vision was given. As we shall see, a similar plan is followed by the Letters to the Ephesians and the Colossians.

God's continuing Plan for the Jews. Chapters 9 - 11.

How wrong to think of Paul as only a theologian. Again and again, the warmth and passion of his heart breaks through. He agonises over his own people's rejection of the Gospel. Their rich inheritance was being deprived of its fruition, or rather, its fruit was being enjoyed by others while lost to them. What a tragedy!

We have already discussed the idea of God hardening people's hearts. It is the problem of Predestination. Set in a particular time and place, we have freedom of choice. But that freedom is limited by pressures of character and circumstance, and of past choices, that shape our present. Much that we do is predictable, yet we feel within ourselves that a basic freedom remains. God, who lives in timeless eternity knows the future. His Plan for His Creation is being slowly worked out. Ultimately God is responsible for evil as well as good. This is another mystery we will never fathom. Like Job, we question God. God did not rebuke Job for this. Instead He questioned Job on the wonders of Creation, reducing him to unknowing silence. Job was given no answers, but he was given a vision of God that led to a new relationship. God had always trusted Job. Now, Job was content to trust God. "I love the mysteries of God. They make Him so great." (Janet Erskine-Stuart)

A young Jew once said to me, "You Christians should be grateful to us Jews. Where would you be if we hadn't crucified your Christ?" Where indeed? God has vessels of wrath and vessels of mercy. He can weave both into His Plan.

The Promise to Abraham was that, through him and his descendants, God's blessing would be poured out on all the nations of the world. (Gen. 12:1-3) Now Jewish and Gentile Christians must take up the task of spreading the good news of the Gospel.

There are those who say that we should not preach to Jews. But if God holds his hands out to them, so must we. (Rom. 10:21) What hinders us is not just their resistance. We meet this from people of all races and religions. It is rather our guilt that holds us back: the appalling record of persecution that Jews have suffered from Christian hands. Recently a group of young Christians from many nations joined in a March of Repentance. It followed the route of the Fourth Crusade, the most iniquitous of them all. They were welcomed with love and tears. In the first century many Jews accepted Christ as their Messiah. Today, Messianic Jews, who have become Christians, but continue to observe their Jewish traditions, are proclaiming Jesus as Messiah to their own people with considerable effect.

From chapter 11 verse 13, Paul speaks specifically to Gentile Christians. The imagery of Israel as a Vine was familiar. (Ps. 80:8-15) He sees unbelieving Jews as branches that have broken off, and believing Gentiles as branches of a wild vine that have been grafted in. They must not presume on superiority. Those who cease to live by faith can be broken off, while Jews who find faith in Christ can be grafted in again. God has no favourites. Paul's hope is that eventually the whole of Israel will be thus restored. This is the hope of Messianic Jews as they witness to their own people today. "The gifts and calling of God are irrevocable." (v. 29)

New Life in the Church. 12:1 - 15:13.

Out of the life of faith flows a new ethic based on the law of love. Paul's first statement is revolutionary. What does "spiritual worship" bring to mind? Charismatic praise? Taise? Quaker silence? For Paul it meant an active life of sacrificial service. But, once again, he stresses that it starts in the mind. "Consider yourself" and "set your mind on" is now followed by "be ye transformed by the renewal of your mind." (2:2) Spirituality is down-to-earth and practical.

The teaching given to the Corinthians, based on the allied themes of love and unity, are here repeated. They involve humility, mutual respect, genuine affection, hospitality, and the sharing of joys and sorrows. Very important is the injunction not to judge a brother in matters of food or the observance of special days. Total abstainers, Vegetarians and Sabbatarians, take note! Love rather than the tut-tutting of others may prompt us sometimes to restrict our own freedom.

New is the instruction with regard to government authorities. This is something Jesus both taught and practised. Paul calls such authorities servants, ie ministers of God. He uses the same word as that used for those elected to look after the feeding of the widows, *diakonos*. As such they are to be respected and prayed for. His instructions include the payment of taxes. Today this would cover the honest filling-up of income tax forms.

Though Nero was Emperor, it was early days, and the government was largely in the hands of the philosopher Seneca, who died in AD 65. Paul's experience of Roman justice had been mostly good, apart from minor clashes in Philippi and Ephesus. It had frequently protected him from violence at the hands of Jewish mobs. Soon, Rome would become the persecutor. Then the church would have to reconsider some of Paul's teaching in this respect.

This letter ends with personal messages. How easy it would have been to write, "My love to you all." That was not Paul's way. How each one would have cherished the special commendations given. Paul's last words typify the man. His final appeal is for unity. His final assertion is Christ's command to make the Gospel known to all nations. His final word is, "To God be the glory for ever, through Jesus Christ."

Adventures at Sea. Acts 27:1 - 28:16.

The Christians in Rome had plenty of time to absorb Paul's letter before he came, even if the postal services were somewhat slower than ours! His two years in Caesarea were followed by months of delay caused by storms at sea and shipwreck. The story of his voyage is grippingly told by Luke his companion on the journey.

The date was AD 60. Winter was approaching. Sea travel was dangerous. No mariner would venture to sea after the season of winter storms approached. Paul had been born and brought up in a busy port. He had already been shipwrecked three times, and adrift in the sea for twenty four hours. (2Cor. 11:25) No wonder Jews had no love for the sea! Paul had plenty of experience of its dangers.

Even though he was a prisoner, Paul, as a Roman citizen, is treated with respect by the centurion. He is given freedom to go ashore at Sidon to visit his friends. The voyage, starting late in the season, is further delayed by winds, and the ship badly needed a safe winter harbour. Reaching Fairhaven with difficulty, Paul warned the centurion that to sail further would endanger lives. The centurion, a landlubber, naturally heeded only the captain, who heeded the ship owners. Their concern was for profit rather than lives. In this respect things have not changed much. "Safety first" is a slogan more mouthed than observed.

The result was predictable. Tossed and driven off course, first the gear, then the cargo, and finally the tackle were thrown overboard. Only when human hope was abandoned were those in charge ready to hope in God. Hope came through another vision given to Paul. All in the ship were to be saved for the sake of God's purpose for Paul. (cp. Jonah 1:11-15) Reassured by his faith, Paul was able to awaken some hope in others. Later, when shipwreck was imminent, the crew, under cover of darkness, planned secretly to abandon ship, leaving the centurion, as well as the prisoners, to their fate. Paul discovered this. Calm and confident, he took charge. Now, at last, the centurion was ready to listen to his advice and the sailors' plan was foiled. Paul urged everyone to eat and regain their strength so that they could cope with the final and inevitable crunch. When it came, the centurion saved Paul from the soldiers who would otherwise have killed him, a small reward perhaps for the 276 lives that Paul had saved, including that of the centurion.

All landed safely. Very soon, two miracles raised Paul to a position of high honour. Active to serve his fellows, he gathers firewood. A viper seizes on his hand. Paul shakes it off and is unharmed. Here is a literal fulfilment of Jesus' prophecy recorded later and added to Mark's Gospel. This incident preceded, and may even account for the prophecy. Then Paul heals the father of the Governor of the island, which happened to be Malta. This led to the inhabitants streaming to Paul from all over the island, seeking to be cured of all their diseases. What an opportunity this gave him to preach the Gospel! Paul was given three months to sow the precious seed. Then he left it for others to reap the harvest the Spirit would give.

With spring came more favourable weather. Another ship was boarded, and Paul and his escort finally disembarked at Puteole. Here, Paul and Luke were allowed to spend a week with a group of Christians they found there.

News of Paul's coming was relayed to Rome, and Christians came out to meet him. The centurion, by this time, must have been more than impressed! On arrival in Rome, Paul was allowed to live in a house which his friends must have rented for him. It had to be shared with a guard, to whom he was evidently chained. This was a burden he found hard to bear. Paul, being the man he was, would have used it as an opportunity for witness, and befriending all those members of the guard who were equally forced to be chained to him. Paul was more free than they were.

The End of the Road. 28:17 - end.

Paul's first action was to contact the Jewish leaders. As we have seen, they had close contacts with their fellow Jews in Jerusalem. They had second-hand information about what they regarded as a sect, but they knew nothing about Paul. So they were willing to come and hear what he had to say. He concentrated on giving them a detailed bible study, no doubt an expansion of that given by Jesus on the road to Emmaus.

I was once part of a bible group that was asked to discuss, "Was the preparation given in the Old Testament sufficient to enable a seriously searching Jew to recognize Jesus as Messiah?" We complained that we didn't know the Old Testament well enough to give an answer. That discovery was, we were told, the point of asking the question. I leave it to the Reader to take up the challenge, and so discover what Paul might have said.

The result, as ever, was division. Many do not want to hear. To break away from past ways of thinking takes courage. The old ways are safe and well trodden. Responding to the call of Christ is costly. Pure intellectual honesty is rare.

Rome was not interested in hearing Paul's case. His enemies in Jerusalem would not be so keen to pursue the matter as to cover the vast expense of sending witnesses. It was enough that he was, so they thought, out of their way. So Paul continued for two years, receiving streams of visitors, and, no doubt, writing many letters.

Some time during that period, Peter must have come to Rome. A letter written by Clement, Bishop of Rome, thirty-five years later, tells us that "Peter and Paul were the greatest and most holy pillars of the church. They both preached there, but were victims of jealous zeal and envy, and were denounced to the Romans". Was this a reference to Jews, or to strongly conservative Jewish Christians, a precursor of fratricidal strife that continues to the present day?

Both apostles were put to death some time between 64-67 AD. It was then, according to Tacitus, that Nero made scapegoats of the Christians for causing the fire of Rome. It is now believed that he himself started it so that he could fulfil his grandiose plans for its rebuilding.

Peter was crucified in the Roman Circus, close to where the Basilica of St Peter's now stands. There is good reason for believing that the high altar is sited directly above his tomb in the old Roman graveyard. Paul, as a Roman citizen, was beheaded on the Ostian Way.

Summary

So Paul comes to the end of his journeying. From Antioch he had travelled throughout Asia Minor, Greece, and Macedonia until finally he reached Rome. Did he ever make it to Spain? A period of release before re-arrest and execution could have made this possible, but, if he went, it is strange that no record of such a visit has remained. It is more likely that, like his Master, his life of strenuous activity ended in enforced confinement. Like many others, he found captivity provided him a good opportunity for thought and for writing.

He was a man of many worlds: Jewish and Christian, Roman as well as Greek. He was also a balanced all-rounder: intellectual and practical, a mystic with a host of friends which included many women, all of whom he cared for deeply, and for whom he constantly prayed. As a contemporary of Jesus with personal knowledge of Peter and other apostles, he was the first to think through the theological implications of the Gospel.

There are those who complain that Paul changed the simple Gospel of Jesus into Christianity with its complicated set of beliefs. At first sight it may seem so, but the Gospel in practice is not so simple. Skating looks simple until you get on the ice! The simple gospel whittles down the painful truth: no cross, no crown.

Paul is struggling to make sense of problems and conflicts he himself was experiencing. The difficult words he used were the common parlance of his day. Today they may sound like theological jargon, but all disciplines of study use technical term as a form of shorthand. One of my aims has been to translate them back into the ordinary language of today.

Paul explored the relations between Law and Grace, Sin and Salvation, Jew and Gentile. His letters became the basis of all Christian thinking from his day until the present. At the Reformation, it was this Letter to the Romans that influenced Luther's thinking and became a major cause of his break from Rome.

In the following chapter we see how further letters written by Paul or in his name, show how his thought developed. They spread through all the churches, and became the first writings to be accepted as Christian scripture, the beginning of a New Testament.

Questions for private meditation

1. Can you see God's hand at work in the troubles and disasters of your life? (Acts chaps 24 to end)

2. In what sense are you free to do as you like? What are the consequences?

3. Might the faults you see in others be faults in yourself that you may not want to face up to? (Romans chap. 2)

4. What does the Cross mean to you? (Romans chap. 5)

5. How deeply are you aware of being loved by God? What impact has such an assurance on your life?

6. How great is your desire for the "much more" of the spiritual life? (Romans

chap. 5)

7. How do you "consider yourself"? (Romans chap. 6) How does this affect your life?

8. Do you accept that suffering is part of God's package for you? (Romans 8:12-37)

9. What does your Jewish inheritance in the O.T. mean to you? How do you relate to the faith of the Jews?

10. How do you face times of crisis in your life? (Acts 27:9 - 28:10)

Questions for group discussion

1. How do God's purposes work through, as well as in spite of, disaster? (Acts 21 - 25:12)

2. God finally allows us to pursue our self-chosen path to self-destruction. Discuss.

3. How can the church proclaim the Gospel to those of other faiths whose lives are morally superior? (Rom. 2)

4. What witness to the power of the Cross in their lives can members of the group give? (Rom. 3:21-26. 6:1-11)

5. God's love is unlimited, inescapable, unearned and everlasting? Discuss.

6. Why do some Christians and churches keep growing while others seem to get stuck? (Romans 5 & 6) What is the difference between thinking *In God* and thinking *About God*? (Rom. 8:6-11)

8. What does our Hope consist of? (Rom. 8:18-25)

9. What can be done in your area to help Christians and Jews grow in mutual respect and understanding? (Rom. 9)

10. Do verses 35-37 in Romans 8 sum up Paul's life and experience? What echoes do they ring in yours?

Chapter 9

Four Letters from Prison

Philemon, Philippians, Colossians, Ephesians

Paul's letters are more permanent than his preaching. His pen has proved more powerful than the sword that beheaded him. These letters have inspired and nourished the church for nearly two thousand years.

The letters to Philemon and to the Philippians belong closely together. Clearly, both are written from prison, but where and when? Paul was in prison in Ephesus, Caesarea and Rome. Tradition favours Rome. Today, many scholars favour Ephesus. It does not really matter. What matters is not where Paul was, but why he was writing, and what he said.

A good way of studying both Philemon and Philippians is to read the whole letter straight through several times in a modern translation. Then note down what you think the situation was that prompted the writing. Finally, make a summary of the points made, and see how they shed light on the problems. If you would like to try this exercise, read no further until you have completed it. Then compare your findings with mine. Take Philemon first. It is shorter and easier to work on.

Letter to Philemon.

Paul must have written many private letters to individuals, but this is the only one we have. That we have it at all is only due to what has been called "a happy accident".

Philemon was a wealthy member of the church in Colossae. His home was the meeting place for the House church there, or one of them. His son, Archippus, was their leading Elder. (Col. 4:17) Paul knew the family well and had probably stayed there more than once.

While in prison he had received an unexpected and surprising visitor. Onesimus, one of Philemon's house slaves, had run away. He had stolen from his master, probably to enable him to travel as far and as fast as he could. Ephesus would have been dangerously close. Anonymous safety was more likely to be found in Rome.

In the market place he may well have met Christian slaves who could have told him how to find Paul. Could some small act of gratitude or even recognition of service by a passing guest, have made a deep impression on a slave who would expect to be ignored as invisible? Anyhow, penniless, and probably hungry, he turned up on Paul's doorstep. Paul took him in, listened to his story, and gave him a home. Christ's love and forgiveness, flowing from Paul, soon captivated Onesimus' heart and he became a Christian. What an upside-down experience! The slave discovered freedom. To serve Paul was not servitude but a ministry gladly given, even a privilege. It was Paul who was in chains, yet no one was more free than he. The two became very close. Paul came to look on Onesimus as a son.

Then Paul began to have qualms. It was a duty to return runaway slaves to their masters. The law regarded them as property, to be bought and sold. The penalty for running away could be death. Paul must have been sure that Philemon would not exact such a penalty, but Onesimus may well have been frightened. Paul was not concerned for the legal rights and wrongs, but for reconciliation. Philemon and Onesimus were now brothers in Christ. But Onesimus would never be fully free until he had asked Philemon to forgive him.

Paul had to wait until Onesimus was ready for this. If Philemon had been an understanding and merciful master, Onesimus would probably not have wanted to run away. Even today, we know that highly respected Christian leaders can have blind spots when it comes to the way they treat their servants and employees, let alone their wives! Onesimus' return would give Philemon an opportunity to grow in Christian social awareness.

To smooth the way, Paul wrote this letter to Philemon. Further encouragement seems to have been given in the provision of an escort. Tychicus had been with Paul on his third missionary journey, (Acts 20:2-4) and had visited Paul in prison. Now he was returning home to Colossae, with a packet of letters to deliver.

This letter is a masterpiece of tact: that gentle consideration for people's feelings, which is an aspect of love. There are however, as we have noted earlier, occasions when an almost brutal bluntness is appropriate.

Paul introduces himself as a prisoner for Christ. He greets Philemon as a fellow worker. He also greets his family by name, and the church, meeting in his house. He speaks of his prayer for them all and of his appreciation of Philemon's ministry.

Then he makes his plea on behalf of Onesimus, in some manuscripts as an ambassador of Christ, in others, as an old man. Each would have its own special appeal. Philemon would have had a shock to read that name, Onesimus. Onesimus is now Paul's beloved child. Paul can hardly bear to part with him. He has also been so useful, giving Paul the service that Paul is sure Philemon himself would have been only too glad to give to this "poor old man in chains"!

But Paul would do nothing without Philemon's consent. So he is sending Onesimus back. If Onesimus owes anything, let Philemon regard it as a debt owed by Paul. Gently Paul reminds him that he is indebted to Paul for his own salvation! So great a debt would give Paul a right to command what he now only humbly requests. Let Philemon receive Onesimus back as if he were Paul himself.

Philemon must have been stunned. Here was Onesimus, standing on his doorstep, perhaps with Tychicus at his side! What was he to do?

To forgive Onesimus and accept him back into service might seem a reasonable option. To treat him as a brother in Christ, or as Paul himself, would create problems. How would the other slaves react? A new relationship with Onesimus would involve changes on all sides. If Philemon had not been a model master, he would now have to alter the way he treated all his slaves. Was the runaway to be favoured because he had become a Christian? That might encourage the others to become what, in India, are called *rice* Christians. It would certainly generate bad feeling. For Onesimus the problem would be that of coping with jealousy. If he now served his master with loving care, he might be accused of sucking up.

Of course Philemon could set Onesimus free. Would we recommend this treatment for prisoners converted in jail? Perhaps the best solution, the one that Paul was probably hoping for, was that Philemon would send Onesimus back to him.

Paul never taught that slavery was wrong. The Gospel provides no easy answers to social problems. But, like Jesus, he was turning accepted ways upside down. Instead of breaking down the mores of the old society, the Gospel was breaking it upwards, Godwards, propelled by the dynamic energy of the Holy Spirit.

Philippians.

The church at Philippi was special. They loved Paul very much, and showed it in their generous support. They had already sent him gifts of money while he was in Thessalonika. Now they had sent him further gifts through Epaphroditus.

He had stayed on with Paul for some time, helping him, perhaps in place of Onesimus, meeting his personal needs as well as helping to spread the Gospel. Epaphroditus had been extremely ill. He had in fact nearly died. Now he had recovered, and Paul was sending him home with a letter of thanks for the loan of his services, and for the gifts he had brought.

A second cause for this letter was news of the sad rift between two women, Euodia and Syntyche. Both of them were dedicated and experienced Gospel workers who had worked alongside Paul. Their disagreement was threatening to tear this loving church apart. It was the old old story. Wherever Satan sees the Spirit powerfully at work, he attacks, usually by stirring up division.

Again we see how gently and how wisely Paul deals with this situation. He introduces himself and Timothy as fellow servants of Christ. There is no apostolic claim of special authority as there is in his other letters. He makes no distinction between himself and his son in the faith.

He writes to the Philippians as saints, not just called to be saints, as in Romans and Corinthians. They are saints now. But not because they are faultless. The greatest saints have always been those most conscious of their sins. The Philippians are saints, as we are, because they have been set apart for God's use. How God uses them is God's business. (Rom. 9:21) To be a saint is to be a servant.

What Paul valued most was their partnership in the Gospel. Joys and sorrows were shared. They too were suffering as they shared with him in prayer. He rejoiced in them and was confident that the Spirit would bring His work in them to perfect fulfilment. His unspoken assurance is that their division will be overcome. When problems are dragging the church down, the need is not for criticism, but encouragement and hope.

Joyfully now he shares his own experience. All the bad things he is suffering are having a good effect. The whole Praetorian Guard has heard his witness to the gospel. If the circumcision Party is using his incarceration as an opportunity to preach their own version of it, Paul is still able to rejoice. One way or another, Christ is preached. Can Catholics rejoice in the success of Protestants, or Anglicans in the success of 7th Day Adventists, and vice-versa?

Nothing could stop Paul rejoicing. In Christ he can rejoice in life and death. In fact, death would be preferable, but to go on living would be more useful to them. He is confident that he will soon be released, and looks forward to visiting them again. He longs for news of their fearless and united witness; with one mind and one spirit, striving together for the Gospel. Slowly he is warming towards his theme.

What are the underlying causes of division? Theological and pastoral disagreements often conceal and are exacerbated by personality problems. Selfishness and conceit drive out love and humility, and take over control.

Paul points the Philippians to Christ, who emptied himself of glory. Becoming Man, he lived as a servant, and died an agonising and ignominious death. "Therefore", note that therefore, "God exalted him to the heights". Self-exaltation, like pride, leads to a fall. Only God can exalt. (Lk. 18:14)

Living the Christian life is hard work. Forgiveness and salvation come, it is true, not by striving, but by letting go, and trusting ourselves into the hands of God. It is only then that the striving starts. We have to work out in practice what God works within us. "Trust and obey." How often arguments and grumbling can disunite and make a job difficult, or even impossible to fulfil. The connection between such arguments and selfishness have been well illustrated in The Archers, and TV Soaps. Jesus called his disciples to be lights in the world. Such blemishes hide the light.

Then Paul rejoices in believing that his work amongst them will not be in vain. How much we depend on the trust of those we love and look up to. Paul trusted his friends, though some of them, like Demas, (2Tim. 4:10) let him down. He is sure of Timothy and of Epaphroditus. Their care for others is genuine. A church can very quickly assess whether or not their pastor really cares for them, and is not just doing "gospel work" as an extension of himself and his own ambition. Christly love is unmistakable.

"Rejoice!" This is the heart of Paul's message. Selfishness and conceit usually spring from a lack of satisfaction and true self-esteem. When God's love flows into the soul, the need for such defences ends, and with such freedom comes joy.

A brief warning is now given to beware of those preaching the necessity of circumcision. Maybe they are those to whom he has already referred. (1:16) The hearts of his friends in Philippi are already circumcised. The outward symbol of being God's People has become an inward reality.

Has it? In Paul's case, certainly, yes. In fleshly terms, Paul had a lot to boast about. He had the right racial and family background. He had had the right education. He'd held the right opinions and observed the right code of behaviour. He could boast that, on those terms, he was blameless, A-plus in all subjects! But, in Christ, he saw that all this was a pile of garbage, in other words, dung.

Starting from square one, he was growing into a greatness already given him by God. It had to be grasped by faith, obedience, and a willingness to suffer. Paul longed to share in Christ's sufferings, the pain of loving and longing for his friends' completion in Christ. He longs too for his own completion. He has not "arrived". Like an athlete, he presses on. (cp. 1Cor. 9:24-27) There is no looking back. His eyes are fixed on the goal: fullness of life in Christ.

This parallels the self-emptying and exaltation of Christ, which he has described earlier. In his letter to Philemon we see the upside-down reversal of values applied to freedom and slavery. Here we see them applied to status in a church congregation. Views commonly held on this subject, whether or not expressed, are stood on their head.

Paul dares to conclude, "Be like me". First he applies this to those whose concerns are fleshly. Then, at long last, with exquisite tact, he briefly refers to the two ladies whose quarrel helped to spark off this letter. While teaching in a College in South India, I was once faced by a problem of religious faction. Dr Max Warren, then C.M.S. General Secretary, advised me to be like a metal worker straightening out a bump in a bronze dish. "Do not bang the bump. Tap persistently all round it." That is what Paul has done.

So, back to rejoicing, trusting, thanking, and living in the peace of God. How important is this control of our thoughts and imagination. TV and the popular press flood us with so much that is ugly, unclean, and goads to greed. It is hard to switch off, and it takes a lot of determination to select programmes wisely. When we do so, we are accused of ostrich behaviour. "This is life", we are told. Yes, but it is only that part of life the advertisers choose to present. Constant loud noise deafens our ears, and the continuous confrontation with sex and violence deadens the sensitivity of our souls. We are, as we think. How important then to quieten our mind and fill our imagination with what makes for goodness and peace.

Paul ends his letter by thanking the Philippians for their gifts. His body is so disciplined that he can endure hunger and plenty alike. He has no need of gifts, but he is deeply grateful for them as tokens of their care for him, and he rejoices in their loving generosity. Paul has sublimated his natural pride, but he loves to boast of God. "My God is able to supply all your need." All God's riches are ours in Christ Jesus.

Colossians.

This epistle, with its vision of the Cosmic Christ, stands out from the other epistles, awesome, like a Colossus. Such an all-embracing view was not just Paul's invention. As we have seen earlier, he has been accused of complicating the simple gospel by imposing on it his own theology. It was when this simplicity was endangered by pagan philosophy, that the church was driven to formulate truths about Christ which were implicit, and had grown through their experience of him in their lives. In this the Holy Spirit guided them, as Jesus promised He would. (Jn. 16:13)

Paul had never visited the Colossians. The gospel had been brought to them by Epaphras. He was with Paul when this letter was written. Paul refers to him as a beloved fellow-servant and minister of Christ. In Philemon he is called a fellow prisoner. This might indicate that, like Onesimus, he was sharing Paul's confinement to meet his needs and help him proclaim the gospel.

Together with Laodicea and Hierapolis, Colossae had been recently destroyed by the earthquake of 62 AD. Maybe the fear, generated by this elemental catastrophe, encouraged the infiltration of pagan philosophy into the church.

The Greeks saw the world as threatened by the conflicting elements of earth, fire and water. Only Zeus or the Logos, could hold them together. A few years before Colossians was written, Plutarch had completed his ten books on the theories of Empedocles. According to these, souls after death ascended to the moon. They could only complete their ascension to heaven by giving back to each element what belonged to it. If they were still weighed down by earthiness, they were driven down again into the elements, or became semi-divine beings, demons, which Philo, a contemporary Jewish philosopher, interpreted as angels. These entered the shrines of the oracles, to help initiate men into the mysteries. These were the source of hidden knowledge (*gnosis*). Only by acquiring such knowledge could souls be purified and attain blessedness. This led to angel worship, and ascetic practices, especially those relating to food and sex. Synchronism with Jewish beliefs led also to stressing the importance of observing rituals and festivals. Philo complained that heathen cults were infiltrating even Jewish families.

For Christians, these beliefs obviously downgraded Christ to becoming only one among many saviours. Salvation depended, not on faith in him, but upon the possession of secret knowledge. Today, our world faces the threat of increasing violence from the elements, and even cosmic calamity from a colliding astronoid. In their insecurity, people are again turning to pagan cults, and the philosophy of eastern religions is infiltrating their thinking, and even that of some Christians. The problems of the Colossians are ours. This letter is written to us.

Greetings and Prayer. 1:1-14.

Paul's greetings and introductory prayers are always related to the people and situations he is addressing. Being personally unknown to the Colossians, he stresses his authority as an apostle. He thanks God for their faith, and the fruit it is producing. These all depend upon the security of their hope of what awaits them in heaven. It was this hope that pagan philosophy was undermining.

What a wonderful prayer follows! First Paul prays that they may be given knowledge, not the esoteric knowledge of the mystery cults, or the head knowledge of philosophy, but the knowledge of God, and of His will. (cp. 1Cor. 1:20-25) From this, a life of active service will flow naturally, bringing further experience and a yet deeper knowledge.

Paul then prays that they may be strengthened with power. Surprisingly, this is not power to overcome and destroy these elemental demons. It is power to endure with patience all attacks on their faith. How? Joyfully. Why? Because God has already qualified them for "final blessedness". They are already in Christ's Kingdom. No one has the right to rob them of their birthright. Though we, like Esau, may lose it, by preferring present gain!

Hymn of praise and acclamation. 1:15-21.

What follows is a Hymn. The J.B. translation makes its echoing strophes clear. The first, (v. 15-18a) proclaims Christ as the Image of God, the Firstborn of all Creation. All things were created through him and for him, and in him all things cohere. The terrifying forces of nature are under his control and are included within his purpose. The second strophe, (v. 18b-20) hails Christ as the Firstborn from the dead. In him God fully dwells. Through him, all things in heaven and earth are reconciled.

Some years ago a book was published entitled "Your God is too small". Today we need the challenge of "Your Christ is too small". He is more than the Jesus of Galilee, of the simple gospel, a figure-head for other men's beliefs. He is more than the risen Lord and personal Saviour, more than the Church's Head. He is also the Cosmic Christ, Teilhard de Chardin's Omega Point in which the whole creation attains its final goal.

The church very soon came to believe in the pre-existence of Christ. When Paul wrote about Christ emptying himself of glory, (Philip. 2:5-6) he was referring to an accepted belief in order to challenge his readers to practical humility. In the O.T. were promises that God Himself would come and save his people.

(Ezek. 34:15-16) Many Psalms, and Isaiah 64:1 express this longing. Paul saw God in Christ reconciling the world to Himself. (2Cor. 5:19) Christ was the New Adam, restoring what the first Adam had lost. (Rom 5:15-17. Gen. 1:27) Paul could even see Christ as active in all God's saving acts in the O.T., eg, the Rock, which, stricken, produced life-giving water, and followed them, providing continual refreshment, as the fire and cloud gave continual protection and guidance.

The cosmic Christ was a new understanding. We have already noticed the key importance of recognising Christ as the Word, and Wisdom of God, the Logos of John's Prologue. This Epistle was probably written earlier. It was the missionary urge to communicate the gospel to the Greek world that led to this breakthrough. To the Athenians, Paul had quoted Greek poets in speaking of a God in whom we live and have our being. But he could not speak of Christ in these terms until he had first preached Christ crucified and the forgiveness of sins. The philosophers of the Areopagus were not interested in or even conscious of their sins.

Which is the most difficult to believe: that God Himself was expressed in Christ crucified, or that this same Christ was His active agent in creation? Both concepts blow the mind. Yet, within an extraordinarily short time after the resurrection, the church came to believe both.

What relevance has the Cosmic Christ for us? It means we live in a purposeful universe. The changes and mutations which science describes are not merely random, or due to laws such as the survival of the fittest. Even top scientists are now conceding that the universe may be purposeful! There is a hidden dynamic that seems to work even through destruction and pain. Hindus ascribe it to the god Siva. Fires, which sweep the forests, clear the way for growth. Elemental disasters, such as earthquakes and typhoons, destroy our worldly security, giving us an opportunity to reconsider our priorities. We were not created to be comfortable. Boredom arouses destructive forces within us. Our security lies only in God.

Nature red in tooth and claw poses a problem for belief. Genesis sees it as a result of the Fall. (Gen. 1:30) Isaiah interprets it as an aspect of nature that the coming Messiah will transform. (Is. 11:1-9) Science sees it as an efficient manner of preserving life and maintaining the balance of the species. But in Christ, we see Man, as the crown of creation, willingly laying down his life for others. Sacrificial love is man's noblest attribute, the strongest power on earth, a revelation of God Himself.

Become what you are. 1:21-23.

To avoid any misunderstanding, it seems that the writer may have inserted two additions to the hymn: "the church" in verse 18, when the original may have been "the universe", and "the blood of his cross" in verse 20. The power of the cross to save is a mystery beyond our efforts to explain, but for 2000 years, countless Christians have witnessed to the life-changing experience it has brought them.

The Colossian Christians had themselves experience of this. Now they are reminded that God has reconciled them to Himself in order that they might, from now on, live lives "beautiful for God". Many think that when they've been "converted", that's it! Oh no. God has by no means completed His purpose for them. To become blameless and irreproachable, we've all got a long long way to go! How can we ever get there? The Colossians are told to hang on to their hope; to cling to it like limpets, and not get sucked away by the shifting sands of heresy. Hope is the life-line that draws us safely to shore. Hebrews compares it to an anchor. (Heb 6:19) In Philippians, Paul speaks of pressing on to the goal of the upward call of God in Christ. He wouldn't have pressed on at such a cost had he not been confident of the prize that awaited him.

Until now the church had been mostly thought of as a collection of small house churches dotted in various towns. Now a vision of a world church was emerging. To a small local church, engulfed in a sea of paganism, this must have been encouraging. Today, ageing and dwindling congregations, surrounded by a pagan culture of consumerism, must have found similar encouragement in the TV programme on the 1999 Lambeth Conference, which showed the joyous and confident faith of the overwhelming majority of bishops now coming from the younger churches of the Third World.

Suffering and striving for the Gospel. 1:24 - 2:7.

Paul frequently spoke of his sufferings, but here is something new. What did he mean by "filling up what was lacking in the sufferings of Christ"? Suffering was clearly part of his original call. (Acts 9:16) In Galatians he refers to his scars as the marks of Jesus. They were the inevitable consequence of his special mission to the Gentiles. He could rejoice in suffering, for, in his weakness, God revealed His strength. This was a comfort he could share with others. (2Cor. 1:3-6) It formed a bond of fellowship with them.

In Philippians Paul spoke of his longing to share in the sufferings of Christ. But how could he fill them up? There was an idea that, before Christ's return, a fixed amount of suffering had to be endured by the church. A hint of this can perhaps be found in the cry of the martyrs. (Rev. 9:1-11) Stated baldly this is far too simplistic. However it is possible to see Christ still suffering in his Body, the church. Paul might see his own suffering as an extension of Christ's own. Jesus never experienced shipwreck or stoning. When people ask "Where was God when His people were perishing in Belsen?", the answer is, "There, suffering with them".

Part of Paul's burden was due to his continuing care for the churches. Preaching the Gospel wasn't enough. How many Missions have failed through lack of proper follow-up? But to become what we are, to grow from babyhood to maturity, what more do we need other than hope? (cp. 1Cor. 3:1-3)

The answer lies in the revelation of God's mystery. Unlike the Orphic mysteries, here lay real power. The Old Testament prophets had longed to see it. (Lk. 10:23-24) Now it was revealed to Jew and Gentile alike. Its influence was seen in the "riches of glory" already transforming the lives of the Gentiles. It was the mainspring of Paul's own life. "Christ in you, the hope of glory."

Later, Paul speaks of being "in Christ". Can these two experiences, like two hands clasped together, be distinguished? Comparison of the texts where they are used indicate that they can. The indwelling Christ is sometimes synonymous with the Holy Spirit. The emphasis is individual and related to personal growth. Being "in Christ" is used four times more often. It involves us in community, and is what unites the church. We can't be Christians on our own. An isolated ember soon dies. Even the enclosed contemplative prays as a member of the church, and for the church. Those isolated by circumstance, the sick and those imprisoned for their faith, rely on such prayer.

The church is divided, so are congregations. Life together is not always either easy or comfortable. Only in Christ can the church find its unity; not in definitions of credal statements, not in constitutions, though these may have their place, nor in hived-off groups of the like-minded. It is God in Christ who reconciles us to each other, and commissions us to proclaim the gospel of reconciliation by demonstrating it. (2Cor 5:19-20. 1:21) When we concentrate our energies on caring for our neighbours and sharing the gospel with them, our differences tend to fade in importance. Inward looking societies tear themselves to pieces.

How to refute false teaching. 2:8 - 3:4.

First, don't let anyone downgrade you. With Christ within you, you are Victors not Victims. The bonds of our sinful indebtedness, together with the legal demands of the Law, have been cancelled on the cross. The cost of debt cancellation falls on the one to whom it is owed, as the EU Nations know only too well! Christ has freed us from the domination of every hostile power. He has disarmed them. (Matt. 10:28. Heb. 13:6) They are like conquered prisoners, displayed to public humiliation, chained to the tail of a Roman triumphal procession.

Secondly, don't let anyone disqualify you. Alas, Christians are continually doing this to one another. There are also forms of self-abasement that minister to pride rather than humility, and spiritual experience that can puff up. These pander to our sensuality and divide the church. It is Christ who nourishes us and knits us together. So don't let arguments about what the joints and ligaments represent divide us further!

Seek and set your minds on things of the Spirit. Techniques of prayer can help us, but beware lest they become another form of bondage!

Hold only to Christ. He lifts us up, with himself, into God. Our real life remains hidden there, until with Christ, we will reappear in glory! How's that for a hope to hold on to!

Some practical advice. 3:5-17.

Meanwhile, we come down to earth with a bump; meanwhile, we are to put to death what is earthly. Two lists of sins are given. The first are those of generally recognised "badness" that "respectable people" would turn their back on, let alone God! (cp. Rom. 1:18) The second group of five are sins that destroy community. In some of these even "good" church folk sometimes indulge. These must be "put away". Having "put off" the old nature, don't go on doing the things that belong to it.

Instead "put on" the virtues belonging to the new nature. These will unite people of every race, class and status. Another list of five is given. They are clearly seen in the picture of Jesus given us in the gospels. Added is forgiveness, without which life in a community can become hell on earth. A Christian, who, for a time, tried living in a Hindu Ashram, told me that the leaders were continually suffering breakdown. This seemed to be the result of their monist philosophy, which denies the existence of sin. This makes any admission of fault and the receiving and giving of forgiveness impossible.

Love alone keeps community life healthy, and the virtues listed above, which spring from it, can't be produced by conscious effort. They are fruits of the Spirit that grow naturally out of a life lived in Christ. (Jn. 15:5) What a lovely picture of such a Christian community is given in verses 15-17. Renewal in the church always leads to an outpouring of new songs.

A Household Code. 3:18 - 4:1.

Virtues and graces need to be translated into practice in all our relationships. Social codes already existed. The tiny minority of Christians had to accept the existing structures and transform them from within, the Spirit acting as leaven.

Codes regulating Greek society appear in the writings of Aristotle and Plutarch. Jewish practices were based on the Law of Moses and the Talmud. Jesus, in his teaching, had provided a set of principles by which to interpret them. Directed towards Jewish society, they also applied to the Greeks. It took time for Christians to work this application out. We see Paul struggling with this in his first letter to the Corinthians.

Here, in this letter to the Colossians, we find the first Christian Household Code. Others follow. (cp. Eph. 5:21-6:6. 1Peter 2:18-3:7. Titus 2:1-10) One big difference between these Christian codes and the others is that the latter were addressed solely to men. It was a Male-dominated Society. In Christ, women, children and slaves, all are equally important. The problem was, then and now, how to give appropriate expression to this in a society in which the structures deny it, and where such equality, even when accepted in principle, is interpreted in purely spiritual terms.

Women are to obey their husbands "as is fitting in the Lord". What does this caveat imply? We have already noted Paul's concern that their new freedom should not give rise to public scandal. Husbands are to love their wives. The word used is "agape", the selfless caring for the good of the other, which is described in 1 Corinthians 13. This would totally transform any marital relationship.

Children are to obey their parents. Nothing new here. But Fathers are told not to provoke them to anger. The reason given is interestingly modern. Nothing arouses resentment so much as a continual put-down. Children thrive on encouragement and on being shown respect.

The main emphasis is on the relationship of masters and slaves. In view of the arrival of Onesimus, this is hardly surprising. Slaves are to obey, but to think of their service as service to Christ. Then, like Onesimus, they would discover a glad willingness to give of their best, springing from inner freedom and a new self-respect. Bad work and bad treatment will come under equal judgement from the One who is no respecter of persons! So Masters are to act justly. Christ is their Master. Let them learn from him how to exercise their mastership. Thus, without either revolution or legal change, the upside-down principles of Jesus are set to undermine and alter the unjust structures of society.

Last words and greetings. 4:2-18.

Finally Paul calls them all to prayer and thanksgiving. He asks them to pray for him that he may be given opportunities to preach the gospel with clarity. Clarifying one's thoughts to oneself is only half the battle. Difficulty lies with making them clear to those whose thought-world and experiences are totally different. I remember a Hindu lady trying to convince me that there was no real difference between her beliefs and mine. She used all the Christian words but meant something quite different by them. It made me more conscious than ever of the different worlds in which we lived. Here, today, the thought-world of Buddhism is less foreign than that of the church. We have to listen to others with a lot of patience and a will to understand, if we are to find a way to bridge the gap. Concern and respect for the person addressed is as important as the message we want to give. It is in fact part of the message.

The Colossians are also called to use every opportunity to witness to their neighbours. Their problem of communication would be less than ours, for they had only recently come from being one amongst them. It is often the quality of loving relationships within a Christian home that first attracts and arouses interest in the gospel. Different translations of verse 6 make interesting comparison: "seasoned with salt" (RSV), "tact flavoured with wit" (JB), "pleasant and interesting" (GNB). All stress the need to tune in to individual listeners.

Those who send greetings are the same as those mentioned in Philemon, with the addition of Justus, about whom we know nothing. Archippus is called to be faithful in his ministry as an Elder. Had he been slack, and perhaps fearful of speaking out boldly against the Colossian heresy?

The letter was brought to Colossae by Tychicus, who accompanied Onesimus. Presumably the delivery of Paul's letter to Philemon, and the reconciliation of master and slave would have taken place before this letter was read out to the church. The introduction of Onesimus as a faithful and beloved brother must have caused quite a sensation. How would we react to a similar situation? The teaching given in 1:21-22 and 3:10-15 would have certainly faced a practical and searching test. Note that the church was told to pass this letter on to the church in Laodicea, and to read a letter that the Laodiceans would have sent on to them. Sadly, this letter has not survived.

Paul's authorship of Colossians has been questioned by many reputable bible scholars. Their main reasons relate to differences of content and style. Other scholars reject their arguments and ordinary readers can be upset by this uncertainty. Critical problems are not part of my brief, and I keep an open mind. The importance of this wonderful letter does not lie in its author but in its content. Its authenticity has been sealed by the Holy Spirit in the experience of the church.

Ephesians

Ephesians has been called the crown of Paul's epistles. It is the culmination of all his teaching. If Colossians, with its view of the Cosmic Christ, blows the mind, Ephesians, with its panoramic view of God's Plan of Salvation, lifts the heart to awe and wonder.

Like a crown, it is packed with jewels. In the first 14 verses the writer tries to convey this with words like "riches" and "lavish". He multiplies and duplicates words, "wisdom and insight", "will and purpose". Tightly packed, these verses, read as prose, are hard to digest. Rewrite them as a hymn of praise, as I once tried to do, and it sings.

A Song of Praise. 1:3-14.

"Blessed be God". This is a typically Jewish introduction to prayer. All the blessings that follow come to us through Christ. Verse 3 provides a chorus to sing after each of the six verses that follow.

Note in verse 3 the expression "heavenly places". It appears in four other places. (1;20. 2:6. 3:10. 6:12) In early days, Heaven was thought of in spatial terms, as "up there". Despite the imagery of some hymns, not even children would think like that today. Gregorin's claim that his space flight had proved God's non-existence, was childish atheist propaganda. Heaven is a dimension of Spirit.

We will now look at the six blessings:

1. We have been chosen, not at our baptism or conversion, not even in our mother's womb, before we were born. (cp Jer. 1:5) God chose us in Christ, before the

world began! The perfection of our loving relationship with Him was the purpose of His whole creation! ! Note the revision of the R.S.V by the J.B. and N.E.B. which add "love" to verse 4, in line with the R.S.V. footnote.
2. We too are destined to be "sons of God". The Spirit within us inspires us to call God "Abba", the equivalent of a child's "Daddy". No other religion offers such a tender and intimate relationship with the Almighty. We can approach Him with the confidence of beloved children. What a privilege!
3. All our past sins have been written off, like a cancelled debt. We are released from the fears that bind us and the bad habits that enslave. We can walk free, given the desire and faith to do so.
4. In Christ, God has revealed yet another mystery. In Colossians this mystery was "Christ in you, the hope of glory". Here it is "Christ in whom all things, both on earth and in heaven, are brought into perfect unity". In Christ, through the Spirit, we are drawn into the oneness of the Holy Trinity. Rublev's icon helps us to contemplate the wonder of this.
5. Our life is given a purpose: to live to the praise of God's glory. What gives meaning to our life? Our family and friends? Our job? What happens when we lose them? When life has lost its meaning people drift into depression. Often they seek refuge in drink or drugs. Here is a purpose that will stick with us to the end of this life, and beyond. It's final fulfilment is sure.
6. We are sealed with the Spirit. These wonderful things seem too good to be true. We are horribly aware of our faults, inadequacies and miniscule faith. The Spirit is God's down payment, His guarantee, that this glorious inheritance is truly ours.

For all this, "Blessed be God", Halleluia!

Paul's First Prayer. 1:15-23.

It is one thing to read about these wonderful things, it is quite another to grasp them and make them part of our experience. It is possible to study theology and remain spiritually as blind as a bat. So Paul first prays that God will give his readers a spirit of wisdom; to know all that He has revealed, not just with their heads but with their hearts. Above all, God wants them to know Him, love Him and desire Him for Himself, and not just the gifts He offers.

What are these gifts? Top of the list comes Hope, not our assurance of it, but what it consists of. Endlessly playing harps and singing hymns is not a very attractive hope for the non-musical! We can't picture life after death. All we know is that we shall be with Christ.

Paul also wants them to know what a glorious inheritance is theirs. All the blessings given in the past to the Jewish nation, are now theirs, as well as all the blessings given them in Christ. Added are all the blessings promised them in the future. Riches indeed!

Thirdly Paul wants them to know the greatness of God's power. Revealed in Christ's resurrection, it is available for them, to work through them. Again, this isn't head knowledge. It is to be the knowledge of their experience.

Christ is Lord both of this world and the next. All things are under his control. Are they? It doesn't look like it. National and economic forces that dominate our lives don't seem to be under his control. To be honest, not even the church, or we ourselves, always show convincing signs of it! Christ chooses to wait for our willing consent. Though all things have been put under his feet, he will not tread them down arbitrarily until the Day of Final Reckoning. But the question boomerangs, Christ is the Head of the Church. We, as members of his Body, are called to assert his sovereignty over all rival powers, human and demonic. But, another awesome but, Christ's power is that of sacrificial love. We are empowered to assert his sovereignty, using only the methods he himself demonstrated.

The gift of New Life. Chapter 2.

In chapter 1 we were given a panoramic view of God's Plan of Salvation. Now, in chapter 2, we have a close-up of what it means, first as individuals, and than as a community. For individuals, it is "Life from the dead". That is what it feels like, especially for those whose conversion is sudden. "Life from the dead" is what in fact it is. Fleshly sins of self-indulgence, and the still more dangerous sins of the mind, pride and self-will, these dull the conscience and blot out God, leaving our spirits to wither and die. Note the change of pronoun. The writer is equally involved. So are we. It is not just our animal nature and human desires that lead us astray. We are pressured by society and by active forces of evil.

Rationalism led to the denial that such evil powers exist. Only primitive people, we presume, still fear and seek to placate the spirits, which they think can affect their lives for good or evil. But don't we too? Who doesn't touch wood, and avoid the number 13? Notice the way house numbers omit it. I rejoiced that mine was No. 13. It made a good talking point! Superstitious practices abound and are widely practised, though we laugh them off. They include the consulting of stars. Belief in the occult is returning. We need not fear evil powers, but we should be aware, and on our guard against them. Never play with them! Evil powers even invade our "heavenly places." (6:12) The closer we come to God, the more dangerous their attack.

"Children of wrath." Is God angry with us? Julian of Norwich, in her Revelations, saw no anger in God. Evil harms and destroys us. Of course God is against it. When we choose to do wrong, we turn our back on God. Then we think that God has turned His back on us. The feeling is the same, not the fact.

With Christ, God has raised us from the dead. Looking back over their past, many declare that they'd been "dead" all their lives. New life dawns. The grass is greener, bird song is sweeter. Joy brings new energy. Notice again the piling on of words, "rich in mercy", "immeasurable riches of grace". We are raised up to sit with God in "heavenly places". This isn't just an after-death experience. It is a spiritual relationship joyously experienced now. We are to see the future moving towards us bringing ever new blessings in Christ. This isn't mere optimism. It is "blessed assurance". It puts a song in our hearts and a desire to share the good news with others. We see all this in the joyous and courageous witness of Christians in the young churches of the 3rd world, and in many converts in our own society. If we lack this joy, what's gone wrong? Has conventional "tribal" christianity inoculated us against an experience of the real thing? Have we been short-changed? Or are we afraid to claim, or even acknowledge, all the riches that are ours in Christ?

Verses 8-10 contain the Gospel according to Paul, in a nutshell. The Gospel is pure gift. Those who try and earn salvation either suffer continual insecurity about attaining it, or become smug like Jack Horner, or, worse, like those Pharisees who opposed Jesus, become blinded by spiritual pride. (Jn. 9:41)

Someone once said to me "God has given you faith. Lucky you. He hasn't given it to me." That, for her, seemed to end the matter. Was it a cop out? Did she really want the gift of faith? Scientists take risks, testing out their theories with experiments. Faith isn't irrational, but reason can take us only so far. Finally we have to take a jump of faith, invite Christ into our lives, and take an active step of obedience. Faith is a gift, but it is by taking such active steps that we claim it, It isn't a one-off experience. We have to keep taking such jumps of faith. Each time we land on solid rock, we are encouraged to take the next jump. But it is never easy. Such jumps of obedience lead us to discover the Rock of our security. (Matt. 7:24)

So what about good works? We aren't saved by them. We are saved to do them. Salvation isn't a selfish preoccupation. We are saved to be members of

Christ's Body; to continue his ministry of love and service in the world. When individual Christians are alive, the church is alive. This is seen in the quality of their life together.

From verse 11, Paul now addresses the Gentile Christians as a group. They too are to remember their past. This will increase their wonder at their new relationship with Jews within the new community of the church.

Gentiles had been "outsiders". The Covenants and Promises had been made with the Jews not them. (Gen. 12:1-3. Ex. 19:3-6) They were excluded from the Kingdom of the Messiah. They were excluded from being a chosen people, not just by their lack of physical circumcision, but by the Law. Like the Berlin wall, it shut them out. To cross it meant death, as Paul knew only too well. (Acts 21:27-33)

Had they indeed no God, no hope in this world? At that time no other nation had a firm belief in One Creator God. No other had more than a shadowy conception of life after death. Even for Jews, belief in a resurrection was fairly new. Significantly, it was their belief in God's justice, coupled with their experience of martyrdom during the persecution of Antiochus Epiphanes, that led them to this assurance. God's character demanded it.

Lacking such belief, the Greeks sought comfort and meaning in sensuality, or in the stoic courage of Bertrand Russell's "Foundation of despair". Today, such despair has led to a soaring rate of mental breakdown, suicide, and a desperate need for belonging.

In Christ, the Wall of the Law had broken down. For Law, he had substituted Love. It was this that led to his rejection. He was cast out of the city, and put to death in the manner of one whom the Law had cursed. (Gal 3:13. cp. Deut. 21:23) On the cross, both the power of sin and the Law were broken. Jew and Gentile, equal as forgiven sinners, found themselves, not only reconciled to God, but to each other, united in the new life they now shared. As at Antioch, where this breakthrough first occurred, their neighbours must have been astonished. "See how the Christians love one another!" Within the recent charismatic revival many have found a similar joy in the breaking down of barriers between Catholics and Protestants, and Black and White Christians. The barriers were not so much broken down as swamped and submerged by the rising tide of the Spirit.

Stones can be laid. People have to allow themselves to be laid, and built together. Even those whose lives have been radically changed by their conversion, find this hard. Learning to live together takes a long time, a life-time of growing in maturity. The Spirit chips away at our sharp edges. His love smoothes and cements us together.

Such a unity is learnt first in the family, or in small communities. Then it spreads outward to extend world-wide. Today, rapid mobility and a shifting population creates problems for all communities, not just those of the church. Air travel and telecommunications may help, but they can't provide a substitute. The problem is only now beginning to be realised and, in a few places, addressed.

Paul and the Gospel. 3:1-13.

Paul now speaks of his own role. He was a prisoner "of" Christ. (Not "for". The R.S.V. has been corrected by later translations eg. J.B., N.E.B. and G.N.B.) Christ captivated Paul on the Damascus road, and later called him to proclaim the gospel to the Gentiles. (Acts 22:17-21) The Gentiles were now co-heirs with the Jews in all the O.T. Promises. They were co-members with them in Christ's Body. They were co-sharers in the future glory promised in Christ. This was a unique insight. Later the other apostles came to share it, but, so long as they themselves felt bound by the Law and its food regulations, full integration with Gentile Christians remained difficult.

A similar problem arose in S. India. Even today, some caste Christians object to taking communion from the same cup as Dalits. Some even built separate churches. Apartheid separated the churches in South Africa. Even in England, Black and White Christians are far from integration. It isn't just style of worship that keeps them apart.

The mystery of God's Plan was even greater than this new status as God's children. From now on, as members of Christ's Body, they were to be the means of making God's glory known to the principalities and powers in the heavenly places. These are the forces that claim men's prior allegiance. They take many forms: nationalism, consumerism, addiction. The witness is to be that of an united church, taking an united stand against them. Only in such unity can the church fulfil its mission of witness to the world.

In witnessing, the church will, like Paul, share Christ's sufferings. They are to be bold. All God's resources, everything they need, is available to them, through faith in Christ.

Paul's Second Prayer. 3:14-21.

The first generation of Christians were dying off. In verse 15 we get the first reference to God's other family in heaven. This points to a dawning belief in the communion of saints.

If the Church is to engage in such a mission, each member is going to need the inner strength that only the Spirit can give. So, in this second prayer Paul prays that the Spirit, who is Christ within them, may be given a permanent home in their hearts. He is not a visitor, to be confined to a front parlour. As a loved elder brother, he is to be given free run of the whole house, and the authority to take charge. We aren't perfect. Sometimes we may not obey. We may even hide from him. But, so long as there are no locked doors, he will find us. Then Paul prays that, with such inner security, "deep roots and firm foundations", they may take into themselves, with Christ, his deep and all embracing love. As the fullness of God was expressed in Christ, so, through Christ, it may now be expressed in his Church.

That's enough to take our breath away. "It's too much! Paul is making it up. Give us back the simple gospel, which we can cut down to size." But it was Jesus who said, "You must be perfect as your Father in Heaven is perfect." We can't shake that off!

These verses are not only the high point of the letter, but the crowning peak of God's Plan of Salvation which forms the theme of the whole Bible. We must keep our eyes on the top. "O God of hope, Let us die climbing." (A Carmichael)

Paul ends his prayer with an ascription of praise. This wonderful God is able to do far far more, the Greek is emphatic, than we dare ask or even imagine. He wants to do great things through us, if only we will let Him. What He longs for above all, is not songs of praise, but glory, radiating from a loving, united and obedient church. This is the praise that Paul, in faith, offers Him on our behalf.

Building up the Body. 4:1-16.

How is the church to grow to maturity and fulfil its high calling? First, by being united.

The J.B.'s translation of verse 2 is a lovely introduction to this. "Bear with one another charitably, with complete selflessness, gentleness and patience." Instead of looking at the things that divide, look at those that unite us. In at least six basics we are already one. Ponder them. (4:1-6) Aren't they enough? Must we do to them what the scribes did to the Ten Commandments of Moses; interpret, expand and apply them with such detail and rigidity, that they divide rather than unite?

Secondly, we grow by sharing our gifts. Verse 8 is either a deliberate or an inspired misquotation of Psalm 68:18!

The short list of gifts given here (cp 1Cor. 12. Rom. 12) are those that pertain to leadership. The A.V. put a comma after "saints". (v. 12) The result was to imply that all that follows is the work of the clergy. Pew members are left with only a passive role. This reflected the situation at the time when the translation was made. Greek has no comma, and later translations have omitted it. This has transformed the attitude of the clergy to the members of their congregations. The clergy are to draw out of their people the gifts the Spirit has given them. No one is without a gift. They are given to all. It is the laity who are to serve their neighbours, share the gospel with them, and draw those who respond into the fellowship of the church as active members. Christians, trained to evangelise and teach others, are not likely to be led astray by sectarian teaching and heresy, whether by 1st century Gnostics or present-day Jehovah's Witnesses and Mormons.

It isn't easy to hold together love and truth. Without love, evangelism can degenerate into scalp-hunting, or pew-filling. Without truth, both our gospel and our service descend into wishy-washy sentiment. To hold back from sharing the gospel when opportunities are given us, is to fail both in truth and love.

Catholics, Protestants and Pentecostals have each a vital contribution to make. Church, Bible and Spirit must be held in balance, or there is distortion. Similarly, every individual is needed to contribute their special gifts. Christ as Head of the Body, sends the signals that maintain the unity and coordination of all the members. In this, the sinews and ligaments are important. Discussing them in Colossians, I warned against arguments about who or what they represent. But there are people, like Barnabas, who seem to have a special gift of encouragement and of keeping people together.

New Clothes for Old. 4:17-32.

Now we come down to the nitty-gritty. As already noticed, the background of these Gentile Christians was one of unlimited sexual licence. In Romans 1:18-24 the same sins are listed as shown here. In Romans however Paul wrote that "God gave them up to do them". This was a typically Jewish way of expressing God's ultimate responsibility for evil. Gentile Christians would have misunderstood. Here we read that "they gave themselves up". The two are not incompatible.

Note in verse 21 how the name of Jesus stands out. "Christ" can sound conveniently abstract and morally vague. Jesus, in his life and teaching, presents a specific challenge. No wonder that films are now presenting us with a distorted Jesus, whose attitudes to sex are dragged down to the level of our own society.

Like Colossians, Ephesians speaks of the New Life in terms of putting on new clothes. The old clothes listed here are the sins that destroy community. Lying especially destroys the mutual trust upon which every community is built. Anger shakes it, but is recognised here both as a sin and an emotion. In close family relationships, it may be better to "have it out" than leave it to smoulder as resentment that piles up and corrodes. There is also a place for righteous anger. Jesus himself showed it. It is a reaction to hypocrisy and to injustice done to the poor and under-privileged. It is totally non-selfregarding. Those who claim it can easily kid themselves in this respect.

Stealing and scrounging are also to be "put off", together with the greed of "I want, I must have because I'm worth it" of the TV Ads. Instead, put on honest work and generosity. Paul set a good example in this. (2Thess. 3:7-8)

Also put off unkind gossip, sly criticism of people behind their backs. Like Barnabas, be an encourager. Living in a community, where an ethos of mutual appreciation has been created by a few resident Sisters, I know what a binding influence this can be.

The Holy Spirit is resident among us. When we flout His gentle pressures He grieves. We have a tender-hearted God. So, despite, or even because of our faults, we need to be tender-hearted towards each other. The Greek word for "kind" is *chrestos*, which also means a "yoke". The yoke of Christos fits kindly on our necks, easing our relationships and enabling us to pull together.

Walking Together. 5:1-20.

Being yoked to another affects the way we walk. That, we can understand. But "Be imitators of God"! What are we to make of that? Paul told the Corinthians to be imitators of him, as he was of Christ. (1Cor. 11:1) Jesus not only imitated God himself, he told us to do the same. (Jn. 5. 19. Matt. 5:44-48) We are called to be, in common parlance, the image of our Father, especially in caring for everybody, good and bad, friend and foe: no snobbery, or racism, no "them" and "us". Loving doesn't depend on liking. We are called to walk in love.

We are also called to walk in the light. It comes as a shock to find ourselves back in the sordid sins of the flesh. Gnostic permissiveness was by now probably such a threat to the life of the church that this teaching needed ramming home. Today, Hindu Rishis, popularized in the west, offer spiritual experience through yogic exercises, often coupled with drugs and promiscuous sex. Many caught up in this dangerous mixture have, sadly, experienced the natural "retribution" of disillusionment and HIV. It is a Darkness. We are children of Light and must live as such.

Thirdly, we are to walk wisely. Life is short. There is a lot of evil around, but opportunities of doing good are given us. Don't miss them. We need prayerful consideration to discern them, otherwise good intentions can lead us to rush off in all directions, or crash in like a bull in a china shop.

Wisdom is a gift of the Spirit. He is to intoxicate us. This is what is prayed for in the Anima Christi. It means being lifted by Him beyond our own control. This doesn't mean spiritual hysteria, which is what many fear may result from charismatic revival. We are to be blown into the control of the Spirit of order. (1Cor. 14:33) We need to be topers, with an unquenchable thirst for God. Drunkards are matey. They are joyful and given to song, until the inevitable hangover flattens them. God's topers also love to be together and to sing. But their joy is lasting and leaves no hangover!

A problem arises in verse 20. It is almost a copy of Colossians. There it says "Do everything giving thanks". As with 4:8 we may ask if this is a misquotation or a deliberate change. I incline to the latter belief. We can give thanks in every situation, but can we always give thanks for it? Not at the time perhaps. But, like the patriarch Joseph, (Gen. 45:5) and, in our own day, people like Terry Waite, we can often give thanks afterwards. It is in our worst experiences that we learn most about God's love for us.

Another Household Code. 5:21 - 6:9.

This new way of living affects all our relationships. This, and the earlier Code in Colossians, spells out how they are to be worked out in the existing society. We cannot lay them down as rules for our own very different one, but the principles on which they are based were given us by Jesus.

The first most important principle is that all are to be servants of all. Jesus himself set this pattern. (Jn. 13:13-17) A comparison is made between the way Christ loves the church and the way a man should love his wife. It includes care and protection but retains his headship. However the comparison becomes complex and the writer finally returns to basic simplicity. Note just two points: the unity of body, mind, and spirit, found in a truly happy and life-long marriage, not only fulfils God's purpose, but provides a training ground for the building blocks of a congregation. Also, here is the first portrayal of the church as the Bride of Christ. It is presaged in the O.T. (Hosea 2:16) It culminates in the Vision of the Holy City. (Rev. 21:9-10) It has coloured our interpretation of Psalm 45:10-17, and the Song of Songs.

Compared with Colossians' Code, fathers are given extra responsibilities. They are to discipline and teach their children. Jewish fathers had always done this. Greeks left it to slaves. Our society leaves it to the schools. The result is disastrous.

The 5th Commandment is quoted to the children. In the light of Jesus' rebuke to the Pharisees, (Matt. 15:4-5) this must include grown-up children. They are given responsibility for their aged parents. Today, the abandonment of the elderly to state relief and loneliness has raised many problems for our society. Glimpses of what we miss can be seen in what remains of the warmth and unity of Asian families living in our midst.

Slaves are to look on service to their masters as service to Christ. Slaves were mostly either captured in war, or sold to pay off debts. Many were educated men and skilled craftsmen. Such an attitude would restore their dignity and self-respect. What is new is that their masters are to behave in the same way to their slaves. Mutual respect, treating a slave as if he were Christ! Threats would be unthinkable. Courteous request and appreciation would become the order of the day. It would probably be also more rewarding! In all these relationships God shows no regard for status. All are equally important and precious to Him. Talents and types of service may differ. Faithfulness is awarded equal praise. (Matt. 25:19-23) This is a recipe for a silent social revolution.

The Armour of God. 6:10-20.

"Finally," - this is Paul's last word - "be strong in the Lord". In the Greek it is "be made strong". A sense of helpless inadequacy is OK. In fact it is an advantage. It throws us back on God.

We are engaged in spiritual warfare, splendidly portrayed in C.S.Lewis' Adventures of Narnia. To be a Christian, is to be enlisted in God's army. Unlike Dad's, it has a splendid Commander who provides his soldiers with all they need by way of equipment. It enables them to beat off attack, hold their position and advance in counter attack. The enemy is wily. He infiltrates behind our lines. He gulls us into attacking him in the wrong place. He lulls us into a false sense of security and then launches a lightning strike. Most dangerous of all, he appears as a friend; as Lucifer - Pride disguised as an Angel of Light.

We need to keep our armour polished, and to put it on every day. Like Nehemiah, be always at the ready. (Neh. 4:10-23) One lady I knew, first thing every morning prayed on her armour, piece by piece, miming it as she did so. Let the Spirit pray in us as we react to the day's events. Let us also pray for our fellow Christians, especially for those persecuted because of their courageous witness.

The Blessing. 6:21-23.

This contains all Paul's favourite words; peace, love, faith, and grace, through which the others are all poured out. It ends with a surprising twist. Surely it is God's love for us that is undying. Yes, but here it is ours for him. The grace to love God with undying constancy, is the greatest gift of all.

Paul's authorship of Ephesians has also come into doubt. Many reasons are the same, but there are others. Paul knew the Ephesians so well. Why then are there no personal messages? In the oldest manuscripts, Ephesus is not mentioned, yet without it, there is an awkwardness as if a space had been left, rather like Dear - . The letter may have been meant for circulation. The passage commending Tychicus is lifted from Colossians. (Col. 4:7-8)

Other reasons for doubt are harder to explain. It seems to have been written at a later date. Christ's return is no longer imminent, so the attitude to marriage has changed. (cp 1Cor. 7:26-31) Also Gentile circumcision is no longer an issue. Yet it is a truly Pauline letter containing the crème-de-la-crème of his thought and writing. Its emphasis on the central importance of the church in God's cosmic plan of salvation has caused it to become a central reference point for Christian leaders of different churchmanship in today's ecumenical debate. So let us read it as God's Word for us today.

Summary

In these letters themes and phrases used in Romans reappear. There is, for example, the insistence that we are saved by grace not works, (Eph. 2:8-9) and the call to "set your mind on", and to "put on" virtues. (Col. 3:2, 9-12)

There is also development of thought. Paul the prisoner has much to say about suffering. It is a sharing in the sufferings of Christ which Paul counts as a privilege. He also rejoices that he is suffering for the sake of the church. In

Colossians this is developed into the thought that, in such suffering, he is completing what is lacking in Christ's sufferings. This takes us out into a wider stretch of water.

Another theme is reconciliation. In Philemon, this is between master and slave, in Philippians between two church workers, and in Ephesians between Jews and Gentiles who are reconciled to each other by the cross. (Eph. 2:14-16) In Colossians the whole of creation, both in heaven and on earth is reconciled to Christ through his cross. (Col. 1:20)

There is also an emerging doctrine of Christ. In Philippians we meet the doctrine of *Kenosis,* ie "emptying". Christ laid aside his glory to be born as man, live as a servant and die on a cross. This became the foundation of a doctrine of the Incarnation. In Colossians the doctrine of the Cosmic Christ became a basis for countering gnostic teaching that was becoming a growing danger for the church. In Ephesians, Christ is seen in relation to his church, the Body of which he is the Head, a Temple for which he is the Corner Stone, and citizens of a Kingdom of which he is the King. There is also, perhaps, a foretaste of the Bride that he takes to wife.

Three of these letters contain beautiful prayers that Paul prays for his friends. They also contain fragments of hymns. These may include Philippians 2:5-11. In the following chapters we shall see how both a creed and a liturgy slowly came into being as churches continued to be linked to each other by apostolic letters and visits.

Questions for private meditation

1. How do you relate to those who serve you, eg. in shops etc.? (Philemon)

2. Are there any fellow Christian you can't get on with? What can you do about it? (Philippians 4:2-4)

3. Are you still able to rejoice when things are going wrong? (Philippians 1:18 & 4:4-20)

4. Has Humanist or Oriental philosophy any influence on your life? Think through these influences with Christ.

5. How do you relate to the different members of your family. How central is Christ in this? (Colossians 3)

6. How important is it for you to be comfortable?

7. Ponder on the 6 blessings that are yours in Christ. (Ephesians 1:3-14)

8. In this age of doubt, what "blessed assurance" do you have? (Ephesians 1)

9. What sharp edges does the Spirit need to chip away to fit you together with others as stones in Christ's Temple? (Ephesians 2:19-22)

10. Put on the whole Armour of God prayerfully, piece by piece. (Ephesians 6:10-18)

Questions for group discussion

1. Should the church be involved in changing the structures of society? If so in what way? (Philemon)

2. Why does Paul call the Philippians "saints"? Are all Christians saints?

3. How appropriate is Paul's warning in Colossians 2:8 for us today?.

4. As our behaviour results from our desires, how can the Church influence people's desires Godwards? (Colossians 3:1-4)

5. Try to draw up a Christian Household Code appropriate for today.

6. How do you answer the problem of the destructive forces of Nature?

7. As spiritual millionaires, why do we seem so impoverished? (Ephesians 1)

8. How can we increase our faith? (Ephesians 3 & 4)

9. How can you and all the members of your church be more closely built together ?

10. What experience has your church of spiritual warfare? In view of the rise of Satanism and occult sects, what training is needed to counter them? (Ephesians 6:10-20)

Chapter 10

After the Apostles

By the end of the sixties, the Church was moving into a new situation. Its three most important leaders were dead. In AD 62 James, leader of the Church in Jerusalem, was stoned to death. Some time during the reign of Nero, 64-67, Paul was beheaded and Peter crucified. Without these "pillars", how would the Church be supported?

One way was to continue their teaching through letters that seemed to bear their authority. We have already seen that this may have begun in the writing of the Epistles to the Colossians and Ephesians. At the time, this was a widely used and acceptable practice. We mustn't judge it according to our modern ideas of copyright. What mattered was that the content of these letters should be true to the Gospel originally preached by the Apostles, yet adapted to meet the needs of the present.

Thus we meet letters purporting to be written by Peter, James, Jude and John. In our Bible they are arranged in order of length. Here we shall comment on them, partly in order of their possible dating and partly in the development of their teaching.

The first epistle of Peter.

What a lovely warm and personal letter! Scholars differ, and, despite what has been said above, many believe that Peter was its author. Eusebius, Bishop of Caesarea and church historian, 260-340 AD, claimed that Peter's authorship was never in dispute. The date of 1 Peter could then be early AD 63-64. The doxology of 4:11 seems to end the letter. 4:12-5:11 partly recoups previous points and seems to refer to a later time when persecution was more serious. It ends with a similar doxology and could have been added later. The final verses refer to Babylon, often used as a code name for Rome, and to Mark, known to be there at the time. (Philemon v. 23) The debate continues. We can keep an open mind and concern ourselves with the letter's contents.

It is written to Christians in Asia Minor. Most of them seem to be converts from paganism, who are facing some kind of persecution. They are perplexed by their suffering. Why is this happening to them? How are they to cope with it? This letter brings them encouragement and wise advice.

"Blessed be God." It was customary to start a letter with thanksgiving. In these circumstances it might sound like "Praise the Lord anyhow!" It is far more than that. Every sentence brings reassurance, seven joyful facts to hang on to. Note the pile-up of words like imperishable, kept, guarded.

Privileged People. 1:10 - 2:10.

How privileged they are! They are not to be surprised at their suffering. In the strange prophesies of the Suffering Servant, (Is. 53) the Suffering of Christ had been predicted, together with his final glory. This was the pattern of salvation which Jesus had accomplished on the Cross. What the Prophets had longed to see, they had experienced. Not even the angels were so privileged!

So, what were they to do? First, be alert and disciplined, ready for Christ's return. When the going gets tough it is easy to slacken one's efforts. Christ died to set you free, so don't fall back into old bad habits. You are saved by faith, but will be judged by your actions. Hang on to hope.

Note the belief in the pre-existent cosmic Christ, and also the reference to the Lamb of the Passover. (Eph 2:13. Ex. 12:6-11) The Christian experience of salvation is linked to the deliverance from Egypt. Only in John's Gospel and the Book of Revelation do we see Christ so clearly portrayed as the Lamb of God, though there is a hint of it in 1 Cor. 5:7.

The distinguishing mark of the new life in Christ is love of the brethren. This leads on to the special vocation they all share.

They are a Special People, so they must grow strong. Newborn babies need mother's milk. Tinned or powdered milk is no substitute. Not only does it lack that special substance that protects the child from disease but it can be contaminated. Young Christians grow by drawing on the life of Christ by close personal contact. The reference is to Psalm 34 verse 8, but the whole psalm is bang on target for Christians facing trouble.

After baptism, these new-born Christians are built together into a spiritual house. (cp Eph. 2:19-22) While the imagery of Ephesians stresses unity, here it is linked to persecution. The corner-stone, which determines the building's shape, is Christ, who was rejected. They have joined a rejected Community. They are a Temple where sacrifice is to be offered.

But the rejected stone is now head of the corner. Those not built into it will stumble over it. They are not just stones but priests. What Ephesians 2:20-22 hints at, is here spelt out. They are the New Israel. Israel's great inheritance, claimed by Christ, is now theirs. It is not a privileged status. It is a call to witness to the world, out of their own deep experience of the saving acts of God.

Witness of Life. 2:11 - 3:12.

How is one to witness when one is being persecuted? Mainly, they are told, by the lives they live. Christians are watched. If one Christian goes off the rails, all the others get tarred with the same brush. But practical caring, especially when extended to those outside their own community, is also noted.

These verses, together with 3:13, indicate that the persecution may not be either continual or organised. The call to be subject to Roman Governors and the Emperor hardly points to official persecution. This teaching would make Christians still more unpopular with Jews, but would help to disassociate them from the Jewish rebels in the mind of the Romans.

Verse 17 sounds like an extract from a baptismal teaching manual. Note the rhythm and parallelism of verses 22-25. These may have been based on a Hymn. The churches were now developing a body of such material, which, circulating with letters through visiting preachers, slowly built up a deposit of teaching common to all the churches. Included in this were the Household Codes, another example of which is included here.

What is special to this code is that it is not given for the negative reason of not shocking pagan neighbours, but for the positive reason of giving a good witness.

Slaves are to be like Christ, not only in their service, but in their suffering. They have received healing and forgiveness through Christ's wounds. They are to witness to this by the Christ-like way they accept wounds inflicted on themselves.

Many early converts were women, whose pagan husbands may have beaten and abused them, forbidding them to attend meetings of the church. Taking Sarah as their model, a rare mention of that lady, they were to be submissive and loving. Their beauty would lie not in clothes and jewels, but in a quiet spirit. St Monica was a lovely example of this, winning over both her husband and her famous son. Christian husbands are to honour their wives, even accepting mutually agreed sexual restraint to facilitate special times of prayer. For Greeks, though not for Jews, this would be a new idea.

In verses 8-12 we get another block of common teaching material which again quotes Psalm 34. Note that the Psalmist's question is here turned into positive teaching. Much of the Old Testament, and especially the Psalms, is being interpreted so as to become part of Christian teaching. Set in a hostile environment, the bonding together of Christians in love and loyalty was especially important.

Chapter 3:13-18.

We now return to the problem of coping with ill-treatment. This teaching comes in recurring waves, but each wave takes us deeper. There still seems to be hope of winning over some of their oppressors, but Christians could be hauled before a magistrate on a trumped-up charge. This is true in many places today such as Pakistan where there is no official persecution. Tacitus wrote that Christians were loathed for their "abominations". This may relate to the secrecy of eucharistic celebration, all but the baptized being excluded, and to the popular rumour of cannibalism! Besides fear of an alien cult, there was the suspicion that it posed a threat to the absolute claims of the State. This also is very prevalent today in totalitarian states.

Though the writer's purpose is clear, the material he uses is thick through with theology. There is a growing consensus of belief expressed in Paul's letters, hymns, liturgies and teaching manuals. Verses 18 to 21 are crammed with doctrine concerned with Christ's sacrificial death. It is unique, vicarious, and atoning. (cp Rom. 6:10, 5:6-10) It is important to understand "flesh" and "Spirit" in terms of the Old Testament, and not in terms of Greek philosophy, which separates body from soul. "Christ in the flesh" refers to his life on earth. His life in the spirit refers to his life with God into which his resurrection body was taken up, as ours will also be. (1Cor. 15:44) So much deep theology! In verse 22 we can see the emerging of our Creed.

Chapter 3:19-22.

These are very difficult verses. Traditionally verse 19 has been linked to paintings of the Harrowing of Hell, and Christ giving those who had died without hearing the Gospel, a chance to repent. But this does not seem to fit either the context or the writer's theme. Kelly, in his Commentary, links it to the apocryphal teaching based on Genesis 6:1-5. It is referred to in Jude 1:6 and 2 Peter 2:4-5, where it is also linked to Noah. Fallen angels were seen as the powers of evil behind the enemies of God and His Church. If this interpretation is correct, then it is to these evil powers that Christ's victory is proclaimed. They know their power is broken; heartwarming news for the Church!

For the Jews, Noah was the man of faith who obeyed God, and was saved through water. God made a Covenant with him, and told him to people the earth anew. In later apocalyptic literature, the Flood was seen as a foretaste of the Last Judgement. The Church used all this in teaching those preparing for baptism. Saved from sin by water, they were united to God in a New Covenant which involved rejection of evil and acceptance of a moral way of life. This is now to be found in the questions and responses made in our Anglican baptism service. They link us to our fellow Christians of 2000 years ago! The creed we are apt to recite as a mere ritual, contain the assurances that have given Christians both then and now, courage to witness and die for Christ. They are worthy of joyful proclamation, with a Halleluia after every phrase. Graham Kenrick has set them to a Marching Song.

New Life in the Flesh. 4:1-11.

Hearts may soar, but faith is also earthy. Like Jesus, we live in the flesh, a very earthy word. (cp Jn. 1:14) Note its use four times in six verses! Sharing Christ's death in baptism, we now have to give flesh to this resolve. So, if we start doing again what we know is sinful, we can say to ourselves, "As a baptized Christian I have ceased from sin", and, claiming the power of Christ's victory, stop! I think this is what this passage is saying.

In verse 4 we see another reason for petty persecution. It is a situation familiar to members of street gangs, who, converted in prison, come out pledged to go straight. Their gang mates do all they can to draw them back into their old life. If they refuse, they are taunted, tormented and even beaten up. Their new life, taken as a criticism and rejection of their old, is bitterly resented. Yet some, envying their joy and freedom, may enquire into its source and come to share it.

What is meant by preaching to the dead? It is not a reference to 3:19-20, but, like those verses, has been interpreted differently by different church traditions. First-century Christians had a problem about what happened to baptized Christians who died before the Lord's return. Paul addressed this problem in his second letter to the Thessalonians. His answer was in terms of life and resurrection. Here the answer is that even the baptized undergo the judgement of death, but their life in the spirit continues, as does that of Jesus.

Since the time of Paul's early letters, the expectation of Christ's imminent return had faded. But, with the rising tide of persecution, it was coming back. Whenever persecution becomes rampant, or catastrophe threatens world security, expectation of the End grows and apocalyptic sects multiply. We have seen it in our day. At such a time, how are Christians to live?

They are to stay calm, sober and prayerful, in contrast to those who, without faith, take to drink. They are also to keep close together and loving. Love covers, ie doesn't show up, others' faults. On the contrary, our faults become a bond of our common humanity. A friend once said to me, "If you were faultless, I shouldn't love you as much as I do!"

Hospitality was important. The churches were linked together by visiting teachers, who would often bring letters such as this. As "stewards of God's varied grace", they were to minister to each other. In Ephesians (4:11-16) this is a means of growing to maturity. Here, avoiding the exhibitionism of the Corinthian church, it is to be a means of revealing God's glory.

Chapter 4:12-19.

As noted earlier these verses, together with 5:1-11 may have been added later. Partly they are a re-cap of most of the earlier main themes. One new thought is that judgement begins in the household of God. This belief was taken from Malachi 3:1-4. Whether to suffer for doing wrong or for doing right, that was the question! If the latter, then we, as well as they, can trust ourselves into the secure hands of our Father.

Words of advice to Leaders. Chapter 5.

In times of testing, mutual trust between leaders and the members of their congregation is vital. The elders here are *presbuteroi*, pastoral leaders. In Acts 14:23, we read that Paul appointed them in every church. The difference between them and *episcopoi* will be dealt with later. A group of elders would share pastoral oversight of teaching and disciplining the local church. It was a pattern of leadership taken over from the synagogue.

The writer himself is an Elder. It is attractive to see Peter in the role, but "to witness" was to testify from experience, not necessarily by eyesight. It doesn't seem as if there was any rush to take on the job, and some may have been paid to do it. They were not to be bossy or greedy; no career structure offered here! They were pastors, feeding their flock after the example set by Jesus. Suffering and sacrifice were involved in this role. (Jn. 10:11-15)

How important is humility in a Christian leader! Jesus had turned the conception of leadership upside down. Mark, in his Gospel gives two examples of

Jesus rebuking his disciples for competing for pre-eminence. (Mk. 9:33-35. 10:35-37. 42-45)

Humility is for all, both young and old. It is an attitude of mutual acceptance and respect, for the Holy Spirit who resides in each one.

What a lot is packed into the last 5 verses. The call to resist the Devil is repeated by James, who adds, "and he will flee from you." Dominion belongs to God, now and for ever. Amen.

Link with Mark's Gospel.

A word here about St Mark's Gospel. Mark is mentioned in 5:13, and his Gospel, which is the earliest, is specially relevant to the time and situation addressed in this letter.

We have already noted his stress on humility. In chapter 12 he quotes Psalm 118:22-23 about Christ as the Corner-stone. (cp 1Pet. 2:6) Christ's warnings of wars and persecutions in Chapter 13:9 find echoes in this letter. These are just three examples. If you read the Gospel in this light, you will find many others.

Two further points about the Gospels generally are worth considering, I hope without too much shock. One is that when the writers of the Gospels decided what to include, (cp Jn. 21:25) they would select what the churches they were addressing most needed to know. Each Gospel reflects the life and times of the church in which, and for which it was written.

It is equally true that all that has been recently discovered about the life and times of the church in the first two centuries helps us to understand the gospels. If the preaching of the Gospel gave birth to the church, it is also true to say that the church gave birth to the Gospels, both by influencing the viewpoint of the writers, and in recognising their inspiration and authenticity. Scripture, church, and Holy Spirit cannot be separated or set over against each other in terms of authority.

The second point is that it is not possible to separate what Christ is reported to have said from what he actually did say. Those who heard him told others, who told others. Only later was it written down. By then the basic teaching he had given, his stories and pithy sayings, would have been expounded and expanded by teachers and preachers, explaining them and applying them to different situations. In doing this they would speak out of their own experience. It was a living Word they passed on.

In John 16:12-15, Jesus spoke of this. We can't be sure that even these words are verbatim, they were written so many years later. But their truth had been experienced, not just by the writer, but by the church over many years.

This links up with Luke's introduction to Acts. Jesus continues to act and speak through his Spirit. There is no guarantee of verbal infallibility. As we shall see, different writers did not all see eye to eye on every matter. Truth had to be acted out, and tested by shared experience. Hence the vital need of humility and of staying together.

The Epistle of James.

What a different world we enter when we turn to the Epistle of James! And yet it is the same. There are the same trials that are to be met with joy, and the confidence that these will mature their faith which will be finally rewarded with the crown of life. There is the same call to put away the sins of the flesh. (1:21. 3:13-15) Chapter 4 verse 7 echoes Peter's call for humility and resistance to the Devil.

It is the atmosphere that has changed, and the point of view. A glaring omission is reference to Christ. His name is used only once and that only impersonally. Peter's letter, of almost identical length mentions Christ 21 times. Peter's teaching is based on Christian hymns, liturgies, and baptismal teaching manuals. In contrast, James refers everything to the Old Testament, quoting largely from Proverbs, Ecclesiasticus, and the Wisdom of Solomon. The last two books are not included in the Hebrew Scriptures. James, like other Christian writers, used the Greek translation, the Septuagint, which did include them.

For these reasons, this Epistle nearly failed to be included in the Canon of the New Testament. Many churches however continued to value it, so it was eventually given a place.

It purports to come from James, the brother of Jesus, leader of the Church in Jerusalem. As we have already noted, he was martyred in AD 62. From the earliest days, his authorship was questioned. Had he been the author, would it have been ignored for so long? However, some scholars date it very early, possibly before a doctrine of the atonement had been worked out. There are so many theories to explain the absence of teaching about the cross and resurrection. But the practical application of doctrine rather than doctrine itself may have been the author's intention. If it was written with the intention of countering the false implications of Paul's teaching, its date would be later. Though its thought is Jewish, its language shows a sophisticated knowledge of Greek.

It is written to the "Twelve Tribes of the Dispersion." This normally referred to Jews scattered throughout the Empire. Jewish leaders in Jerusalem used to send them annual letters to keep them loyal to the practices of their religion. This may have provided a model for an encyclical sent out to Christians, seen as the New Israel. (1Pet. 2:9) If so, it would need the authority of a name equal to that of Peter. Though James probably did not write it, it reflects the Jewishness of his Christian faith.

If Jews in dispersion had needed such letters of encouragement, how much more would Christian converts, especially those coming out of the lax morality of pagan society. Today, Jews and Moslems as well as Christians, especially the young, are vulnerable to the enticements of the modern city.

Luther, with his emphasis on justification by faith alone, called this letter an epistle of straw. But Paul, who had first preached this doctrine, had been aware that it was open to distortion. He had rebuked this justification of sin. (Rom. 6:1-2) James's Epistle also rebukes the absence of positive good.

The key to understanding this letter lies in the argument that we are justified by good works, and that faith without works is dead. (2:14-26) The dialogue is somewhat confused, but the main point is clear. The challenge of verse 18 seems irrefutable. But what about the good deeds of pagans? For centuries this dilemma has split the western church. Only in 1999 has a formula been drawn up by Catholics and Lutherans, mutually acceptable, at least to the signatories! It is a sad fact that many who have a strong faith can not only fall into the type of sin that The Sun likes to publicise, but can also be blind to social injustice in some of their own relationships. Humanists can be more sensitive and morally active.

Faith doesn't lie in doctrinal propositions. It means trusting and committing the whole of one's life to God. There will be lapses and blind spots. We aren't yet perfect. Our commitment, as well as our expression of it, needs to grow. What matters is that we see the two as interdependent. This letter also teaches us to leave judgement to God. The Parable of the Last Judgement (Matt. 25:31-46) and the House built on a Rock, bears out James' main contention.

Jesus came to fulfil the Law, not to abolish it; to free it from legalistic accretions and reinterpret it in terms of love and trust. His life was steeped in the Scriptures. It is good to have this Letter to remind us of how much we owe to our Jewish inheritance. So now let us turn to look at some of the spiritual treasures to be found in it.

First a note of personal thanks for chapter 1 verse 4. At a time of great need, a friend quoted it to me in the King James' version. "Let patience have her perfect work." I pass it on to any reader with similar need.

Another gem is verse 5: a promise to hang on to. But note the condition attached. That's the rub! (Prov. 2:3-6. Eccles. 2:12-15. Matt. 9:28-29)

In verse 13 we meet the problem of fatalism. There are those who say sin is God's fault. To put a tree in a garden and then forbid Man to eat its fruit, is asking for trouble. The answer given here depends on a Greek play on words. The word for "untouched" sounds like that for "untempted". Everyone knew that God is untouched by evil, so He cannot tempt. The real answer is that evil deeds spring from misdirected desire. (cp Lk. 6:45) James isn't advocating a morality of rigid self-control, but the centering of our life on one overmastering desire: to do the will of God. Look in the mirror. Am I God's man, or my own?

With regard to the common sins of which others had written, James has some special contributions to make. Writing about anger, he warns that the wrath of man does not work the righteousness of God. We often think that it does, at least when the anger is our own! The righteous anger we claim is often provoked when we see our own faults reflected by, or projected upon, our neighbour. Which is why so often we are critical. (cp 5:9) This leads on to saying quite a lot about the tongue. (1:26. 3:1-12. 4:11. cp Matt. 7:1-5. 16-17)

James also has a lot to say about partiality. Prophets had thundered against the corruption of justice; power and money securing one justice for the rich and another for the poor. The Law forbade partiality being shown either to the rich or to the poor. This was closely linked to the Law of love for one's neighbour. (Lev. 19:15, 18) Respect of persons is here applied to snobbery shown at church meetings, when the rich were welcomed with obsequiousness and the poor with disrespect. We all know how easy it is for this to happen even in our own democratic society. How much more was it almost inevitable in a small congregation where most were slaves or poor workmen, and very few were wealthy. (cp. 1Cor. 1:26-29. 11:20-22)

Another problem was ambition and jealousy due to the coveting of position. (3:14-16. 4:1-2) It led to a battle for power among church members. As in all churches composed mainly of underdogs, the church was the only place where there was any hope of rising to positions of importance and respect. I remember in India how hard people would fight to get elected on to Committees. It is not unknown in our own church! We say we only want to serve, but we need to search our hearts. The C of E provides a career structure that can entice. So can our own need to feel needed.

Closely linked is pride, the preferring of our own will to God's. James gives as an example of this the failure to consult God about our plans and business dealings. Every entry into our diary needs a D.V. put against it. Moslems are good at this. "Inchallah" they say, "God willing", though it can be an empty formula like "touch wood". James challenges us to submit all our plans and decisions to God; to keep alert with our radar communications switched on, ready to read God's signals, green, amber and red. (Is. 30:21)

Another important emphasis is on the sins of omission. As the Prayer Book puts it, "We have left undone the things we ought to have done." Only we know what they are. Others may point us to various duties they think we ought to undertake. We have to learn when to say no. But God's directions, especially when they are unexpected and call for instant response, can easily be missed or ignored. We look back and regret an opportunity missed. When we do respond, we often find a situation prepared for us. "Thank God you've come, just when we needed you. How did you know?" The only honest answer is, "God sent me." Take special note of chapter 4 verse 17.

The "above all" in 5:12 is not to be interpreted as condemning bad language as the worst of sins. It needs to be taken in the context of Jesus' teaching in Matthew 5:33-37. Using God's Name or Christ's in bad or obscene language is certainly a nasty though often unconscious breaking of the second commandment. It is not what is referred to here. It means using God's Name to back up our own statements. Quakers fear that this is involved in the oath taken in a Law Court. To meet their objection they are allowed to take the oath of affirmation. But nowadays, the intention of the Legal oath is not to use God to back up a statement, but to create a crime. Anyone caught lying after taking such an oath can be legally prosecuted.

Next to the teaching of faith and works, the teaching on the healing ministry has had the most influence on the church. (5:13-18) Jewish beliefs related the cause of sickness to sin. This over-simplification was rejected by Jesus. (Jn. 9:1-3) But Jesus accepted the fact there was a connection. (Jn. 5:14. Mark 2:5) The sin might not however be that of the person suffering. (Lk. 13:16)

In Ecclesiasticus 18:1-15, the relationship between God's healing activity and that of the doctor is beautifully portrayed. The renunciation of faults is one of the first steps to be taken by the sick. James speaks of confession to ensure there is no blockage to the healing flow. (cp. Mk. 2:5)

The Holy Spirit had given special gifts of healing to individuals, (1Cor. 12:9) but, for the local congregation, James gives this special work to Elders who had been chosen by the congregation and officially commissioned. Note that the sick person should invite them to come. If conscious, his active cooperation is needed.

After confession of sin, three ingredients of the healing activity are mentioned: the prayer of faith, the anointing with oil, and the use of the Lord's Name. Jesus had used spittle as well as touch in some of his healings. When his disciples went out on their first mission, they anointed the sick with oil. (Mk. 6:13) Oil was regarded as having healing properties. (Lk. 10:34. Is. 61:3)

Of these three ingredients the most important was faith, not just that of the sick person but of those praying for him. While faith is a gift of grace given to all, it is also a special gift given to a few. Power in prayer is linked to special closeness to God. The example of Elijah is, perhaps deliberately, not given a healing context, as other factors might also have been at work. (1Kings 17:21-22)

James' last word is concerned with his care for those led astray from the truth, either by sin or false teaching. Every effort is to be made to win them back. Love, not denunciation, is the means to use. (Prov. 10:12)

The Fall of Jerusalem and its Consequences.

We have seen how the death of the three great apostolic leaders affected the Church. The destruction of Jerusalem in AD 70 had even greater consequences. When the Roman armies closed in on the city, the Christians, remembering Jesus' warning, fled, many to Perea, east of Jordan, others to Egypt.

The destruction of the temple brought an end to the sacrifices, the Priests, and the Sadducean Party. The Zealots fought on until their resistance ended in AD 73 with mass suicide at Masada. Only the Pharisees remained. Giving up their sectarian title, they now just called themselves Rabbis. Like the prophets of old, many of them saw the fall of the City as God's punishment on a people who had failed to keep the Law. Their zeal for the Law was even greater. Jamnia, a coastal town, became the centre for the study of the Torah, and a Rabbinate was set up. It became the Law's authoritative interpreter, and worked towards an accepted Canon of Scripture. The synagogue was now the centre of Jewish life. There the Law was taught, and elements of temple worship were introduced and thus preserved.

Up to this point, Jewish Christians like James were still able to worship at the synagogue. Now they began to be excluded. In AD 130 a prayer was added to the 18 Blessings, recited by Jews every morning. In it Christians were included among the Sects blotted out from the Book of the Living. (cp Phil. 4:3) Might this perhaps partly account for the sweeping condemnation of the Pharisees as a class found in most of the Gospels?

Jewish Christians now had to rethink their relationship with their Jewish past. Previously they had looked to the church in Jerusalem for leadership. After the Jewish War some Christians trickled back to the City. Their leaders bore the names of Jesus' other brothers, and they may have been so. But authority was now fragmented, and became established in four different centres: Rome, Antioch, Ephesus, and Alexandria.

Antioch and St Matthew's Gospel.

The last we heard about Antioch was of the clash between Peter and Paul, temporarily resolved by the Council of Jerusalem headed by James. After AD 70 the balance between the different parties changed. The mission to the Jews became fruitless, but the Gentiles kept pouring in. To them the Council's decision seemed irrelevant. Holding to the views of Paul, they considered themselves free of the Jewish Law. But the Jewish Christians, now in a minority, were concerned to preserve their Jewish heritage, especially its emphasis on traditional morality. Hence the importance of the Epistle of James.

There was a political factor drawing the two parties together. The Jewish religion had been officially accepted by Rome. As the Christians became separate, they lost this protection. Continual threat of persecution helped to draw Jewish and Gentile converts together. Peter was seen as a central figure round whom they could rally.

In his book "The beginnings of the Church", F.J.Cwiekowski shows how St Matthew's Gospel sought to meet the needs of this time. Jesus condemns the legalism of the Pharisees, but, in his Sermon on the Mount, he gives fresh positive teaching on morality. Jesus' own Mission was confined to the Jews. He is constantly quoting Scripture and consciously fulfilling it. But Matthew's Gospel begins with the coming of the Magi, and ends with the Great Commission to preach the Gospel to all nations. To Mark's version of the Parable of the Vineyard, Matthew appends the warning that "The Kingdom of God will be taken from you and given to a nation producing the fruits of it." (Matt. 21:43. cp Mk. 12:1-12)

There are also many stories about Peter. Only in Matthew do we read that the church is to be built on the Rock, Petros, and of the Keys of the Kingdom being given to him. But Matthew also makes it clear that all authority in Heaven and earth is Christ's alone. (Matt. 28:18)

In Peter's commissioning the word church, *ecclesia* is used for the first time. It is used again in Matt 18:17 in the context of church discipline. Slowly a structure of authority and discipline is being built up. This brings us to the Pastoral Epistles, the Letters to Timothy and Titus.

The Pastoral Epistles.

These letters appear to have been written by Paul to his two colleagues, Timothy at Ephesus and Titus in Crete. Problems of authorship however abound. In comparison with the energy and depth of Paul's writing, the Pastorals appears pedantic and doctrinaire. The virtue most commended seems to be obedience, not just to God but to the authority of the church. For this and other reasons the letters seem to belong to a later age.

Fragments, apparently taken from Paul's unpublished letters, seem to give authenticity, yet some of them describe events that can't be fitted into what we know of Paul's life from Acts and his other letters. We are faced by this problem right from the beginning in 1 Timothy 1:3. According to Acts, the only time Paul left Ephesus for Macedonia is recorded in chapter 20 verses 1-5. This, taken with 1 Cor. 4:17 is almost impossible to reconcile with Paul's charge to Timothy to remain in Ephesus. Similarly, in Titus 3:12, we read of Paul's plan to visit Nicopolis. The only possibility for this would have been during a time of temporary release between his first trial in Rome and a re-arrest prior to his execution. As noted earlier, there is no record of this. Had there been such a release, a visit to Spain would have been more likely. Some scholars believe that some of these controversial fragments may even have been composed to give the letters added authenticity. At that time this was an acceptable practice. Such scholars differ as to which, if any of these, may come from Paul. However, 2 Timothy 4:9-18 appears in most of their lists of acceptable texts. Despite all this, many reputable scholars do accept Paul's authorship, giving many different reasons for explaining away or disregarding these difficulties. Theories abound, but I confess that, in general, I side with the doubters and plump for a later date. The church was acclimatising and adapting itself to the Greek world, while holding on to the essential deposit of teaching given by the Apostles who had direct experience of the Gospel events. For this there was need to strengthen the authority and organization of the leadership and teaching ministry. These letters have been called Pastoral, because they contain advice to such leaders on how to shepherd their flock.

How does one adapt new thought to new situations and yet hang on to essentials of Christian teaching? This is a very contemporary dilemma. High Churchmen put great value on these letters. Others find their moralising conservatism prosaic. Those facing persecution may look for more revolutionary solutions.

In working out His Plan of Salvation, both through the Old Israel and the New, God leads His people through different and developing situations, tensions and disputes. In recording this, Scripture provides a rock to stand on which is a wide platform of varying terrain. There is space for exploration and discovery. It is the Holy Spirit who authenticates its truth and interprets its relevance for today.

The three letters are closely related. 1 and 2 Timothy seem to have been written for predominately Greek churches in Asia Minor, while the letter to Titus was sent to a more Jewish church in Crete. Otherwise Titus is a shortened version of 1 Timothy. 2 Timothy differs in that it contains more Pauline material, making the letter more personal, and stamping all three with greater authority. What I call "golden verses", those of deep personal value, mostly come from these fragments, eg 2 Tim. 1:7 & 12. Because of their similarity, and to avoid repetition, I shall deal with these three Letters together, under headings related to their subject matter.

False Teaching. 1 Tim. 1:3-12. 4:1-4 & 7. 6:3-10. 2 Tim. 2:16-19. 3:1-9. Titus 1:10-16.

In Acts 20:28-31, Luke records in great detail Paul's farewell to the Elders of Ephesus, warning them that, after he left them, false teachers would arise from among themselves and draw away many. This comes very close to 2 Timothy 4:1-8. There is a close connection between the Pastorals and Luke, in vocabulary as well as points of view. There are 37 words which they use in common that are found nowhere else in Scripture, an added problem for the dating of both!

As in Colossians, (Col. 2:8) the heresies were a combination of Gnostic philosophy and imaginative interpretations of Jewish scripture, found in popular Jewish literature. Different aspects of this are denounced: myths, speculation and genealogies. Today we find a fascination with numerology and fanciful interpretations of the later chapters of Daniel. It can be a form of escapism, a bolt hole from the radical moral challenge of true faith.

The Law is a negative force, directed against evil behaviour. Christians should not need such rules. The aim of faith is to live according to the positive Law of Love. In Titus, greater detail is given. It reflects the fact that the writer is addressing mainly Jewish converts and Cretans. Cretans evidently had an unsavoury reputation!

The problem was not the Mosaic dietary rules, but gnostic beliefs that downgraded the body, separating it from the soul. As we have seen earlier, this could lead either to extremes of asceticism or to licentiousness.

Craving for controversy and arguments over words is linked to the desire for gain. These teachers made a lot of money out of their converts, as many do today. Love of money is not confined to heretics! Simplicity not asceticism should be the Christian response. Note that it is not money, but the love of it that is the root of all evils. (1Tim. 6:10)

Another dangerous form of heresy was the teaching that the resurrection was past. Paul had faced this problem in his letter to Corinth. (1Cor. 15) Heretics taught that in baptism, Christians had died with Christ and risen to new life with him. That was the resurrection. After that, salvation was secure and after death immortality awaited them.

Resurrection of the body seemed crude to gnostic ears, as it does to many today. To dodge the issue by using another word is hardly "handling the word of truth rightly". Is the church to jettison its doctrine when it runs counter to popular opinion? 2 Tim 2:19 is a quotation from Numbers 16:5. Korah was considered an example of those who sell out on the true faith.

In 2 Tim. 3:1-9 we read of men who worm their way into the homes of weak women burdened by their sins, and, by gaining control, exploit and make money out of them. This too goes on today. Jannes and Jambres were the traditional names given to Pharoah's magicians who tried to outdo Moses. (Ex. 7) They are examples of counterfeit faith, of those who hold to the form of religion while denying its power.

Encouragement and advice to Timothy.

Most of such encouragement given in these letters comes from the fragments of St Paul, and so are mostly found in 2 Timothy. What an inspiring first chapter!

In it three special words of advice are given. The first is, "Rekindle the gift of God given you through the laying on of my hands." Verse 7 is really a golden verse to memorise and hang on to. The second is, "Do not be ashamed", of witnessing to the Gospel. Like Paul, he is to be sure that "God will guard what has been entrusted to me", ie the Gospel. No one will ever be able to stamp it out. Another possible meaning is that He will "guard what I have committed to Him", ie my life, and the service to which He has called me. Both are true. The third word is closely connected. "Guard the truth", ie the deposit of faith, "entrusted to you". Compare this with the author's moving final word, ending his first letter. (1Tim. 6:20)

Timothy's mother and grandmother had handed on the faith to him. Now he is charged to hand it on faithfully to others. The metaphor of a deposit, implied rather than used, comes from Greek and Roman Law regulating the placing of money or valuables into the keeping of another who, on demand, must return the deposit intact. Today, a deposit can also mean what remains after the goodness of something has been drained away. This could lead to dangerous misunderstanding if applied to the deposit of faith!

The word "charge" is used many times with the utmost seriousness. Timothy is charged to hold the faith with a good conscience. (1Tim. 1:18-19) He is charged to teach preach and rebuke, in season and out. (2Tim. 4:1-2) He is charged to keep the rules of discipline, and the commandments. (1Tim. 5:21 and 6:14) He is also to charge others. (1Tim. 1:3,. 6:17. 2Tim. 2:14) The word "command" is also used. But the aim of these charges is love. (1Tim. 1:5)

In teaching and preaching, Timothy is to use the Scriptures wisely. (2Tim. 3:16-17) Scripture can be used to prove all kinds of doctrines and give rise to the profitless controversy over words that Timothy was to avoid. Scripture is inspired by God to be used for sound teaching, correction and training in godly living. The Jews did not accord all scripture equal authority, and Jesus, though referring to it constantly, was selective and original in his interpretation. For the author of the letters to Timothy, as for that of James, its chief value was the ethical teaching it provided.

To guard the truth is costly. Christ had died. So had Paul and most of the Apostles. In these letters there is no hint of persecution. The suffering was caused by hostile opposition of heretics within the church, and the defection of some of its members.

Timothy is to be like a soldier on duty, an athlete who has to keep in constant training and to abide by the rules. Note the author's emphasis and contrast it with that of Paul. (1Cor. 9:24-26) He is to be like a farmer who is to work hard if he is to be rewarded. He is to be a workman who has no need to be ashamed of his handiwork. (2Tim. 2:3-7. 15)

The first requirement is to set a good example. (Titus 2:7) Timothy is to shun youthful passions, avoid controversy, and be gentle and forbearing with his opponents. (2Tim. 2:22-26) He is to treat Elders with respect, and regard all women as if they were members of his own family. (1Tim. 5:1-2) By his own integrity he himself is to command respect despite his youthfulness. (1Tim. 4:12. cp Titus 2:15) He is also advised to take care of his health. A little self-indulgence in this respect is good! (1Tim. 5:23)

Doctrine.

Although these letters stress the importance of teaching, most of the teaching given is ethical and practical. Comparatively little is said about doctrine. The deposit of belief is expressed in formulas, sometimes accompanied by "This saying is sure and worthy of all acceptance." (1Tim. 1;15. 4:9. 2Tim. 2:11-13. Titus 3:4-8) They may be extracts from baptismal creeds. (1Tim 2:5-6) Some are rhythmic, easy to memorise. (1Tim. 3:16. cp 2Tim. 2:11-13) One might even reflect a hymn. (1Tim. 6:15-16) It may have inspired a deeply loved one of our own.

In this last quotation, and in 1 Timothy 1:17, the writer expresses the transcendence and majesty of God in words that accord well with Greek philosophy. Nowhere else in Scripture is the word "immortal" to be found. Otherwise, seven times, God is referred to as Saviour. This is special to these letters. Christ is referred to as the one Mediator between God and man. (1Tim. 2:5) This is an explicit rejection of Gnostic belief in a hierarchy of such mediators. In other passages however, God and Christ are brought so close together that they seem almost identical. Titus 2:13 is an extreme example of this. Translators vary slightly but all agree in the verse's ambiguity.

Right from the beginning, the unity of God, Christ, and the Holy Spirit was experienced and believed in. Jesus himself had taught this. But thinking out the implications, and expressing it as a doctrine took time. Words can't define mysteries. It was the false teaching of heretics who tried to simplify and rationalise that drove the church into drawing up doctrinal formulas that refuted them, while leaving the mystery undefined.

There is no reference to Christ's death on the cross, but 1Tim. 2:6 speaks of him as giving himself as a ransom for all. Sin is not mentioned, though it is in 1 Timothy 1:15. This later text refers more to salvation through knowledge of the truth. Titus 2:11-14 teaches that Jesus came to redeem men from sin in order "to purify for himself a people who are zealous for good deeds." Compare this with Titus 3:4-7 which sounds more typical of Paul. The two viewpoints have to be held together. The balance is apt to vary according to particular needs of the time and place, It continually needs to be righted. Compare the emphasis on hope in 1 Peter and on good deeds in James.

False teaching about the resurrection being already past has been rebuked, but no direct mention is made of Christ's own resurrection. The word is avoided. Jesus was "vindicated by the Spirit". (1Tim. 3:16) He "abolished death and brought life and immortality to light through the Gospel." (2Tim. 1:10) The proof that Jesus has risen and is alive, lies in the experience of the Spirit at work within the life of the church.

The writer's problem is also ours. He is refuting teaching that denies the basic fact on which the Gospel rests. At the same time, he is seeking to avoid words that, outside the church, can create misunderstanding and give offence. An example familiar today is the difficulty of talking to Moslems about Jesus as the Son of God. To the pagan mind, immortality was an acceptable belief. Resurrection was not. (Acts 17:32) When is the use of a more acceptable word selling the pass? This is a problem with which Bible Translators sometimes have to wrestle.

Appointment and qualification of Church Leaders.

Much space in these letters is devoted to this. We read first about bishops, ie Overseers of the local church; stewards of God's Household. (1Tim. 3:1-7. 5:17-22. Titus 1:5-9) Bishops, *episcopoi*, and elders, *presbuteroi*, often seem to refer to the same people. Paul appointed elders to take charge of the churches he planted, but in his letters, he only speaks of bishops. (eg Phil. 1:1)

There was however a difference, not of order, but of function. A body of elders would appoint one of their number to oversee a particular task on a temporary or ongoing basis. Several might be appointed to supervise different tasks.

Elected elders could thus, in some places, be seen as Overseers working together as a group. Those who laboured at teaching and preaching were to be specially honoured. They may even have been paid more. (1Tim. 5:17) Other Elders may have been more concerned with administration and finance. We seem to accord these latter functions greater priority!

Bishops are to be men above reproach, temperate, hospitable, and self-controlled, as well as sound in doctrine and able to teach it with devotion. (cp 1Peter 5:1-5) Note the importance given to their ability to manage their own family. Today so many clergy marriages are breaking down. They face the same pressures of society as do others. Devotion to duty, unreasonable expectations and demands made on them by their congregation, heighten the pressure. Now battle is raging over clerical celibacy and its abuses, as well as over the ordination of Gays. All this does immense damage to the church.

As for discipline, Timothy is directed to look into charges against Elders only if they are substantiated by at least two or three witnesses. (Deut. 19:15) If misconduct is proved, the Elder is to be warned privately, but if the wrong-doing is persisted in, he is to be rebuked in public. Nothing here is said of dismissal from office, though in extreme cases of immorality, excommunication was possible, and Paul had used it.

Deacons were a second group or order, recognised by the church. (Acts 6:1-6) The same qualifications were required of them. They were also to be trained and tested before being given office.

A third order was that of women. In 1 Timothy 3:11, the word correctly translated as "women" can also refer to wives. This is probably intended here. In Romans 16:1, we read of Phoebe, also called Diaconus, and in Philippians 4:2, Paul writes about Euodia and Syntyche who had worked side by side with him. However the Order of Woman about whom Timothy and possibly Titus writes is that of Widows, supported and employed by the church. (1Tim. 5:3-16. Titus 2:3-5)

The Church had always recognized its responsibility to care for widows left destitute. (Acts 6:1) Families had an absolute responsibility for maintaining their elderly members. (cp Mk. 7:10-13) Young widows are advised to remarry. Only those over 60 were to be enrolled. They could devote their time to prayer, as nuns do today. They could also offer hospitality, visit, and train younger women in domestic virtues: a Grandmother's Union perhaps?

In 1 Timothy 5:22 and 2 Timothy 1:6 there is reference to ordination by the laying-on of hands. This practice goes back to the ordination of scribes who had completed several years of study under a teacher. It qualified them to act as theological teachers and make decisions on religious Law. It consisted of a heavy pressure of both hands being laid on their heads (*samkak*). This was quite different from the gentle touch (*sim sit*) used for blessing and healing. Timothy himself received the laying-on of hands twice, once by Paul, (2Tim. 1:6) the second time by a Council of Elders (1Tim. 4:14) accompanied by prophetic utterance. The first was probably when Timothy received a special blessing and gift of the Spirit before joining Paul as a junior colleague on his missionary journeys. The second sounds more like his ordination as an elder. Both have elements that recall Paul's own experiences. (Acts 9:17, 13:2-4) As time went on, an efficient bishop would tend to be re-appointed, and more and more work might be laid on his experienced shoulders. Roman ideas of centralized administration would encourage this process.

In this early period, organisation in the church varied somewhat from place to place. Catholics, Protestants, and Pentecostals can all claim some primitive sanction for their different methods of church organization. The first place where a single bishop had real control was in Antioch under their outstanding leader St Ignatius, who was martyred under the Emperor Trajan (98-117 A.D). Ignatius presided over a Council of Elders and a group of Deacons. The first reference to three orders rather than two, is to be found in his letters. At the time, this situation was only to be found in Antioch.

Peter and James as well as Paul exercised some authority over a number of churches in many places. It had to be accepted and could not be imposed, as Paul knew from bitter experience. Paul had delegated his authority to both Timothy and Titus as well as to others. After these great leaders died, the need for such wider oversight grew, both because of the spread of heresy, and the beginnings of Imperial persecution. It was important that those appointed as leaders should have credentials that would ensure, and assure the local churches that their teaching was sound. Hence the need to link them to one of the great Apostles. Ordination could provide just such a link. As in the case of doctrines, statements, theories, and regulations concerned with Orders of Ministry, developed later.

The Letters also contain general moral teaching, some of it drawn from household codes. (1Tim. 2:8-15. 6:1-2. Titus 2:1-3:2) The writer justifies the submission of women to men by laying the whole blame for the Fall on Eve, which is rather unfair! Equally unfair, in the light of all the doubts about the Pauline authorship of these letters, is the widely held belief that this teaching was given by Paul.

The virtues upheld in these letters are those of integrity, gravity, sobriety, godliness, good deeds, and, very important, steadfastness. Nothing is said about evangelism, winning outsiders to the faith. Good behaviour is the witness that is called for, and a steadfast holding on to the deposit of sound teaching, It was this that was under attack, as it is today. So let us not dismiss these rather prosaic letters. The Holy Spirit working in the church has seen to their inclusion in sacred scripture. There is much we can learn from them. I confess, that, in studying and writing about them, I have come to appreciate them more.

Summary

In these letters we have seen different churches, facing different problems, requiring different virtues, being encouraged by writers with very different points of view.

The problem of dating makes it difficult to discuss them in terms of historical development with any easy confidence. The situation with regard to persecution could vary from place to place. That being said, we can however recognize that development is taking place.

1 Peter was probably written to a church composed mainly of Gentile converts facing harassment from their neighbours and, probably later, threatened by real persecution. The call is therefore to stay together, firm in faith, united in love, and looking forward in hope for Christ's early return.

James, writing for Jewish converts, also facing trials, sees a greater danger stemming from the lax morality of their pagan neighbours. Their need is to stick to the moral principles of the Law, and not to be fooled into thinking that faith alone can save them. The faults rebuked are primarily those that are divisive. Unity is a moral virtue.

The Pastorals reflect a more ordered society. Danger came mainly from the infiltration of gnostic beliefs. The virtue most commended is that of steadfastness in holding on to the Apostolic deposit of truth, passed on by those authorised to teach it.

Ministries, originally gifted by the Spirit, and freely exercised, slowly changed into ministries authorised by the church.

Extracts from hymns, emerging litanies, and credal statements, begin to be circulated among the churches. Slowly they will develop into a common body of doctrine, and a structured form of worship. The seeds are sown. It is remarkable how quickly they will grow.

The one thing all these writers had in common was the value they placed on their Jewish heritage, and their use of the O.T. scriptures. Peter saw the church as the new Israel, freed from the restrictions of the Law, to proclaim God's salvation to the Gentiles.

There were however others who believed that, with the old Israel having been superseded, the church could now leave its Jewishness behind. This view is expressed in the writings of John and the Book of Hebrews, which will be studied in the following chapter.

Questions for private meditation

1. Would you regard suffering for Christ a privilege? Pray for those who are suffering for Him, and do. (1 Peter 4:12-14)

2. What sort of witness do you present in your own home?

3.Give thanks for each clause of the Apostle's Creed.

4. How do you relate to the clergy of your church? (1 Peter 5:1-5)

5. How much control have you over your tongue? (James 3:3-12)

6. Apart from church-going, what evidence do your neighbours have of your Christian faith?

7. Do you consult God about your future plans? (James 4:13-15)

8. God will guard all I have committed to Him and all He has committed to me. Let Paul's assurance of this sink deeply into me. (2 Tim. 1:12-14)

9. How do you experience the Holy Trinity? Which of the Three Persons do you usually centre on?

10. What virtues would you consider the most important in today's world? Compare them with those emphasized by the Pastorals.

Questions for group discussion

1. When things get tough, what helps you most?

2. "As Christians we belong to a rejected community." Discuss. (1 Peter 3:14-18)

3. In what ways can wives witness to unbelieving husbands? (1 Peter 3:1-6)

4. How can the bonding of mutual respect be strengthened between the leadership and ordinary members of your congregation? (1 Peter 5:1-5)

5. Is partiality a problem in your church? How can it be dealt with? (James 2:1-5)

6. How would you explain the relationship of faith and works? (James 2:14-26)

7. How can you become involved in the healing ministry?(James 5:13-16)

8. What do you regard as the essential "deposit of Apostolic faith"? (2 Tim. 1:14)

9. How does "Resurrection" differ from "Immortality"? Why is this regarded by the church as so important?

10. Should the historic structures of the church be changed to meet today's very different situation? Is God's Spirit already starting to change them?

Chapter 11

The Epistles of John and Hebrews

Before we study the Letters of John, let us look again at the fourth Gospel. We have seen how research into the life of the early church has helped us to interpret the gospels of Mark and Matthew. In a similar manner, a study of John's gospel can throw light on the church with which the author was probably closely connected.

Whether the Gospel and the three letters have a common author is now a disputed point. What is not in dispute is that they all emerge from a common Johannine tradition of a community centered on Ephesus. Here the "beloved disciple" was believed to have settled down and lived to a great age, thus attracting a number of disciples who would absorb his teaching.

His Gospel may provide clues as to what sort of people they might have been, and where they came from. Some may have originally been followers of the Baptist. Repeated stress is laid on the Baptist pointing his disciples away from himself to Jesus. In Ephesus Paul had met some of the Baptist's disciples who had never heard of the Spirit or been baptized into the Name of Jesus.

Another group may have been Samaritans. Early persecution had led to Philip's mission to Samaria followed by the visit of the apostles, Peter and John. Samaritan worship was independent of the temple, and the Messiah they looked for was a Saviour rather than a Jewish King. Central to John's Gospel is Jesus' teaching about himself and his oneness with his Father. He is the light and the life of God dwelling with men. This was highly offensive to Jews who, as we have already noted were, in John's Gospel, depicted as Jesus' main opponents. In the nineties, anti-Jewish feelings would have been increased by the persecution of Christians by some synagogues close to Ephesus. They are referred to in Revelation as the synagogue of Satan. (Rev. 2:8-10, 3:3-10)

There were also the growing number of Greek converts. John's Gospel mentions Greek enquirers asking to see Jesus. Such converts would not owe loyalty to the Jewish Law. Also, a growing number of Jewish Christians, including Paul no longer felt bound by it. Valuing their Jewish inheritance less than Paul, they may have become part of this Johannine community.

It is in Colossians, possibly written at Ephesus, that the pre-existence of Christ is first clearly stated, and, in the Epistle to the Ephesians, further developed. In John's Gospel the Cosmic Christ is identified with the Logos, a word that bridged Jewish and Greek thought. John's Gospel, like 1 Timothy, which was addressed to Ephesus, deals with the same problems of gnostic teaching. Works of faith are similarly stressed, but the emphasis is on the love which inspires them and makes them fruitful. These similarities link the author to Ephesus and so to the Johannine community.

As the church became growingly Greek in its membership, there were two tendencies at work within it, represented by different factions. Should the church, freed from the legalism of the Law, continue to value its Jewish inheritance, or abandon it? There was a danger of the church splitting over the issue. Though the Gospel refers to the Twelve only as disciples, giving special prominence to the unnamed "beloved disciple", Peter's special position is recognized. From the very beginning, Jesus names him Peter the Rock. His confession of faith, though given a different setting, still marks the turning point of the story, which ends with his special commissioning. As noted earlier, this chapter was probably added later, possibly at the time the Letters were written, and the unity of the church was under attack. Peter was seen as a central figure round whom all the different factions could unite. But the Gospel makes it clear that it is the Holy Spirit who would guide the church, preserving its truth and unity. Orders and organisation are no substitute.

The 1st Epistle of John.

So we come to the first of the letters, one of the loveliest of all New Testament writing. Both author and date are matters of dispute. The author may have been the beloved disciple, or the Elder of the other two letters. Even these could have been different men. Note that in none of them is the name of John mentioned. Dates suggested vary from the earliest suggestion of AD 70 prior to the Gospel, and the latest fairly early in the second century when it is quoted by Polycarp, bishop of Smyrna. His disciple, Irenaus, bishop of Lyons believed it was written by John the apostle. In commenting on the text I have tentatively accepted a later rather than an earlier date.

What a strange opening, more like a treatise than a letter. But chapter 2 starts with a very personal appeal. The author is soaked in the language and thought of the Gospel, yet the warnings about the Antichrist belong to a later time. It is possible that, while the writer could have known and been taught by the "beloved disciple", he might have been writing ten or more years later.

He is writing to a church facing schism. Some of them had misunderstood John's Gospel, or were twisting it to accord with gnostic ideas. Exalting Christ as the Divine Word of God, they disregarded his humanity. Later, Docetists taught that Jesus only appeared (*docet*: to seem) to be a man. Like some of the Greek gods who walked the earth, his humanity was a masquerade. Typically gnostic was their disregard for all things material. Sure that they had eternal life now, morality was irrelevant. Some of these men had already left the church and were drawing others after them.

This letter appeals both to the Tradition and to personal experience. It insists that morality is the essential witness of true faith, but it is to be interpreted in terms of love. It also gives assurance to those whose faith was being shaken. "We know" rings out as a constant refrain.

Chapter 1:1-4.

A witness testifies to personal experience. The tradition was a living tradition. Even if the writer had never known the Jesus of history, he could still, as we can, see, hear and touch him by faith. Jesus' contemporaries had no advantage over us, if as much! (Jn. 20:29)

The writer's motive for writing (from now on we shall refer to him as John) was that they may share in fellowship with "us", ie the church. It is a deep sharing in the life and unity of Christ and his Father. How we have cheapened the word! Without such unity there can be no wholeness, no fulness of joy in the church.

Chapters 1:5 - 2:15.

How is such fellowship possible? It depends on walking in the Light. (Jn 3:19-21) In our baptism we renounce evil, and turn away from sin. But despite our good desires, our feet tend to stray and daily we need Jesus to wash them. Joy depends on continually receiving his forgiveness, his saving life and the benefits of his continuing intercession. (Heb. 9:14. 7:25)

Danger stems from those who claim to know Christ while disregarding his command to love. Their knowledge is mere intellectualism. "Matter is unreal" they say, "so sins don't matter."

This is a lie. Here is the first thing John's "children" can be sure of. If they keep Christ's commands, their knowledge of him is genuine. (2:15) You only really know someone if you love them and stay close to them. Similar assurance is given in verses 5-6. If others can see Jesus in the way we live, then we can be sure we are abiding in him. To love is to live in the light. To hate is not only to live in darkness, but to be blind to the fact. (Jn. 9:40-41)

It isn't clear why John singles out three groups of people and, in almost identical language, gives different reasons for writing to them, but it emphasises three things they are sure of: their sins are forgiven, their knowledge of Christ and his Father is real, not just intellectual, and through the Word of God and the Holy Spirit within them, they have already experienced the power to overcome sin. While it is a lie to say sin doesn't matter, or to claim to be sinless, it is equally a lie to say, as many still do today, that sin is inevitable; that "you can't change human nature". We can't, but the good news of the Gospel is precisely this, that Christ has done so. To worldly people material things do matter. Hence the consumer society. Such a life is ephermeral. Life lived with God is for ever.

Antichrist and the Schismatics. 2:18-28.

The Jews believed that as the End of the Age approached, before God brought in His Kingdom, there would be a final upsurge of Evil. Christians inherited this belief. Christ had taught that before his Return, they were to expect many disasters and persecutions. They linked this to the appearance of an Antichrist or a series of Antichrists. (Matt. 24:5-14. 23-25) John identified as Antichrists these schismatics, whose false teaching was splitting the church.

How could this happen to men who had received baptism and Holy Communion? They had never been truly "of us" says John. Today we might call them nominal or uncommitted Christians. They had gone through the motions, receiving the outward signs of faith without their inward truth.

It was not just indifference to morality that led to John's indictment. They denied that Jesus was the Christ. The Man Jesus was not the Son of God. The Divine Logos could not take flesh.

Gnostics claimed to have gained spiritual knowledge through a special rite of initiation - anointing. Christians had already been anointed by the Spirit at their baptism. They had to hold to what they had been taught.

In verses 24-28 John uses the word "abide" six times. Abiding was one of the key words in Christ's last Discourse. John links it to anointing three times. Note the build-up of meaning.

"Let what you have heard abide in you". John doesn't argue. Assurance of faith was what they needed, not head knowledge. Like the writer of the Pastorals he takes his stand on the truth entrusted to the church. If you abide in that, he tells them, then you will abide in the Father and the Son, and that is the meaning of eternal life. Note that this abiding is conditional on the other two.

He then speaks of their anointing. The Holy Spirit given them in baptism was abiding in them, continually at work, teaching and pointing them to Christ and what he had said about loving and abiding. So let them abide in Christ. Then, when he returns, their confidence will be sure.

Loving, Knowing, Abiding. Chapter 3.

Six times in this chapter John refers to the things they know. First in verses 1-3 they are privileged to be God's children in a very special way. The analogy of child-father relationship implies a recognizable likeness. Despite their frailty, they knew that when Christ returns, they would come to perfection, ie completion in him. What that would be like was beyond imagining, but, if they really believed this, they would strive towards that completion now.

Secondly, sin is lawlessness. Those who indulge in it give evidence of their true paternity. (Jn. 8:43-44) But John's "children" know that Christ came to take away sin. Here we meet the contradiction of continuing sin expressed in 1:8. A child of God can't sin because "the divine seed remains in him." (NEB translation)

Perhaps our new understanding of the effect of genes on our character may help us here. When the Spirit is implanted, it acts like a spiritual gene. It affects the whole of our life by creating a new tendency towards God. To change the metaphor, we are then like the needle of a compass, which, when pushed off course, always swings back to true north, The Spirit, like a magnet, continually draws us back to Christ. Paul dealt with the same problem using the illustration of the Old and New Adam. He spoke of "considering" our old self to be dead. John speaks of abiding in love.

The third thing they know (verses 11-15) is that they have already passed from death to life. Proof of this is their love for each other. Human love isn't enough. A small segregated community can generate a lot of mutual hostility as well as provoking the hostility of outsiders who distrust it as something alien.

John here contrasts love not with hate, but with murder, its end product. (Matt. 5:21-22) When this letter was written, persecution had become more active, and some Christians had already faced martyrdom. They were not to be surprised at this. Cain had murdered Abel. The world had crucified Christ.

They also knew the quality of this love. They had seen it in Christ who had given his life for them. They should be prepared to do the same. It might not come to this extreme, but they should at least show practical caring for brothers in need! (3:16-18) John is saying much the same as James, (James 2:14-16) but links deeds to love rather than faith.

The last verses, 19-24, sum all this up but with such compression their meaning is somewhat obscured. They include two more things these Christians know. They know that they are truly children of God because they have no sense of God's condemnation. The Devil loves to discourage us by making us feel guilty. But God knows our hearts better than we do because He has made His home in them. His indwelling Spirit gives them assurance.

Testing the Spirits. 4:1-6.

The coming of the Spirit at Pentecost revived in the church gifts of prophecy. The Old Testament is full of warnings about false prophets. The test of a true prophet lay in his personal integrity, his closeness to God, demonstrated by his life, and by his willingness to suffer persecution.

The church's prophets also had to be tested. Paul had said their words must be weighed. (1Cor. 14:29) The heretics John was condemning also prophesied. They claimed the Spirit inspired their teaching. How was this to be disproved? John provides a simple test. Did their "spirit" confess that Jesus had come in the flesh? If not, it was the spirit of Anti-Christ, and they should have nothing to do with it.

Today it is equally important to know how to test the spirits. People have no trouble in believing that Jesus was a man. It is his Divinity they doubt. Worldly people will not listen to the Gospel. Christians today have been labelled by Communists in various countries as liars, evil people, children of the Devil. Jesus warned his disciples of this. (Jn. 15:18-19, 16:2-4). Such hatred and refusal to listen is in fact another test. (1Jn. 4:6) What confident joy rings out in verse 4, and again in chapter 5 verse 4 with its assurance of victory.

The Test of Love. 4:7 – 5:5.

We can learn so much from noting the number of times John uses the key words of the Gospel. In this section, love is mentioned 32 times! It is the key to the whole epistle.

God IS love. His love, flowing through us and out to others, is proof that we belong to Him. So let us unblock all that hinders the flow and be what we truly are.

God demonstrated His love by sending His Son to free us from sin by laying down his life for us. That should be the measure of our love for each other. (cp. 3:16 and the Gospel 3:16. A coincidence of numbering!) Only when God's love flows out of us can others "see" the unseen God. Only in this can His loving purpose come to fulfilment.

This brings us back to the vital importance of abiding: God in us and we in Him. This is not just a spiritual experience, let alone a feeling. It depends on active belief in the doctrine, that Jesus is the Son of God. Jesus was truly a man of flesh and blood like ourselves. He was also so continually filled with the Spirit and abiding in God that he could say, "I and my Father are one. He who has seen me has seen the Father." Because he perfectly united our humanity to God, this can become true of us. To climb Everest, men had to believe it possible. All who died on its slopes bear witness to this. Despite faults and failures, our love for God can be seen in our love for others. If this is true of us, we need not fear God's judgement.

John's eye is again on the heretics who claim to love God without loving their fellow Christians. To claim to love the invisible God and care nothing for the visible members of His Family is bogus. It is also disobedience to Christ's clear command. The Law is no longer an impossible catalogue of dos and don'ts. It is simply to love, not a feeling but an attitude toward people, coupled with practical caring, something possible for us all.

The Test and Confidence of Truth. 5: 6-12.

John now refutes the heretics as if in a Court of Law. God Himself has declared that Jesus Christ is His Son. (Matt. 3:17, 17:5) Here are the three witnesses required by the Law: the Water of Baptism, the Spirit which descended on Jesus at his baptism and is given to us at ours, and the Blood of his sacrifice communicated to us through the Eucharist. John emphasises the latter because the heretics said Christ never died. They taught that the Spirit which descended on the Man Jesus at his baptism left him before his death. But these three witnesses all agree that Jesus was the Christ the Son of God, and all three are part of daily experience in the life of his church.

Another thing they know is that God hears and answers prayer. Loving involves praying. Are they then to pray for these heretics?

John makes a distinction between those who had chosen to leave the Church, the Ark of Salvation, and others. For the Antichrists he cannot ask for prayer.

But for others, disturbed but still hovering, and for all who do wrong out of human frailty, they should pray, believing that God would bring them safely through to eternal life.

John ends with three strong repetitions of "we know". (cp. 2:12-14) They sum up and need to be interpreted in the light of all that has gone before. As in the Gospel, John's style of writing is spiral, a constant repetition of basic themes with an ever increasing richness of content.

The final injunction to keep away from idols seems surprising. But John is not referring to images of pagan deities, or even to Mammon and the love of material things. The idols of the educated Greek were those of philosophical speculation. In our day too these provide alternatives to faith in the living God. The consequences are the same: the downgrading of morality.

The 2nd and 3rd letters of John.

These are real letters with the usual personal greeting at the beginning and the end. But they are quite different. The 2nd Letter is written to a church, the 3rd to an individual.

It was customary to refer to a local church as "the lady", and to the congregation as "her children". (cp 1Peter 5:13) So this 2nd Letter is designed to be read to a church. The children of the elect sister refers to the congregation of John's church.

In both letters he calls himself The Elder. Elders were members of collegiate bodies, but this Elder is obviously someone very special and is writing to a church, other than his own, with an authority they recognize. We have seen how Elders could also be bishops, with responsibilities for oversight, and their power was growing. We have also seen how Paul exercised some oversight over churches, especially those that he had founded. But an Elder could also denote a man respected for his age. By the mid to late nineties, the church would increasingly have consisted of second generation Christians. Those who were old enough to remember first generation leaders such as the first Apostles, were deeply respected, and their authority and status were widely recognised in the church.

His concern is the same as that of the writer of the 1st Letter. He could be the same man, or someone who knew him well. In none of the letters does the name John appear. As in all of them, the command to love is basic. He is warning this sister church of the danger of these "deceivers", the Antichrists of the first letter, trying to infiltrate and spread their false teaching there. He calls it "going ahead".

He tells the elect lady to refuse to receive them and to shut her door against them.

We talk of the need of the church to keep abreast of the times and adjust to modern ideas. There is conflict between Liberalism and Fundamentalism in the church. These are the tags of extreme positions. When does faithful adherence to the deposit of faith once handed to the church become a dogmatic rejection of all the fruits of biblical scholarship? When does openness to what the Spirit may be saying to the church today become a betrayal, a selling of the pass? Churches differ as to where the line should be drawn. This makes it all the more important that they keep together, abiding in love, patiently listening to and learning from each other, testing the spirits.

The 3rd Letter is a personal one to Gaius. The Elder has had news of him from visiting brothers and rejoices to hear that his life is reflecting his faith. As noted earlier, the church depended for much of its teaching on such itinerate preachers. This is why the offering of hospitality was so important. The Elder thanks Gaius for being generous in providing for such travellers and asks him to go further by helping them on the next stage of their journey. This would be a means of sharing in their mission.

The letter complains with some feeling about the actions of Diotrephes, the leader of a local church, possibly that of Gaius. Certain brothers, vouched for by the Elder, had been sent to visit his church. Diotrephes had rejected the Elder's authority, not only by refusing to welcome them, but by expelling from his church those members who wanted to meet them. The Elder ends by testifying to the "truth" of another brother, also on the move. Perhaps, in view of Diotrephes' rebuff, the Elder is sending Demetrius to Gaius where he would be sure of a welcome, taking this letter with him.

What lay behind this conflict? The Elder calls Diotrophes evil, but does not accuse him of heresy. We find it hard enough to get to the bottom of conflicts about authority in our own church today, and we have no way of knowing why Diotrophes acted as he did. It is possible however that a new stage was being reached in the life of the early Church. The authority of the old men who remembered the leaders of the first generation was being challenged by new second generation leaders elected by their congregations. The danger of heresy taking over in a democratically elected Church was great. It explains the emphasis on tradition and the increasing importance of presiding bishops, whose appointment had some form of apostolic recognition.

There was also a danger of local leadership falling into the hands of power-hungry men. Gathering a party round them for support, they could get themselves elected. Such men would brook no questioning of their authority either from within their congregation or from without.

The Elder was not the only leader to exercise some influence and control over other churches than his own. At about the same time, in the mid 90s, Clement of Rome wrote to the church at Corinth where a group had created schism by ousting some of their leaders who had done no wrong. Their action seems to have been prompted by jealousy. Significantly, Clement writes that it was a similar jealousy in Roman Christians that had led to the deaths of Peter and Paul, no doubt through their betrayal to the Roman authorities!

Hebrews. Shadows of the True.

From the deep well of John's Ist Epistle we come to Hebrews, which, like a great mountain soars up at the end of our journey, not only through the New Testament, but the Old as well. It interprets their relationship.

For the first four centuries it was anonymous. Then Paul's name was pinned to it. It didn't fit, so now it is again accepted as being anonymous. It seems to have been written to Jewish Christians in Rome. Scholars differ over its date. Some put it early, just before Nero's persecution. Faced by approaching danger, some such Christians may have been tempted to return to the security of the Law of Moses, and perhaps the immunity given to Jews by Roman Law. A later date seems to fit better with chapter 13:7 & 17. So do the rebukes given to complacency and unbelief, more typical of second generation Christians. However, untroubled by these uncertainties, let us open ourselves to the author's vision which can speak to us today.

The first problem that confronts us is the author's method of handling scripture. Jews were fundamentalist. Orthodox Jews still are. The Greek Septuagint was regarded as having the same infallibility as the Hebrew Bible. Differences were interpreted as God's way of revealing new truth. Some texts make God seem cruel, which is why heretics like Marcion said that the God of the Old Testament was different from the God of the New. Some people think the same today; but it is our understanding of Him that has grown, especially since the coming of Christ. Jewish Rabbis got round these and other problems by interpreting scriptural texts by means of allegory as Paul did in Galatians. (Gal. 4:22-31)

The early Church took over all this, but, like some Jews, they saw in the history of Israel a gradual unfolding of God's plan of salvation. This led to a different method of interpretation, that of typology. The Law, the Priesthood, and the Sacrifices were shadows of things to come. Jews already saw in many of the Psalms a foreshadowing of the Messiah. Jesus shared this view and not only quoted them but fulfilled them. The author of Hebrews sometimes pushes this method to lengths that to us may seem far-fetched, but let us concentrate on what he is trying to say.

Christ the Word of God. 1:1-4.

"God has spoken." This is pretty well what the whole of Scripture is about. God spoke in Creation. He spoke to Moses giving him the Law. He spoke continuously through the Prophets recalling Israel to faith and obedience. Then, after a long apparent silence, He spoke again through His Son, the most authoritative Word of all.

What a compression of doctrine is found in these verses! Christ the Word of God, creating and sustaining the universe; Man, as God made him to be, God's image stamped with the glory of His likeness, bearing His authority; descended to be our Saviour, ascended to be our King.

Greater than the Angels. 1:5 - 2:18.

Gnostic teaching exalted angels to a status even higher than Christ. Even some Jews had to be rebuked for worshipping them. (cp Rev. 19:10) Using a string of quotations, mainly from the Messianic Psalms, the writer sets out to prove the superiority of Christ.

The first comes from Psalm 2:7. The words originally referred to Solomon, but pointed back to God's promise to David. (2Sam. 7:14) But they were also spoken by the Voice at Jesus' baptism. Psalm 110, was quoted by Jesus himself when the Pharisees questioned his authority. (Matt. 22:44)

In chapter 2 verse 1, the writer breaks off to warn his readers of the danger of not heeding a word of such authority. Jews believed that God had given the Law to Moses through the intermediacy of angels. This was to avoid anthropomorphism implied by the text. In Christ, God's Word was spoken directly to the disciples who passed on the message of salvation faithfully to others. Its truth was also attested by the Voice spoken at Christ's Baptism and Transfiguration and by the Spirit through the signs and the gifts poured out at Pentecost. Woe to thosc who neglect it.

Woe also to us. Do we believe that, in Christ, God has spoken a unique and authoritative word of truth? Or do we think of Christ as just one among others such as the Buddha and Mahomet? If a poll were to be taken on this amongst even regular members of our church congregations we might get a shock. Or wouldn't we? If Christ is God's unique word to us, then it is the most important thing that has ever happened. The whole meaning and purpose of our life depends on our response.

In verse 5, the writer now returns to comparing Christ with the angels. He quotes Psalm 8, not obviously a Messianic Psalm. Here he sees Jesus, made for a time lower than the angels, then raised again to glory.

The problem of verse 8 is our problem too. We sing "Jesus is Lord of all the earth", but to most people it is patently obvious that he isn't. Yet, surprisingly, while the triumphant Jesus today has little appeal, Jesus in his suffering draws the hearts of those of all religions and of none. It is not in the triumphalism of a powerful church that God is being seen today, but in the poverty and pain of Christians facing persecution. We identify with Jesus, our brother in adversity. He shares our pain, and imparts his own power to endure, to forgive, and to overcome fear. The teaching that perfection, ie spiritual maturity, is only reached through suffering may sound repellent, but we recognize its truth when we have experienced it. "Pioneer of our salvation." What a lovely title for Jesus Christ!

Today, fulfilment of life is measured in material terms. We don't like to think about death which can make a mockery of our success. Paul saw death as a friend. For him eternal life had already begun. (Phil. 1:21-23) What worried the Christians to whom Hebrews was written were their sins. They feared condemnation and fear eroded their joy and power to overcome. They needed a compassionate Priest.

This brings us to our next problem in relation to Hebrews. "Sin" doesn't ring bells with people today. High priests and sacrifices are completely foreign. Before we go further we need to connect with O.T. ideas on these subjects.

Sin wasn't primarily murder and adultery. It was disobedience to God's Law. Such disobedience, whether deliberate or accidental, set off a chain of consequences that involved not just the sinner and his family but the whole of his society. A cigarette stub insufficiently put out can ignite a forest fire with consequences quite as disastrous as a fire started by arson. Drugs and AIDs can damage even an unborn child. Similarly we are all involved in the sin of the world, however "good" we may think we are.

Sacrifice was God's provision of a remedy. The shedding of blood was seen as the release of innocent life offered to God to expiate, ie to cover the sin. By laying hands on the victim's head and confessing his sin. the worshipper identified himself with its vicarious sacrifice. (Lev. 4:27-31)

Once a year, on the Day of Atonement, a similar sacrifice was made by the High Priest on behalf of the sins of the whole community including his own. (Lev. 16) In our day, the deaths of martyrs like Martin Luther King, and Archbishop Oscar Romero have had a similar cathartic effect on their communities and the world. The point made in verses 17-18 is that Jesus, despite his sinlessness was, like the High Priest, truly identified with his people. How else could he represent them to God?

Greater than Moses and Joshua. 3:1 - 4:13.

Two key words stand out in this passage. Both come from Psalm 95. "Today" repeated four times gives a sense of urgency. The decision to be faithful is NOW. It always is. We meet it all the time. Straying starts in the heart. The feet follow the heart's dictates.

The importance of "today's" decision lay in the promised "Rest" repeated eleven times. After a long march through the desert, rest was to be found in the Promised Land. Because of their unbelief, most of the Israelites who started that journey never made it to the end. (Deut. 1:26-36) Even those who settled in the land proved faithless and were driven out of it. So where was true rest to be found?

God's Rest, and His promise that His People would enter it remains. God's Sabbath, (Gen. 2:3) when God rested after His work of creation, typifies the joy and peace of fulfilment which awaits us at the end. It is the same paradox of striving and letting go that we met in the Pauline epistles. Just because it is a paradox, we need the sharp sword of God's Word to cut through our rationalising and expose the secrets of our hearts. We can hide from ourselves but never from God. Is this an awesome thought, or a relief?

Greater than the High Priest. 4:14 - 7:28.

When we discover we are running away from self-knowledge, we face the fact of sin. This can lead us to Christ. He stands before God on our behalf. So often pictured in Art as Judge, here Christ is seen as the compassionate Priest. He understands us for he has shared our weakness and our temptations while triumphing over both. We can come to him confident of his loving understanding and support.

Two objections could be made against this teaching. Priests had to be members of the tribe of Levi and descendants of Aaron. Two points are made in reply. First, Aaron was called to be a priest by God. (Ex. 28:1) True. But, quoting Psalms 2 and 110, the author of Hebrews shows that Christ also was given both his Priesthood. and his Sonship by God. Secondly, Priests shared a common identity with their people and had to sacrifice for their own sins as well. Christ was sinless, yet he shared in the sins of others through suffering and bearing their weight. He also shared the pain of obedience, a fact dramatically illustrated by his agony in Gethsemane.

In verses 5:11 - 6:12, the writer again breaks off his discourse with a heartfelt reproach to his readers. His teaching is solid meat to be chewed and digested by the spiritually adult. But they are immature still needing baby food. Many today who come to church Sunday by Sunday still haven't absorbed the basic teaching on sin and salvation. They too lack spiritual discernment. The more they hear it preached the more they can become gospel hardened.

Here the situation seems to have been worse. Apparently some had once experienced the joy of salvation and received the gifts of the Spirit and yet given it all up. How could this be? Had their experience ever been real? Had it been mere emotion? Had some sin they were not prepared to relinquish, or family pressure made them give up? Or, as seems most likely in this case, was it fear of persecution? The writer's verdict is harsh. A flame that has gone out can't be relit.

There are many indications of faith that is flickering, but can we ever be sure that it has gone out? Here is the problem of continuing sin we met with in John's first Epistle. For John, darkness fell when a disciple left the fellowship of the church. (cp. Jn. 13:30) But he was dealing with heresy. Can even this be final?

The author of Hebrews hopes that his readers, who remain within the church, are children capable of growth. So from now on let them prepare for meaty teaching and a tough journey. Let them join the ranks of those who by faith made it to the end and received the promised reward. Note that besides faith, they needed patience, an underrated virtue with a root meaning of both acceptance and suffering.

From verse 13, the writer returns to Jesus, in whose Priesthood lies our hope. To keep going when it is tough depends largely on hope. Writing this in Wimbledon week, it is clear from the player's eyes when hope dies. At that moment the match is lost. In some players it never dies. They fight on to the bitter end and even though they may lose, someone has to, they are essentially winners.

The writer gives two grounds for hope. The first is God's promise to Abraham. (Gen. 22:16-17) An oath needed two witnesses. He argues that these are provided by the promise and the oath itself. We may not find this very convincing. We anchor our hope on Jesus.

The imagery is taken from the Day of Atonement, the one and only occasion when the High Priest entered the Holy of Holies through the Veil. Matthew's Gospel tells us that, at the moment of Jesus' death, the Veil was rent from top to bottom. (Matt. 27:51) Whether fact or symbol or both, it denotes the glorious reality of the Ascension. Jesus has entered into the presence of God, taking our humanity with him. Things can never be the same again.

Remember that drowning man being rescued by a life-line thrown him from the shore. His final safety depends both on the rope being firmly anchored, and on his keeping tight hold of it until he reaches land. Our hope is firmly anchored on Jesus who is our Rock. So hold on tight.

Chapter 7 brings us to Melchizedec, this strange character referred to in Psalm 110. The only other mention of him is found in Genesis 14:17-20. It is worthwhile taking the trouble to read it. Melchizedec is a Priest of God most High. He is also King of Salem, meaning Peace, the name given to Jerusalem. Jews were known by their father's names. No such names are given here. This is interpreted to mean not just that they were unknown, but that he was parentless and so was unique.

Melchizedec does two things. He gives Abraham symbolic gifts of bread and wine. Then he blesses him. Abraham recognizes his sovereignty by giving him a tithe. This was the offering required by the Law to be given to the Levites, the priestly tribe that was landless. The writer notes that Levi, Jacob's third son, was, in one sense, inside the body of Abraham. Thus the ancestor of the levitical priesthood recognized the superior priesthood of Melchizedec.

This again may seem a far-fetched argument to us, but to Jewish Christians, used to this method of handling scripture, it would be convincing. Like Melchizedec, Jesus was both King and Priest. Though born and dying as a member of the royal tribe of Judah, his priesthood was also unique. It was an everlasting priesthood. Other priests died. Jesus lives for ever. Through him we draw near to God. We need no other mediator. As our High Priest, he stands before God continuously holding us up in prayer. The sacrifice he offers is also unique. He himself is the sinless victim, the Lamb of God, offered once and for all. Christ's sacrifice is unrepeatable. Like Christ himself, it is in God's eternal "Now".

Christ and the New Covenant. 8:1 - 10:18.

If the new was both superior and unrepeatable, what now was the meaning and future of the old? Our Writer's answer is clear. By fulfilling the old sacrifices, Christ abolished them.

That didn't mean they had been valueless. Moses had been told to copy a pattern shown him on the Mount. The old was a foretaste and a foreshadowing of the new. But the Law, with its regulations and its priests and sacrifices was faulty. It was unable to save from sin. It could not change hearts and lives. The Prophets had realised this. Jeremiah had spoken of a New Covenant that God would make with His People, a Law written on their hearts springing out of a personal relationship with Him. (Jer. 31:31-33)

The Old Covenant was based on the Law. (Ex. 24:3-8) The tablets of stone were kept in the Ark which was known as the Ark of Testimony. Other items, if they were ever stored in it, had disappeared by the time of Solomon. (1Kings 8:9-11) Enshrined in the Holy of Holies, covered by the Mercy Seat, the Ark was thought of as the throne, or as the footstool of God who was invisibly present in a Cloud.

In his brief description our writer's interest lies in the division between the outer and inner sanctuary. Incidentally, the altar of incense is wrongly placed. It stood in front of, but outside the inner sanctuary. The mistake may be a misunderstanding due to translation. So long as the outer court and priestly rituals continue, he says, the way into the Presence of God is blocked. Verse 9 may imply that Jewish Christians who still cling for assurance to the old ways are cut off from the benefits of the new. For them Christ is not all sufficient. Christ our High Priest has entered into the presence of God through the Tent (Temple) not made with hands, ie his risen body. (Mk. 14:57-58. Jn. 2:21) Through the Spirit he has made the one perfect offering of himself to God. Salvation doesn't come through rituals or anything we do. It comes from identifying ourselves with Christ by faith and love.

In verses 15-22 our writer continues to forward his case with Rabbinic legal arguments. From the Sin Offering of the Day of Atonement, he turns to the Covenant sacrifice described in Exodus 24:6-8. How did Christ mediate the New Covenant? Use is made of a pun. The Greek word for Covenant is very like that for a Will or Testament. Before a will can be implemented, the Testator has to die. The analogy can't be pressed, but two points are made. First, our promised inheritance of eternal life has been realised by the death of Christ. Secondly the old Covenant, like all binding agreements of those days, was ratified by a sacrifice. The victim's blood bound the two parties together. The Covenant and the forgiveness of sins were thus linked together by sacrifice. The bald statement of verse 22 shocks like a plunge into icy cold water. We have already noted one aspect of its impact on our lives today.

Christ, now in God's eternity, has dealt with sin once and for all time. Modern physicists are exploring the relation of time to eternity, but as yet it remains a mystery. The opportunity to reap the benefits of Christ's sacrifice is always Now and Today. He will return, not to deal any further with our sin, but to bring us to our final Rest. (Jn. 14:3)

This "once for all" is so important that further quotations from the Psalms are given to prove the ineffectiveness and obsolescence of the sacrifices that preceded the sacrifice of Christ.

In chapter 8 verse 13 Jeremiah was quoted. The New Covenant would make the Old Covenant obsolete. Psalm 40 is now quoted applying the same judgement to the sacrifices of the Law. Like all N.T. writers, the author of Hebrews is quoting from the Greek Septuagint, which differs from the Hebrew original by giving these verses a Messianic interpretation. Read Psalm 40, which is translated from the Hebrew, and you will see the difference. It expresses the feelings of a man rescued from deep trouble. He feels that ritual sacrifices are inadequate to express his gratitude, but God has opened his ears to understand that these are not what God wants. (It is interesting to compare the N.E.B., J.B. and G.N.B. translations) "A body Thou hast prepared", points however to the Incarnation. As we have mentioned earlier, the Septuagint was regarded as equally inspired and differences were taken as new teaching inspired by God, so the Writer would be perfectly justified in his use of this text. Christ had abolished the ineffective and endlessly repeated sacrifices. He had substituted the single perfect sacrifice of his life and death as an offering of loving and total obedience to God.

His priestly task completed, Christ now sits enthroned as King, waiting for the final Day when all things shall be put under his feet.

The repetition of the quotation from Isaiah brings us back to the main point. God's forgiveness is free. Sin offerings and all attempts to earn it are therefore pointless.

Chapter 10:19-39.

"Therefore brethren". As in other epistles, doctrine leads to exhortation. The Veil of the Temple, like the Jesus' body, had been rent. The way to God is now open. He is the way. They go to God through him. Freed from guilt and fear, and freely forgiven, they have been cleansed by the waters of baptism. On that momentous occasion they had made a public confession of faith. They must cling to this, and encourage each other to go on living lives of loving and active service.

Today people may not think much about sin, but many do feel crippled by feelings of guilt and a sense of worthlessness, especially if they have been abused in childhood. They may not be looking for forgiveness so much as acceptance. They have a desperate need to belong. What is this but a need of At-One-Ment with Someone, God, whose love is unconditional, and with a Body, His church, who will welcome them? Does it? That's where the challenge hits us. One of the best ways of experiencing acceptance is by being co-opted on to a team that is working on a project to bring health and happiness to others.

For the early Christians, the approaching End was a major incentive towards making the best use of the time that remained. The Day of Judgement was seen in terms of both a destructive and refining fire. Both are awesome. Neither Jesus nor any of the N.T. writers minimised this. Mediaeval Artists painted horrifying pictures of the Last Judgement and Hell. In rejecting their imagery have we gone too far in dismissing all idea of a final Reckoning, and in doing so, trivialised our life? At some point we have to face the truth about ourselves, but in the words of T. S. Eliot, it is "*the wounded surgeon*" who "*plies the steel that questions the distempered part*".

It seems clear that the main reason for these Christians giving up and turning back was fear of persecution. They are now reminded of their past courage, when persecution first hit them at the time of their conversion. "You have gone so far, borne so much, don't give up now. Hold on. Christ is truly coming." The writer associates himself with them in his confidence that they will do so.

Heroes of the Past. Chapter 11.

This chapter, like Westminster Abbey, is where heroes of the past are remembered. The one thing they all have in common is their faith, not an intellectual acceptance of doctrine or personal experience, so much as a practical commitment. They staked their lives on God and His eternal purpose. It meant rejection of this world's materialistic values and involved taking risks. For each it was different.

First, Abel. (Gen. 4:3-8) Why was his sacrifice accepted and Cain's refused? The sin that spoiled Cain's sacrifice seems to have been jealousy, but was it also a desire to gain something by it? Even our worship can be materialistic. Prayers and offerings are made with the expectancy that material benefits will follow: a good harvest, fertility, success in battle or business, or even in an exam. It can be a form of bribery! Worship offered purely out of loving devotion is comparatively rare.

This leads on to Enoch. (Gen. 5:21-24) He "Walked with God". Then, in extreme old age, he seems to have disappeared. Elijah was taken up into a whirlwind. Paul had an experience of being taken up into Paradise, (2Cor. 12:3) but returning to earth for there was still much he had to do. Great contemplatives, like John of the Cross, learn to live in eternity while still on earth. How much we owe to the "craziness" of saints.

How crazy of Noah to build a huge boat in the middle of a desert! Yet his family and livestock were saved by his obedience to his inexplicable "hunch" from God.

Abraham, well past the age of retirement, uprooted his family, and, leaving the comforts of the big city, embarked on the wandering life of a Bedouin. God promised him a Land, but the author of Hebrews tells us he was really seeking a City of God. He didn't find it in his lifetime. He could have given up and gone back, but he didn't. His whole life was a venture of faith into the unknown. His readiness to sacrifice Isaac, the beloved and only true son on whom the promises rested, was a leap of faith. He trusted God with death. He and Sarah had discovered that there was nothing God could not do. (Gen. 17:17, 18:13-14)

In the Exodus story, Moses flees Egypt out of fear rather than faith; but in killing the Egyptian overseer he showed that his decision to identify himself with his people may have already, perhaps unconsciously, been taken. God sometimes catapults us into action, the seeds of which may have been germinating for some time. Unlike Abraham, there was for Moses no possibility of return. The Passover foreshadowed things to come, but Christ was already there in the Exodus event. Moses predicted his coming. (Deut. 18:15. Jn. 5:46)

Despite archaeology and textual criticism, the stories of the crossing of the Red or Reed Sea, and the taking of Jericho testify to extraordinary experiences on which the faith and the subsequent history of Israel came to rest. Miraculous experiences of deliverance still take place. Enemy walls still crumble before the assault of believing prayer. Victories are still won by faith rather than numbers. The tortures of the Greeks could not force the Jews to give up their religion. Despite many defeats, the faith of the Maccabbean brothers won back freedom. The sufferings described in verses 36-38 are being endured by Christians facing persecution today. According to tradition it was Isaiah who was sawn in half in the reign of Manasseh. (2Kings 21:16) Worse brutalities are being perpetuated today.

These earlier heroes had no hope of resurrection. The after-life was to them a grey shadowy existence in an underworld. Their trust was in God and His purpose for His People. Their part was to forward this by active faith and obedience and by passing it on to their descendants. Martyrdom and belief in God's justice led many Jews, from the second century on, to believe in resurrection, but they died without the assurance of the resurrection of Christ. Verse 35 probably refers to the resuscitation of children by Elijah and Elisha. (1Kings 17:17-22. 2Kings 4:32-37)

Chapter 12

Therefore. Again the purpose of presenting his readers with this portrait gallery of heroes is to encourage them to emulate and press on. (cp Psalm 73:13-15) These heroic ancestors are portrayed as spectators at a sports arena: champions of the past cheering on their successors. "Keep going. You'll make it!" Singleness of purpose was what the runners needed, no entanglements, no backward looks, just perseverance, with eyes fixed, not on the finishing tape but on Jesus, their Pioneer. Certain of the joy that lay ahead, Jesus disregarded the cost and won his crown of glory. What he had done, they could do.

They hadn't yet faced martyrdom. Quoting Proverbs 3:11-12, their troubles are to be seen as God's Fatherly discipline. It is like training given to athletes which can be very tough.

To teach that God deliberately sends us hardship is unacceptable to most of us. But to offer our hardships to God and receive them back from His hands is altogether different. Everything God takes He transforms. Positive thinking? Making the best of things? Yes, but with the added dimension of faith and Spirit and joy.

A second "therefore" calls for a practical response. Like athletes they must strengthen their weak points. Verse 13 can mean "keep your steps from wavering" (N.E.B.) ie don't by-pass difficulties. But it is a quotation from Proverbs 4:26 which J.B. translates, "Let the path you tread be level". To fill in pot-holes and clear away stones of stumbling, fits in with a concern for lame legs and weak joints.

They should strive for good relationships and single-hearted devotion to Christ. But the root of bitterness doesn't refer to the nursing of resentment, though this too can destroy a community. Verse 15 is a quotation from Deuteronomy 29:18. It refers to those who, in their hearts, have already given up on the church and chosen the world. Like Esau they have sold their birthright. For them too there is no going back. Outside the church, the visible community of God's people, there is no salvation. In this the writer takes the same hard line as John. Heretics who stay physically within the community are a dangerous source of infection.

Israel's experience of God at Sinai was terrifying. Christians have come to Mount Zion where God is worshipped by angels and saints at a feast of joy and song. Jesus, at the centre, pleads for our mercy. This doesn't mean we can take sin lightly, or think we can barge in to heaven without bothering to put on our wedding gown of righteousness. (Matt. 22:11-16) God is no longer terrifying, but He is still awesome. Haggai prophesied that God would once again shake the earth. When that Day comes, all that is not of God will crumble. His Kingdom alone will remain. Let them rejoice that they belong to it, and worship Him with awe, for His love is a refining fire. (Mal. 3:2-3)

Chapter 13.

With these *therefores*, the writer is letting us descend from the mountain-top by a series of stages. The moral teaching given in this last chapter is traditional and could have come from the writings of James or the author of the Pastoral Epistles. The virtue of hospitality, the evils of adultery and avarice together with the need to respect and obey their leaders are repeated, as well as the warning against false teaching about food regulations.

In verses 10-13, a last appeal is made. According to the old Law, animals sacrificed as sin offerings could not be eaten by priests or people. Their bodies were taken out of the camp and burnt. Jesus too was cast out of the city to be crucified. Christians, fed by his Body in the Eucharist, in which only the baptized can share, are called to share also in their Lord's disgrace as voluntary outcasts of society. If Hebrews was written after AD 70, the fate of Jerusalem would be known. But all earthly cities crumble or are destroyed. Like Abraham we seek for the City of God.

In verse 18 for the first time we find a personal note. The blessing that follows, echoing I Peter 2:25 and 5:4, refers to Jesus as the Good Shepherd, but the blessing flows from the blood of his sacrifice. The mini-epilogue includes a reference to Timothy. There is no other indication that the companion of St Paul was ever imprisoned, so this may be a different Timothy. The greetings sent by those from Italy make it probable that the readers addressed are in Rome. This is confirmed by the fact that the earliest mention of Hebrews comes from its being quoted in a letter from Clement of Rome in AD 96.

Before we leave this great book we need to examine further its implications for the early church and for our church today.

After the destruction of the temple and the end of the Priestly sacrifices, The Lord's Supper came more and more to be thought of, not just as a Remembrance, but as a sacrifice, not repeated, but continually pleaded and re-offered.

At the turn of the first century, the same Clement of Rome, in his letter to the Corinthian church, pointed to the divinely appointed pattern of temple worship with its hierarchy of High Priest, Priests, and Levites who officiated and performed the sacrifices. He saw Bishops in terms of the Priests, and Presbyters and Elders in terms of the Levites, known as *klericos*, ie "belonging to the inheritance". Clement was the first to apply the word *clericos*, "of the people", to these members of the church rather than to all God's people. Thus he created a distinction between clergy and laity.

As already noted, the increasing danger of heresy had been leading to greater authority being exercised by bishops. For the sake of good order, licence to celebrate the sacraments had to be granted by him. What began as a wise ordering developed into a doctrine. As only priests could celebrate the sacrifices of the old Law, so now it was only a priest who could celebrate the sacraments of the new. As Jewish priests had to be men, so the ordination of women was deemed impossible. The fact that Jewish priests also had to be without any physical blemish (Lev. 21:16-23) was not however regarded as an obstacle to the ordination of Christian priests!

The Epistle to the Hebrews was possibly a protest against the development of this kind of theology in the church in Rome. It teaches that there is now only one Priest, Christ. The Ist Epistle of Peter provides an alternative view. All are God's priests. (1Pet. 2:9) This was scriptural and Mosaic (Ex. 19:6) and it avoided drawing any line of division. The people of God differ in gifts and ministries, but all share in the priesthood of Christ.

If Hebrews was a protest, it went unheeded. Further developments took place after the conversion of Constantine. Bishops became officers of State. Hierarchy became entrenched. Where was the guiding hand of the Spirit in all this? The church divided over the issue. When the Empire fell to marauding pagan hordes, the church remained. Bishops, who had absorbed and learnt to apply Roman law in the affairs of the church, now became Lords, standing at the right-hand of newly converted Kings, teaching them the ways of civilised government and the rule of law. Christendom, despite its faults and failings, provided Europe with a form of peace and justice as well as a knowledge of the Christian faith.

Today Christendom has collapsed. We are experiencing a new dark age of paganism. The church has lost most of its power and authority. House churches are springing up. Persecution has led to small cells of secret believers and a scattering and constant migration of individuals and groups evangelising wherever they go, prison included. It is all very similar to the early church as described in the book of Acts.

While the core deposit of faith remains generally accepted, the form taken by the church is thus changing rapidly. In all this we need to ask what is the Spirit saying to us now? What is He actually doing? Holding to the apostolic tradition isn't to be backward-looking and conservative. It means being led by the Spirit into new situations and new structures appropriate to them. Like the early church, we will have to explore and suffer, cope with controversy and disagreements, to say nothing of dealing with old heresies rearing up in new forms. Like Christians in the past we will make mistakes, but all the time we have to go on in faith and hope, keeping our eyes on Jesus. and striving to maintain the unity of the Spirit and the bond of love in the fellowship of the church which is his Body.

At such a time the message of Hebrews can speak to us afresh.

Jude and 2 Peter.

This chapter ends with a discussion of two epistles, both probably written some years later though some have put Jude earlier. Both initially faced opposition to their inclusion into the canon of the New Testament. The fact that they did get in indicates that through them, the Holy Spirit had something of permanent value to say. So let us study them and dig for it.

Jude.

We don't know who Jude was. The writer may have assumed the name of Jude, (Judas) a brother of Jesus, (Mk. 6:3) which would also link him with James and the epistle written under his name. Verse 3 could hardly have been penned by a first generation Christian, neither could verse 17 which refers to the apostles in the past tense. The form of heresy and the type of arguments used against it also reflect a later period. (cp 2Tim. 3:1-9)

The readers were either Jewish or Gentile Christians with a very good knowledge of the Jewish scriptures. Gnostic teaching had led them to see no harm in indulging in licentiousness while continuing to attend the church's love feasts and take holy Communion. They act as if they are so sure of their own salvation that it doesn't matter what they do. Jude quotes examples taken from Jewish scripture and legend to illustrate how God had judged those who disobeyed His laws through arrogance and unbelief. The licentiousness of Sodom and Gomorrah was notorious. Recently a large amount of brimstone has been found in that area. If thrown up by an earthquake and ignited, fire would indeed have rained down from heaven. An earthquake also put paid to Korah and his fellow Levites who challenged the authority of Moses and Aaron. (Num; 16:1-35) Not even angels were spared from punishment when they sinned. In interpreting this, we need to remember Jesus' words in Luke 13:1-4.

Of the three accusations made in verse 8, the third needs some explaining. There was a Jewish legend that when Moses died the Devil rudely stopped the Archangel Michael from taking charge of his body. He claimed that Moses had killed the Egyptian overseer and so was a murderer. Some Gnostics denigrated angels.

The stars referred to in verse 13 were planets, which Jews believed were stars that had wandered off course, and were heading for darkness and destruction: black holes?!

Verse 14 is a quotation from the Book of Enoch. It was compiled during the first and second centuries BC, but never accepted as scripture. Quoting from it nearly cost the writer his own scriptural authority! Enoch predicted that before the End came there would be an explosion both of disasters and of heresy. (cp. 1Tim. 4:2. 2Tim. 3:1-5)

In verses 22-23 we again find the problem of how to deal with heretical church members: whom to try and save, and whom to excommunicate. Today many will find Jude's harsh language offensive, but perhaps much of our toleration stems from indifference which allows evil to flourish. Jude's anger stems from a deep caring for the church and for those being led astray. Verses 20-23 express a passionate loving concern that has inspired countless people to venture and reach out to others with the gospel.

The beautiful blessing that concludes this letter resembles that at the end of Romans. It may have been drawn from a first century liturgy. and is now part of our own, included as an alternative blessing to end Morning and Evening Prayer.

(A.S.B.) How wonderful it is to be linked in this way with our fellow worshippers of the 1st century!

2 Peter.

This is probably the last book of the New Testament to be written. The style, tone and the situation addressed are completely different from that of the 1st Epistle of Peter. The claim that Peter wrote it was challenged very early. The writer is acquainted with the collected writings of Paul which had by then acquired the authority of being scripture. He leans heavily on Jude which he sometimes quotes verbatim, though a minority, favouring an earlier date, think Jude may have been quoting 1 Peter.

Chapters 1:1 - 3:13.

Why Simeon? It is the Hebrew/Aramaic form of the Greek Simon. This may provide us with a clue for understanding the whole format. Apart from these opening verses, what follows does not seem to be a letter, and it is not addressed to any particular church.

Contemporary Jewish writing sometimes took the form of a Testimony supposedly written by one of the Patriarchs just before his death. It would include moral teaching and refer to incidents in his life. Simeon was one of the Patriarchs as well as being Peter's original name. So this letter could be a Testimony of Simeon Peter, one of the twelve Patriarchs of the New Israel. (Rev. 4:4) It is an attractive theory which I shall follow through.

This letter or testimony seems to be pointed towards Christians whose culture was Greek but who had a good grounding in the Jewish scriptures. Phrases like "divine power", "escaping the corruption of this world", and "becoming partakers of the divine nature", were expressions common to Greek philosophy. The writer is at home in the language of his surrounding culture. Today, biblical and churchy language form an almost insurmountable barrier to the communication of Christian truth to people within the church as well as outside it. The problem is that words can convey different meanings to different people, which is why the Roman Church took so long to give up the Latin liturgy. Unless meanings are defined, the use of contemporary idiom can enable popular philosophies to infiltrate the church.

There are two important sayings in this first chapter. The first is a "jewel". Verses 3-4 speak of God's precious promises. These are countless. I'll quote just two: Acts 2:38-39 and 1 John 2:25. Look them up, claim and rejoice in them.

Listing virtues was another familiar feature of both Jewish and Greek literature. (cp. 1Tim. 6:11) A similar list is given by Paul in his letter to the Galatians, but there they are fruits of the Spirit, flowing naturally from His indwelling presence. Effort is needed only to express them in action. In 2 Peter it is the virtues themselves that have to be striven for, and only then will the knowledge of Christ prove fruitful. Is he saying the same thing as Paul, or is his thinking different?

The danger of forgetting an initial experience of Christ and returning to the old ways is a mysterious and tragic fact. John doubted that in such a case the experience could have been real. (1Jn. 2:19) Jude and 2 Peter don't discuss the problem, they only condemn and warn of the resulting judgement. Jesus in his parable of the Empty House (Lk. 11:24-26) warns of the consequence of a House cleaned up and then left empty. Its final degradation was not a punishment but an inevitability, but it gave a similar warning. God calls and chooses, but, in the words of the N.E.B. translation, "we have to clinch His choice."

Death is approaching. (verse 14) This is another mark of a testimony. Jesus' prophesy of Peter's death is found in John 21, the chapter that was added later. The reference to the Transfiguration is told as a personal life experience, which is another such mark. In the Gospels it is presented as an awesome experience, a revelation of the true glory hidden within Jesus' manhood. Here it is used to prove his divine status and confound the heretics who denied it.

This leads on to a warning against the free-for-all interpretation of scripture. It follows the second important saying which is a warning. (1:20-21) God speaks through men, but prayerfully His church must "test the spirits". (1Jn. 4:1) Scripture could be twisted by heretics to justify their beliefs. This danger later led the Mediaeval Church to ban the bible from the laity. Gnostic writers also produced Gospels, such as the Gospel of Thomas, as well as many Epistles. These were excluded from the canon of scripture but they were widely available, and are quoted today to support the revival of Gnostic beliefs. There was a real danger of Gnosticism swamping the Church, had not the Spirit inspired men to battle against it on behalf of the faith handed down by the Apostles.

Chapter 2.

This is a repetition, sometimes verbatim, sometimes more violent of the denunciations found in Jude. The same O.T. characters are quoted. Although Lot chose to settle in Sodom despite its reputation, he later became included in a list of righteous men. The story of Michael is omitted, perhaps because it was so well-known. The denunciations conclude with the rather nasty but apt illustration of the habits of a dog!

Waiting for the End. Chapter 3.

We don't know if the writer had in fact written an earlier letter or if perhaps he was referring to Peter's first Epistle. It was typical of a testimony to remind readers of what they had already been told. It gave the present teaching added weight.

Increase of heresy was seen as a mark of the approaching End. Belief in its immanence had long since faded. "It will never come" sneered the heretics. But to denounce all belief in a final reckoning is to undermine morality for which it provides powerful motivation. Gnostics were influenced by eastern philosophy, which, being cyclic, denies a final End, but nevertheless retains a moral motivation through its doctrine of karma and rebirth.

Two replies are made. First, in the days of Noah, God did very nearly destroy the earth. In the days of the dinosaurs, He nearly destroyed it with an asteroid. He could do so again in our own day! God had promised never to flood the earth again. Jews and Christians both believed that the End would come by fire. (Is. 66:15-16. 2Thess. 1:5-8)

Secondly, God's time is different. Verse 8 quotes Psalm 90 verse 4. Based on the 7 Days of Creation, astrologers of the time predicted that the earth would last 7,000 years. Paul interpreted the delay as a sign of God's patience with sinners. (Rom. 2:4) Jesus had indicated that God might shorten the time out of mercy for the righteous. (Mk. 13:20) He made two things absolutely clear that The End, when it came, would be both sudden and unexpected.

Some Pharisees believed that if every Jew kept the whole of the Law perfectly just for one day, then Messiah would come. The author of 2 Peter urges his readers to live spotless lives at peace with one another. By doing so they might hasten the Day. Let them desire it, however terrifying, and, trusting in God's promises, look forward to it in hope. (cp Lk. 21:28)

His final injunction reverts to the problem of interpreting scripture. Paul himself had complained that his teaching of salvation by faith was being twisted to justify immorality. (Rom. 3:8) Our Writer, while quoting scripture to support orthodox teaching, fears for its wrongful use by others. By this time the old tension between Peter and Paul is over. The situation that created it has gone. They stand together in people's memories as two giants of the church's faith and authority.

His final comment is very appropriate for our own unstable times. "Don't be carried away by the persuasiveness of the lawless. Hang on to your stability in Christ, and grow in grace." To that we add a fervent Amen!

Summary

Both John's first Epistle and Hebrews point to the Gospel's basic simplicity, illustrated by the Taise chorus, *ubi caritas, Deus ibi est.*

For John, this *caritas* is the love seen in Jesus, profound beyond definition, but, at the same profound level, unmistakably recognizable. Thus to know God the Father is to know the Son, and vice-versa. As Michael Ramsey has said, "there is nothing unchristlike in God".

To say that we all worship the same God is misleading. What matters is our concept of Him. This is what affects our attitudes and actions. God is not a philosophical abstraction. Nor is He the all-powerful Boss figure, like some Victorian fathers. The power of God as defined by Jesus is that of sacrificial love.

For John to know is to love. The word "know" is that used for the intimate consummation of sexual love. (Gen. 4:1. Matt. 1:25). It is self-revealing through self-giving, and expression beyond words and conscious analysis.

This experience of divine love, and of being personally loved, is communicated through the Spirit's anointing. It is a contagious love that is compelled towards active expression. If all such expression is lacking, there must be some disconnection or blockage. Since the Spirit's anointing has not been lost, i.e. taken away from us, (Jn. 1:1:27 JB version), the failure to connect must lie in our lack of abiding. Hence the repetition.

In Hebrews the simplicity lies in seeing in Jesus our Way through to the Father. He is our High Priest, Mediator, and Intercessor. We need no other. The complexity of the book is due to the efforts made to demonstrate this!

1 Peter speaks of Christians as being a nation of priests. We are privileged to share in Christ's priestly ministry. Our prayers and offerings are taken up into His. Only this gives them meaningful effect. The history of the church has shown that this derived office has been widely misunderstood, and can degenerate into clericalism. The stark simplicity of the teaching of Hebrews provides a cathartic counterbalance.

Questions for private meditation

1st Letter of John

1. What experience have you of the power of God to conquer sin?

2. Have you ever been tempted to give up your faith? What held and holds you to it now?

3. Can you write down six things about the Christian faith to which you could testify from personal experience?

4. How are you able to "abide in Christ"?

Hebrews

5. Have you any sense of urgency in the challenge of God's "Today"?

6. What sort of Saviour do your neighbours need?

7. Think of three people whose faith and example have influenced you? Give thanks for them.

8. What importance has the Communion of Saints for you?

9. Do you know of any House Church in your area? How would you feel about visiting and learning more about it and its members?

10. Claim and give thanks for the two promises of God given in the Commentary on 2 Peter 1:3-4.

Questions for group discussion

1st Letter of John

1. As Christ has changed human nature, sinning is not inevitable. Discuss.

2. Does the balance of the 1st great commandment (Mk. 12:24) safeguard your church from intellectualism, emotionalism, and activism?

3. How can we "test the spirits"?

2nd and 3rd Letters of John

4. How does falsehood infiltrate a church? How can it be guarded against and prevented from spreading?

Hebrews

5. Can comfortable middle-class priests communicate Christ to needy people who are neither? If not, what can be done about it?

6. "When we discover we are running away from self-knowledge, we face the

fact of sin." Discuss.

7. Jesus has taken our humanity with him into heaven. What meaning has this for us?

8. Is sin today experienced as alienation and lack of worth? How should this affect our presentation of the Gospel?

9. What disciplines are important in your Christian life?

10. Do you see the world-wide growth of House Churches as the work of the Spirit equipping God's church for the New Age, or do you oppose this development?

Chapter 12

The End Unveiled

The Book of Revelation

The Book of Revelation stands at the end not only of the New Testament, but the whole Bible. The "End" evoked is not the terminus, but the fulfilment of our journey and of God's purpose for us.

Looked at from that point of view, the book would seem to be important, yet most people steer clear of it. Why? Obviously it is difficult, a jungle rather than a mountain. Before we start to explore it let us look briefly at three more emotional issues.

The first is the craziness of the interpretation some people have set upon it. Armageddon and the Millennium are two of the subjects that, taken literally and given specific dates, have led to fantasy sometimes resulting in catastrophe. The remedy is not avoidance but sober study with the aid of reputable scholarship. That means effort and discrimination. Hopefully this chapter may be a start.

Another problem is its bloodthirstiness. The saints cry out for vengeance, Christ wades through a sea of blood, and John seems to applaud. Where is the love and forgiveness of the Gospel? These problems will be faced as we study the text, but briefly three points can be made. First, the bloodthirsty bits are almost all based on Old Testament quotations and need to be given a New Testament interpretation. Jesus conquers in the power of his Cross. Secondly vengeance is exacted on the powers of Evil, not persons. The saints cry for vindication not revenge. In our own time we have seen how violent events have overturned unjust regimes and vindicated those who suffered for the truth, even at the cost of their lives. The battle between good and evil will go on to the end of time, but we must believe that finally evil will be destroyed, and those who resisted it will be vindicated.

As for John's attitude, he may well have been affected by memories of the appalling horrors of Nero's persecution. Even Romans like Tacitus were sickened. Could Jews who survived the death camps be expected to weep for Hitler?

Revelation means unveiling. Apocalypse, the Greek equivalent, means uncovering. The book emerges from a whole collection of apocalyptic writing of which Daniel was an early example. Daniel was written in the 2nd century BC at a time of horrendous persecution. Prophets began to have visions that the end of the world was close at hand when God would intervene to save them.

The style of such writing is symbolic, cryptic and allusive. No wonder it is difficult to understand. The reader needs to be clued up, first to the decoding of numbers.

2 = Truthful witness. 3 = What belongs to heaven. 4 = what belongs to earth. 5 : a round number, not large. 6 or 7-1 = Evil; the Antichrist. 7 or 3+4 = completeness. Similarly $3^1/_2$= incompleteness; a limited period. It can also mean a time of evil. 8 or 7+1 is the day of resurrection, ie of Christ.

10 is an undifferentiated round number. 12 or 4x3 = wholeness, unity in diversity, eg the 12 tribes and apostles.

Multiplication by 10, 100 or 1,000 intensifies. A square, and still more so a cube, denotes perfection.

Geography is also symbolic. Sodom, Egypt, Babylon, and sometimes even Jerusalem, can refer to the Evil City, and any of them can point to Rome for which only a cryptic allusion was safe.

Some of the images are archetypes, and some have links with the signs of the zodiac, but overwhelmingly it is in the Old Testament that their context and meaning is to be found. Within Revelation's 404 verses there are 518 O.T. quotations as well as countless other allusions, the most important being taken from the visions of Ezekiel and Daniel. The apocalyptic sayings of Jesus, recorded in Mark 13 and Matthew 24, are also important. The latter helps to give John's book its shape. Important references will be given with the heading of each chapter and section. It will be helpful to look them up before reading comments on the text.

Hearing was, for Jews, more important than seeing. Throughout the book what is seen is interpreted by what is heard. Visualising the visions would result in pictures more fantastic than a Picasso! Like a Picasso they aim to create an emotional rather than an intellectual response. Listen to the bells they ring, of meaning soaked in scripture.

As with the Epistles, it is important to understand the situation being addressed. This raises the problem of dating. Some scholars opt for an early date, soon after the death of Nero, but the majority place it between 90-95 AD towards the end of the reign of Domitian. Divinity had been first claimed by madmen like Nero and Caligula, but wise Emperors retained the title. The Empire embraced a multiplicity of races and gods. Emperor-worship as a state religion, without abolishing such diversity, provided a bond of unity and strength.

Under Domitian, Christians were, for the first time, persecuted, though only spasmodically, primarily on grounds of their religion. Nero was generally suspected of having had his own private reasons! The threat was greatest in Asia where the Empire had brought peace and prosperity and Emperor-worship was popular. Local Governors were not eager to kill Christians and did not seek them out. But if Jews denounced them as enemies of State, the Governors had to take action. Christians would then be ordered to deny or even curse Christ and offer a token of worship at the Emperor's shrine. If they did this they would probably be let off. If they refused, the penalty was death, usually by burning.

They would not be mourned by the general public. Christians were regarded as atheists and antisocial. They did not take part in public feasts and religious celebrations or contribute to the expenses involved. There were some within the church who taught that involvement in civic events was good and their religious aspect could be ignored. This teaching was a greater danger to the church than persecution. Martyrdom strengthens, compromise weakens. It was a dilemma that faced the church in Nazi Germany and Communist Russia.

Who was the author? The short answer is that we don't know. The book was accepted into the canon because it was believed to have been written by John the Apostle. There are references to the Gospel and similarities of thought, but the same could be said about Paul. The style is very different, and the writer makes no apostolic claim. He is "John, a servant of God and your brother." He is obviously well-known and respected by the churches to which he writes and has suffered exile for his witness. He is steeped in the Scriptures, both the Hebrew and Greek texts. He doesn't just quote but uses them creatively, applying them to his visions and the problems of his own day.

He has also shaped his Visions into a plan which aligns them to the temple worship, the eucharistic liturgy, and to the 7 major Festivals of the Jewish year. Some commentators link them also to the days of the week.

The book can be read meaningfully without understanding all the complexity of its structure, but, so that its richness can be better appreciated, references will be made at the heading of each section together with the bible texts.

General plan of the Book.

This can be seen as a drama with a Prologue and Epilogue enclosing 7 Acts. The number 7 dominates. There are 7 Churches, 7 Seals, 7 Trumpets, and 7 Bowls. Each Act has 7 Scenes. As in all good drama these are linked by foreshadowing and flashback, by repetition and parody. Scattered amongst them are 7 Images of Evil, of the Church and of Christ, as well as 7 Blessings.

Visions may be given by God, but, like dreams, they can also draw upon images and desires buried deep within the psyche. The bible warns us that visions can even be demonic. (Jer. 14:14) Hence the need for careful reference to scripture and to the experience of the worshipping community. In John's book, visions, biblical study and experience, both conscious and unconscious, combined with an urgent pastoral concern. His message of warning and encouragement is spoken not only to those Asian churches, but to us as increasingly we face similar problems.

Prologue and Opening Letter. 1:1-11.
Daniel 7:13. Zech. 12:10. Ex. 3:14. John 17:4-6.

All the other books of the New Testament rest on the authority, direct or indirect, of an apostle. John claims that the authority for his book comes directly from God. It is designed to be read at public worship, and the first of the 7 Blessings is proclaimed to all who read, hear and respond, for the "time is near".

John begins and ends his visions in the form of a letter. Jesus is the Faithful Witness. It was this that led to his crucifixion. Now he is the risen and ascended Lord whose love and salvation the church has already experienced. When he returns, all the nations will recognise his Lordship. Will the wailing express repentance as in Zechariah's prophesy, or will it be angry grief at worldly loss? It could imply both. The "even so Amen" is a prayer for his coming echoed at the end of the book.

Jesus is also the Alpha and Omega, the first and last letters of the Greek alphabet. The Beginning and the End, in him all things are enclosed and held together. (Col. 1:17) Note the unusual sequence, "Who is and was and is to come." (cp Rev. 4:8) Jesus is God's great I AM, echoed by Jesus at his arrest. God, the eternal Now, reflects backwards and forwards in earthly time. "Almighty" doesn't mean one who is able to do anything, but rather, one who holds all together in final control.

Opening Vision and Letters to the 7 Churches. 1:12 - 3:22.
Vision. Daniel 7:9-14. 10:5-6. Ezekiel 1. Psalm 29. Numbers 25:1-3. 31:15-16. Isaiah 22:19-23, 45:14. Matthew 16:18-19. John 10:7-9.

Temple worship began with the opening of the gates and the lighting of the lamps.

It is the Lord's Day, the first day of the week. Exiled and alone, John joins his people in spirit as they gather for worship. Praying, he is caught up into a state of visionary consciousness. He hears a loud trumpet, a call for action. He is to write the vision and send it to the churches.

In the vision Christ is seen with the attributes of God: white hair conveys antiquity, fire the glory of Sinai, and the sword, the Word of God. He truly died. Docetists denied this. Now Christ lives. The keys symbolize his control over death and the powers of evil.

He stands amid the churches represented by the Menorah, the 7-branched lamp-stand that stood in the outer sanctuary of the temple. Its light is their witness. Zech 4:2 and Matt 5:14-16 are good examples of an inspired transfer of meaning. The 7 stars, representing heavenly dominion, may be the guardian angels of the 7 churches.

Part of the Passover ritual was the search for and casting out of any scraps of the old leaven. The Eucharist began with self-examination and confession. Those unbaptized or excommunicated had to leave.

Starting with Ephesus, nearest to Patmos, the 7 cities stood on the main Roman road forming a circuit. With their different problems they represent all the churches of Asia Minor and beyond.

John is writing for them too. Of seven of them he has a very intimate knowledge. Each church is first presented with an aspect of Christ most relevant to its need. Under his judgement their strengths are commended and their weaknesses exposed. Warnings are given and rewards promised to those who heed them. These promises are all summed up in the final vision of the Heavenly City. The Spirit's call to hear runs like a refrain. It is a call to prepare for the trials ahead. The first 4 churches are all facing the problem of compromise.

Ephesus was the chief city of the Province famous for its Temple of Diana and for its Games. Paul had worked there for many years. The beloved disciple and John the Elder had both probably lived there.

The church at first seems to be scoring well. They are specially commended for their hatred of heresy. The Nicolaitans held Gnostic views about the separation of body and spirit. So you could eat what you liked, where you liked. Fornication, often a synonym for idolatry, could also, as here, refer to sexual indulgence with temple prostitutes. But, and it was a big but, their orthodoxy had created in them the proverbial self-righteousness of the Pharisees. They had to go back to square one and learn what it meant to love and be loved by Christ. To eat from the tree of life was Paradise restored.

Smyrna had been totally destroyed by an earthquake in the 6th century BC and it had only been restored 300 years later. Thus it had experienced death and resurrection. It was famous for the beauty of its buildings built like a crown around the top of a hill. Wealthy and prosperous, thanks to Rome, it had three Imperial Temples. Its large Jewish colony was very hostile to the church, hence the reference to "the synagogue of Satan". The vision is of Christ who had died and risen. No faults are rebuked, but warning is given of coming persecution. Those who are faithful to death will be rewarded with the crown of life. In 155 AD the Jews instigated the martyrdom of Bishop Polycarp. Smyrna is the only one of the 7 Churches still standing.

Pergamum was the first centre of Imperial worship, hence "Satan's throne". There had already been one martyr. Balaam and Balak prefigure the Beast and False Prophet of a later vision. Balaam was blamed for encouraging the mixed marriage that led Israel into idolatry. The real problem was the teaching of the Nikolaitans, ie compromise with the immoral practices of the surrounding pagan society. Both the Vision and the warning is that of a sharp sword, the Word of the Spirit. (Heb. 4:12) Manna was the food of Heaven of which the Eucharist was a foretaste. White stones were used as votes for judicial acquittal, as entrance tickets, and as electoral voting slips. All point to final salvation. The new name, ie identity, bestowed at baptism, finds its fulfilment. Secrecy gave power over enemy attack.

Thyatira was a commercial city. Its government was based on trade unions, which, like the mediaeval craft guilds, and Masonic Lodges today, had religious origins and ceremonies. To get on in life you had to join them as in Nazi and Communist states where it was impossible to get a good education or job without holding a Party card. Jezebel was a self-styled prophetess. Like the Nicolaitans she advocated compromise. Christians in Thyatira were only too happy to be persuaded and she was obviously popular. "The deep things of Satan" probably refer to sorcery, a darker aspect of Gnostic belief.

Christ's eyes burn up the camouflage of lies. His feet of bronze are immovable. Christians who stand firmly for truth will be given a power greater than that of commerce. Christ, the Morning Star, overcomes the darkness of Satan.

Sardis, once the capital of Croesus, had twice been taken by surprise attack. Its glorious Acropolis was a deserted ruin. The church, like the city, was living on past reputation, outwardly in good shape, inwardly hollow. Christ is seen as the source of their spiritual renewal. They are to wake up and face reality. Their name, thrice mentioned, refers to their true character. To Asians, the Book of

Life was a register of citizens. Jews now cursed Christians as heretics, blotting them out from membership of God's People. Jesus would not blot them out. But they are warned that if they continue to sleep, the enemy will overcome them by a surprise attack.

Philadelphia in contrast is a church very much alive. Like Smyrna, its members are true and devoted. Their oppressor is not Rome but Jews who have excluded them from Messiah's Kingdom. The vision is of Christ holding the Keys of David. They have been taken away from the dishonest steward. It is Christ who controls the Door of the Kingdom. He is himself its Door. Isaiah's vision of the Gentiles coming to bow before the Jews has been significantly altered.

The J.B. Bible translates verse 10 as "I will keep you safe in the time of trial." The promise is of becoming a Pillar in God's Temple, strong and able to support strain. Jews may strike out their name from the pages of a book, but God will engrave His own Name upon them indelibly as in stone; a fulfilment of their baptism.

Laodicea was a prosperous commercial and banking city, with a Medical School famous for its eye specialists. Proud and self-sufficient, it had refused Imperial aid to rebuild the city after its destruction by earthquake.

The Church shared this self-satisfaction. Confronted by a vision of Christ as the True Witness, their shabby poverty stands revealed. Like the city's water which came from hot springs outside the city, their faith was lukewarm and unrefreshing. Their eyes needed more than their famous eye-salve to enable them to see their true condition.

Theirs is the harshest of all judgements, but it proceeds from love. Christ knocks at the door of their hearts. He will not force the door. The reward to those who open it to him is the best of all: an enduring holy communion, and a sharing of his throne. But sharing Christ's victory means sharing in his witness and sacrifice.

We can recognise these churches in our world today. What about our own?

"Repent" cry the angels. "The Lord whom you adore
In judgement and in mercy is knocking on your door. "

Vision of Heaven and the 7 Seals. 4:1 - 8:1.

Worship of God. Chap. 4. Ezek. 1. 10:18-20. cp Ex. 25:18-21. Ps. 99:1. Also Gen. 1:1-2. 9:8. Ex. 19:16. Is. 6:1-3.

Again the opening of the temple gates and the Trumpets. The door into heaven is open, and John is summoned to enter the Holy of Holies, into the presence of God. (Heb. 10:19-20. cp Rev. 3:8)

God cannot be imagined or described. His sovereignty is indicated by a throne, his glory by jewels, his awesome majesty by the thunders of Sinai. The seven Spirits speak of His active Presence. The sea of glass rings many bells: of Original Chaos, of deliverance through the Red Sea which prefigured Christian baptism. Here it lies subdued under the feet of God. The glass, reflects His glory. Through it He sees all that happens on earth.

The Cherubim, winged creatures that overshadowed the Ark, are here seen as the 4 Orders of God's creation. It is in the worship of Creation that God's glory is made known. (Ps. 19:1-4) The 24 elders representing God's faithful people, both before and after Christ, join the 4 Creatures in the 3-fold worship of the Sanctus. Originally part of temple worship, it was already used at the Eucharist.

Worship of the Lamb Chap. 5. Ezek. 2:8 - 3:4. Dan. 12:1-4. Gen. 49:9-10. Is. 11:1. 29:11-12. Feast of the Passover.

In the morning service of the synagogue, the praise of God as Creator leads on to celebration of the teaching of Scripture.

God is the ultimate source of all that is and all that happens. Heaven is timeless, but the key to understanding God's meaning lies in an event in history and has a date.

The scroll contains the meaning and purposes of God as revealed in the Scriptures. A sealed roll is like a legal document. When the seals are broken its contents take immediate effect. No wonder John weeps. Are we never to understand the meaning of Creation? Will God's purposes ever be finally fulfilled?

He waits expectantly for a Lion coming in power. Dramatic surprise! A Lamb appears with the marks of death. But its horns symbolise power, and its eyes wisdom. Christ is both Lion and Lamb. It is in his death and resurrection that the meaning of Creation and history is revealed. How wonderfully C. S. Lewis pictures this in Aslan.

The Lamb's appearance leads to the New Song of the Redeemed. All creatures of earth and heaven join in the 7-fold ascription of praise. Christ the Lamb is enthroned and worshipped as God. It is an unbroken worship, belonging to time and eternity. We enter it not just at the Eucharist, but anywhere, at any time, always.

The 7 Seals. Chaps 6-8:1. Zech. 1:8-11. 15. 6:1-8. Ezek. 5:8-12. Matt. 24:6-8. Luke 23:28-31.

The Feast of Pentecost was a thanksgiving for the first-fruits of the Harvest and for the giving of the Law.

Here are the disasters Jesus predicted as the birth-pangs of the New Age. We know these 4 Horsemen only too well. They ride across history as wars of conquest, civil war, famine, disease, and death. They are an interconnected sequence and the consequences of man's ambition and greed. Man brings these judgements on himself, but God allowing this, is still in control.

The disasters are limited. A poor man's wage for his daily rations would only tighten belts. His staple food is untouched. But the black horse creates a black market. Though these disasters are outside time, John may have in mind particular events. In AD 62 the Romans were defeated by Parthians whose deadly arrows fired in retreat became proverbial. Nero's murder in 68 AD led to Civil war. In 79 Vesuvius erupted. This was followed by fire and plague, while the year 92 brought severe famine. Such an unprecedented series of disasters led to fears of Divine judgement and End Time predictions, as they do today.

The 5th seal is broken and the cry of the martyrs is heard, "How long?" They are the first-fruits of the Harvest, and, as we have seen, their cry is for vindication. As long as history continues, the Riders will ride, but the Visions assure us that a Day of final reckoning will come.

We have a foretaste of this as the 6th seal is broken. Creation is shaken and Chaos returns. There are times in history when an Empire or civilisation gets so tyrannical and corrupt that its destruction is the only way forward. The ground needs to be cleared as by a forest fire for any possibility of new growth. Assyria and Babylon both reached this point and, like the Tower of Babel, were destroyed. Jesus had predicted the destruction of Jerusalem. The inevitable consequence of national pride, it had been destroyed only about 20 years before John was writing. When men's world collapses, they hide in their bunkers and turn to suicide.

Before the 7th seal is broken there is a total change of scene and a different kind of seal. To stamp anything with a personal seal is a sign of ownership and protection. In Ezekiel 9:4 those who deplored the Temple's idolatory were sealed with the last letter of the Hebrew alphabet, *tau*. Its sign was + and sometimes written as x. For Jews it signified the Name of God. Given to Christians at baptism it signified Christ's cross. The woes to be ushered in by the 7 Trumpets were spiritual and satanic. The 4 angels hold them back until God's people are protected.

The number of those sealed is heard. It is symbolic. God's People ie 12, squared and intensified, a number that happened to be that of a military formation; God's army! They are seen as peoples of all nations and tongues. Jesus had said that before the End, the Gospel had to be preached to all peoples. In one sense this might have been seen as fulfilled by Paul's missionary journeys. The sealed multitude join the myriads round God's throne singing the Song of the Redeemed with its 7-fold ascription of praise.

Note the forceful use of opposites in the symbolism: robes made white in blood; the Lamb as a shepherd. The imagery is taken from Isaiah's prophesies (Is. 49:10. 25:8) and the Psalms. (121:6-7. 23:1-2)

The vision of heaven takes John back to the seals. The 7th seal is broken. Unexpectedly the result is silence! What could be more dramatic. What could it mean?

In the Temple Liturgy the sacrifice offered on the altar outside the Temple was followed by the offering of incense in the inner sanctuary. At a signal, the people fell down and prayed in silence for half an hour. (Lk. 1:9-10) Their worship and intercessions were carried by the smoke up to the Cloud of God's Presence. Was John thinking of the Talmud tradition of heaven hushing to hear the prayers of earth?

Other bells ring in scripture. Silence preceded Creation. Does this silence point beyond the word of Judgement to a New Creation? For the reader, the silence induces a sense of awed expectancy.

Vision of the Altar of Heaven and the 7 Trumpets. 8:2-13:18.

Vision. Ezek. 10:2. cp Lk 12:49. Ezek. 33:1-6.

In the calamities that follow, God's People are increasingly revealed in their witness, their suffering and their self-sacrifice. Their prayers mingle with the prayer of the saints in heaven. "How long must evil prevail?" In response, coal from the altar in heaven is thrown to cast fire on the earth. Then, one by one, the trumpets are blown.

Trumpets that summoned the faithful to worship were also used to warn the city of danger, much as church bells do even today. The plagues of the first 4 trumpets are based on the plagues of Egypt. Their power of destruction is again limited but this time to one third.

The First 4 Trumpets. Ex. 9:23. 7:18-21. 10:21-23. Jer. 51:24-25. Is. 14:12-17. Amos 5:7.

The first trumpet ushers in a storm of hail and lightning which destroys the green things on earth. The second throws a burning mountain into the sea destroying the fish. Memories of Vesuvius? Maybe, but more importantly Jeremiah's prophecy of the fall of Babylon. Jesus had said faith could cast mountains into the sea. (Matt. 21:21) The resulting splash would certainly sink ships! (Rev. 18:19)

The third trumpet causes a Star to fall on the rivers and fountains. In Isaiah's Taunt Song, the morning star that fell is Babylon. Wormwood, a bitter herb, is linked by Amos to the bitterness of injustice. In John's day Rome, by her tyranny and injustice, was poisoning the springs of her own life.

The 4th trumpet puts out the lights of heaven. The darkness of original Chaos returns. Darkness was the penultimate plague before the final death-blow that forced Egypt to free its Hebrew slaves.

The Unjust City is in its death throes. The vulture screams 3 Woes to the earth summoning its fellows to gorge on the feast. (Matt. 24:28) What a parody of the heavenly banquet!

Unlike the plagues of the 4 Horsemen, these plagues are not directly caused by man, but, though seemingly supernatural, John could see Rome's involvement. Today it is we who are literally poisoning the trees with acid rain, and polluting the rivers, seas and atmosphere. Our judgement will be that, knowing this, we refused to take the drastic steps needed to reverse the process, blinding ourselves to the consequences, with the irresponsibility of Louis XV's *Après moi le déluge.*

The 5th and 6th Trumpets. Ps. 68:17. Num. 21:1-10. Ps. 91:2-3.

The Fallen Star points to Lucifer, an aspect of Satan. (Lk. 10:18-19) Here again is the problem and mystery of evil: God lets Satan loose but stays in control. We wrestle with the fact of it. Somehow God meets us within it.

Chaos and Evil are now released and the 3 Woes are loosed on earth. The first is an attack by what Niles calls "The Devil's Vanguard". The imagery is taken from Joel 2:4-11. It is good to read his whole chapter as he links an invasion of locusts with a call to repentance and a promise of salvation. This army, poisonous as scorpions and attractive as women, has as its king Apollyon, ie "destroyer", which in Bunyan's "Pilgrim's Progress" is the name given to Satan. Niles interprets this Woe as the bitterness of doubt and disbelief that, when nemesis strikes, attacks those who have no resource other than themselves.

The 4 angels of destruction, previously held back are now released. (cp Rev. 7:1) The hoards of cavalry parodies God's army described in Psalm 68. The fire and sulphur, ie brimstone, recall the destruction of Sodom. Like the Parthian cavalry that attacked Rome from the east, they are powerful in attack, equally dangerous in retreat, and deceptive as the Serpent in Eden. Echoes of the poisonous serpents in the desert links this army to the scorpions of Rev. 9:5. From all such plagues the sealed faithful are protected. Niles interprets this attack as apostasy and lawlessness. Civilizations break up from within before they are conquered. Loss of faith, moral corruption, and lack of social cohesion make a society fragile. A crisis could lead quickly to the law of the jungle.

The Little Scroll. 10:1-11:14. Gen. 9:16-17. Ezek. 2:8-3:8. Luke 24:25-27, 44-48.

Before the 7th Trumpet sounds there is another pause. A mighty angel appears with a message of mercy. It is a scroll which John is commanded to eat and digest. The earlier scroll, (Rev. 5:1) revealed scripture in the light of God's purpose. This reveals it in the light of the Lamb. The Gospel is sweet to those who accept it, bitter to those who refuse; bitter also in its consequence for those who proclaim it in a hostile world. Now is the time to proclaim it to all nations. The following visions spell out its meaning and consequence to the churches.

a) **The measuring rod.** Ezek 40:3-5. 42:15. Luke 21:24.

Measuring is a sign of protection. The sanctuary is protected but not the outer court. The Gentiles would be allowed to trample it. Jesus had predicted the destruction of the outer, ie the earthly temple. The inner spiritual temple, the members of his Body, were already protected by his seal. The 42 months, ie 3½ years, meant that the period of their trials would be limited. It echoes the time of Greek oppression described in Daniel. (Dan. 7:25)

b) **The 2 Witnesses.** Zech. 4:12-14. 1 Kings 17:1. Ex. 7:17. Dan. 7:25. Ezek. 37:10. Matt. 16:24-25. 24:28. Jn. 2:19. 16:20. 1Thess. 4:17.

The lamp-stands take us back to chapter 1:20. The vision unfolds the pattern of life to be experienced by a witnessing church, a pattern already set by the life of Jesus: initial success, persecution and even death, followed by final vindication. The time of persecution coincides with that of the trampling, the same situation in another guise.

The witnesses are tormented because they torment the consciences of the powerful and worldly. This pattern has to be worked out in some sense by all who follow Christ. (Matt. 16:24-25) "A comfortable church cannot stir the world either to salvation or opposition." (Morris)

Like Ezekiel's dry bones, Christ's faithful witnesses rise to new life, and, like their Lord, ascend to glory. An earthquake symbolises the shaking of the foundations of a godless world. It forms the climax of the plagues, and is the Vulture's 2nd Cry of Woe

The 7th Trumpet. Psalm 2. Matthew 27:51.
The "Last Trump" doesn't bring about a sudden end to the world, as popularly imagined. It signals the Days, God's Days, of the End Times.

All John's warnings of calamity begin and end with a vision of heaven. In words made famous by Handel's great chorus, we hear heaven's Halleluias of joy at the establishment of Christ's universal Kingdom. Note the omission of the future ascription of Rev. 4:8. We are living in these future events now. In the Eucharist we celebrate them. (2Cor. 6:2)

Note also how the Messianic Psalm 2 is continually referred to in the following chapters. (12:5, 14:1, 16:14, 17:18, 19:15)

The Powers of Evil. Chapters 12 & 13.

The Woman. Gen. 3:15-20. Is. 7:14. S. of S. 6:4-10. Dragon. Is 27:1. Gen. 3:14-15. Job 1:6-12. Heavenly War and the Wilderness. Dan. 12:1. Ex. 19:4. Deut. 32:10-12.

The Woman is not just Mary. She is Eve, Israel idealised, the Bride of Christ, the Church. She is kept safe in the Wilderness. Her Child, though "bruised", is caught up by God. The Dragon is the Serpent (in Greek *drakon*) in Eden. He is Leviathan the Sea Monster representing the forces of Chaos and of Evil underlying the persecution of God's People. He is Satan the Accuser, both God's servant and Devil's Advocate.

How can the God of Justice pardon sinners? Sweet, in his commentary, points out that the "war in heaven" is a legal battle. On the cross Jesus defeated evil, and all who share in his death share in his victory. In the spiritual sphere Satan's power is broken. On earth it rages still. This is the Vulture's 3rd Woe. (v. 12) Verse 13 echoes the trampling and the protection described in 11:1-12. It is similarly limited.

The two Beasts. Chapter 13. Dan 7. Matt 24:23-24.
John now moves from symbolism to allegory. He is specifically referring to the danger of Rome and Emperor worship. The first Beast is an incarnation of the Dragon, a parody of Jesus as the Incarnation of God. With the attributes of all four empires represented by the beasts of Daniel's vision, it stands for Rome with its claim to divinity. For us it represents all rulers and powers that claim total allegiance.

The 10 heads represent 10 Emperors. The one with a mortal wound may refer to Nero's suicide and the myth of his return. Rome was worshipped by its citizens because of the benefits it provided. Through this they were drawn into worshipping evil. How true this was of Hitler's Germany. The power to persecute was permitted but limited. God was and is always in final control. "You cannot serve God and Mammon". But individuals have freedom to switch allegiance, either way.

The second Beast from the earth is a wolf in sheep's clothing. It represents the Priesthood of the Imperial shrines. Later it is referred to as the False Prophet. As a parody of the Holy Spirit it works signs and wonders, parodying the miracles of the Witnesses. (11:6) Priests at these shrines used magic and ventriloquism to stun people into belief, a method Jesus had rejected. Its mark may refer to some proof of conformity given after sacrifice had been offered. This too is a parody of the sealing of the faithful. (7:3). In all this, what John has in mind is not Rome and her Priesthood but the Nicolaitan teachers and the Christians seduced by them, like those in Pergamum. Failure to produce a Party card has been used by many modern dictatorships to exclude Christians and others who refuse to conform, from economic and educational advancement, and even to reduce some to near starvation. In verse 18 John is specific. The number of the Beast is the number of Evil intensified. It could represent the Antichrist. Greek and Roman letters had numerical values. 666, transliterated, could be made to fit Nero Caesar. John's readers would certainly know to what or to whom he was referring.

Victory of the Lamb and Reaping of the Harvest. Chapter 14.

The Victory. Ps 75:8. Jer. 51:6-7. Gen. 19:24. 2 Pet. 2:6.
The Harvest of Grain. 14:13-2. Mark 4:28-29 13:24-27. Matt. 3:11-12. Heb. 4:1-11. See also Ps. 126:6.
The Harvest of Grapes. Is. 63:1-6. Joel 3:13.

We now return to the Lamb and his triumphant multitude. Theirs is a song that not even angels can sing. It is a song of salvation. Chastity here refers to singleness of heart.

The 3 cries of the Angels counter the Woes cried by the Vulture. The first proclaims Christ's victory and the second the fall of the Evil Empire. "Babylon" recalls Jeremiah's call to escape from her. The third cry warns of the terrible consequences of compromise. It is clearly aimed at the Christians in Thyatira.

The cup of wrath again refers to Jeremiah and to Psalm 75:8. God's judgements work slowly through the events of history. They can be seen prophetically as nemesis, or recognised in recall by eyes of faith.

The decision between loyalty and compromise is stark. John paints in black and white. Christians facing persecution today know this. They have no problem in relating to this Book. The world of Western Democracy is however a grey world. We are grey people struggling in grey areas to make grey choices. In thick fog it is easy to cross unmarked frontiers and enter enemy territory without noticing. Returning is very difficult, though not impossible.

What is meant by "eternal torment"? The points made at the beginning of this chapter are relevant here. This book is not concerned with doctrine and future event so much as picturing the awesome and eternal consequences of choosing worldliness in preference to God. What Jesus taught in parables, John portrays in symbols. It is love that drives him to warn.

There are two harvests. First the *Harvest of Grai*n. The Reaper is Christ, He is also the Sower who sowed in tears and brings home his harvest with joy. In the 2nd of the 7 Blessings, the Righteous enter into their promised Rest.

Secondly the *Harvest of Grapes*. This gory picture comes from Isaiah and a modern reader is apt to feel revolted. But translate it into New Testament terms. The winepress outside the city brings Calvary to mind. (Heb. 13:12) An Angel, not Christ is the Reaper, for it is Christ's blood that is shed, and that of his faithful Servants. It is they who have washed their robes in his blood. (Rev. 7:14) The blood also points to the wine of the Eucharist and all that it stands for. The Trampler is the trampled grape.

It is we who are responsible for the rivers of blood that flow. We inflict our judgement on ourselves. It is the Beast that conquers by killing Christ and his followers. Christ conquers by dying; another parody!

Song of Salvation and the 7 Bowls. Chapters 15 & 16.

Ps. 86:9-10. Ps. 145:17. Deut. 33. Ex. 15:1. Armageddon. Jud. 5:19. 2Chron. 35:20-25. Zech. 12:1-9. 12:10-11. 13:1-2.

The Feast of Tabernacles, or Booths, was celebrated at the end of the harvest. Those sacrificing boil the flesh of their sacrifice in bowls. (Zech. 14:16, 20-21) Here, the last sacrifice is the burning up of Evil.

In this introductory Vision we hear the Song of those who have conquered the Beast and its Image. They rejoice that all nations will come to worship the King of the Ages. His power and glory have been revealed to the world.

The plagues let loose by the Bowls, like those of the Trumpets, echo the plagues of Egypt, but now their destruction is total. The first 4 punish the followers of the Beast for their complicity in the murder of Christ's followers. Nero's atrocities were still fresh in John's mind as those of the Holocaust are in ours.

The altar cry of chapter 6 has been answered. The martyrs are vindicated. The "scorching" recalls memories of our own burning cities. These are still man-made but God-permitted events. The innocent suffer with the guilty, but at the spiritual level they are safe. (Dan. 3:19-25. Ps. 91) The awfulness is that men still do not repent.

The last 3 plagues destroy the Beast's Kingdom. As such it is a special warning to Pergamum. (2:13) The 5th Bowl brings Darkness, graphically described in the Book of Wisdom (Chap 17) as a place of fear made worse by a bad conscience. It indicates a breakdown in Roman administration as during the Civil Wars of AD 68-9.

The 6th dries up the river Euphrates that protected the Empire from invasion from the east. Cyrus had actually dried up a river in order to defeat Babylon. "Dried up" and "prepare the way" ring many bells of ironic contrast. Magic was prevalent in Roman society and is growingly popular in our own. Demonic forces lie behind it for its attraction is power. The Harry Potter books may not be as innocent as they appear. They can hook. All this leads on to the 3rd Blessing upon those who take heed and keep awake. Note the warning of Jesus' parable. (Matt. 24:36-44)

Despite various problems, Armageddon has been traditionally identified with the present Megiddo. This would ring memories of decisive battles in which God's power had been displayed both in victory and defeat. Some fundamentalists link it to Zechariah's prophesy to predict an End coming in history to be preceded by a final assault on Jerusalem. The Israeli-Palestinian conflict could of course spark off another world war. but this is to misread John's intention. The nations are assembling against Rome. This was an historical fact. In John's day, Jerusalem, the corrupt city Jesus had wept over, had already been destroyed. In his Visions John saw it purged of idolatry and unbelief, descending as a Bride from heaven. (Rev. 21:1-2)

The 7th Bowl leads to the final destruction of the Evil City. Admittedly the hail does somewhat resemble a massive use of atom bombs! This is how at least two cities in our day have been obliterated. John's mind is here focussed on Rome, but what he writes applies to all corrupt centres of power. The City falls and breaks up. Those who survive remain unrepentant.

Vision of the Great Harlot and Fall of the Great City. 17 - 19:4.
Ezek. 28. Is. 47.

Who is this Scarlet Woman? She is the embodiment of the evil city from Sodom up to those of our own day. Some extreme Protestants refer her to the Papacy. Fox's Book of Martyrs, still popular reading, is partly responsible for this. But Protestants have persecuted too. This is only one aspect of the Harlot. London, a centre of commercial trafficking and exploitation might also fit the bill, together with other great centres of power from Chicago to Hong Kong. Bin Laden has dramatically pointed this out!

John hears the interpretation in the wilderness. (Mk. 1:13) This links the Harlot to the Woman in chapter 12 verse 6, yet another parody. Rev. 21:9 links her as a reverse image to the Bride. She is a mystery. The evil concealed by her splendour goes unrecognised. It is revealed to John. It is Lawlessness, ie total rejection of the rule of God, the essence of The Fall.

Verses 8-11 are obscure, but the 10 Kings are the eastern tributary kingdoms of Rome. These collaborated in the persecution of Christians, but finally attacked and destroyed the City. Evil is self destructive.

Lament for the City. Chapter 18.

Based on the Taunt Song of Ezekiel and others, this is a lament for the Great City by all who profited from her, and enjoyed the goods she provided. They were mostly good things in themselves, but pride and greed led to injustice and waste. What lost potential! One feels that John shares in the grief. Note the link between verse 7 and Laodicea, also the warning of verse 4 which links with Isaiah 52:11 and 2 Cor. 6:17. Over the destruction looms the warning myth of the Tower of Babel.

The Great Halleluia and the Last Judgement. 19:5 - 20:15.
The Great Halleluia. Ps. 113:1-4. Ps. 117. Ps. 118:1-4, 14-16. Hos. 2:5, 14, 19-20. Is. 61:10. Eph. 5:25-27.

The Liturgy of the Passover celebrated the betrothal of God to His redeemed People in the Wilderness.

Here at last is the real Halleluia Chorus! It is in two parts. The first celebrates the vindication of the martyrs. We can think of the thousands killed in our time, more than at any other period in history. The second celebrates the marriage of the Lamb. In keeping the Passover, the Jews looked forward to the Messianic Banquet. In John's Vision this is seen as fulfilled in the consummation of perfect unity between Christ and his Bride. It is the fulfilment of God's Purpose in Creation. The 4th Blessing is on the Wedding Guests, invited and joyfully present, clothed in their wedding garments of righteousness. (Matt. 22:2)

Verses 9-10 repeated in Chapter 22:8-9 are a warning against prevalent angel worship.

Christ Rides to Victory. Ps. 2. Is. 63:1-6. Ps. 45:3-5. Deut. 10:17. Ezek. 39:17-21. John 1:1. Heb. 4:12.

What an array of familiar symbols of Christian power! The white horse is foreshadowed by the 1st Horseman. (6:2) Eyes of fire. (1:14) The Crown and the secret Name. (2:17) The robes dipped in blood. (7:14 and Lk. 12:50) The Word of God, (Jn. 1:1) and again the reference to Psalm 2. The wrath of God as His absolute hostility to evil. Christ's armour is a sword able to prick the conscience (Zech. 12:10. Heb. 4:12) and convert enemies. The painful trampling causes life-enhancing wine to flow. Grapes escaping this process live only to shrivel and die, to be useful only as compost.

The feast of the birds is a horrible parody of the banquet of the Lamb. It is drawn from Ezekiel where the evil army of Gog is destroyed. But here the army is slain by the Word. Only dead flesh is destroyed. Their spirits await final judgement. Only the Beast and False Prophet are killed, and they are abstractions.

The Millennium. 20:1-10. Is. 65:17-25. Ezek. 38-39. Ps. 90:4. 2 Peter 3:8. Is. 10:5-6.

This is another happy hunting ground for literalists and those given to making predictions. It is a difficult chapter. Let us learn what we can from modern scholarship and then try and see what relevance it may have for us.

John's thinking was influenced not only by Old Testament writings such as Isaiah, Ezekiel, and the Book of Daniel, but also by later apocalyptic writings and current Jewish and Christian beliefs.

The Old Testament Prophets believed that the Messiah would set up his Kingdom on earth, thus bringing in an endless Age of prosperity. By the second century BC, this hope had faded. Belief in resurrection led to it being spiritualised and transferred to heaven. But hankering for a golden age continued, and some Jewish thinkers in John's day believed in a limited period of Messianic rule. John links this to the old Creation myth of God chaining the Serpent of Chaos and imprisoning it beneath the earth. The only escape was a shaft to which God alone had the key. (Rev. 9:1) There was a parallel belief that the Devil's kingdom had 4 exits opening up at the four corners of the earth.

The 7 days of Creation were understood as 7000 years. The 6th Millennium was to be an Age of Triumphant Evil. Hindus have a similar concept of Ages having differing characters. The 7th was the Age of the Messiah, the Jubilee Year of Sabbath, when God's captive people would again be liberated. The 8th Millennium, the Age of Sunday, the Day of resurrection, would be the Age of Christ's reign ushered in by the Day of Judgement and the End of history.

John saw this in terms of two deaths. The first was natural death, the second would be the total destruction of all whose final choice was Satan, (vs. 14-15) ie Darkness. (Jn. 3:19) There would therefore be two resurrections. The first would be that of the martyrs and saints. (2:4. cp. 11:11-12) On these the 5th Blessing would fall. (20:6) This Millennium would be a limited period of their rule. The second resurrection would be of all the dead, who, with those still living, would face The Last Judgement.

Who then are Gog and Magog? Gog was Israel's mythical enemy, an ally of Satan. The Septuagint translated Magog, Gog's territory so as to transform him into Gog's ally and thus a second enemy. The story of Gog's invasion follows Ezekiel's famous vision of the Valley of dry bones and of a restored Israel. (Ezek. 37) In previous historical invasions God had allowed Israel's enemies to punish Israel with defeat, but in this last visionary assault, Israel's victory would be a mighty demonstration of God's power to save His People. (cp Armaggedon. Rev. 16:5-6)

What can we make of all this? A rule of the Saints followed by a final fling of the Devil is still a popular belief. John could not know that in just over 200 years, the Roman Emperor would become a believer. Nor could he have foreseen that, after the decaying city had been overrun by pagan tribes, these too would be converted, bishops would become their advisors and Christendom would be born. It was far from perfect. Power corrupted the church. But if goodness was not always practiced, saints and martyrs were honoured. Now Christendom has collapsed, dark demonic forces are returning and many Christians are again facing the stark choice of compromise or martyrdom.

How and when life on earth will end is a question we can leave to the speculation of scientists and others. We are facing our hour of decision and judgement now, as the Christians of those Asian churches were when John was writing. He used these spiralling visions of evil assault and divine protection to hammer home his point. Like them we need to realise the ultimate importance of the choices we make and take heart from the assurance that Christ will ultimately triumph.

The Opening of the Books. 20:12-15. Ex. 32:32. Dan. 12:1. Is. 9:18-19. 66:15-16 & 24. Mark 9:48. Matt. 13: 41-42. 25:34-46. Luke 23:23-30.
Two Books will determine our final destiny. They will be opened beyond Time, but they are being compiled now. The first contains a record of deeds. But good deeds are motivated by love, Brownie points are disqualified! The second is the Book of Life, a register of the citizens of God's Kingdom. Whose names are there? Jesus refused to answer that question. What matters is our decision to turn to Christ now, ie whenever that decision confronts us.

Christ appears not only in Jewish dress. He is the "Light that lighteth every man". The response of faith is to say Yes to the light we see, an act of trust in God, of whose loving mercy we are given assurance in the Person of Jesus.

What of the lake of fire? How are we to view the doctrine of damnation? The lurid literalism of Mediaeval paintings and Church dogma is rejected by the modern mind. To dismiss the doctrine altogether is to ignore the warnings of Jesus himself and to trivialise our life. To say "Oh it will all be OK in the end" is to close one's eyes and avoid questions. Is this how to comfort an alcoholic drinking himself to death?

It is better to examine the biblical imagery. Fire depicts the glory and holiness of God. It is the consuming fire of love which refines and purifies. God will not be content with anything less than the best for us, in us and of us. Fire cauterises to make way for healing. Those suffering in Dante's purgatorial flames do not complain.

After-death experiences recently reported by those who died and were resuscitated have described how, after death, they experienced a flash-back of their whole life. While aware of being held in a loving security, they found themselves feeling and sharing in the pain they had caused others. Was it just remorse, or the sympathetic pain of a newly discovered loving awareness?

But there is another fire that Jesus, quoting from Isaiah, speaks of as "a Worm that dieth not." It is a fire that can feed for ever on unforgiving resentment and hatred. We start experiencing it in this life and can hold on to it even after death. It is wholly destructive.

God will never force his love or healing upon us in this world or the next. We choose our own hell. But for those who are willing to face the pain of "withdrawal symptoms" and the refining fire of love, there is the assurance that, in God's economy, every fragment of good will be gathered up.

A New Heaven and a New Earth. Chapters 21 & 22.
Is. 65:17-19. Ezek. 37:27. Zech. 8:7-8.

In these last two chapters we reach the end not just of John's Book but of the Old as well as the New Testament. In them we see the final fulfilment of God's Plan of Salvation worked out from the dawn of Creation. Here we see the full flowering of the 8th Age of the Victorious Christ. It reaches beyond space and time but, like our spiritual bodies, it is germinated from seeds planted on earth in this present time. (cp 1Cor. 15:36-37, 53-58. Jn. 11:25-26)

The old heaven refers here to the spiritual realm. We know only too well that even our holiest moments are tainted. The sea symbolised Original Chaos. For John, exiled on the Isle of Patmos, it would also represent separation. The Vision is, as ever, interpreted by the Voice. "The dwelling of God is with men." The perfect intimacy of Eden before the Fall is restored. To describe the indescribable, John, as ever, uses thematic images developed in both Old and New Testaments which he now shows perfectly fulfilled. There are 4 of them and we will look at them one by one.

1. The Tree of Life. 22:2. Gen. 2:9. 3:24. Ezek. 47:12. 1 Peter 2:24. Rev. 2:7. 22:2 & 19.

Here is another sign of Paradise regained. Put out of reach by the Fall, the Tree of Life now reappears, not just as one Tree but as an Avenue of Trees watered by the River of Life. Note John's significant addition to Ezekiel's vision. Its fruit is for the healing of the nations. Though John does not make the point, we cannot ignore how this Tree of life connects with the Cross.

2. The River of Life. 22:1. Gen. 2:10. Ex. 17:5-6. Is. 43:19. 51:1. Ezek. 47:1-12. Zech. 13:1. Jn. 4:13-14. 7:37-38. 19:34. Rev. 21:6.

This too appears in Eden. It is provided by God in the wilderness where it streams from a stricken Rock, which Paul identifies with Christ. (1Cor. 10:4) Isaiah visualises the River issuing forth as "streams in the desert", God's provision for His pilgrim people. It matures in Exekiel's wonderful vision. If you read no other text, read this. As "streams of living water", it flows from Jesus. Through his Spirit it springs up like a fountain in the hearts of his followers. Mingled with Christ's blood, and flowing from his pierced side, it is related in John's Gospel to the Eucharist.

3. The Holy City and its Temple. 21:2,10-27. 22:3-5. Ex. 33:7. Num. 2:17. Lev. 16:16. 1 Kings 8:6 & 10-13. Is. 1:21. Ezek. 10:18-19. 11:22-23a. 43:3-7. Is. 60:19. cp Gen. 11:3-9.

In 21:2 John sees the New Jerusalem coming down from heaven. What a contrast to the city and Tower of Babel erected by Man's pride. The city of Jerusalem was also seen by the prophets as a Harlot city, notorious for its unholiness. Pilgrims today who complain of this with shocked surprise have in fact experienced its authentic mixture of fanatical religion and worldliness.

Its holiness depended on the Presence of God, concealed in a Cloud of Glory, the Shekinah, located in the darkness of the Holy of Holies. In earlier times this Cloud was depicted as either resting on, or filling the Tent of Meeting. Exodus stations the Tent outside the Camp, in contrast to Leviticus that places it within, "in the midst of their uncleanness", thus expressing both the transcendence and immanence of God.

Before the city and temple were destroyed, Ezekiel had a vision of its evil and idolatry and of God's withdrawal of His Presence. In his later vision of a newly restored temple he saw that Presence return. It was from under the altar of this ideal temple that the River of Life had its source.

Herod's temple was based on Exekiel's measurements and design, but Jesus, when he entered it as Malachi's "Messenger of the Covenant", quoted Jeremiah in calling it a den of thieves. The Shekinah had departed. Was it ever there? God's Presence was now embodied in Jesus. In him God became present among men. Now He is present in His church and in us, His People. But, as with Jerusalem, there is ambiguity, for His Presence is not only concealed within the church but, sadly, by the church and, from a harlot church, His Presence can be withdrawn.

So we return to John's vision of the Holy City descending out of Heaven from God. The measurements are symbolic. (cp. 7:4 14:4) Like the sanctuary of Solomon' temple it is a perfect cube, for the City itself is the temple, filled with God's Presence and Light. It is founded on the 12 Apostles and their testimony: their "deposit of faith". It is a Holy City of priests. (1Pet. 2:9) The High Priest wore a square breastplate bearing 12 jewels inscribed with the names of the 12 tribes. This probably accounts for the jeweled walls. Ten of the jewels are the same, a sardius probably being a carnelian. John is creative in his use of images and quotations and he may also have had in mind Ezekiel's "jewels of Eden". (Ezek. 28:13)

The Light of the City is the Glory of God, no longer hidden in a Cloud. Light is yet another great Biblical image. The lights of Creation are replaced and God's Light shines, perfectly reflected through the Lamp which is the Lamb. The Light of the World has kindled the lights of his church, and, in the first of John's visions, the 7 churches are called upon to be like wise virgins and "trim their lamps" so that they will burn brightly. By their light the nations of the world will be led to the Holy City. There the Lamb Himself will be their light. Here again Time present and Time future interplay and overlap. At long last they shall "see

His face". (22:4) What a glorious and longed-for conclusion! Nehemiah and Ezra had closed the city gates against foreigners. The gates of this City were never closed, and people of all nations could enter freely. These are people who were witnessed to by prophesy and martyrdom. (Rev. 10:11, 11:11) They are the people who were deceived by the Beast and False Prophet. Yet they are people who are still able to repent and find their true home in the Holy City of God.

So who is excluded? All that is evil. In chapters 21:8 and 22:15 John is specific. He is writing to meet a particular situation. Remembering this helps us to interpret and apply what he says to ourselves.

Top of his list comes cowardice. This not only silenced witness but led to the public denial of Christ and token worship at the Imperial shrines. Peter had been scared into denial, but his love and repentance was deep. Jesus forgave him and Peter finally died as a martyr. Continual denial by word and deed can cause such inner pain that, apart from repentance, the only escape is by deadening the heart to all faith and feeling. This is visibly the case in many unrepentant war criminals today.

Next come a list of sensual sins still indulged in by some Greek converts, not through human weakness, but deliberately. "Dogs", an epithet given by Jews to Gentiles was, in John's day used by Christians to denote such people. "Liars" were those who, denying the Truth witnessed to at their baptism, had turned to the teaching of the Devil, the Father of lies. (Jn. 8:44) It is difficult to discern when such people are hardened beyond repentance. This is illustrated by the changing attitude in the Pastorals and late Epistles as years went on and heresy hardened. (cp. 2Tim 4:1-4. Jude 22-23. 1John. 5:16. 2Peter. 2:12-22)

The Bride. 21:2 & 9. Hos. 2:19 -20. Is. 62:5. Matt. 22:14.

Hosea was the first to see Israel as a Bride. She had turned into a harlot, but Hosea discovered, from his own sad domestic experience, that God still loved her despite her unfaithfulness.

Isaiah had a vision of God rejoicing over Jerusalem like a Bridegroom over a Bride. The Song of Songs is included in the Canon of Scripture because it was interpreted as a love duet between God and His People.

In the Gospels, Christ becomes the Bridegroom and the Kingdom of God is pictured as a wedding feast. In Ephesians Paul links Christ's relationship to the Church to that of a husband and wife.

John sees the Holy City as the Bride. In contrast to the Harlot clothed in rich and gawdy finery, the Bride descends from Heaven clothed in the glory of God. Jasper was regarded as being His special jewel. If the Church is viewed as a City in the width of its embrace, and as a Temple in its priestly office, the Church is seen as a Bride in her interior devotedness and in her consummation of perfect love and unity with her Lord.

Last Words. 22:6-21.

Last words are important. John's can be summed up in four words: "I am coming soon."

Authenticity was vital. John's visions were revealed by an angel who, like the prophets, was directly commissioned by God, and like them, a servant not to be worshipped. The warning of 19:10 is repeated. Now, for the first time, God Himself speaks and gives His own testimony. (cp Jn. 5:37). This is echoed by Christ, the Alpha and Omega, who first commissioned John to write to the churches.

The 7 churches were struggling with compromise. The danger of heresy and persecution was growing. The call to hold on and be faithful had to be coupled with assurance that Christ's victorious Return was certain and would be soon. The word "soon" is repeated four times.

Daniel had been told to seal up his prophecies. (Dan. 12:4) They purported to have been written in the 6th century, but they related to the events of four centuries later. John's visions were for his own time and he believed the End was near. For us, living in the End Times, Christ's victory and his Coming is both Now and something still expected.

The last two Blessings now appear. The first, found in verse 7, is given to those who keep the words of "this prophecy". The warning quoted from Deuteronomy 4:2-4 related to the idolatry that seeped into Israel through intermarriage, which was traditionally blamed on Balaam. In Revelation 22:18 it connects with Christ's warning given to Pergamum. (2:14) This text in Revelation has been used by some fundamentalists to insist on the whole Bible as being verbally as well as divinely inspired. It can perhaps be used to question those who water down the Gospel's challenge to all forms of unholy living.

The second and final Blessing (verse 14) is on those who have washed their robes (cp 7:14). They are wedding guests clothed in their wedding gowns. (cp. Matt. 22:11-14. Is. 61:10) They can eat from the Tree of Life and enter the City by the gates. This recalls the promises given to Ephesus, Sardis and Pergamum.

The promise is given by Jesus, "the bright and morning star", foretold by the same Balaam who was blamed for Israel's sin. (Num. 24:17) The "root and stump of David", another Messianic prophecy, is more familiar. (Is. 11:1) The morning star had been promised to Thyatira. Note how the promises to all 7 churches are fulfilled.

The four "Soons" are followed by the four "Comes" of the Spirit, the Bride and all who hear and desire the Bridegroom's return. The prayer is answered by Christ's sure promise, to which all the faithful reply AMEN, MARANA THA, Amen Come soon.

Verse 17 sounds like the antiphonal response of worship. John's letter would probably have been read at a meeting of the church and been followed by a celebration of the Eucharist. The Grace, a traditional form of opening and closing a letter, was also used at the beginning and end of public worship, as it is to this day.

So let it then conclude this book of mine. The Grace of the Lord Jesus Christ be with us all.

Summary

Our Journey through the N.T. has ended. It has been the continuation of a journey begun in the O.T. with Abraham. The Drama of God's Cosmic Plan of Salvation has been unfolded, and, in the Book of Revelation, we have seen a vision of the final curtain beginning to come down. But for us, both the Journey and the Drama continue to be worked out in our lives.

As we look out on the world, we may be tempted to wonder if the Plan has succeeded. Little seems to have changed. What difference has the coming of Christ really made? Many answers can be given, but the question remains to haunt us. We have seen the transformation of the lives of the first apostles and their converts, but how quickly sin, heresy, and institutionalism dimmed that early brightness. Yet, over the centuries, the light has never been quite extinguished. In the darkest of times it has revived and shone most brightly.

The answer lies within ourselves. What difference has it made to us? Today, as the church is being stripped of its worldly power and wealth, it is rediscovering the power of the Spirit and the riches of Christ.

The relevance of the N.T. is clearer than ever. In it we see reflected our own experience. From the depths of faith, and the variety of understanding of these early writers and disciples of Christ, we can learn how to enter into, and possess, all the spiritual treasures that Christ has given us.

These books are like an inexhaustible gold mine. Like the treasure hidden in the field, it has to be dug for. I pray that this book may have provided some help in the digging.

Questions for private meditation

1. In John's opening Vision, which aspects of Christ speak to you most strongly? Let meditation lead you to worship.

2. In what areas of your life is the temptation to compromise most pressing? (chaps 1 & 2)

3. In private and public prayer, how conscious are you of sharing in the worship of heaven? (chaps 4 & 5)

4. Have the foundations of your life and faith ever been shaken? Is Christ truly the Rock on which you stand? (chaps 6 & 7)

5. How practical is your concern to protect the ecology both locally and world-wide? (chaps 8-11)

6. "God allows evil to attack us but meets us in it". What is your experience? Strengthen confidence with thanksgiving.

7. What does Christ's death and victory over the powers of evil mean to you? Are you sharing in it? (chaps 14-15)

8. What does heaven and hell mean for you - in this life, and in the next? (chap 20)

9. Rejoice in those aspects of heaven of which we have a foretaste now. e.g. The Presence of God. Rivers of living water.

10. What has God been teaching you through this study of the Book of Revelation? Give thanks for it.

Questions for group discussion

1. What thoughts, feelings and questions come to mind as you start this study of The Book of Revelation?

2. What clues about heaven do John's images and symbols provide? How should we interpret them?

3. How does the death and resurrection of Christ provide us with clues to the meaning of history? (chap. 5)

4. In times of disaster, what protection does God provide for His people?

5. What has caused the breakdown of morality and rising tide of lawlessness in our society? Do we bring our judgement upon ourselves? (chaps. 8-11)

6. What threatens the church most today?

7. The Devil would argue that forgiveness is destructive of morality. How would you answer him?
8. Are multi-national corporations the Evil Empire of today? In a grey world, what frontiers are we in danger of crossing? (chap. 14:1-12)
9. Do people choose their own hell? How do you view hell? (chap. 20)
10. What does the prayer “Marana tha” mean to you? What is your view of the Second Coming? (chap. 22:6-21)